JOHNNY DEPP
A KIND OF ILLUSION

JOHNNY DEPP
A KIND OF ILLUSION

DENIS MEIKLE

Research Associate: Dr Robin L Moody

Reynolds & Hearn Ltd
London

To Jane

This maiden she lived with no other thought
Than to love and be loved by me
EDGAR ALLAN POE, *ANNABEL LEE*

First published in 2004 by
Reynolds & Hearn Ltd
61a Priory Road
Kew Gardens
Richmond
Surrey TW9 3DH

A CIP catalogue record for this book is available from
the British Library.

ISBN 1 903111 86 2

Designed by Kate Pankhurst.

Printed and bound in Great Britain by
Biddles Ltd, King's Lynn, Norfolk.

CONTENTS

Being an actor is the loneliest thing in the world. You are all alone with your concentration and imagination, and that's all you have. Being a good actor isn't easy. Being a man is even harder.

JAMES BYRON DEAN, ACTOR (1931–1955)

Troubles and trials almost over,
Now see what the Lord has done.

'KEEP YOUR LAMP TRIMMED AND BURNING' (TRADITIONAL)

ACKNOWLEDGEMENTS

THE AMOUNT of material which has been put into print about John Christopher Depp since he first came to the attention of a larger public in 1984 is simply staggering, and yet many gaps in the record of his life and career still needed to be filled. Individuals who aided me in this task need to be singled out for special mention. They are Yves Bouhadana, Rose Moody, Donna Weaver, Cheryl Hollar, Mary Wells Walton, the staff of the Daviess County Public Library Kentucky Room, and Wes Walker. My thanks go to them all. Additional thanks must also be extended to Robin Moody, whose devotion to the task of tracking down information on Depp's early years in Kentucky and Florida contributed immeasurably towards my being able to include in this work much biographical detail which had never before been in print; Robin was equally instrumental in the acquisition of many rare materials, without which the present volume would be only half the book that hopefully it is.

I have quoted extensively from extant interviews conducted over the years by numerous journalists from all parts of the world, many of whom are mentioned in the main body of the text. Among those whose work was consulted are the following: Bill Zehme, Elaine Warren, Ian Spelling, Emily Blunt, Cindy Pearlman, Johanna Schneller, Karen Hardy Bystedt, Steve Pond, Christina Kelly, Chris Willman, Stephen Rebello, Johanna Schneller, Glenn Collins, Tom Burke, William Norwich, Christophe d'Yvoire, Leesa Daniels, Susan Morgan, Jamie Diamond, Betsy Israel, Chris Heath, Pauline Haldane, Jim McClellan, Larry Karaszewski, Scott Alexander, James Ryan, Cindy Pearlman, Peter Galvin, David Blum, Brendan Lemon, Thomas Beller, Holly Millea, Kevin Cook, Kevin Sessums, Karen Schoemer, Richard Schickel, Steve Goldman, Christopher Hemblade, Dana Shapiro, Elizabeth McCracken, Christopher Lawrence, Susan Morgan, Tom Shone, Douglas Brinkley, Dagmar

Dunlevy, Thomas Quinn, Kyle Smith, Jenny Peters, Chiara Mastroianni, Bridget Freer, Nancy Mills, Steve Runyon, Jessamy Calkin, Louise Finlay, Donna Walker-Mitchell, Martha Frankel, Morgan Bell, William Keck, Chris Pizello, William Georgiades, Brenda Levin, Jean Cummings, Paul Cullum, Tiffany Rose, Victoria Pandrea, Philip McCarthy, Sandra Benedetti, Gregory Katz, Ron Dicker, Robert Abele, Sophie Grassin, Philip Berk, John Millar, Gabrielle Donnelly, Lucy Kaylin, Isabelle Caron, Shelley Levitt, Marjorie Rosen, Danny Leigh, Polly Vernon, Sophie Cooper, Mark Ebner, Mark Salisbury, Jenny Dyson and Mara Reinstein. There are sure to be more. To those whom I might have missed, my sincere apologies and most grateful thanks in their inadvertent absence.

BACK STORY

The instinct of nearly all societies is to lock up anybody who is truly free. First, society begins by trying to beat you up. If this fails, they try to poison you. If this fails too, they finish by loading honours on your head.

JEAN COCTEAU, POET AND FILMMAKER (1889–1963)

ACTORS ARE DIFFERENT from other people. Committed actors are more different still. Johnny Depp is nothing if not a committed actor-although it was not always that way.

Actors come in all shapes and sizes, psychologically as well as physically, but they fall into two main categories: the technical, stage-trained or 'classical' actor and the 'method' or intuitive actor, whose rise to prominence began in the 1950s and whose technique is more suited to the art of film. Adherents to either discipline have one thing in common: they find it more comfortable to submerge their identities beneath the mask of another than they do to be themselves. Those who follow the path to acting are often more at ease in a make-believe world than they are in the real one. And yet actors, for all their frailties and their failings, their foibles, their dysfunctionality and their pathological need for adulation and attention, are the necessary conduits for the dream-lives of the rest of us. They are the means through which our collective fantasies find common expression. 'Acting,' said Victorian poseur and playwright Oscar Wilde, 'is so much more real than life.'

Some actors strive at the profession, considering it to be an old and honourable one, its history peopled with many of the most famous names of this and previous centuries. Others come to it by accident, through a quirk of personality or physiognomic attribute, or simply through sheer good looks – it is, after all, the most glamorous job in the world. The primary assets of the screen actor are physical attractiveness and the facility to exude 'charisma' that a camera lens can see. Of secondary importance is the ability to utter dialogue passably well. The wonders of make-up and technical effects, as well as lights, sound and carefully chosen camera angles, all contrive to compensate for a multitude of unprofessional sins. 'Acting is easy,' the 20-year-old Depp was advised by fellow thespian Nicolas Cage. 'They keep their eyes open for a look, and you've got that look.'

In the past, great actors would have learned their trade on the stage, whose intimacy with its audience allowed them the freedom to interpret and experiment; in the theatre, presence, vocal projection, manner and movement were more important than physical perfection, and success was dependent on talent alone. But, increasingly, the 'stage' of the twentieth century was film. Many would-be actors gravitated to performing on-screen without ever having set foot inside a theatre, with its singular disciplines, and without going through the rigours of playing to near-empty houses that did so much to put the steel into the performances of their forebears. Acting was seen to be within reach of all, and thus it became the career of choice for many a pretty boy or girl whose talent, in truth, was no more than skin deep. In consequence, it was doubly difficult for film actors to convince the public of their worth, let alone of their integrity towards the profession which had spawned them.

This paradox is central to any appreciation of the life and work of Johnny Depp. He fell into films through a simple twist of fate and the fact that he was possessed of teen-idol good looks, both of which arraigned against his chances of being taken seriously as a practitioner of the craft. But a painful childhood (in part) and confessed lack of self-esteem had invested him with a hunger for acceptance on a less superficial level. They had also provided him with the fuel for a series of characterisations which ran counter to the manufactured persona that the image-makers of the industry had seemed intent on foisting upon him. Instead, he sought recognition by different means and in unconventional quarters, preferring to play not to type but to instinct. Johnny Depp, in many respects, is the stereotypical 'crack'd actor' – confused and sometimes contradictory in life, but incisive and purposeful, and supremely gifted in his capability to create the illusion of life through role-play. It is the hallmark of his talent, as it was for all the great film actors in whose illustrious footsteps he follows. Depp, the man, is far removed from most of the characters he has portrayed on-screen, but his chameleon-like ability to become many men is what distinguishes him from his peers.

Acting is an intangible, and most actors reveal little of substance to the interviewer that is instructive about themselves, or about how or why they practise their craft. Like all artists, the actor can best be understood through his body of work, the product of his individual endeavour. The films of Johnny Depp exhibit the growth and development of a prodigious talent, one that he undoubtedly fails to recognise himself, beyond a modest desire to do the best that he can with whatever is to hand in any given situation. But Depp has transformed himself from teen idol into cinematic icon. The process has been a long and arduous one, which is partly his own doing and partly because his time to 'strut and fret his hour upon the stage' had not yet come. Though he still looks deceptively youthful, Depp has been in the business for 20 years; those two decades have been a period of learning and refining his craft, with some highs and many more lows. With the release in 2003 of *Pirates of the Caribbean: The Curse of the Black Pearl*, however, the film-going public – as well as the powers-that-be within the industry itself – started to look with new eyes upon Johnny Depp, and to see something that previously they had demarcated as arty and eccentric and of minority taste. The recognition for which he has striven for so long, and in largely uncompromising fashion, is now waiting around the corner; it may be overdue but it is unarguably deserved. With his quirky, stylised and characteristically individual turn as Captain Jack Sparrow in *Pirates of the Caribbean*, Depp has finally arrived on the world stage and on the Hollywood A-list.

Good looks or bad, talent will out at the end of the day if opportunity presents itself, and Depp has always shown himself to be attuned to opportunity. His story is one of a wannabe Punk rocker who has risen to become the pre-eminent screen actor of his generation. It is the Abe Lincoln American Dream saga of the poor white boy from the backwoods who, by hard work and dedication – as well as sex, drugs and rock 'n' roll – came through it all to be the undisputed king of the modern movie world.

For Johnny Depp, currently sailing the high seas of a success that was always destined to be his, it is only just beginning.

What follows is the story so far...

INTRODUCTION

INT. GLEN'S ROOM. NIGHT.
The boy lies sprawled, still clothed, in the middle of his bed.
Save for the bedside lamp, the room is dark.
There's a heartbeat's pause. Then with tremendous force, two
powerful arms shoot up beneath the red and yellow bed-
spread and grab GLEN around the waist!
Next moment the young man's body is dragged straight down
into the bed, as if some huge beast had grabbed him and
heaved him down! His feet and his arms shoot up – there's
another hauling yank – and the boy disappears except for his
hands and fingers-down into the pit in the middle of the bed!
His hands are last to go, clawing for a hold. But soon they
vanish as well, dragging blankets and bed-sheets, wires and
stereo across the caved-in bed and into the abyss...
from the screenplay of A Nightmare on Elm Street (1984)

A NIGHTMARE ON Elm Street – 44-year-old ex-humanities
teacher Wes Craven's breakthrough feature – almost single-handedly revived a genre which more than ten years before had fallen
into disarray and disrepute through repetition and a dearth of
original ideas.

The film itself was unappealing and somewhat controversial
in content: ostensibly about a child molester named Fred
Krueger, who had been hunted down and burned to death by a
mob of vigilantes, the storyline expeditiously sidestepped that
issue to concentrate instead on Fred's return from the grave as
a 'dream demon', out to revenge himself on the offspring of his
erstwhile persecutors via the incisive employment of a neat line
in switchblade glove. Through inventive staging of its set-piece
murder scenes, and the iconic look that its creator had given to
the talon-wielding villain of the piece, *A Nightmare on Elm
Street* managed to rise above its unsavoury theme and garner

sufficient box-office revenue to engender no fewer than six (now seven, with the belated *Freddy Vs Jason*) sequels, as well as a measure of respectability for the more contentious 'splatter' film to which it was heavily indebted.

A Nightmare on Elm Street made a minor horror star out of Robert Englund, whose only other genre outing of note had been a sympathetic alien reptile in the sci-fi teleseries *V*, but who played the role of the phantom paedophile with such relish that he stole the show from the rest of a cast of similar unknowns.

As was the way with 'stalk-and-slash' thrillers, the girls and boys who found themselves on the receiving end of the relevant maniac's attentions were largely dispensable – there to look pretty and act dumb until the time came for them to be shredded, or worse. Thus, none of the ensemble casts of victims in these films seemed ever to fare as well in any subsequent screen careers as the ubiquitous bogeyman to whom they were offered in sacrifice. Englund went from here to star in horror fare for other low-budget directors, including Tobe Hooper (*Night Terrors*, 1993; *The Mangler*, 1995), before making his way to the convention circuit in his trademark fedora and ultimately a reprise of his most famous role in 2003 (*Freddy Vs Jason*). In *A Nightmare on Elm Street*, however, another among the featured players turned out, eventually, to be an exception to this rule.

The role of Glen Lantz, a typical suburban teenager unwittingly embroiled in the gory goings-on, had gone to a young newcomer to films by the name of Johnny Depp. Like many of his peers, the slight but sharp-featured 20-year-old, who originally had hailed from the small Kentucky town of Owensboro – self-styled Barbecue Capital of the World – had spent the previous three years playing guitar in a number of unsuccessful 'Punk' bands by night while holding down a variety of equally mundane jobs by day.

His screen debut in *A Nightmare on Elm Street* brought Depp no closer to success than it did any of his co-stars in a film which turned out to belong solely to its monster, but it did bring him regular work as a actor.

It took another ten years for Johnny Depp to become a recognisable star. Ten years after that, however, and he was to become a superstar.

> Next moment what's left of GLEN is vomited up from the pit of the nightmare bed...a horrible mess of blood and bone and hair and wires...streaming out and over the bed. Then the pit in the bed is gone as if it were never there...
>
> from the screenplay of A Nightmare on Elm Street (1984)

1 IN SEARCH OF IDENTITY

STRETCHING OUT for more than five miles along the meandering south bank of the mighty Ohio River lies the sprawling steel town of Owensboro, in the Bluegrass state of Kentucky. St Louis, the second largest city in Missouri, is 200 miles to its north-west, while some 120 miles south is the home of country music itself: Nashville, Tennessee. To the north, on the other side of the river, lies Indiana; to the east, Virginia, of which Kentucky was originally a part. During the American Civil War, Owensboro was a town of split loyalties: it fought with the North, but its heart lay in the South.

According to anthropological studies, Native American culture in the locality dates back 12,000 years, though the last Shawnee Indians were forced to vacate the area before the end of the eighteenth century. Legend has it that Kentucky as a whole is 'dark and bloody ground' – a myth which arose out of the popular belief that Indian tribes were happy to hunt the land but were unwilling to settle it, rather than a reference to any hostilities which might have taken place in the territory between 1861 and

1865. Owensboro's only claim to fame in the civil war was that, in August 1864, the town was subject to a raid by a band of Confederate guerrillas from Tennessee led by Captain Jake Bennett, an officer in Johnson's Partisan Rangers. Bennett's men rode into Owensboro, tried and failed to rob a local bank, took 13 Union soldiers of the 108th Coloured Infantry prisoner, executed them, burned the bodies on a supply boat, and hot-footed it back to Tennessee having covered a total of 300 miles on horseback inside six days. At that time, Owensboro was less than 70 years old. It had initially been settled in 1798, becoming Owensborough after the name of its founding father, Colonel Abraham Owen, in 1816, before finally opting for the shortened version of its original name in 1893.

The end of the Second World War had brought civil engineering projects, which helped turn Owensboro from a sleepy industrial rump into a modern, expanding community by the turn of the 1960s. Many of these had been set in motion by Johnson, Depp & Quisenberry, a firm of consulting engineers then engaged in a runway redesign at the County Airport; the 'Depp' in question was but one member of an old and prodigious Kentucky family which was about to endow the town with its most famous son. Its retail heart was then the Lincoln Mall shopping centre on New Hartford Road, a site which now houses the $5 million Owensboro Christian Church. When the Lincoln Mall was a-buzz with shoppers, the resident population of Owensboro was something less than a third of its present 110,000.

With all of its roads leading to the imposing, blue-steel Ohio River Bridge, Owensboro formed the commercial hub of Daviess County – itself the crop capital of Kentucky in soybean production and a major source of its tobacco revenue. Two centuries earlier, the state had been home to Daniel Boone, one of the great American folk heroes. In the 1960s, it was more famously the home of Colonel Harland Sanders' Fried Chicken.

In June 1963, when a satisfactory resolution to the Cuban Missile Crisis of October the previous year had put a new spring in the step of the Kennedy administration, America was basking in the warmth of a summer that many of its citizens had thought they might never see. President John Fitzgerald Kennedy himself was not to be gunned down, officially by a Marxist fanatic, for another five months, and the country as a whole had not yet had time to come to terms with its government's covert incursions into the Southeast Asian trouble-spot of South Vietnam.

On the other side of the Atlantic, scandal, in the form of call-girls Christine Keeler and Mandy Rice-Davies, was rocking the British establishment to its very foundations: on 5 June, the Secretary of State for War, John Profumo, was forced to resign from office for having lied to Parliament about his association with Keeler.

The race for space between the USA and the USSR, whose rockets had been ignited by a presidential address to Congress in May 1961 that raised the curtain on this 'new frontier of human adventure,' was now being run in earnest. Within a year, John Glen had become the first American astronaut to orbit the earth; twelve months on, and Russia was preparing to send the first woman cosmonaut in his wake.

Nevertheless, all was not well on the home front. The burgeoning civil rights movement, under the charismatic leadership of Rev. Martin Luther King, Jnr., was gaining momentum. Prejudice and long-running tensions had once more been brought to the surface as a result and, on 12 June, Medgar Evers, the movement's field secretary in Mississippi, would be shot and killed outside his home. Hispanics and Native Americans, whose life expectancy was only two thirds that of whites, were also growing increasingly militant in their demands for equal rights and social justice. University campuses were becoming a focal point for this unrest: student populations were slowly being politicised, both from inside and out – on the very day of Kennedy's death, handbills were to be found circulating in college grounds with the words 'Wanted For Treason' emblazoned over a picture of the President. While Middle America tuned to *The Flintstones*, *Dr Kildare* or

The Beverley Hillbillies on television, the youth of America was grappling with a raft of new causes in a seedbed of disaffection.

Little of this was being reflected in the national culture of June 1963, however. Girl groups dominated the pop charts, from The Chiffons to The Crystals: in the top spot on both sides of the Atlantic was Lesley Gore's 'It's My Party'. The falsetto tones of Del Shannon and Jan and Dean still resonated close behind, as did the vocal harmonies of The Drifters with their unique brand of New York soul, but waiting in the wings was a four-piece band from Liverpool, England, who were destined to consign all of them to the pages of pop history.

In movie theatres were *The Birds* and *Dr No*, with the long-delayed *Cleopatra* now lined up for release. John Frankenheimer was filming *Seven Days in May*, while Stanley Kubrick was in England, shooting *Dr Strangelove; or How I Learned to Stop Worrying and Love the Bomb*. Robert Aldrich had already put the finishing touches to *Whatever Happened to Baby Jane?*, and Otto Preminger was doing likewise to *The Cardinal*. Jack Lemmon was working on Billy Wilder's *Irma La Douce*, Vincent Price had just tucked *The Haunted Palace* under his belt, and Marlon Brando – still one of the biggest box-office stars of the day – was soon to embark on *The Quiet American*, having been mauled by the critics for his dandified performance in *Mutiny on the Bounty*. Every other available actor in Hollywood was either featuring in George Stevens' *The Greatest Story Ever Told* or Stanley Kramer's *It's a Mad, Mad, Mad, Mad World*.

Hollywood remained resolutely in the mainstream, but small-scale 'kitchen-sink' dramas from British studios, like recent releases *The L-Shaped Room* and *This Sporting Life*, were starting to have an impact on world cinema, while directors like Italy's Federico Fellini and Polish-born Roman Polanski were fast becoming as well known to young audiences as their more illustrious American counterparts were to the old.

Kentucky's connections to the film business go back to its very beginnings: David Wark Griffith, pioneering director of *Birth of a*

Nation (1915) and *Intolerance* (1916) and 'father' of the entire American industry came from La Grange. Tod Browning, director of *Dracula* (1931) and *Freaks* (1932) was born in Louisville, as was beefcake actor Victor Mature and, more recently, Tom Cruise. George Clooney hails from Lexington; fellow-actor Harry Dean Stanton from West Irvine. Tom Ewell, who famously played opposite Marilyn Monroe in Billy Wilder's 1955 comedy *The Seven Year Itch* was a native of Owensboro itself, as was Florence Henderson, who is perhaps best known for television's *The Brady Bunch*. Patricia Neal, for many years married to author Roald Dahl, came from Packard. Neal is Kentucky's sole Oscar-winner to date; in 1963, she had just gained the Best Actress Award for *Hud*, in which she starred opposite Paul Newman.

It was a schizophrenic age, of hot chicks and cold war, and the generation gap that had appeared with the advent of rock 'n' roll in the 1950s was growing wider by the day as other art forms sought to side with the armies of youth that were readying themselves for the long march. The previous year had seen publication of Anthony Burgess's *A Clockwork Orange* as well as Ken Kesey's *One Flew Over the Cuckoo's Nest*, though 1963 had so far produced only one book worthy of note: *On Her Majesty's Secret Service* – Ian Fleming's latest outing for secret agent 007. The month of May had brought a screen version of Tennessee Williams' *Period of Adjustment*, starring Jane Fonda and Jim Hutton – and that, ironically, was what America was about to undergo. Whether it would be for good or ill, no one could yet foresee.

Either way, this was the world into which, at 8.44 am on the morning of 9 June, Betty Sue Depp gave birth to her fourth child and second son, whom his proud parents decided to christen with the names John Christopher, after his father. This was the tumultuous sea onto which the young 'Johnny' Depp opened his baby-blue eyes (later to turn brown).

The latest addition to the Depp household was duly transferred from the Catholic Mercy hospital in downtown Owensboro to the family's modest, timber-framed home on Stockton Drive, in a residential neighbourhood off the southbound highway of Frederica Street, to the west side of town. John junior found himself with a two-year-old sister named Elisa Christine (nicknamed Christi), as well as a half-sister and brother named Deborah and Daniel, aged seven and nine respectively, who were the offspring of his mother's previous marriage but had since been adopted as John Depp's own. His 25-year-old father had gained a Bachelor of Science degree in civil engineering from the University of Kentucky in 1961, and he was presently employed by his father, Oren, in the family firm of 'O L Depp, General Contractor'. (In his final year at Owensboro Senior High School in 1956, John Depp senior had been voted Best Looking student.) His 29-year-old mother, the former Betty Wells of Butler County, worked as a waitress in a coffee shop.

Depp's mother had waited on table in diners and coffee shops since the age of fourteen. Because of her lowly status in life, she had developed a feisty temperament and a fiercely independent nature – much like the stereotypical waitresses of so many Hollywood movies. Betty Sue's youngest son soon grew to admire these traits in his mother, wearing her sense of self-respect in the face of disparagement as a badge of honour in his later years. 'One of the greatest pieces of advice I've ever gotten in life was from my mom,' he was subsequently to recall for Karen Hardy Bystedt. 'When I was a little kid, there was a kid who was bugging me in school. And she said, "I'm going to tell you what to do. The kid's bugging you. If he puts his hands on you, you pick up the nearest rock, or whatever you can get your hands on, and you lay him out." And I did! And I felt better.'

Aside from being one of four siblings, John Christopher Depp was the newest recruit to an extended family whose roots went back to the Revolution and beyond, and most of whose present members lived in the near vicinity. Consequently, he had no lack of aunts, uncles or cousins. He also possessed two sets of grandparents. Both were in their late fifties at the time of Johnny's birth but Walter and Bessie, on his mother's side, were hard-working tobacco farmers who lived near the state capital of Frankfort, while Oren and Violet (whom he knew as 'Mattie') were a middle-class couple who lived in a wealthier neighbourhood on the other side of Frederica Street, in the lush heart of the Owensboro suburbs. Right across the street from his paternal grandparents' home were his Aunt Sheila and Uncle Bobby; Bobby was soon to find himself drafted into service in Vietnam.

The American branch of the Depp line was effectively begun with Pierre Deppe (the 'e' was later dropped), the son of French Huguenots who had settled in Virginia around 1697 to escape persecution in the land of their birth. By the time his grandson, William, had married and raised a family of his own, the Depps had moved on to Barren County, Kentucky, where their descendants were to remain from 1792 on. John Depp Snr was the ninth generation of naturalised Depps and he and Betty were married in Lexington in 1961, six months after the birth of their daughter and his graduation from college. By 1963, in preparation for the birth of their son, they had moved into the house on Stockton Drive.

In August that year, more than 200,000 people joined a civil rights march in Washington to hear the Reverend King deliver a speech on the steps of the Lincoln Memorial. It turned out to be one of the great speeches of the twentieth century, if not of all time: 'I have a dream,' King began, 'that one day this nation will rise up and live out the true meaning of its creed – We hold these truths to be self-evident: that all men are created equal.' Less than three months later, the same Democratic President of the United States of America who had ordered the National Guard onto university campuses to safeguard the very rights of black students that King had spoken about was brutally assassinated.

The young John Depp was less than six months old when the 'liberal' Kennedy was shot to death in Dallas, Texas – an event which was condemned as an act of 'monstrous stupidity' by a 26-year-old Kentucky journalist named Hunter Stockton Thompson, a native of Louisville, who later condensed his reaction to the gunshot whose reverberation was heard around the world into two words: 'fear' and 'loathing'. The America that the Depps' baby was about to grow up in would now be a very different place from that into which he had been born.

Despite this, Depp's Owensboro childhood was essentially a happy one. He passed it by watching the world-famous Harlem Globetrotters while nurturing an ambition to become the first white member of the all-black basketball team. He followed the exploits of 'Daredevil Legend' Evel Knievel, until the motorcycle ace crashed his bike after jumping the fountains in front of Caesar's Palace in Las Vegas in 1968, bringing his stunt-riding career to an abrupt halt. He fancied himself as one of 'Hogan's' television 'Heroes', jollying their way through wartime internment in Stalag 13. Alternatively, he thought to be a master-spy in the laid-back style of Dean Martin's Matt Helm or James Coburn's Derek Flint, both characters that had featured in Bond-style film series in the mid-1960s. His somewhat unusual surname might have weighed in against that prospect, however. 'It spawned nicknames,' he confessed. 'I was "Johnny Dip". "Deppity Dawg". "Dippity-Do".'

Two years after Johnny was born, the family had moved to a marginally larger and more modern house on Freeman Avenue, a mere five blocks away from the paternal grandparents' home on Griffith Place West and a few minutes walk from 'Elm Street', a place-name which the young Johnny Depp would come to know much better in another couple of decades. By 1966, the Depps and their children had moved again, only on that occasion it was more than 120 miles east towards Frankfort, where his mother could be nearer her parents. 'We moved constantly,' Depp later complained. 'My mom just liked to move for some reason. It was hard. Depending on how far we'd move, you'd have to make new friends. We never stayed in one neighbourhood for long. At the drop of a hat, we'd go.'

In ultra-conservative Kentucky, Depp also grew up listening to the music of Sinatra and the big bands of the 1930s and 1940s; in addition, he was weaned on gospel music and the Blues, courtesy of an evangelical preacher in the family – 'an "Elmer Gantry" uncle', as film director John Waters later christened him – and cousins who provided choral harmony for the Sunday sinners who came to repent and be saved. With his mother's genes predominant in his make-up, young John soon showed himself to be an altogether rougher diamond than his largely middle-class heritage might have indicated. He exhibited an especial affinity for his maternal grandparents – she with her habitual tobacco-chewing and ever-ready spittoon; he with whom Johnny often went tobacco-picking and affectionately nicknamed 'Pawpaw'. And he developed a fascination for insects of all kinds – 'bugs', as Americans term them – which would last throughout his life. Long summer evenings spent trying to catch 'lightning bugs' (fireflies) with neighbourhood friends were to become an enduring childhood memory, as Depp remembered, wistfully: 'Beautiful, fascinating bugs ... There was a little girl who lived next door who had a brace on her leg. We used to play on the swing set, and the night the astronauts landed on the moon, her father came out and looked up and said, in all seriousness, 'When man sets foot on the face of the moon, the moon will turn to blood.' I was shocked. I remember thinking, Jeez, I'm six and that's a little deep for me. I stayed up watching the moon. It was a big relief when it didn't change.'

But watching the moon was not the only thing which kept the young Depp from sleep at night. Another was the sound of his parents arguing. And there was a recurring dream which was inspired by the popular TV sitcom *Gilligan's Island* (which had run on CBS from 1964 to 1967), in which the otherwise amiable Alan Hale Jnr character of Skipper Jonas Grumby gleefully chased after the impressionable Depp; an equally inexplicable sense of dread was engendered in Depp by the smiling countenance of crooner John Davidson, who played host to Kraft's *Summer Music Hall* in 1966 before graduating to his own show in 1969. In the same period, Johnny had his first exposure to the silent movies of John Barrymore, Buster Keaton and Lon Chaney, through the auspices of *Silents Please*; he was told 'The Legend of Sleepy Hollow' at Halloween, watched Bela Lugosi in *Dracula* and consequently became a devotee of a daytime Gothic soap-opera called *Dark Shadows*, in which Canadian actor Jonathan Frid stalked Collinsport, Maine as a vampire named Barnabus Collins.

That the various house-moves would eventually have a disruptive and long-lasting effect on the youngest member of the Depp family almost goes without saying. But there was more to it than the metaphorical 'ants' which Johnny Depp naively assumed his mother must have had in her proverbial pants. Since the birth of their son and the increasing financial burden which it naturally placed on the family unit, his parents had not been getting along. Nor did 'starting over' at regular intervals appear to solve the problem; if anything, matters only got worse. His father's seeming unwillingness to feed off the family business had forced him to search for independent employment, but it also put an intolerable strain on the relationship. Even at elementary school age, Depp had become sanguine about the situation at home: 'As young as seven or eight, I remember looking at them and thinking: "Come on, this is torture. Just split up",' he would tell Gabrielle Donnelly of *You* magazine.

As his parents moved further apart, so Johnny had moved closer to his 'Pawpaw', whose sagacity he had come to admire and who had taught him to fish and to roll tobacco. In 1970, Pawpaw died quite suddenly, at the age of 65. Depp was heartbroken; he would never forget the Kentucky tobacco-picker who had inadvertently became his first real role model in life, or the profound impact that his homespun philosophising had made on him: 'I have always had this feeling that an inner force, coming from nowhere, guided me, as well for the bad or the good things happening to me. That force-I do believe my grandfather gave it to me. At least, I like to think it. We were really close. I do love him and I think he liked me.'

With the prospect of a more attractive job in civil engineering now on offer in the south, and little left to hold them to Kentucky, John and Betty Depp decided to make a clean break of it and head for Miramar, which at the time was a relatively new residential community in the Fort Lauderdale district of Florida. Less than ten miles to the east of it was a beach-side resort called Hollywood. Little did Johnny know that his warring parents' next step on life's highway was to put him firmly on track for the real thing.

DISSOLVE. MIRAMAR, FLORIDA. 1970.
SCREEN CAPTION:
The City of Miramar was incorporated May 26th, 1955. At the time of incorporation, the City had a population of less than two hundred people. Robert Gordon, the first Mayor of the City, gave the City its name. 'Miramar', which is Spanish for 'Look at the Sea'. The City seal is inscribed with its motto 'Beauty and Progress'.
OFFICIAL CITY OF MIRAMAR WEBSITE

Miramar was not exactly Small-town USA, but for the young John Depp, it might just as well have been. He was enrolled in Miramar's Sunshine Elementary School while he and his family spent the first year in their newly adopted state of Florida holed up in a motel. But in the beginning, there were compensations. When the Depps were finally able to rent a place for themselves, Johnny found a kindred spirit in the ebullient form of Sal(vatore) Jenco, and a friendship was born which would last till the present day. The resulting invitations to dine with his new friend enabled him to see for the first time 'how the other half lived', in a more harmonious home, not always riven with acrimony and discontent. Depp recalled: 'I was very mischievous as a boy; I loved tape recording people when they didn't know. One time a friend and I dug a really deep tunnel in my backyard. We covered it with boards and leaves. I was attempting to dig a tunnel into my room. I liked to push it to see how far I could go.'

By the time the Depp family settled in Miramar, the *Easy Rider* era of pot-smoking and 'peace and love' was well and truly at an end; an orgy of murder in the Hollywood hills by the self-styled Family of Satanic guru Charles Manson had sounded the death-knell for the hippie dream, and 'Lucy in the Sky with Diamonds' had faded into 'The Long and Winding Road' as the pop phenomenon that was The Beatles ended in legal separation. In 1968, the dystopian cinema of the American underground had disgorged *Night of the Living Dead* and with it had been born the 'splatter' film, whose graphic violence was a visceral metaphor for a national psychosis and wholly emblematic of the empty materialist philosophy from which it had sprung. The times, they were a-changin', as one-time folk-poet and icon of the youth movement, Bob Dylan, went electric, his bemused audience went ballistic and everyone else of impressionable age either went into denial or sought to escape through drugs.

Man had landed on the moon but two out of the three Kennedy brothers were dead, both assassinated. Martin Luther King had similarly been gunned down outside his hotel room in Memphis, while leading cultural lights like Jack Kerouac, Jimi Hendrix, Otis Redding and Janis Joplin could also now be numbered among the fallen. On 4 May 1970, at Kent State University in Ohio, members of the National Guard had opened fire on a number of students who were demonstrating against the bombing of Cambodia and clandestine expansion of the war, wounding nine and killing four – one down for every second of the salvo. America was killing its own children and the American Dream was turning to nightmare, an unappetising truth which became inculcated in popular iconography by part-time sports commentator and full-time dope-head Hunter S Thompson, in his seminal work of 'gonzo' literature, *Fear and Loathing in Las Vegas* (1971).

Twelve months later, Watergate loomed and an air of desperation crept over the land; an air of despair, typified by films like Richard Sarafian's *Vanishing Point*, as the names of the 58,000 American dead from the battlefields of Southeast Asia were being etched in a roll of honour onto granite monuments nation-wide. The Depp's home state of Kentucky's loss had been more acute than many: 80 miles south-west of Owensboro lay Fort Campbell, home to the 101st Airborne Division.

Before he was 11, Depp's parents had moved into more suitable accommodation at SW 68th Avenue, near Miramar Parkway: 'The house was a three-bedroom, built in the sixties,' he recalled. 'It constantly smelled of my mom's cooking: soup, beans and ham. I remember my brother and sister fighting. I had a poodle named Pepe, and I shared a bedroom with my brother.' He later described his immediate neighbourhood as having 'A Winn-Dixie [food] store, a drugstore next door, and next to that a card and gift store. Across the street was a Publix [food] store that had its own drugstore and card and gift store attached to it,' adding pointed-ly, 'You were just *there*.' Miramar: a 'bedroom' community of sun-drenched palms, sun-bleached houses, sterile conformity, 33,000 souls and… food stores. To a country-boy, it was all a far remove from the rolling crop-fields of Kentucky.

Johnny had now graduated to the Henry D Perry Middle School and had temporarily lost touch with Jenco along the way. Sal's immediate replacements were not of the same calibre, and the adolescent Depp fell under the influence of what he was later to term a 'bad crowd', at what was to be the most vulnerable time of his life. The result was a period of petty theft, petty vandalism and all-round petulance; still to come were the drink and the drugs.

Like most Americans, Johnny Depp could trace his family tree back to pioneering days. Despite that, he soon affected to declare that he came from humbler origins – 'white trash', as he was to colloquialise his roots in his more outspoken moments of early fame. This was not strictly true: his mother was a waitress, but his father was a white-collar worker and both had been in regular employment throughout most of his childhood. Part of this feel-ing of alienation stemmed from his lowlier background on his mother's side; it was an aspect of his make-up of which he was made increasingly aware by the time he had started to run with the big boys in the more reactionary outpost of the Florida Keys. (He was later to claim that his antecedents on his mother's side were of mixed blood – specifically Cherokee – which was not, in itself, unusual in the area of Kentucky from which they originated, although there is no clear evidence for this in the Wells lineage.) 'Living in Florida, there's tons of rednecks out there. I mean, these guys want to hear "Sweet Home Alabama" twenty-four hours a day,' was a typical reflection. One incident in particular left an indelible mark on the youngster: Depp was standing outside the gates of his school when a stranger walked past him, staring at him intently. 'God, what an ugly kid!' the man suddenly exclaimed, before going on his way. The callous remark cut deep: 'He fucked with me really bad,' Depp was to say of the experience years later. (During his two years at high school, he would become accustomed to being referred to as a 'dirty Indian' because of his ethnic looks.)

As Depp looked towards his years as a teenager, his parents' marriage grew increasingly rocky. Their relationship had been fraught for some time and the situation was not improved by the move to Florida; by the mid-1970s, the downward spiral towards a parting of the ways was already on the cards and, as the youngest child, he was particularly affected by the ongoing animosity, withdrawing ever more into a world of his own devising in order to flee the constant quarrels which had now become a feature of daily life.

In common with many of his contemporaries, Johnny had read *The Catcher in the Rye*, J D Salinger's chronicle of disaffected youth and the growing-pains of adolescence. Other influences were also being brought to bear on his emotional susceptibility: his elder brother Danny, now 21, was naturally possessed of a cultural sensibility which was altogether more sophisticated and almost a generation removed from the ragbag artistic tastes of his younger sibling. The teenage years are a time to seek out role models in the human male and Depp's disenfranchised father was now in no position to fit the bill. Enter Big Brother, with his Van

Morrison LPs, his penchant for art-house films like Bertolucci and Brando's *Last Tango in Paris*... and his dog-eared copy of Jack Kerouac's *On the Road*.

Jean-Louis 'Jack' Kerouac was a writer of French-Canadian blood, but native to Lowell, Massachusetts. In his mid-twenties, he and fellow freethinker Neal Cassady had taken off on an arbitrary series of travels by Cadillac across the USA and Mexico, essentially to see what was out there. Their adventures along the way were to form the basis of *On the Road*, in which Kerouac characterised himself as Sal Paradise and friend Cassady as Dean Moriarty; drugs, alcohol, sex, jazz and literature had fuelled these trips, and in 1951 Kerouac began to try to capture his experiences on paper, in a narrative form which was heavily influenced by his admiration for Marcel Proust but which Kerouac described as 'spontaneous writing'. The book was eventually published amid some controversy in 1957, and it immediately became a bible for the restless youth of the Eisenhower era, whose institutional disaffection with the extant social order had already found an outlet in rock 'n' roll

The counter-cultural philosophy expressed in *On the Road* was a quintessential to the politics of the 'Beat' movement, a term which Kerouac coined to represent the New Vision that he sought to explore with fellow 'Beatniks', New York poet Allen Ginsberg and novelist William S(eward) Burroughs. The broad aim of the Beats was social and sexual liberation, coupled to artistic freedom of expression and, in these respects, the movement represented a modern American incarnation of the Pre-Raphaelites of the 1850s or the Bloomsbury Group in the early decades of the twentieth century.

Every age has its antithetical element and the more conformist the mainstream, the more extreme has been the opposition to it. The ultra-conservatism of 1950s America had ushered in the Beats, rock 'n' roll, artists like Jackson Pollock and movie stars like Marlon Brando and James Dean. The influence of the Beats – many of whose leading proponents were also the product of broken homes – was profound; it continued to inform the hippie movement a decade later, and actor Peter Fonda had unashamedly pilfered *On the Road* for the plot of *Easy Rider* in 1969.

Kerouac had died in 1969 at the age of 47, disenchanted by his role as cheerleader for the Beats and a victim of 'fame burnout'. But his influence remained undiminished, and his philosophical flame was kept burning well into the 1960s by Ginsberg, a die-hard dissenter and confirmed subscriber to new-wave ideologies. Ginsberg had demonstrated against the war in Vietnam, been an outspoken advocate of gay rights in an age when there were none (he was himself homosexual), worked with acid-guru Timothy Leary to promote the mind-expanding properties of LSD, and went on to contribute to The Clash's *Combat Rock* album in 1982, as well as performing with them on stage, before eventually succumbing to cancer in 1995.

Dan Depp urged Kerouac's book on his younger brother, and Johnny obliged by reading it avidly; it opened his eyes to a cultural universe which previously had been inhabited only by a biography of legendary football coach Knute Rockne, the Kung Fu films of Bruce Lee and the music of the 'face of the seventies', Peter Frampton. In 1999, he recalled this period in his life for *The Rolling Stone Book of the Beats*, in an article that consciously referenced the style of Hunter S Thompson but which was honestly expressed, and revealed something of the sensitivity which by then had benefited him as an actor: '*On the Road* was life-changing for me. I wanted my education to come from getting out there in the world, moving among the other vagabonds who had had the same sneaking suspicion I had, that there would be no great need for high-end mathematics, nope... I was not going to be doing other people's taxes and going home at 5.37 pm to pat my dog's head and sit down to my meat-and-two-vegetable table, waiting for *Jeopardy* to pop on the glass tit, the Pat Sajak of my own private game show, in the belly-button of the universe, Miramar, Florida. A beautiful life, to be sure, but one I know I was destined not to have, thanks to big brother Dan and the French-Canadian with the name Jack Kerouac.'

Within two years, Depp had taken refuge in his room and learned to play a guitar which his mother had bought for $25, lost his virginity to a girl four years his senior in the back of a pick-up truck, experimented with drugs ('I just wanted to find out what was out there') and looked helplessly on as his parents' shaky marriage crumbled inexorably to dust before his eyes. He was now fourteen and, with only the youngest of his sisters still domiciled with him in the troubled home, he could see little future either for himself or the family of which he previously had felt so much a part. It was at this point that he started to cut himself – or 'self-harm', as psychologists prefer to describe what has become an increasingly prevalent psychosis among disturbed teenagers. 'It was anger and unhappiness,' he was to confide to *Time Out*, 'a form of self-loathing.' It was also an impotent response to the growing sense of alienation which was induced in him by the never-ending series of house moves (which had continued in the interim), as well as the strong probability of impending divorce. 'We'd go from neighbourhood to neighbourhood, sometimes from one house to the house next door. I don't know why; my mom would get "ants" somehow. There's a huge history of my family out there: furniture, my toys, schoolwork, everything. Everything was abandoned, left in attics or garages. All gone.'

The man falling isn't permitted to feel or hear himself hit bottom.
He just keeps falling and falling.
J D SALINGER, *THE CATCHER IN THE RYE* (1951)

The political black hole which had been left by Republican President Richard Nixon's ignominious impeachment from office in the wake of the Watergate scandal had now been plugged by the squeaky-clean administration of Southern Democratic peanut farmer, Jimmy Carter, but the cultural vacuum was to be filled through the loudmouthed antics of a bunch of British anarchists who were about to put 'Punk Rock' on the map – the very antithesis of the musical mood which it rampaged to replace.

Punk Rock was officially acknowledged on Thames Television's *Today* show of 1 December 1976, when a band called The Sex Pistols, comprising lead singer Johnny Rotten (Lydon), Paul Cook, Steve Jones and Glen Matlock, was goaded by host Bill Grundy into unleashing a four-letter tirade over the London airwaves at an unseemly 6.15 in the evening. *The Daily Mirror* headline on the following day was 'The Filth and the Fury!', which typified the response that greeted the Pistols' introduction to a larger audience than the denizens of the pubs and clubs of the capital to whom they had previously plied their wares, but it shrewdly launched both them and the musical movement which they came to represent on a rocky road to pop riches.

The Pistols had opened the floodgates for other Punk bands on both sides of the Atlantic to try to emulate their lead, and their unorthodox route to success had pricked up the ears of every wannabe rock musician who heard the news.

It was the cue that Johnny Depp had been waiting for. He had already found the love of his life and it had turned out not to be the cheerleader on whom he had a crush in 7th grade: instead, it was music, and a chance encounter on CB radio with another guitar-picking teen from his own school set the ball rock 'n' rolling. Depp and his CB-buddy, Yves Bouhadana, got together with Joe Quinones (bass) and Bernie Phlum (drums) to form a band which they christened Flame. 'I followed the Jimmy Page school of guitar playing and Johnny followed the Eddie Van Halen school,' Bouhadana was to note. This first band lasted only one gig, at a Catholic school during a local carnival. They played two songs, one of which was Lynyrd Skynyrd's 'Freebird'. But it was a beginning, and it had given both boys something to focus on as they switched from Henry D Perry to Miramar High School.

The Clash, the Pistols, Bowie and Iggy Pop were required listening for any young rock 'n' roller on the make, but with the help of his brother, Depp's musical tastes had now been broadened out to include Tom Waits, the Georgia Satellites, Aerosmith and the florid antics of Kiss – especially Kiss. (In his last year at middle school, Depp had revealed his talent for mimicry by imitating lead-guitarist Ace Frehley in a talent show.) His new school proved to be of little interest to him, and his evenings were spent practising with his band in a rented warehouse. 'I wasn't big on participating in school activities,' he admitted. 'I used to bring my guitar to school, and I'd skip most classes to sneak into guitar class.' Flame had been a serious business for all involved: guitarist Yves Bouhadana missed one practice session and was summarily booted out of the band. 'Johnny was sympathetic and compassionate about the sadness I felt,' Bouhadana said of the affair, but the decision stood. 'Another kid joined the band, but it didn't last very long after that.' One of the reasons for that was that Johnny Depp now had much more than music on his mind.

While he was still fifteen, Depp's parents divorced. It was hardly unexpected, but it was a shock to him all the same. With that final, irrevocable split, he found himself cast adrift in an unpredictable sea of perceived rejection, with little sense of belonging left to him as he wandered the sun-baked streets of a bland, middle-class suburban landscape for which he had never felt any affinity. 'When my parents split up was when I think I realised these are the most important people in my life,' he was to confess to *US* magazine. 'I was fifteen, and it just sort of happened. You deal with it, but there's no escaping the hurt.'

'When he did go, it was a relief,' Depp said of his father in an interview with *Metro*. 'A cloud of violence was lifted.' But when John Senior moved out, his daughter Christi opted to join him. Being the youngest, Depp had felt for some time that it was his presence in the home which had delayed the inevitable, and so he felt equally obliged to stay put in support of his mother. As things turned out, this was just as well: Betty Sue suffered a breakdown as a result of the split. 'When they finally did it, I thought it was the right thing for them to do, then my mother became ill and the focus was on getting her well.'

*The teachers didn't want to teach, and I didn't
want to learn from them.*

J D SALINGER, *THE CATCHER IN THE RYE* (1951)

The pressures which were created by the break-up of his parents' marriage saw to it that Depp's high school career was over almost before it began: he flunked out inside two years, choosing instead to hang with friends who found themselves in positions which were similar to his own: Sal Jenco (with whom he had been reunited in 11th grade) was sleeping rough in a Chevy Impala, so Johnny decided to join him there. While he was still in high school, he had also joined another band called Bad Boys, one of a dozen more which would utilise his musical talents before he finally managed to form The Kids, an outfit that he described as 'Muddy Waters meets The Sex Pistols'. Jenco went along for the ride, acting as 'roadie' to the band as well as lighting technician.

The Kids turned out to be Depp's salvation: 'When the home front went into a tailspin, you needed to believe that somewhere, somehow, something was going to be okay,' he said. 'You had to believe that you just keep moving forward regardless, and you'll get to a place where you can breathe better.' They were his passage out of Miramar High as well, and he and his new band were soon playing parties, functions, 'roller rinks' and the Balkan Rock Club in nearby Dania, for $25 per band-member per gig.

By the turn of the 1980s, the Miami rock scene was buzzing, with bands like The B-52s, The Pretenders, Talking Heads and Iggy Pop playing clubs like Blue Waters, Tight Squeeze and the aforementioned Balkan Rock, all of them long since gone. Through hard work and dedication, The Kids met with some success on the club circuit, where they were soon hired to play opening sets for the bigger names on the bill. (After a concert in Gainesville, Depp's opening salvo to current bill-topper Iggy Pop, in typical Punk style, was allegedly a juvenile retort of 'Fuck you!', endlessly repeated. This forced nod to anarchic convention failed to achieve the desired effect, however, as Pop took the verbal assault to indicate the presence of a 'little turd', rather than a kindred spirit. When Depp eventually retreated from what he had perceived to be Punk conformity, the two later became friends.)

Depp's proclivity for cutting his arms as a neurotic means of self-expression in the face of overwhelming trauma had since given way to a more focused fixation with the tattooist's art, and the first in an eventual tally of fourteen 'skin illustrations' – as author Ray Bradbury had christened them in his novel *The Illustrated Man* – had now found itself emblazoned on his left shoulder: 'Betty Sue', in honour of his mother. To the bewilderment of many, Depp now seemed determined to become The Illustrated Boy.

The Kids eventually played the clubs of South Florida for more than three years, during which time their reputation and standing as a band grew, though not fast enough for their 20-year-old guitarist. In 1983, at the invitation of Don Ray, booking-agent for a Hollywood music-spot called The Palace, Johnny Depp and The Kids decided to take Horace Greeley's oft-quoted advice and head west to Los Angeles, in the hope of finding the fame and fortune which still eluded them at home. Depp now possessed all of the attributes of the typical teen rebel of the 1980s: he had the Punk credentials of tattoos, earrings, torn jeans and an unruly mane of hair, and he smoked, drank, swore like a marine and did drugs. California was to be his oyster, he thought. It was only a matter of time. But still he hankered for the family life which had brutally been snatched from him in his youth. It was music and the freewheeling philosophy of Jack Kerouac which drove him on, but it was an unconscious need to recreate the security that he had lost which ultimately was to set him on course for stardom.

In his reading of Kerouac's existentialist muse, Depp had uncovered allusions which struck a chord in him in relation to his own life, like the fact that Jack's wife had worked as a waitress while he was writing the novel (though he left her after it was published). It was natural that he would pick up on the idea that he, Cassady, Ginsberg and the rest experimented with drugs as a way of opening their minds to new means of artistic expression. Depp was profoundly affected by the text and, as he packed his bags for LA, he was taking more from *On the Road* along with him than he could ever have realised.

Among a disaffected youth, the culture of soft drug-use had begun in earnest in the more affluent 1960s; by the 1970s, it had become indigenous on both sides of the Atlantic and was being catered for on an industrial scale, its bill-of-fare having expanded from marijuana and variants of psychedelic hippie-favourite LSD to include 'harder' drugs like heroin and, later, cocaine. Drugs had been freely available in the clubs and bars of Florida – more so in the night-haunts of LA – and Depp had no compunctions about their use: 'I did drugs when I freaked out,' he would admit. 'I was in a rock 'n' roll band in Florida, the cocaine capital of the world, and drugs are really prominent in the club scene. Especially there.'

Drugs had been every bit as prominent on the club scene in Los Angeles for some time past, as Depp would find out to his cost in the years to come.

> 'Sal, we gotta go and never stop going till we get there.'
> 'Where we going, man?'
> 'I don't know but we gotta go.' Then here came a gang of young bop musicians carrying their instruments out of cars. They piled right into a saloon and we followed them. They set themselves up and started blowing. There we were!
> JACK KEROUAC, *ON THE ROAD* (1957)

Sal Jenco chose not to go to LA with The Kids, and he remained in Miramar to work in the construction industry. But Depp was determined to make his mark on the music scene no matter what, and despite having to leave his boyhood friend behind, he and the rest of The Kids waved Florida goodbye. 'Nothing else mattered for Johnny,' Yves Bouhadana recalled. 'For most of us, we had family, school and a few other functions. But for Johnny, music consumed 95 per cent of his life.'

In the later 1980s, the Punk movement in the USA was to be exemplified by the 'grunge' look, a ragbag fashion statement of sorts, in which articles of clothing long past their sell-by date were combined with items of ethnic or historical origin, culled from charity shops and embellished with ephemera of pop-cultural significance, like VW badges or a medallion of Coke-bottle tops. It was an outfit which The Kids and their precarious financial position had already adopted out of necessity after reaching LA, as they set out upon the steep climb towards musical recognition. The next year brought only a small number of supporting gigs and no breakthrough: unlike the situation which they had left behind in Florida, competition was fierce and The Kids were neither good enough nor different enough to make the grade. 'There were so many bands, it was impossible to make any money,' Depp explained. 'We all had to take menial jobs to avoid starving to death.'

Torn jeans, spiked hair, a modishly casual attitude to drug-taking, a head-banging stage presence and a pounding guitar-style notwithstanding, Depp was still a young man to whom commitment meant everything, and the hedonistic allure of life in a band had proved to be only skin-deep. The oft-cited adage of 'sex, drugs and rock 'n' roll' had been seen as a panacea by many a social outcast since the notion was originally coined in the hedonistic days of the 'swinging sixties'. Depp had found an outlet for his pent-up frustrations in 'drugs and rock 'n' roll', but the 'sex' part of the equation had come a poor third. By the age of 20, and in defiance of rock convention, he had already met, hurriedly wooed and this time married an 'older' woman (as had his father), in the shape of 25-year-old Lori Anne Allison, sister to one of The Kids and an aspiring musician in her own right. For a brief moment, the pair were in love, though Depp was to become less sure of Lori Anne's affection for him as time went on. Depp's nuptials had taken place in Florida (on 20 December); his honeymoon was to be spent in California.

But with marriage came responsibility and more dead-end jobs designed to help support himself and his new bride on the fringes of Hollywood: he had been a construction labourer, a gas-station attendant, a mechanic, a screen printer, and now Johnny Depp was a telephone salesman, employed to persuade reluctant purchasers to part with their hard-earned dollars for 'junk' items like ballpoint pens: 'We got paid a hundred bucks a week to lie to people,' he said. 'I got very good at it, but guilt started to get to me. I felt like I was ripping people off. The last couple of times I did it, I just said "Listen, you don't want this stuff, man".' The 'lying', as he put it, was to come in handy; for his next job, he would be asked to lie in front of millions.

Depp continued to play with his band – now renamed Six Gun Method – in the evenings and at weekends, a situation which put him into conflict with his wife and led to the dissolution of the marriage inside two years ('I was a child of divorce and I didn't know how a marriage worked,' he said later). Freed from the ties that bind, Lori Anne introduced him to an actor friend of hers, who was also now the new man in her life, by the name of Nicolas Coppola. Coppola was the nephew of *Godfather* director Francis Ford Coppola, and he had recently adopted the alternative stage-name of Nicolas Cage; he had played in several films to date and was presently shooting *Rumble Fish* along with Matt Dillon, Mickey Rourke and Dennis Hopper, with his uncle in the director's chair. Depp's parting from Lori having been amicable, he and Cage became friends and drinking companions and it was Cage who urged him to try his hand at acting. Cage made good the suggestion by offering to set up a meeting for the young Punk rocker with his own agent, Ilene Feldman.

Reluctantly, Depp agreed. Feldman was impressed with the young man's looks, if not his attitude or potential ability: 'He came in with long hair and an earring, and a tee-shirt with cigarettes rolled up in the sleeve,' she recalled. 'He wasn't what someone usually looks like when they're coming to look for an agent. He just wasn't into it.' Despite her reservations, Feldman sent Depp along to a casting-call for director Wes Craven, one of the instigators of the splatter movement of ten years before, who was presently on the lookout for new faces to feature as fodder for the murderous entreaties of his latest movie monster, in a film called *A Nightmare on Elm Street*.

In spite of recent mainstream thrillers like *Deadly Blessing* and *Swamp Thing* (1981 and 1982 respectively), Craven was best-known in fan circles for *The Hills Have Eyes* (1977), a savage gore-fest about a cannibal assault on a family of tourists who inadvertently stray into their hostile desert domain. But he had risen in the ranks of directors to watch in the splatter stakes of the 1970s on the back of a semi-professional film that he had written, directed and edited in 1972 with *Friday the 13th*'s Sean Cunningham, after the two had collaborated on a comedy feature called *Together: The Last House on the Left* (alternately known as *Krug and Company* or *Sex Crime of the Century*) was notion-ally adapted from Ingmar Bergman's *The Virgin Spring* (Jungfrukällan, 1960) and it achieved instant notoriety for its tale of rape and revenge by pushing hard at the envelope of what had previously been acceptable on-screen in terms of violence and sexual explicitness. Promoted under a tag-line of 'Mari, seven-teen, is dying. Even for her, the worst is yet to come', the film was banned by censors in Britain, Australia, New Zealand and much of Europe, and heavily cut everywhere else, including the USA, where it received an R rating for prolonged scenes of torture, dis-embowelment, fellatio and castration – the dynamic of which was allegedly informed by the American experience in Vietnam. Consequently, no self-respecting distributor in the States would touch it, though it turned a respectable dollar, regardless. In the UK, it was totemised as a 'video nasty' and as a result was respon-sible, with others, for legislative measures which had a profound and, for a time, deleterious effect on the fledgling home-rental market. Given that all publicity is good publicity, however, it's director's star had inexorably ascended amid the furore.

The political dimension having been removed from the collec-tive unconscious of horror filmmakers in the meantime, the cine-ma of splatter had undergone a puritanical reversal and transformed itself into one of 'stalk-and-slash', in which homogenous groups of pubescent teenagers indulged in the typical adolescent pastimes of partying and premarital sex before being hunted down and slaughtered by a variety of reactionary knife-wielding maniacs. Wes Craven had so far failed to participate in this insalubrious sub-genre, after a five-year search to secure funding for *Elm Street* had resulted only in disappointment. But, in May of 1984, he had finally been enabled to mount the production with the help of distributors, New Line Cinema.

On paper, Craven's latest project appeared as unappetising as those of his recent past: *A Nightmare on Elm Street* centred on the vengeful activities of a child molester named Fred Krueger who, having been burned to death by a lynch-mob of aggrieved parents, returns from the grave in dreams, to torment and murder the children of those who did him down.

The story proper then focuses on Nancy Thompson (played by Heather Langenkamp), and her recurring nightmares about a sinister fedora-clad killer in a striped sweater, who lurks in the boiler-room of an old school. Her friends soon experience the same dream until, one by one, they are murdered in their sleep. Nancy realises that the killer must be Krueger, and that she and her boyfriend Glen must stay awake. By a process of logic which only a horror film would entertain, she then concocts a plan to lure Krueger out of her dreams and into the real world, where she and Glen can turn the tables on him. Before they can act, Glen falls asleep and is murdered. But Nancy still succeeds in trapping and killing Krueger. Or so she thinks. A twist ending reveals this, too, to be a dream, and Freddy lives to slay another day.

Depp was to audition for the role of Glen Lantz, Nancy's high-school beau and nominal male lead in the story. Glen was barely described in the script, but what few pointers there were suggested an archetypal all-American boy: 'GLEN wears one of the school's football jerseys; a good-natured, bright kid.' 'Depp wasn't even close to the way the Glen character was written,' Craven said of the screen-test, which he conducted along with Annette Benson, casting agent for New Line. 'Johnny was a chain-smoker; he had yellowish skin.'

Depp himself was no more complimentary than Craven had been of his qualifications for the part: '[Glen] was described as this big blond surfer jock type and here I was, this little scrawny, pale little guy, with long dark hair starched to death with five-day old hairspray.'

Craven later reviewed the footage of the various actors who were in the running with his 16-year-old daughter, Jessica, who plumped for the 'scrawny, pale little guy' with the penetrating brown eyes. 'She just flipped for him,' Craven told biographer Christopher Heard. 'She found him hypnotically good looking and very charming,' reflecting on another occasion to a different journalist that he possessed 'sort of a James Dean attraction-that quiet charisma that none of the other actors had.'

Depp was given the role, and his first chance to make serious money in Hollywood.

FADE IN.
EXT. HIGH SCHOOL. DAY.
FADE UP ON SHOT OF this large high school and its crowds of STUDENTS. FOREGROUND, Tina climbs out of a cherry-red 1959 Cadillac convertible with two other students, best friend NANCY WILSON, and Nancy's boyfriend and owner of the car, GLEN LANTZ.
from the screenplay of A Nightmare on Elm Street (1984)

On the face of it, *A Nightmare on Elm Street* was no more original than any other of the many stalk-and-slash thrillers which had followed in the wake of John Carpenter's seminal *Halloween* (1978), nor was it any more inventive than Sean Cunningham's own *Friday the 13th* (1980) in having a seemingly invulnerable and predictably regenerative monster. Where the film ultimately scored in the novelty stakes was in its over-the-top death-scenes and through its devilishly perverse villain, with his iconic taloned hand.

In Wes Craven's imagining, Fred Krueger was an amalgam of a former school bully and a homicidally inclined hobo whom the director had come across. His chaste yet ultra-violent pursuit of – specifically – children charged him with the archetypal characteristics of the classic bogeyman, and his cinematic design, coupled with the zeal of actor Robert Englund, had ensured him a place in the pantheon of movie monsters even before his fire-scarred features appeared on-screen. Being quite literally a creature of the imagination, Krueger's ability to mangle and mutilate knows no physical bounds, which opened the way for some of the most outlandish murders in the entire stalk-and-slash cycle. *Friday the 13th* Parts 1 and 2 had run into censorship trouble in both America and Britain, and Craven's own *The Hills Have Eyes* had also been cut in the UK. *A Nightmare on Elm Street* eviscerated its young victims more comprehensively than anything that had gone before, but it did so in such a fantastic fashion that its own sins of excess were allowed to pass without murmur.

For a film about dreams from a director who was said to have studied them in college, *A Nightmare on Elm Street* exhibits precious little comprehension of the psychology involved; only stairs turning to 'porridge' as Nancy tries to flee from Krueger comes close to capturing the overwhelming sense of helplessness that the nightmare can inspire in its percipient. But Craven engenders a strong sense of suspense throughout, and the mostly mechanical effects which are employed in the film's set-piece murder scenes add to its overall effectiveness.

The death of Glen Lantz, Depp's character, is the most overblown of the bunch. Lying atop his bed between sleeping and waking, he is suddenly sucked into a vortex created in its centre until he vanishes from view. Moments later, a geyser of gore gushes forth, to wash in torrents over the ceiling of his room. Craven was content to let a double perform the actual stunt but, excited by the challenge, Depp persuaded him otherwise; after he is seen to vanish down the hole in the bed, a fortuitous jump-cut ensures that he is saved from injury by the heavy stereo-speaker which tumbles in after him. An epilogue to the scene was originally to have had Glen re-emerge from the bed, drenched in blood, but this was abandoned.

With Depp gone, the climax descends into formula: Nancy sets an array of booby-traps for the unsuspecting Fred, whose complexity would tax the ingenuity of the SAS. Krueger is brought forth into the real world and summarily dispatched in the ritual ball of fire. Depp's character of Glen had proposed a more logical ending to the tale earlier in the proceedings, by suggesting that a refusal to accept the possibility of Krueger's existence would be enough to consign him to oblivion. Such an outcome was felt to be insufficiently visual by itself for a Hollywood horror film, however, and Craven supplements it with Fred engulfed in flames, prior to this characteristic demise.

Depp's performance in the role of Nancy's college boyfriend exhibits all the failings of the ingénue: he delivers his lines too fast, mumbling as many as not, though he does display a certain natural grace of movement. A typical example is a comedy scene early in the film, where Glen attempts to persuade his mother that he is somewhere other than Nancy's house by playing a sound-effects tape in the background (only to have it switch from airport noise to a gun-battle in mid-conversation); there were no directions in the screenplay to aid Depp, and he can plainly be seen to flail around helplessly as a result, whereas a professional actor would have supplied a variety of reactions to further the developing gag. Despite being the same age as her co-star, Heather Langenkamp was a professional actress, which only served to point up Depp's own lack of experience.

Most revealing of all is the tyro actor's lack of emotional range. Craven makes much use of neutral close-ups to work around Depp's failings, and his most dialogue-heavy exchange is conducted in an untypical long-shot to minimise the effects of bland delivery. Given that the girl he supposedly loves believes that she is being terrorised by a dream-demon, Glen's attempts at moral support could hardly be more disengaged; Depp exhibits not a modicum of concern, cruising through the action on the strength of a fresh face, a beguiling smile and an air of insouciance. By the midway point in the film, Glen has seen two of his classmates butchered in the most horrendous manner, but nothing of that registers in Depp's expression or on his character in general. (To be fair, this is partly a failing of Craven's script, which has Glen remain sceptical to the end, despite the evidence of his own eyes.)

Glen's spectacular demise at the hand of Fred Krueger may have burst Johnny Depp onto the screen in an unfeasible amount of blood, but it attracted much attention in reviews and more than made up for the overall deficiencies of his debut outing.

> Nancy: You believe in anything?
> Glen: I believe in you, me, and Rock and Roll.
> (dialogue deleted) from the screenplay of A Nightmare on Elm Street (1984)

Glen's dialogue was cut back substantially from that in the original script. Wes Craven undoubtedly noticed how things were playing and made revisions as the filming progressed. From the extant exchanges, the inference is strong that Depp was unable to deliver his lines with sufficient conviction. 'It was awful: I was scared to death,' he eventually conceded. 'I couldn't move right in front of the camera – I couldn't follow the track – I couldn't stop at a precise place and say my lines. All the technical aspects terrified me.' At least he had only a few blocks to travel to be on-set: exterior shooting took place in and around the suburbs of Los Angeles, at Marshall High School and the old Lincoln Heights Jail. But *A Nightmare on Elm Street* was never intended to be a showcase for Johnny Depp.

The idea for the film had originally come about when Craven was allegedly intrigued by news reports of children who had experienced nightmares which were so terrifying that they were unable to return to sleep. The notion of literally dreaming oneself to death has a sound physiological base but, as played out in Craven's story, what begins as psychological horror ends as supernatural farce when Freddy – formerly the figment of a fevered imagination – leaps fully formed into the Thompson household at the climax to wreak material havoc, not least of which is the attempted murder of Nancy's mother. This turnaround shoots the premise of *A Nightmare on Elm Street* in the foot and ultimately demarcates it as exploitation schlock, no matter how high the concept may have been when it started out.

Craven's film proved one thing beyond question: instead of playing rock 'n' roll, Depp had rediscovered his bent for role-play, his innate willingness to submerge his own identity beneath a mask of make-up and walk in someone else's shoes. He was also commensurately at ease in front of a camera, in spite of his comments to the contrary and in stark contrast to how ill-at-ease he sometimes felt in life. They were both character traits which singled him out from others of his peers, but they happened to be primary attributes of the screen actor. To cap it off, he had turned into an exceptionally good-looking young man.

While Depp's acting career was shoved into gear by *A Nightmare on Elm Street*, his co-star Heather Langenkamp's was put on ice; she returned to the *Elm Street* fold for the third in what by then was regarded as a series – *Dream Warriors* – and again in *Wes Craven's New Nightmare* (as did the original's John Saxon also), the final instalment in the long-running franchise until 2004's *Freddy Vs Jason*, but she appeared in little else in-between, other than the occasional TV spot. Craven made half a million dollars from the film, but he had signed over the sequel rights to New Line, so he had to forego any profit participation in those that followed on.

INT. GLEN'S BEDROOM. NIGHT.
> LT THOMPSON steps into GLEN's room, anxious to be
> done with it. He hits a wall of stench and horror even
> before he takes it in with his eyes, and as soon as he sees

the bed he claps his hand over his mouth, pivots and
walks right back into the hallway.

from the screenplay of A Nightmare on Elm Street (1984)

'Doing *A Nightmare on Elm Street* was a trial-by-fire sort of
thing,' Depp admitted. 'I'd never acted before. I'd never done
school plays. Nothing. The fact that it was totally new to me was a
tremendous challenge. I'd never done anything like this, hitting
marks and saying lines and thinking about why my character was
doing what he was doing.'

Depp had been lucky: he had Craven's daughter to thank for his
break, for he is the least convincing member of the cast. Small
wonder that Wes Craven took a while to acknowledge the fact
that either Jessica or himself had discovered a new young star – it
seems likely that he thought they had *not*. He had been luckier
still to feature in a film which was to prove so potent at the box
office. After *Elm Street*, he could virtually guarantee himself
another stab at acting on sex-appeal alone, and the higher profile
which was bound to be his in the wake of such a pronounced hit.
He had learned little about the craft of acting but something
about the craft of filmmaking, and what he had learned had interested him: Depp had an inquiring mind; he was something of a
cultural 'sponge', and curiosity alone was enough to encourage
him to try his hand at the profession again.

The new Kid on the block remained under no illusions about his
role in the film ('What were they going to write?' Depp said of his
failure to rate a notice. 'Johnny Depp was great as the kid who
dies?'), though the $1200 union-rate fee was giving him pause for
thought: the occasional acting stint could prove a more lucrative
way to fund his sought-after musical career than anything else
which had thus far come his way, so it made perfect sense to see
how much mileage could be extracted from this particular gig. As
things turned out, he was to be left with no choice in the matter.

A Nightmare on Elm Street was a huge success for makers New
Line Cinema, returning almost fifteen times its production cost of

$1.8 million, but it had also meant the end of The Kids, aka Six Gun Method. With Depp on-set and constantly on call, the other members of the group had decided to call it a day. 'What I was planning to do was just do the movie and then keep going with the band,' he said, 'but they broke up when I put them on hold for six weeks, eight weeks, whatever it was. They couldn't deal with that.'

For the first time in five years, Johnny Depp was a guitar player without a band. He was a stranger in a strange and unpredictable land, without any prospects to speak of, or even a place that he could call his home, and he was now without a wife as well. But he had 1200 bucks in the pocket of his jeans and the potential of more where that had come from. He figured that, for the time being, he had little alternative but to give 'this acting stuff' another shot. In any event, what did he have to lose?

How would you like yourself to be credited? Depp had been asked at the completion of the film.

At first, the screen's newest young actor failed to comprehend the question.

'John Depp; John Christopher Depp; John Christopher Depp II..?'

For as long as he could remember, Depp said eventually, he had always been 'Johnny'.

'"Johnny" it is, then. Johnny Depp.'

A Nightmare on Elm Street endowed him both with a screen credit and a calling-card, at one and the same time. After the premiere of the film in November 1984, cinemagoers who turned out in large enough numbers to ensure that Wes Craven's modestly budgeted horror thriller was profitable enough to inspire a total of six sequels in the coming years were also witness to the prophetic caption, 'Introducing Johnny Depp'.

By the end of 1984, while he was still in his twenty-first year, John Christopher Depp II had become a reluctant movie star.

FADE TO BLACK

2 INTRODUCING JOHNNY DEPP

FADE IN. HOLLYWOOD, CALIFORNIA. 1985.
*Hollywood Boulevard was a great, screaming frenzy of cars; there
were minor accidents at least once a minute; everybody was rushing
off toward the farthest palm – and beyond that was the desert and
nothingness. Hollywood Sams stood in front of swank restaurants,
arguing exactly the same way Broadway Sams argue at Jacob's
Beach, New York, only here they wore light-weight suits and their
talk was cornier. Tall, cadaverous preachers shuddered by. Fat
screaming women ran across the boulevard to get in line for the
quiz shows. I saw Jerry Colonna buying a car at Buick Motors; he
was inside the vast plate-glass window, fingering his moustachio.
Terry and I ate in a cafeteria downtown which was decorated to
look like a grotto, with metal tits spurting everywhere and great
impersonal stone buttockses belonging to deities and soapy
Neptune. People ate lugubrious meals around the waterfalls, their
faces green with marine sorrow. All the cops in LA looked like
handsome gigolos; obviously they'd come to LA to make the
movies. Everybody had come to make the movies, even me.*
JACK KEROUAC, *ON THE ROAD* (1957)

> Welcome to Paradise. For the incurably romantic, there is
> Club Med. For the incredibly wild, there is the club
> that's… mad! – Private Resort! Where two eager guys can
> resort to their most private fantasies…
>
> from the trailer to Private Resort (1985)

'IT WAS UNBELIEVABLE, sitting there, seeing Johnny in a
movie,' the now 77-year-old Violet Depp was quoted by
Owensboro's *Messenger-Inquirer* as exclaiming of her grandson,
after she attended a release-screening of *A Nightmare on Elm
Street*. 'I've never been to a horror movie,' she went on. 'I don't
like horror movies. But I got along all right.' It would be fair to

conclude from this sentiment that the venerable lady liked soft-porn movies even less, but that was the direction in which Johnny Depp's fledgling film career now headed.

First, there was the recent demise of Six Gun Method and his career in rock 'n' roll. The news that the band had decided to split was something of a mixed blessing for Depp; he had been sorry to see the dream for which they had worked so hard in the eighteen months since leaving Miramar brought to a close, but he had been bitten by the acting 'bug', even without realising it: 'It was totally the opposite of being in a rock 'n' roll band,' he conceded. 'In a band, you are four people, all working together to write great songs or to get a record deal. In acting, I found it was just me. It all depended on me and my own choices. I didn't have to answer to anyone about what I wanted to do.'

Depp's first choice was one which he would look back on with little affection, however. Having signalled his availability for work, the sexploitation arm of the Hollywood machine lost no time in typecasting him as a typical testosterone-charged teenager on the make, in a raunchy drive-in comedy called *Private Resort*. For Johnny Depp, it was to be the film that in future years would 'dare not speak its name'.

Private Resort was promoted as the third in a notional series of sex comedies whose commonality was only the word 'Private' in their respective titles – *Private Lessons* (1981, starring *Emmanuelle*'s Sylvia Kristel) and *Private School* (1983) – and the fact that both had been written by Dan Greenburg. The film teamed Depp with New York-based actor Rob Morrow, equally pliable in his own big-screen debut. The two were cast as a couple of hormonal high-school graduates, trying to get their rocks off at any opportunity while vacationing at a resort hotel predictably packed to the pool-side with pulchritudinous female flesh. In another irony, the film was shot on location in Miami, barely a stone's throw away from the town of Miramar from which Depp had sought desperately to escape less than two years before!

2 INTRODUCING JOHNNY DEPP

Effectively stricken from the biographical record by its embarrassed star, *Private Resort* is a rather harmless sexploitation comedy which is funnier than it has any right to be, thanks mainly to the sterling efforts of a largely semi-professional cast who extract the maximum mileage from a paper-thin plot in which everyone runs around a great deal, literally chasing one another's tails. In what passes for its storyline, Ben and Jack (Morrow and Depp) book into a Miami beach resort for the weekend, intent on having 'fun' (screenwriter shorthand for bedding as many of the other guests as possible). Once there, they fall foul of small-time crook the Maestro (Hector Elizondo), when they mistakenly believe that they are given the come-on by his buxom wife (Leslie Easterbrook). The Maestro is intent on getting his rocks off Mrs Rawlings (Dody Goodman) – in the form of a diamond necklace – and his fumbling attempts to procure the same, while being thwarted at every turn by the bumbling duo, form the bulk of the film's 85 minutes of screen-time.

> Good afternoon, sir – my name is Jacques. Would you like a manicure?
> Jack (Johnny Depp), Private Resort (1985)

Depp plays second fiddle to film newcomer Morrow, who was also nine months his senior in life –though the youthful-looking pair were no longer the 'teenagers' that their screen roles infer them to be. Depp's character of Jack is ostensibly the more sophisticated of the two and he is given much opportunity to indulge his latent talent for comedy, as rushing from room to room and bed to bed, Feydeau-style, while constantly mugging to camera, is very much the order of the day. He is visibly more confident on-screen than he was in *A Nightmare on Elm Street*, but he still appears somewhat stiff and noticeably more image-conscious than the enthusiastic Morrow, who ultimately pips him to the post in the believability stakes (if such a notion is feasible in a film like *Private Resort*). Acting honours in context are actually stolen by veteran Hector Elizondo who, along with Tony Azito's hapless hotel supervisor, is called on to supply the requisite repertoire of gapes and grimaces as physical misfortunes rain down on him from all quarters in the course of the proceedings. Having been bounced over a balcony by the karate-chopping grandmother, the Maestro clambers back into the room with gun in hand: 'Playtime's over,' he announces. 'First you're gonna give me that diamond. Then I'm going to lock you in the bathroom. Then you can karate the shit out of yourself. How's that sound?'

Unsurprisingly, the film revels in its display of bikini-clad (and unclad) flesh, but it also reveals its egalitarian credentials by undressing its two leads for as much screen-time as it allots to its parade of busty starlets: both are caught coyly in the nude, though not quite in flagrante, at various plot-points along the way, their pert posteriors providing uplift for the females in the audience, while their male partners are catered for elsewhere. In Depp's case, the prolonged (if largely unrevealing) sequence has since become something of a collectable in fan circles. With most new actors or actresses, a nude scene is sooner or later considered to be de rigueur: *Private Resort* was the venue for Johnny Depp's, though a series of carefully contrived camera angles ensure that he manages to escape having to clutch his genitals in the traditional manner as he tries to evade capture by the husband whom he was about to cuckold (that cliché is reserved for Rob Morrow, where shots of him fleeing down hotel corridors make it unavoidable). The script is short on sight-gags and decent one-liners but, when it gets into its stride, it does squeeze the most out of body-blows and extreme physical injury in the grand cartoon manner.

Private Resort is certainly the 'stupid movie' that Depp later designated it to be, but it is professionally shot and directed, and its comedy set pieces are staged with some care. It is not the cheesy, straight-to-video schlock that its reputation in the wake of Depp's subsequent fame has retrospectively caused it to be regarded as; filmed today, with a better-known cast, it would be on a level with the likes of *Porky's* or *American Pie*. (Leslie

Easterbrook went on from this film to become a regular in the *Police Academy* series.) It is an unpretentious romp, leering and lightweight and shamelessly composted from equal parts female flesh and simple slapstick, but it is easy on the eye and soothing to the senses. It is also, on occasion, very funny. The only member of its cast to take the film more seriously than was clearly intended is Depp himself, who is often at odds with the broad comedy in play and whose own sense of screen humour, when it eventually came to be developed, would turn out to require a loftier and more subtle concept to bring it to fruition than that provided by *Private Resort*.

Depp's co-star was marginally more gracious about the quality of Depp's performance than Wes Craven had been: 'He had no idea what he was doing, yet he had an understanding of how people operate,' Morrow commented. 'He had obstacles, but he was aware of them.' It is clear from his largely detached perform-ance in *Private Resort* that Depp still thought of his acting gigs as something of a lark, albeit a lucrative one, and his later reminis-cences about the film were inclined to concentrate on a prankish incident where he and Morrow tried to gain entry to a private screening of the finished product by dressing as a pair of nerds. 'Nobody affiliated with the film could go, but Depp and I heard about it and wanted to see it,' Morrow concurred. 'So we dressed up in the weirdest possible way. He had dorky glasses and a knit hat on, and I put cotton in my mouth so my face puffed out. We walked past all the execs who knew us.' However, it was during the shooting of *Private Resort* that Depp first started to think seri-ously about pursuing a career as an actor instead of a musician. 'It wasn't like I ever kissed the guitar goodbye,' he said, 'but I seemed to be having more steam with acting.'

Depp lost no time in considering *Private Resort* to be 'kind of embarrassing' and would refuse even to refer to it by its title, but it led him to a small role as Lionel Viland in the fourth episode of a short-lived ABC television police series called *Lady Blue*, enti-tled 'Beasts of Prey'. The stars of the show were Danny Aiello and

Ron Dean and the episode in question aired on 10 October 1985; but, by 1986, *Lady Blue* had been fired from the force. His next role, that of a high-school son, came in a made-for-cable movie entitled *Slow Burn*, which was directed by Matthew Chapman and executive-produced for MCA by Joel Schumacher, director of the recently released *St Elmo's Fire*. As though somebody was trying to create a running joke at Depp's expense, *Slow Burn*, like *Private Resort*, was once more set in Florida.

Slow Burn was adapted from a 1980 novel called *Castles Burning* by one-time restaurateur Arthur Lyons. It was the fifth in a series of Chandleresque thrillers to feature private eye Jacob Asch (played by Eric Roberts, older brother of Julia), whom Lyons had first introduced in *The Dead Are Discreet* six years earlier. The novel's sub-noir plot revolves around the kidnap and murder of a Californian teenager, which consequently brings to light the sinister machinations of a scheming stepmother intent on bumping off a wealthy husband. The film is a recognisable retread of territory previously explored to better effect in James M Cain's *The Postman Always Rings Twice* and *Double Indemnity*, with its murderously seductive femme fatale and incidental cast of social misfits. Depp's role was that of kidnap victim Donnie Fleischer, heir apparent to his millionaire father's commercial empire, who winds up on a rubbish tip, beaten, stabbed and with a .22 calibre bullet in his head; needless to say, *Slow Burn* did not offer his fledgling talent for acting anything more by way of a challenge than had its immediate predecessors.

> The police were satisfied with the obvious conclusion: McMurtry kidnapped Donnie, lost his nerve when he failed to collect the money, killed him, and then took his own life. The investigation was closed. But I had something more powerful than facts: I had my instincts back. McMurtry wasn't capable of killing anyone-least of all Donnie; I was certain of it.
> Jacob Asch (Eric Roberts), Slow Burn (1986)

For all its pretensions to film noir, *Slow Burn* is a strangely subdued thriller, with a moody and mumbling Eric Roberts 'burning' studiedly throughout but never quite bursting into flames and having to be rescued from imminent demise at the climax by the very murderess whom he belatedly sets out to apprehend. The prolific Roberts had barely survived a serious car accident some five years before his appearance in *Slow Burn*, but it is Depp who ends in a bloody mess in the film – much as he had in *A Nightmare on Elm Street*. He was joined for the occasion by Emily Longstreth, who paradoxically had been Rob Morrow's love interest in *Private Resort*.

Despite his blink-and-you-miss-them appearances, Depp manages to establish Donnie as one of the few inviting characters in an otherwise tepid bunch of drifters and the dysfunctional rich, and the film would have benefited from providing more of a back story to his eventual murder. The languorous pace is well suited to the mood of casual corruption beneath the surface-gloss of the Miami smart-set with which the script is primarily concerned and, ironically, much of the action was filmed at the Palm Springs hacienda of producer Glen A Larson, the power behind some of the most successful television shows of the 1980s, like *Magnum P.I.*, *Knight Rider* and *Battlestar Galactica*. Good use of locations and some evocative images notwithstanding, even the most indulgent viewer is ultimately reminded of the old adage about the 'watched kettle': it never seems to come to the boil. There is constant straining after a hot and steamy atmosphere, but a curiously passionless female lead (Beverly D'Angelo), unerotic love triangle and largely uninvolving direction all conspire to ensure that the only real evidence of heat in *Slow Burn* are the stains on Eric Roberts' sweatshirt.

> Yeah, I know – he was some father ... I thought my dad was an asshole.
> Donnie Fleischer (Johnny Depp), Slow Burn (1986)

Depp's contribution to *Slow Burn* consisted of two dialogue scenes (and a brief shot of him as a blood-spattered corpse in a scrap-yard): the first of these is an encounter with Asch in the presence of his stepmother, where he utters the line 'Ethics? What's Ethics?' in response to a remark about the teaching of the subject in school; the second is a longer exchange where the two of them discuss his family background. In neither was he given much opportunity to develop a recognisable identity for Donnie Fleischer, but he patently had begun to develop an identity for Johnny Depp. In Donnie can be seen the beginnings of Depp 'cool': the character is presented as a smirking, swaggering, gum-chewing teen, finger-twirling a football as he talks in the self-consciously mannered style of Danny Zuko from *Grease* (1978) or the Fonz in *Happy Days* (which had ended a decade-long run on American television only eighteen months earlier). It was not so much a characterisation in keeping with the requirements of the script as it was a promo reel for a young actor on the make. Depp is clearly more confident, poised and above all appraised of how to appear in front of a camera. He was not yet an actor as such, but he was on his way. *Slow Burn* had begun the process of establishing a screen persona for the guitar player from Florida; it may not have reflected the real Johnny Depp, but it was to be good enough for what the fledgling Fox television network would have in mind in the following year.

Depp's unique composure had not gone unnoticed on-set, if Joel Schumacher's comments in retrospect are anything to go by. Schumacher is on record as the first to mention his name in the same breath as that of James Dean, the most famous teen icon of the twentieth century, with whom Depp coincidentally shared his initials: 'He had that demeanour, like James Dean – now I know how much of a cliché that is, but it happens to be true in some cases,' he told author Christopher Heard. With Depp, it was something rather different, though; he was a Kentuckian, but he was invested with the same psychological swagger and peacock-strutting sensibility that marked out archetypal Southerners like Elvis

Presley and Jerry Lee Lewis. His predilection for tattoos (whose most prolific adherent on the contemporary scene is footballer David Beckham, who also shares Depp's rationale about their employment as biographical 'markers') was a case in point, albeit a contradictory one: tattooing has long been regarded as a mark of the criminal classes, reaching its artistic peak among Japan's yakuza. 'The presence of a tattoo betrays not a daring independence, a need to communicate individualism, but more a feeble-minded need to conform,' design guru Stephen Bayley wrote in the *Independent on Sunday*. If Depp was street-savvy enough to display his nonchalance on his torso, he was also wise enough to realise that he had no need of comparisons like Schumacher's. But any reference to Dean was cultural shorthand for an easily identifiable screen 'type'.

There had been a 'new' James Dean for every decade which had passed since the bearer of the name met his untimely death in 1955, at the age of 24 (notably Christopher Jones, the star of David Lean's *Ryan's Daughter*) – often, there had been more than one. But all were the creation of studio publicists and none stayed the course, let alone struck a similar chord with the public at large. Dean's reputation as an icon of teen rebellion rested on the strength of his appearances in a mere three films, all of them made in the year of his death. In *Rebel Without a Cause*, Dean played Jim Stark, a dysfunctional misfit and focus for the adolescent angst of all the teens in America who were growing up under the picket-fence and apple-pie administration of Dwight D Eisenhower. In *East of Eden*, he was cast as Cal Trask, an even more mixed-up sociopath, in Elia Kazan's masterful adaptation of the John Steinbeck novel. While in *Giant* (which he finished just before he was killed), he was Jett Rink, the lone wolf of Edna May Ferber's epic tale of the Texas oil industry.

Dean's iconic status was typified by the blue jeans, red-jerkin look which he adopted for *Rebel Without a Cause*, but it was cast immutably in stone by his early death at the wheel of a speeding Porsche Spyder. Dean, it was, who initiated for the modern age the 'live fast, die young' philosophy that youth embraced to personify its devil-may-care attitude towards a post-war society in which it seemed to have no place of its own. And the overt expression of this new-found disdain for traditional authority was the jungle rhythm of rock 'n' roll.

Dean's cultural persona and meteoric rise to posthumous fame were owed mainly to the role that he had played in *Rebel Without a Cause* and the mythic qualities which attached to him as a consequence of his tragic end, but his public image belied his personal history. The so-called 'first American teenager' was actually a youthful-looking 24 when he made *Rebel*; he had appeared on Broadway and in some 30 television plays, as well as doing walk-ons in three other undistinguished films, before being signed for *East of Eden*. He was profoundly serious about the profession of acting, and the mien of misunderstood youth that he distilled so brilliantly in both *East of Eden* and *Rebel Without a Cause* was an 'act', a performance, a carefully crafted illusion.

James Byron Dean had also come from a troubled background; his mother died when he was nine and he was raised by an uncle and aunt. His life thereafter was more itinerant than might otherwise have been the case. But he actually came from a different generation to the one to which he became universally enfranchised (his favourite singers were Billie Holiday and Frank Sinatra) and whatever rebellion was in his soul found more conventional outlet in artistic pursuits and a love of motorbikes and fast cars – the latter of which found parallel in the off-screen activities of the 'James Dean' of the sixties, Steve McQueen. The real rebels of the age were the rock 'n' roll stars, with their drinking, their debauchery, their underage marriages, their statutory rape charges, their defiance of racial boundaries, their high-speed bike crashes, their trashing of hotel rooms and their irresistible enticements to shake, rattle and roll – not a clutch of movie actors like Dean, Brando or Montgomery Clift, who became emblematic of youth through a mere one or two in-character impersonations on-screen.

The freewheeling philosophy which Dean embodied was not a product of rock 'n' roll; it had been born out of the experience of war. The baby-boomers were the beneficiaries of the reaction, but its architects were from a generation which had witnessed a world in collapse and the ineffectiveness of established social order in being able to do anything about it. The Eisenhower years were an attempt by those in power to pretend that nothing had changed as a consequence, that all would continue as it always had, despite the intervening glitch. And yet everything had changed. Writers and poets like Kerouac and Ginsberg, as well as those who followed in their trailblazing footsteps, were determined to ensure that not only was this fact recognised and accepted, but also that change to the fabric of society was a fundamental requirement if wars were to be avoided in the future. The Beatnik's rejection of authority found resonance among the young, for whom such an attitude is an instinctive response at a certain age, in any event. Jazz gave way to rock 'n' roll, and the real possibility of rebellion, which the Beats had acknowledged only in passing, became a rising swell which was ultimately to wash away the old values and replace them with new.

James Dean was indisputably the first 'teen' martyr, however. The effect of his death on the constituency which he had quickly come to represent was as profound as those, in future years, of Jimi Hendrix, Elvis Presley and John Lennon. He was perceived to have given his life to the cause, even though, in truth, he had represented it only through his art.

Depp was prone to disavow any too-close identification with James Dean – 'Everybody compares everyone to James Dean these days. If you're lucky, they mention Brando or De Niro or Sean Penn. It's like they have to compare you to somebody' – but as his career progressed, he came increasingly to align himself with the counter-cultural icons who were contemporaries of Dean, and with whom Dean himself is identified. Nevertheless, the image that James Dean manufactured had become part of the American myth, and it was to cast its long shadow onto Johnny Depp.

As one strives to make a goal in a game, there should be a goal in this crazy world for all of us. I hope I know where mine is, anyway, I'm after it.

JAMES DEAN, LETTER TO THE PRINCIPAL OF FAIRMOUNT HIGH SCHOOL (1948)

From *Slow Burn*, Depp went into another ABC TV series: *Arthur Haley's Hotel*. Again, it was for only a single episode entitled 'Unfinished Business' (which was eventually to air on 4 February 1987), in which he was once more cast as a high-school son, only this time to warring parents Cathy Lee Crosby and Robert Forster. Mundane as these roles were, all was not yet lost: no sooner had the new year dawned than he was made an offer which no young actor could reasonably have refused.

EXT. PLATOON PERIMETER-FOXHOLE-DUSK.
   Chris (VOICEOVER, as he digs): Somebody once wrote,
   Hell is the impossibility of Reason. That's what this place
   feels like. I hate it already and it's only been a week.
   Some goddamn week...
   from the screenplay of Platoon (1986)

William Oliver Stone was the typical Vietnam vet, embittered by his experiences in the war and increasingly angered on his return from duty in Southeast Asia by what he perceived to be the indifference of successive American governments after the fact. Unlike the other 'grunts' in the 2nd infantry platoon, Bravo Company, with whom he had been drafted in September 1967, Oliver Stone was a Hollywood screenwriter and director. For ten years, he had tried and failed to bring his own politically incorrect version of events to the screen. By 1986, with the help of Britain's Hemdale Films, he was finally about to succeed.

Along the way, Stone had collected a Best Screenplay Oscar for *Midnight Express* (1978) and on the strength of that, he had made his debut as a director in the time-honoured way with a derivative horror film called *The Hand* (1981), which not even the normally bankable presence of Michael Caine could save from critical derision and commercial disaster. After several more screenplays, including Brian De Palma's *Scarface* in 1983, he was returned to prominence with the politically charged *Salvador* (1986), for which he was again Oscar-nominated as co-writer. *Salvador* had been backed by Hemdale, who felt sufficiently bolstered by the film's reception to entrust Stone with the project which he had carried in both his head and his heart for most of the previous decade.

The starkly titled *Platoon* was designed to document the experiences of raw recruits rudely uprooted from their apple-pie existences and drafted off to fight in a foreign war. The idea was hardly a new one; anti-war sentiment has a long and honourable history in the movies, from *All Quiet On the Western Front* in 1930, through *Paths of Glory* (1957), to the screen adaptation of Leslie Thomas' *The Virgin Soldiers* (1968). But the relaxation of censorship in the interim had convinced Stone that he could tell it like it really is, not only in terms of violence but in the profusion of four-letter exchanges, without which no soldierly vocabulary could be considered either complete or accurate. To bring his vision to life required a total of 30 fresh-faced actors, all of whom had to be prepared to endure two weeks of authentic army training in the jungles of the Philippines, where the film was subsequently to be shot. In January 1986, Johnny Depp was handed his draft papers from Oliver Stone and packed off to party.

Star billing was originally intended for Emilio Estevez, but prior commitments excluded his involvement and his place in the platoon was taken by his half-brother Charlie Sheen. The film was typically an ensemble piece, but the scripted conflict between Sergeants Elias and Barnes, good grunt and bad, promoted Willem Dafoe and Tom Berenger to second and third leads. Depp was hired to play the platoon's interpreter, Lerner – at 23, an unlikely exponent of the Vietnamese tongue. Some of the rest of the squad went on to make names for themselves elsewhere; others were simply left to rot in the jungle. Depp was fated to see his initial enthusiasm for the project turn out to be as short-lived as some of the characters in Stone's script.

Before boarding his flight to Manila, Depp had time to garner some advice from his Uncle Bobby, now a Vietnam vet himself who had been wounded in action: 'He told me about what it was like to be in Vietnam – to be in a firefight.' Despite the team-building rigours of Stone's autocratically imposed boot-camp regime, the preparation that he extracted from his actors for the filming of *Platoon* was not as arduous as publicity made it out to be. For the impressionable Depp, it nevertheless seemed that way. 'It was highly emotional,' he confided on his eventual return from combat: 'You put thirty guys in the jungle and leave them there to stay together for two weeks, just like a real platoon, and you build a real tightness. It's almost like a family. We became a military unit – a platoon. To this day, whenever I talk to Charlie or any of the other guys, it's just like the same deal. We still get together all the time and try to hang out as much as possible, and it takes us right back to the platoon.'

Platoon is a first-person narrative on the part of Charlie Sheen's Chris; a first-hand account of a twelve-month tour of duty on patrol along the Cambodian border, as seen through the eyes of an idealistic believer in the rightness of the cause who becomes predictably disillusioned by the harsh realities of an ultimately unjust, all-out war. Its opening scenes of the decampment of the platoon, their induction into mundane routine, the boredom, the forced camaraderie, and the sudden and shocking intrusion of violent death are handled with skill and comprehension. Even the clichéd moral tussle between Barnes and Elias is absorbing up to a point, though the notion of the mad, scarred, battle-hardened Barnes being more of a threat to his men than the whole of the NVA put together is too pat a cliché, while the upstanding Christ-like figure of Elias – even more messianic in the script than in the film, and crucified in both a jungle clearing *and* on the *Platoon* poster – is too crude a metaphor for the gritty tone of the film as a whole. But when its thoughtful interludes eventually give way to full-scale assaults, *Platoon* loses its way in a blaze of pretty pyrotechnics and half-crazed hysteria.

The actual scenes of warfare, in all their spectacularly stage-managed Technicolored glory, never quite measure up to the more authentic passages in the first half of the film, when Bravo Company's raw recruits are thrust into a world so unlike anything that any of them have known that they are forced to adapt their thinking in minutes, in order to try survive until the following day. The realities of war in Southeast Asia are more effectively drawn by simpler means, such as the bites and blisters from infestations of strange bugs, of which Chris is at constant pains to rid himself; the coming upon a decomposed corpse propped disconsolately against the trunk of a tree; the swift and casual abandonment by all concerned of the basics of civilised behaviour; the over-whelming feeling of alienation; the overriding sense of an inex-orable descent into Hell – and all to the accompaniment of Jefferson Airplane's 'White Rabbit'.

Stone's strident determination to push the idea that Americans at war are every bit as brutal and degraded as the enemy whom they are sent to fight ultimately swamps the more meaningful allusions to which *Platoon* was originally wedded: to show the youth of a nation swept up in, and away by, a geopolitical agenda about which it had little grasp, and with which it was never given time to come to terms. Chris's voice-over rendition of his letters home (a device which in part inspired the following year's *Dear America: Letters Home From Vietnam*, a heart-rending television documentary by Bill Coutourié) is abandoned as things heat up, and along with it the story's contextual base and remaining sense of the long days slowly passing.

Depp's character of Lerner goes down in a firefight a little over halfway through the film, at which point he has to scream a lot before disappearing off-screen for good, laid out bloodily on a stretcher. Previous to that, his presence has largely been imperceptible, and even his cries of pain can barely be heard above the noises of battle. It might have seemed like a good idea at the time to participate in an ensemble piece directed by one of the hottest Hollywood names of the day, but it was to do Depp no favours in the longer run. What was shot of him was reduced by Stone to fleeting glimpses in the edit which, even at a reduced running time of 120 minutes, managed to sacrifice character interplay for battle scenes at ever-increasing intervals.

Even during the opening 'introduction' to the members of the platoon, Lerner is noticeable by his absence, so severely was the part cut back. Whenever Stone conducts a contextual recce of the team, it is Lerner who is nowhere to be seen. His first appearance of substance finds him dragging on a joint, and his only major scene comes when he tries to stop Sergeant Barnes from killing a Vietnamese farmer whom the former suspects of withholding information about troop movements and whose wife he has shot at point-blank range with an automatic rifle. Depp tries hard to convey the rising sense of terror and outrage which the soldier is supposed by the script to feel in the face of Barnes's increasingly psychotic behaviour, but deprived by his director of a close-up during the confrontation, his performance in the scene goes by virtually unnoticed in a mêlée in which attention is focused almost exclusively on Tom Berenger's mad rage.

Johnny Depp may have been in the film, but he was not yet able to be wholly in character. What little is glimpsed of him reveals an actor too clean-cut by half and somehow still detached from the more experienced players working alongside. Oliver Stone seems to have been aware of this too, and he concentrates his directorial firepower away from Depp at every opportunity in order to maintain *Platoon*'s grubby sense of realism, which the novice, by his indifferent air, was unconsciously undermining. It is relatively easy to believe in Sheen, Berenger, Dafoe and the rest as fighting men in the jungles of Cambodia; it is less easy to accept Depp as a character called Lerner, holding onto his life by the thinnest of margins in a far-off war, much less that he is supposed to be versed in the language of the natives.

Other biographies have speculated that his role was cut down by Stone so as not to overpower that of Charlie Sheen. There is no evidence for this, either in the film itself or in the original screenplay. The scenes Depp lost were incidental at best and, while it pained the actor to see them go, *Platoon* itself lost nothing by their excision; nor was he alone in his loss, as others in the cast suffered the same fate in post-production.

Stone's film was potent enough in its rabidly anti-war way, but its US opening on Christmas Eve of 1986 bore little upon the fortunes of Johnny Depp. The time had not yet come when he could hold his own against a cast such as Oliver Stone had assembled to fight in Hollywood's Vietnam, and he was aware of it. The critic of the *Washington Post*, Paul Attanasio, went out of his way to mention most of them by name – but not the young actor who played the translator; in another decade, Attanasio would know him a good deal better. *Platoon* eventually collected four Oscars, including those for Best Picture and Best Director; Depp had merely collected his pay cheque and been granted an honourable discharge from the army.

> Lerner (to Chris): I was home on leave, y'know, and everybody's just worried 'bout making money, everybody's out for themselves, they don't even want to talk about it, man; it's like the fucking Twilight Zone back there-you wouldn't even KNOW there's a war on here.
> (scene deleted) from the screenplay of Platoon (1986)

In the meantime, Depp had begun to take the whole notion of acting for a living much more seriously. Just as he had taught himself to play the guitar, so now he pored over the rudiments of his new-found craft by reading Stanislavsky in his Whitley Avenue lodgings, off Hollywood Boulevard, and enrolling in acting classes at Beverly Hills' Loft Studio, under the expert eye of Peggy Feury, a follower of Lee Strasberg's 'method' school. 'After I saw how bad I was in my first couple of jobs, I decided I'd better do something about it,' he told *Movieline* in 1990. One of his fellow students at the Loft was a young actress named Sherilyn (Cheryl Ann) Fenn, who was to make a name for herself in *Two Moon Junction* (1988) and in David Lynch's surreal TV soap-opera *Twin Peaks*. Depp was cast opposite her in an experimental short for the American Film Institute called *Dummies*. The attraction between the two was mutual and immediate, and he and Fenn were making more than movies together by the close of the shoot; the relationship would later come to be regarded as the first of Depp's many tabloid 'engagements'.

Conversely, the more that Depp immersed himself in his new profession, the more the work seemed to dry up. After that initial flurry of activity in the wake of *A Nightmare on Elm Street* had come little more than a walk-on in *Slow Burn* and the eventual disappointment of finding himself on the cutting-room floor in *Platoon*. Regardless of the way in which its director was to treat his contribution to *Platoon* in the final cut, the experience of working with a maverick like Stone had been such that he nurtured the hope of being asked to participate in Stone's proposed biopic of rock band The Doors, which was currently in preproduction under the working-title of *Wonderland Avenue*, after the book of the same name by Doors' groupie Danny Sugarman. (Depp had eventually to pass on this project: 'It was taking too long to work out,' he said.) For the moment, however, he was effectively back in class and acting in student films.

Johnny Depp's roller-coaster ride through Hollywood had pretty much ground to a halt by the middle of 1986, and taken the wind out of his sails in the process. He had already started to have second thoughts about the whole change of direction on which he had embarked some 30 months before and consequently had re-engaged with the music scene by joining a band called Rock City Angels, only recently formed in Florida by Bobby Durango and Andy Panik. He was philosophical about his retreat into the safe haven of rock 'n' roll: 'I wasn't a singer-songwriter who had a ton of shit to say. I was just a guitar player without a band.'

Just as he was beginning to find his musical feet again with the Rock City Angels, Depp received a phone call from his agent. She had been approached by *A-Team* creator Stephen J Cannell and writer-producer Patrick Hasburgh about a show which they were setting up to help inaugurate the new Fox television network.

'These people want you to come and read for this TV thing,' Depp was informed. 'It's about an undercover cop who busts high-school druggers.'

Depp frowned. 'What's it called?' he asked.

'*Jump Street Chapel.*'

Depp listened patiently as more details were outlined: he was to play the part of Officer Tom Hanson, one of a squad of rookie cops whose job it was to operate undercover, rooting out drug-traffickers and other assorted delinquent criminals from inner-city high schools.

Depp weighed the alternatives. He felt that his profile must have risen a couple of points from having appeared in a film directed by Oliver Stone, the talk of Tinseltown in 1986, and he was still inclined to wait for the better offers which were sure to follow.

'No, no, no,' he said, finally dismissing the idea. 'I don't want to sign some big contract that will bind me for years.'

The pilot episode of the retitled *21 Jump Street* thus went into production without him, and with Jeff Yagher as Hanson, and Depp thought no more about it.

> Captain Briody: The department's got an undercover pro-
> gramme. It's the Mayor's baby. Nobody on the force knows
> about this, except silver shields and up. It's called Jump
> Street Chapel. And the reason it's called that is because
> this particular undercover unit works out of an old, aban-
> doned chapel on the corner of Jump Street and Sixth.
> Interested?

Hanson: Not yet.
pilot episode, 21 Jump Street (1987)

Less than a month after shooting on the pilot had begun in
Vancouver, Canada, Cannell and Hasburgh declared themselves
less than happy with Yagher's performance. Yagher was promptly
released from his contract, and Depp's phone rang again.

More details were forthcoming. 'Listen, the average life-span of
a TV series is 13 episodes, if that. One season. And this thing has
Frederic Forrest in it. He's a great actor.'

No better offers had materialised in the meanwhile, but still
Depp was hesitant.

'Would you please come in and do it?' his agent pleaded. 'It's
$45,000 an episode.'

A convincing argument. 'Okay,' Depp conceded at length.

Captain Briody: Tom, it's either this, or I assign you to
a desk at Progress Centre until you look old enough to be
a cop.
Hanson: I am a cop.
Captain Briody: Hey, genius, why do you think I'm making
this offer? Think it over.
pilot episode, 21 Jump Street (1987)

The producers of *Jump Street* breathed a collective sigh of relief
and were united in their opinions of their new signing: 'When I
first saw Johnny, he had a felt hat pulled down and these deep
brown eyes peering out, with a coat that went to the floor. He was
cute as a bug's ear, but he looked like a waif,' Joan Carson
enthused. 'That's part of his appeal-he can be waif-like, but his
charisma comes through.' Supervising Producer Steve Beers felt
much the same: 'What struck me about him when we auditioned
was that he wasn't nervous. He was laid-back. He had this presence. He's an unusual personality.' The preferred choice of some
of the Fox executives had been Josh Brolin, son of actor James,

but that idea was overruled. Depp had agreed to the role of Hanson on the ground that it could do his career no harm in the short term and the belief that *21 Jump Street*, like so many other shows fed into the maw of American television, would indeed prove a short-term proposition. How wrong he would turn out to be.

On the face of it, *21 Jump Street* was just another example of the television trend for 'cool' cops, which had begun with *Starsky and Hutch* in 1975 and continued on through *CHiPs* to 1984's *Miami Vice*. If there was a hidden agenda to these series in relation to the rehabilitation of the police after the Vietnam War protests of the 1960s and 1970s (and Chicago Mayor Richard Daley's notorious deployment of his local force to suppress the 1968 riots in the city), it had so far gone relatively unnoticed. Cannell and Hasbrugh's series was no different to any other in that respect – at least, not at the start.

The two-part pilot episode for *21 Jump Street* treads familiar ground. Hanson is introduced as a young officer following in the footsteps of a policeman father who was killed in the line of duty. Because of his boyish looks, he is assigned to an undercover outfit run on ad hoc lines by the jocular Captain Jenko (Forrest) and consisting of three other officers of similar disposition: Doug (Peter DeLuise), Harry (Dustin Nguyen) and Judy (Holly Robinson, singer of the series' theme-song); from here, he is patched into a local high school to bust a couple of drug-pushers. This he does, steering a would-be user onto the path of redemption along the way. No surprises there, then.

For all its formulaic plot mechanics, Jump Street's premiere episode is nevertheless a lively affair, thanks in part to a sound-track which featured liberal helpings of Steve Winwood's 1986 Grammy Award-winning Album of the Year, *Back in the High Life*. With its hip dialogue, its smattering of car (and bike) chases, its personable characters and its *Blackboard Jungle*-meets-*CHiPs* ambience, *21 Jump Street* looks like a winner from the off. Depp's initial uncertainty in the role of Hanson is soon replaced by the kind of confidence which can only be inspired by the knowledge that one is part of an ensemble of experienced players, all of whom are there to help their fellows along. The faster pace of television shooting seems to settle him more assuredly to the task in hand and, at long last, he is able to establish a real sense of identity for the character that he is required to play. The drugs element of the story is dealt with as explicitly as current censorship restrictions allowed, and the episode as a whole gives the impression of being on the right side of the moral argument. The attempts to be hip often strain at the leash, with a few too many 'man's and 'you dig's, especially when it comes to the Woodstock mentality of Frederic Forest's hippie Captain Jenko, but overall, the film is slick and efficient. The only jarring note comes at the close, when Hanson breaks into a Clintonesque riff on a saxophone, jamming to a rendition of Junior Walker's 'Shotgun' with Forest on drums. This was shot before Winwood's participation was decided upon and it pales in comparison, investing the finale with the look of a desperate-to-be-with-it Hollywood musical of the 1960s, where extras in floral shirts gyrated to nondescript tunes, and which were sent up to such devastating effect by Mike Myer's *Austin Powers* series. A little background research on the part of the writers might at least have given Depp a *guitar*. But at this stage, no one yet realised what it was that they had on their hands.

One exchange in the show is unconsciously predictive, however. Arriving late for a school production of Washington Irving's *Rip Van Winkle*, Hanson offers his tutor a typically flippant excuse: 'I got hung up with Rona Barrett. After this, she figures I'm gonna be bigger than Paul Newman.' In retrospect, it appears to have been a case of many a true word spoken in jest.

The pilot was considered a success by the executives at Fox and a series was commissioned on the strength of it to run for an initial 13 weeks, which meant shooting 11 more episodes. Hasburgh was delighted, but he was already aware of the potential for trouble which lay ahead of him. 'Fox originally wanted

Jump Street to be a sort of light, *Happy Days* sort of show,' he said. 'They're very young; in some ways inexperienced. They're hard to work with because they think they know more than they do. But the relationship has worked out very well so far.' At the end of 1986, oblivious to the politics behind the scenes, Depp relocated to Vancouver to begin filming. The show was scheduled for a Sunday evening slot, commencing in April 1987.

Two months after Depp started out on *Jump Street*, Geffen Records and Rock City Angels signed a recording deal worth $6.2 million. 'It was like, 'Oh Christ',' he said, on hearing the news. 'All I'd wanted since I was 12 years old was to go on the road.' His dismay was short-lived, as it happened; there was no follow-up album, and the band's career came to a strange and sudden halt only a short time later.

The inaugural season of *21 Jump Street* tried its hardest to adhere to the precepts which its creators had been at pains to establish for it, as 'a show that parents don't want their children to watch,' in Hasbrugh's words. 'My concern is that I don't want to come off being pretentious,' he said. 'We're not trying to preach.' That might have been true of Hasburgh and Cannell, but the executives at Fox were working on their own ideas.

The initial batch of eleven shows was fairly conventionally plotted, and dealt with stalking, car-jacking, teen drinking, pornography, sexual abuse, arson and all-around anarchy in general. Whatever moneys the pilot had expended on its Winwood songs was less forthcoming in series terms, and while the idea of a regular pop-rock soundtrack was retained, the bands whose job it became to supply it now went under decidedly minor-league names like Expose, Timbuk 3 and Agent Orange. 'Name' guest stars were few and far between at this stage (and the fact that the films were shot in Vancouver meant that they were never to feature much), although Brad Pitt, Ray Walston and Mario Van Peebles put in fleeting appearances from Season Two onwards, while the reliable Kurtwood Smith added welcome weight to the current season's 'Low and Away'. The last episode of the First Eleven was 'Mean Streets and Pastel Houses', which had Hanson as a Punk rocker, flinging himself frenziedly from a stage into the collective arms of the waiting audience below. Johnny Depp must have felt quite at home.

After its initial run of a dozen 50-minute episodes (excluding the pilot), *21 Jump Street* was declared a hit and swiftly re-commissioned for a full season of 22 episodes for 1987–1988. With Fox's publicity machine gearing up to make the most of its hot new property, Johnny Depp was now a star of the small screen – and recipient of all the teenybopper razzmatazz that went along with it, like an estimated 10,000 fan letters a month. Among the legions of admirers was octogenarian Violet Depp, who had continued to follow her grandson's career with enthusiasm in the years after *A Nightmare on Elm Street*: 'I think he's done real well in such a short period of time,' she told the *Messenger-Inquirer*. 'I still feel like I'm dreaming when I see him in something.' Depp's own comments about his new-found status as a teen idol were typically bemused, and bemusing: 'I don't hate it; I don't mind it; it's not an ugly thing,' he told Steve Pond of *US* magazine. 'But it's a little strange. I'm still not used to it.' He was never actually to become used to it, as three more years in the series were eventually to prove, but, for the moment, he had pitched his tent on the campuses and mean streets of a fictional LA and he now had to stay the course.

21 Jump Street was turning into a television phenomenon, and the contract which Depp had signed had contained a clause that was designed to cater for just such an eventuality: it tied him to the show for *five years*. 'Once you put your name on a piece of paper, you have no choice. There are people in ties with very big pens and hulking desks who do bad things to you.'

With the news of the show's re-commissioning, Depp settled down for a long haul. Filming in Vancouver was now scheduled to occupy nine months out of every year and to make himself feel more at home, he persuaded his mother and stepfather to move north and join him. He was still dating Sherilyn Fenn, but she was less inclined to leave LA, other than when she was hired to act alongside of him in an episode entitled 'Blindsided'. (Fenn returned to the series in 1989, for a fourth-season episode called 'Back From the Future'.) His popularity as a teen idol was still rising steadily, however, and hardly a week now went by without any number of magazines, from *Tiger Beat* to *Bop* (aimed squarely at the 12–17 age-group), running pictures of him strutting his stuff, Brando-style, on the back of a Harley-Davidson motorcycle, the typical teen rebel's transport of choice.

> Without Jenko, this thing's going to be nothing but Charlie's Angels.
> Tom Hanson (Johnny Depp), 'Gotta Finish the Riff', 21 Jump Street (1987)

Shooting on Season Two started off without incident – but without Frederic Forrest as well. His character had been written out in a hit-and-run accident between Episodes Six and Seven of Season One, and Depp was not best pleased. He made good the deficit by eliciting an occasional walk-on for his buddy Sal Jenco as the character Blowfish.

For Depp, his growing dilemma in terms of the series was not yet the teen adulation with which he nevertheless felt distinctly uncomfortable, nor even the trap of typecasting which would become increasingly difficult to shake off, but his inability to extend himself as an actor. Instead of 'walking through' the part as others in the cast appeared only too happy to do, he began to tinker with the character of Hanson in an attempt to unshackle him from the stereotypical way in which he had initially been conceived – querying lines, questioning motivation. 'I'd done the audition and thoughtlessly put my signature on a piece of paper without realising that by doing this, I'd turned over all responsibilities for my actions,' he was now moved to complain. 'I'm allergic to formula movies. If I have to put words in my mouth that another person has repeated over and over again, I become sick. Television is a hundred per cent prefab. You don't grow; you don't learn anything.' By the second year of *Jump Street*, grittier plots were being concocted in response to his desire to stretch himself in the role.

The season's opener was 'In the Custody of a Clown', a hoax-kidnapping drama which not only reintroduced Kurtwood Smith's FBI agent Spencer Phillips but brought back actor Barney Martin as a well-meaning grandfather who stages a snatch; Martin had played Hanson's partner in the pilot episode for the series. The remainder of the new shows were harder-hitting – within the constraints of their scheduled 7 pm time-slot – and had more controversial storylines (rape; racism; the shooting of Hanson's girlfriend), but the series as a whole had not quite hit its mark. One of the more interesting episodes was 'Brother Hanson and the Miracle of Renner's Pond', which was written by Eric Paul Jones as a retread of the arguments debated in *Inherit the Wind* (1960): Larchmont High is the scene of conflict between a 'creationist' teacher and a principal who demands the teaching of evolution. Someone is burning science books. Hanson is sent into the school, as per formula, but atypically unencumbered by the usual interaction with the rest of the *Jump Street* gang. As a result, the film becomes a virtual showcase for Depp, and it reveals all too clearly why the entire series was marketed around him. According to Christopher Heard, Depp refused to participate in any scenes which depicted the actual burning of books although, from the episode itself, it is difficult to imagine where he might have featured in any event. 'Maybe you found religion,' Williams says to him at one point in the proceedings. In a way, he had.

The character of Officer Tom Hanson was slowly and surely transforming into custodian of the nation's youth: 'The great thing about doing the show is the responses we get from people from the public service announcements we do,' Depp declared: 'We try to broadcast 1-800 service numbers on specific subjects, but if it's a light show, there's no sense in running one. And the response to the announcements has been great. For instance, we did a show about a kid who had a problem with drugs. After we ran a drug-abuse hotline number, the number of calls they received shot right up!'

During its opening season, *Jump Street* had made it only to 140th position in Neilsen's chart of the 163 highest-rated shows, but that was about to change too.

With nearly three dozen episodes now under their belts, Depp had formulated something of a double act with co-star Peter DeLuise (son of comedian Dom), and their knockabout turns as 'The McQuaid Brothers' invested the show with wit and warmth, though the writing in general often left much to be desired: in 'Best Years of Your Life' (which gave a role to Brad Pitt), by series regular Jonathan Lemkin, a psychologist delivers a lecture on suicide in which he states that 'a hundred years ago' the English used to drag a suicide's body naked to a crossroads and plunge a stake through its heart... The *English?* Puh-lease.

By the end of Season Two, *21 Jump Street* had become one of the fledgling Fox network's two big hits, the other being *Married With Children*. 'Apparently, we are the number one show in the country for teenagers,' Hasburgh informed the press. 'I'm real proud of that.' Pride comes before a fall, so the saying goes, and hardly had the words left his lips than he found himself on the next flight out of town, citing the usual 'creative differences'. Other voices were demanding to be heard over the way in which *21 jump Street* was now to be run. Voices in suits. 'The first season, we hit a lot of good issues,' was Depp's view. 'The second season, the same: we dealt with AIDS, sexual molestation, child molesta-tion – things like that. Unfortunately, Patrick left the show after the second season, and the direction seemed to change.' The only direction that interested Fox was up, especially as the show now topped CBS's *60 Minutes* in the ratings.

Desperate to cash in on the one big asset of their first year in business, Fox embarked on an aggressive marketing campaign whose sole aim was to SELL Johnny Depp. And that was when the problems really began: 'They said, "We want you to do interviews for all these magazines." I said, "What magazines?" They said, *Sixteen*! *Teen Beat*! *Teen Dream*! That's how TV's sold.' Depp was reluctant, but he had little choice other than to go along with the plan. 'My first reaction was to close up and put up a wall,' he said. 'Then I got mad. They were selling me as a product, but the product had no relation to who I was, and I had no control over the situation. I wanted them to fire me; they wouldn't. But at the same time, they did good things for me. They gave me a job, they gave me a pay cheque and they put me on the map.'

'They' also gave him an edge, albeit unintentionally: the more disgruntled that Depp felt about the way in which he was treated, the more disengaged that he became from the annual rigours of soap-opera production, the more that the character of Hanson was toughened up. He may not have been aware of the change, but it was evident on-screen, and the situation in which he found himself did as much for him as an actor as the teachings of Stanislavsky or the divergent demands of a successful television series.

> I like to see my guys happy. Get your smiles in now, fellas.
> 'Cause when we get back to the Chapel, there will be none.
> Captain Fuller (Steven Williams), 'In the Custody of a Clown', 21 Jump Street (1987)

Throughout his initiation into the ranks of teen idol as a star of the small screen, Depp's interest in music never waned. 'Grunge' was the latest fashion trend and grunge music was exemplified by bands like Nirvana, Mudhoney and Pearl Jam; grunge was a look with which Depp not only felt comfortable but had also played his part in inaugurating, and he still liked to hang out with musicians more than he did with actors. In March 1988, as shooting wrapped on a second consecutive batch of episodes for *21 Jump Street*, George Michael and Michael Jackson were topping the charts in the USA while, on the other side of the pond, a precocious 14-year-old Parisian *chanteuse* in Edith Piaf mould (and with

Brigitte Bardot pout) named Vanessa Paradis had shot to the top spot across Europe, and to number three in the UK, with a novelty record called 'Joe le Taxi'. On the set of *Jump Street*, Officer Tom Hanson was the only one who was not amused.

In June, Fox sent the five-strong regular cast of the show on a whirlwind personal-appearance tour of major US cities. The teenybopper phenomenon which Depp had become was consolidated in the process. 'Hello, I'm Johnny Depp' was invariably his intro to the hysterical masses who turned out to see their idol. 'My basic message is simple. Protect your mind. Protect your heart. And take care of yourself.' Not quite John Lennon, but more than enough. Next bus; next city; see you next Wednesday.

Two years on *Jump Street* was sufficient for Depp. The very routine of the series had taught him things about himself which he never could have found out any other way – certainly not by acting in one or two features a year. He was the kind of person who needed new challenges; he had the kind of mind-set which could not simply go through the motions of a script but required to treat each new show as though it were a feature film in itself, to be examined, deconstructed, reconstructed afresh. Pretty soon, each and every episode presented problems for the rest of the cast, as he chose to delve deeper into his character and his relationship both with them and with the particular themes in play. Others in the 'Jump Street Chapel' were less than sympathetic: it was a TV series, for Chris'sakes – what was the big deal?

But the 'big deal' for Johnny Depp was the integrity of the storylines. The runaway success of the show had increased the involvement of network executives and raised the stakes in terms of its political profile. Its radical edge was subtly to be toned down, to make it conform to the perceived needs of watchdogs and sponsors. As the series became ever more conservative in its attitudes, so Depp sought single-handedly to fly the flag of liberty over the production, which was moving inexorably out of his control. What had begun with the rewriting of dialogue with which he felt uncomfortable, even in the guise of a police officer, soon developed into a refusal to participate in entire episodes where he disagreed with the approach that was taken, either to the story itself or the response of his character within it. This was not so much a sign of Depp's identification with the role of Hanson ('The only thing that Tom Hanson and I have in common are that we look alike. Hanson isn't someone I would want to hang out with, or grab a pizza or a coke with.') as it was the awakening of his political consciousness as an actor. So central had he become to the ongoing success of *Jump Street* that he had at last begun to realise the power he had to disrupt the proceedings; he could not escape his contract and simply leave the show, but he could make it difficult for those concerned if things were not to his liking.

Depp had moved from the relative sanctity of feature film production in faraway places into the power politics of the closed world of the television industry, and he was starting to wise up. 'I've learned a lot about this business, how political it is, and how people manipulate other people. It's scary. Power is a scary thing.'

But it proved difficult for Depp to subvert the basic premise of the series, the underlying message of which was support for the covert actions of an authoritarian state in infiltrating educational establishments to spy on the nation's youth – an idea that Depp ultimately found unconscionable. 'I played the young Republican. I felt like a hypocrite, sensationalising these guys who bust high-school kids for joints,' he said. 'To me, it was fascist.' No matter how individual episodes of *Jump Street* were rigged to show the student body-politic in an anti-social light and the *Jump Street* team as sole guardians of democratic values, the show smacked unhealthily of a sugar-coated sales pitch for the clandestine activities of the CIA in American and British college campuses during the closing days of the Vietnam War. These guys were spies when all was said and done, and they were spying on their own countrymen. (Depp was to return to this territory in 1996 in *Donnie Brasco*, but that film would operate on a more secure moral base to begin with.)

Many actors might have remained content with the level of fame bestowed upon them by a show such as *21 Jump Street* but, to his credit, Depp was alert to the dangers of too long an exposure in a single high-profile role, especially one with a teeny-bopper fan-base. All of the players in *CHiPs* and *The Dukes of Hazzard* had faded back into obscurity with the eventual cancellation of their respective series. While only Ron Howard from *Happy Days* prevented TV triumph becoming cinematic disaster by moving to the other side of the camera and into directing; even nominal teen-turn Henry 'Fonz' Winkler failed to make the transition to the big screen, despite a starring vehicle which was written especially for him (*The One and Only*, 1978). By the time the third season of *Jump Street* came around, he was telling *Rolling Stone*'s Johanna Schneller, 'I don't want to make a career of taking my shirt off. I don't fault TV stars who do teen magazines. They took a hold of their situations; took offers that gave them the big money fast. But they were dead in two years. I don't want that.'

At this point, Depp was dating Jennifer Grey of the movie, *Dirty Dancing*. He and Fenn had now gone their separate ways, with some 1,080 miles in-between. Along with the individualism which had already earned him a reputation as something of a rebel (a label which automatically attaches to anyone who displays a measure of nonconformity in mainstream society), Depp had developed a strong sense of social conscience which he found himself able to vent in interview. This had encouraged *GQ* magazine to refer to him as 'the philosopher king of the stoners', and he was being hailed as the coolest character to hit the small screen since the Fonz.

Johnny Depp, former Punk rocker, had become a teen idol. But there was a down-side: playing a cop, teen or otherwise, was hardly indicative of an anti-establishment mentality, so he was forced to make up the deficiency off-set. 'Bad boy Depp' was soon the automatic response of the tabloid press when it came to write about his exploits. Just how bad Johnny Depp's behaviour became in contrast to the morally upstanding police officer that he was required to play on-screen was invariably a matter of debate between those who reported on it and the protagonist himself. The headlines told one story, but Depp often told another, and the expressions of artistic temperament which increasingly afflicted his performance as time and the series went on were typically misconstrued as the delinquent antics of a young actor whose head had been turned by too much fame coming far too quickly. The truth was more prosaic: 'My whole life had become engrossed into the show,' he said. 'I worked 15 hours a day on the set shooting episodes, the rest of my time was spent learning lines and scripts for other episodes. I barely found time to sleep, let alone be Johnny Depp.' Producer Stephen Cannell was a little less circumspect, however: 'He had a few drunken hotel parties that we had to straighten out afterwards,' he said.

> He's a kid just trying to leave some kind of a mark.
> They're not hardened criminals, by any means.
> Tom Hanson (Johnny Depp), 'Mean Streets and Pastel Houses',
> 21 Jump Street (1987)

The series began to become 'preachy' from Season Two onwards, segueing in an epilogue at the end of each episode in which a member of the cast, typically Depp himself, delivered a public information message relating to the subject of the preceding episode. At this point, Depp's nose began to twitch and his interest began to wane. Here was the establishment reverting to its traditional role of moral guardian, and though initially he went along with the idea – 'The best thing about the show is that kids learn from it. They're able to see things that go on in their high school and see them objectively. It teaches kids about drugs and safe sex' – he very soon changed his mind. 'It was preachy, pointing the finger. And it was hypocritical, because the people running that show, the very highest of the higher-ups, were getting high. They were getting loaded. Then to say, "Now kiddies, don't do this" was horseshit. I was getting loaded, too; am I really the one to say, "Don't get high"?'

The demise of Frederic Forest's Captain Jenko had been an early warning sign. Forest was replaced by the more utilitarian Steven Williams, whose Afro-Caribbean Captain Adam Fuller was a less irreverent disciplinarian and whose ethnic origins could not even be relied upon to add anything in the way of patois to the series. Of more concern to Depp now was the departure of Patrick Hasburgh, whose philosophy about the show Depp had shared and with whom he had got along particularly well. (Hasburgh also wrote most of the first two seasons' episodes.)

It was during the third season of *Jump Street* that the executives at Fox became aware of the fact that they had a problem on their hands: through subtle alterations in the shading of his character (and less subtle refusals to perform in certain episodes), it was made all too clear to them that Johnny Depp had begun to change sides. 'There were a couple of episodes that I told them I wouldn't do because I thought they were dangerous and basically full of it,' he revealed to the *Los Angeles Times*. 'I got out of those, but it didn't stop them from shooting them anyway.' ('Nemesis' and 'Next Victim' were the shows in question, and he had taken exception to the way in which Hanson was portrayed in the scripts.)

'I don't always agree with him but I see where he's coming from,' Joan Carson soothed. 'He fights hard for what he believes in, and he has a tendency to fight for other people as well, which sometimes puts another strand of grey in my hair.' Though not for much longer. To keep her locks in the peak of condition, Richard Grieco was hired to substitute for Depp at times of greatest disagreement. The network executives at Fox may have been young, but they were past masters at a game which Depp had only just learned to play. Grieco was cast as Officer Dennis Booker, a more Grattan-man version of Hanson (he started out modelling for Calvin Klein), and he was eventually awarded a spin-off series of his own for his pains: *Booker*, which lasted all of one season.

There were even episodes where Sal Jenco had more time on-screen than Depp (as in 'Whose Choice Is It Anyway?')

Depp had been allowed to take time out from *Jump Street* since the end of Season Two, but his virtual absence from the likes of 'Raising Marijuana' only served to show how important he had become to its success. A new set of credits had further emphasised his prominence in relation to the rest of the cast, but it also helped to highlight the anomaly of his diminishing input. In terms of the series' continued ratings success, the move away from the high-school milieu was one thing – any move away from its star was another. 'It was a frustrating time,' Depp recalled. 'I didn't feel like I was doing anybody any good on there. Not them; not the people watching the show. Certainly not myself.'

Grieco was a less convincing cop than those already featured in the *Jump Street* line-up, though, and as Depp gained in strength as an actor and a personality, Booker's appearances were increasingly seen for what they were: the actions of a clone. 'C'mon – you can be just like Fonzie,' Hanson teased his potential replacement in 'Hell Week', an episode with more than a hint of *Tom Brown's Schooldays* about it.

There was now growing animosity behind the scenes from those in the cast who felt that *21 Jump Street* was an ensemble piece, rather than a starring vehicle for one actor, and that Depp was receiving more than his fair share of publicity on behalf of the show. But then somebody always has to captain the Enterprise, and somebody else has to be the ship's doctor or chief engineer. Johnny Depp was the reason that the audience was tuning in, Sunday after Sunday, and it was only reasonable that he should receive the lion's share of any rewards as a result. Actor Richard Grieco failed to see it quite that way. Tales were told. 'There are a couple of people who don't like the fact that I'm outspoken about certain things,' Depp said. 'But as far as temper tantrums and throwing punches at my producers, it's such bullshit that it's hilarious.'

Patrick Hasburgh had always been supportive of his young protégé: 'Most actors who find themselves in the spotlight

2 INTRODUCING JOHNNY DEPP

like Johnny become real assholes, but not this guy. I think the worst thing Johnny has ever done is set his underwear on fire in the middle of the set one day. But he had good reason, claiming that no one had cleaned his motor-home in a while!' With Hasburgh out of the way, others rushed to fill the vacuum with vitriol.

Depp's now terminal dissatisfaction with his lot provided an endless source of copy for the tabloid press, much of which was only too pleased to afford him the space in which to publicly vent his frustrations. 'Dumbfounded, lost, shoved down the gullets of America as a young Republican ... TV boy, heart-throb, teen idol, teen hunk ... Plastered, postered, postured, patented, painted-*plastic*!' were but some of the epithets that he flung carelessly around to characterise how he felt about his situation. His behaviour in the circumstances was hardly surprising: when asked by the *Messenger-Inquirer* if he had 'gone Hollywood', he had stuck firmly to Kerouac's philosophical guns: 'I never will. That's a real big thing with me.'

In the two years since the start of *Jump Street*, the whole cast had literally matured (with the possible exception of DeLuise) to the extent that they had virtually outgrown their roles. The tensions on and off the set had produced the best season yet. The show had grown more formulaic in tone, in the process casting aside its former high-school milieu and the proud badge of liberal conscience which had been key to Hasburgh and Depp, but it was also tighter and dramatically more engrossing. The 1988–1989 season was *21 Jump Street* at the peak of its pulling power; it was now cult viewing. If Depp had wanted to go out on a high, this was it. But a contract is a contract; because of it, he found it increasingly difficult to see the wood from the trees. The rest of the cast were willing to go with the show to the bitter end, but the adulation that was still being accorded to him alone (as well as the numerous opportunities to air his grievances) meant that something had to give. He knew it, and they knew it. Depp decided that it would have to be him.

> Hey, Tom, man – I think you're a real class act. I mean, is
> this an exceptional cop or what? A guy who puts his own
> pain, his own anger, in front of a case.
> Doug Penhall (Peter DeLuise), 'The Dragon and The Angel',
> 21 Jump Street (1988)

Depp was now 25 and staring artistic death in the face. He still had not reached the point where he thought of acting as a career of choice, but the direction in which *Jump Street* had gone was forcing him to arrive at just such a 'career' decision. In essence, he wanted out. 'I want to experiment; I want to express different things,' he pleaded. 'It's just the beginning; I'm not even born yet. I'm still trying. I'm still pushing. I hope I never stop pushing. I don't ever want to get to a place where I feel satisfied. I think if I do that, it will all be over.'

The sense of claustrophobia which Depp felt from being trapped in the straightjacket of his *21 Jump Street* contract did begin to take its toll of his private life, though. In March 1989, he found himself arrested on a charge of assault after engaging in a fracas with a security guard at a Vancouver hotel. 'He got real mouthy with me,' Depp explained. 'I ended up spitting in his face. I shouldn't have done that, but he shouldn't have put his hands on me.' He spent the night in the cells, but the charge was later dropped.

Similarly, while on-board a flight to Canada to begin filming again, he suddenly felt moved to announce aloud to his fellow-passengers, 'I *fuck* animals!'

The outburst was greeted with bemused indulgence. Some of those present turned briefly to stare in his direction, before repairing to their own in-flight pursuits. Then the accountant with whom he was sharing his seat leaned towards him.

'What kind?' the man asked.

Sure, Johnny drank, smoked, ingested the occasional exotic substance and dated a string of young starlets, but this was fairly conventional stuff for a rock-cum-film star in the 1980s and a long way from the likes of Keith Moon or Ozzy Osbourne. The fact that an obligatory brouhaha was made in the American press of his bouts of bad behaviour or skirmishes with the paparazzi said more about the persistent puritan preoccupations of the tabloids than it did about rebellion. Depp's particular rebellious streak took a different form entirely, and it was one which related to his new-found talent for the craft of acting, rather than acting up for the prurient delight of the world's media. Accordingly, after nearly three years in the hot seat of a popular television series, Depp jumped the *21 Jump Street* ship on a ticket-of-leave and swam back to shore and the relative (in)sanity of cult director John Waters.

Did he plan to return? That was the question on every journalist's lips. 'If they want to make the show I signed up for three years ago, I'll be there,' Depp assured. 'And if not…' There was no 'if not' – Depp remained bound to his *Jump Street* contract; it might as well have been a wheel of fire. 'Every day, I mark down the days left. Two more seasons … contractually.'

'My feeling is that it's done about all it can do,' Depp confided to Christina Kelly. 'They came up with some neat ideas and tackled some interesting issues. But at this point it's hard not to be repetitive. How many more schools are in our jurisdiction? How long before we're found out? I mean, you can take artistic license to a point, but after that it becomes surreal.'

To make his point in the most unequivocal way possible, Depp had signed up to be directed by the defiantly gay and outrageously controversial (though well-meaning) John Waters, most of whose previous films – like *Pink Flamingos* (1972), *Female Trouble* (1974) and *Hairspray* (1988) – had tended to satirise provincial American life and had featured a 200lb transvestite by the name of Divine (aka Waters' former high-school classmate Harris Glen Milstead). The project in question was *Cry-Baby*, a thinly disguised pastiche of *Grease* and all the rose-tinted, rock 'n' roll, Romeo-and-Juliet nostalgia which that and television's *Happy Days* had spent the best part of the previous decade wallowing in. 'John's was the best script around,' Depp said. 'The most unique, best-written, funniest. It makes fun of the whole teen dilemma thing, and was such a joke on how people perceive me, or what has been shoved down their throats. I was doing fast food every week ... I wanted to work with an outlaw.' Baltimore-born Waters was being less of an outlaw this time out, however: *Cry-Baby* was to be his first feature for a major studio; in this case, Universal. As such, it had been allocated a budget of $11 million.

Cry-Baby is the story of Wade 'Cry-Baby' Walker (Depp), a kid from the wrong side of the tracks who ends up on the wrong side of a prison wall, simply because he looks like a juvenile delinquent and runs with a biker gang called the Drapes. But mean looks are merely skin deep, and he ends up singing his way out of jail and winning the hand of the Square maiden whom all the fuss has actually been about. Oh, and there are lots of songs. 'Johnny told me how much he hated being a teen idol,' Waters recalled. 'I said, 'Well, stick with us-we'll kill that; we'll get rid of that in a second, because we're going to make fun out of you being a teen idol.'

To Depp, Waters and his film offered an opportunity to free himself from stereotyping at a stroke. On paper, at least, *Cry-Baby* was the very antithesis of the values promoted by Officer Hanson and the whole *Jump Street* ethos, a reading of the material with which Waters clearly concurred ('I have this movie about a juvenile delinquent whose father got the electric chair,' was his pitch to Depp). According to Waters, actress Susan Tyrell, who was to play *Cry-Baby*'s grandmother in the film, liked to indulge in a rite of passage with her co-stars by saying or doing something shocking in their presence, in order to gain a reaction. On her introduction to Depp, her opening gambit allegedly was, 'I've got the pussy of a 10-year-old and I'll mail it to you in a box.' There is no record of his asking her in response why she might have wanted to present him with a child's pet cat.

Juvenile delinquents are everywhere. Right here, in this community. Boys, with long hair and tattoos, who spit on sidewalks...
Mrs Vernon-Williams (Polly Bergen), Cry-Baby (1989)

Johnny Depp was paid $1 million to play the lead in *Cry-Baby* and, if nothing else, he gives the film's producers their money's worth. His wholly unselfconscious performance is a delight to watch for its drive and boundless energy. As Wade Walker in rock 'n' roller mode, he turns in a spectacular impersonation of Elvis Presley in an oversized zoot-suit, whose sharply angled shoulders cunningly call to mind the wolf in the Tex Avery cartoons. Hubba, hubba! No longer was he James Dean or even the Fonz. Now, he was 'the Deppster'.

Cry-Baby is a mildly risqué musical comedy send-up of 1950s teen flicks, like *Hot Rod Girl* and *High School Confidential*, with a large dollop of *Jailhouse Rock* spooned on top, and Depp clearly enjoyed every minute of its making. It is filled with sly digs at the iconography of rock movies: Wade is an orphan, his parents having been sent to the electric chair in his youth: 'My dad was the Alphabet Bomber,' he tells his girl. 'My mother couldn't even spell but they fried her too.' We are given the high-school prom, the gang 'rumble', the courtroom scene and the 'chicken-run' – all of them fair game for their director's water-cannon approach to satire.

Waters' film is an affectionate homage to a bygone era of blue jeans and bobby-soxers, and it revels in its camp recreations of jukebox jive, elaborately choreographed dance routines and endlessly interchangeable harmony groups. It is a conspicuously candyfloss confection and, as such, it has a certain cheerleader enthusiasm and Baltimore-rep charm. But his direction is too often flat and featureless, only coming into its own in the garishly staged musical numbers. It is neither biting enough, nor humorous enough, nor even controversial enough to make much of an impact beyond that of a novelty, and undoubtedly it seemed funnier on paper than it became when translated to the screen.

Part of the problem with *Cry-Baby* is that Depp is miscast. He certainly looks the part and he gives it his best shot, and no longer is there anything amiss in his ability to perform in front of a camera, but he is not a comedy actor and, for all the mugging in which he indulges, he nevertheless appears like a fish out of water amid the plague of weirdoes with whom his director has him surrounded.

Disparate support is offered by Iggy Pop (who presumably thought Depp less of a 'turd' by this stage in his career), one-time Andy Warhol regular Joe Dallesandro, authentic 1960s teen idol Troy Donahue, Polly Bergen (slumming it somewhat in *Cry-Baby* after a career high in the original version of *Cape Fear*, 27 years before) and Kim McGuire, who plays Walker's sister (nicknamed 'Hatchet-face') as a typical Waters grotesque: a role that was designed with Divine in mind, before his sudden death from heart failure in 1988. (Hatchet-face bursting through the screen of the prison cinema during a 3-D presentation of *Creature From the Black Lagoon* and frightening the inmates even more than Ricou Browning's gill-man is one of *Cry-Baby*'s better moments.)

The mainly original songs in the film are faithful recreations of 1950s pop, from boogie to ballad – in particular the title-track, 'King Cry-Baby' (so it should be; it was co-written by Doc Pomus). Their sheer abundance weighs in against individual merit, but among the many, mostly slight, musical interludes, there is at least one memorable and superbly choreographed number, when Allison (Amy Locane) sings 'Please, Mister Jailer' outside the prison walls in the style of Julie London, with the entire ensemble joining her in the chorus. So infectious and well-staged is this Winona Carr-penned Blues pastiche that it almost appears as though Waters might have constructed the rest of the film around it, simply to give it a home. Both of the leads have their singing voices dubbed – Depp by James Intveld and Locane by Rachel Sweet – but they make an excellent job of the required lip-synching; Locane came literally from high school to her role in *Cry-Baby*, but her obvious inexperience is impossible to detect.

2 INTRODUCING JOHNNY DEPP

It is hard to see how Depp could have thought that *Cry-Baby* would dent his teen-idol status, when Waters had asked him to *play* a teen idol – and a singing one at that – though on a purely superficial level, Walker does operate on the other side of the legal fence to Tom Hanson, and Hanson would hardly have engaged in any of the French-kissing or crotch-straightening antics that Walker gets up to here (though some of Depp's recent appearances in *Jump Street* seemed to be heading that way). Its poor showing at the box office on its release does tend to vindicate his thinking, though by that logic, he and Waters would have been setting out to make a flop.

For all of his film's fun and frivolity, John Waters' idea of cutting-edge satire is more akin to the work of *The Goodies* than that of *Monty Python*, and things go resoundingly off the rails at the end when every cliché so far left unexplored is thrown at the screen in the desperate hope that something will stick. He is not quite up to the scope of his material in *Cry-Baby*, and what he lacks in technical proficiency, he attempts to make up for by sheer effervescence. The result is uneven at best, but moderately amusing while it lasts. Waters was to fare better with his next feature – *Serial Mom* – in which Kathleen Turner proved herself a more able foil than Depp for Waters' playful pot-shots at all things American.

When filming was complete, Waters did Depp another favour by agreeing to guest star in a Season Four episode of *Jump Street* entitled 'Awomp-Bomp-Aloobomb, Aloop-Bamboom', which eventually aired in February 1990. By then, Depp's own appearances in the show had become intermittent at best, although he remained its nominal star. In the summer of 1989, he had too much else on his mind to be bothered about the petty criminal concerns of Tom Hanson.

Reporter: How does it feel to be a juvenile delinquent?
Walker: Feels good, man. I've never been so happy in my whole life.
Cry-Baby (1989)

Depp's romance with Jennifer Grey having come to a similar end as that with Sherilyn Fenn, again due to the insurmountable difficulties of conducting it between Vancouver and LA, it was at this precise moment that he met the 17-year-old female star of *Lucas* and *Heathers*, and now much talked-about fellow-traveller on the road to bigger things: Winona Ryder.

Ryder was the former Winona (after her birthplace in Minnesota) Laura Horowitz, first child of Michael and Lucinda Horowitz who, along with two stepbrothers from her mother's previous marriage and a younger sister, had been brought up in a California commune with 'no electricity, no running water, no heating' by liberal parents who had smoked dope and debated the Beat poetry of Allen Ginsberg. The young 'Noni' had taken up acting at the age of 12 at the instigation of her parents, who had her enrolled in San Francisco's American Conservatory Theater, where she was spotted by a talent scout. By the time she was 15, director David Seltzer had cast her in the teen-drama *Lucas* (1986). Other roles in *Heathers*, *Square Dance* (1987) and *Beetlejuice* (1988) followed swiftly, and her latest was *Great Balls of Fire* (1989), about which Rita Kempley of the *Washington Post* wrote: 'Winona Ryder, the homicidal co-ed of *Heathers*, the rebellious teen of *Beetlejuice*, adds another baby doll eccentric to her growing roster ... Ryder's solid sense of character and even better sense of humour play paperweight to this flighty material.'

At a party following the 29 June Los Angeles premiere of *Great Balls of Fire*, in which Ryder played the child bride of legendary rock 'n' roll 'bad boy' Jerry Lee Lewis (Dennis Quaid), her eyes had met with Depp's across the crowded room; over the Tannoy, LA-based band Berlin were singing their number one hit, 'Take My Breath Away'. Two more months had been allowed to elapse before the pair were finally in a position to make a date, but the rest soon became history.

Reams of prose were subsequently expended on this initial encounter. Bill Zehme gave a blow-by-blow account in *Rolling*

Stone: "'I was getting a Coke," Ryder said. "It was a classic glance," [Depp] said, "like that shot in *West Side Story*, where everything else gets foggy." She said, "It wasn't a long moment, but it was suspended." He said, "I knew then."' Suffice it to say that by all accounts, Depp was smitten; Ryder, similarly so.

Depp spent the final few months of 1989 conducting his courtship of Ryder by plane, via 'red-eye' flights from Vancouver to Boston (she was filming *Mermaids* in various locations throughout Massachusetts). By the turn of the year, another 'engagement' was on the cards, tabloid news of which was greeted by the appearance on the streets of a bumper-sticker that proclaimed 'Honk if you've never been engaged to Johnny Depp.' ('Time was when Depp passed out engagement rings the way other guys make passes,' Christopher Connolly later underlined in US *Premiere*.) Depp's so-called engagements and reputation as a serial fiancé were largely the product of media speculation; he was, if anything, a serial monogamist, in a cultural ethos in which such an old-fashioned concept was considered tantamount to sexual deviancy. Nevertheless, the image had stuck.

The young couple did everything that young couples in love do – except for the fact that this was a couple of well-paid movie stars who were in love. Consequently, the Depp-Ryder relationship garnered a disproportionate degree of coverage from the world's presses during the three-year period that the affair was to last. He proposed; she accepted. He had 'Winona Forever' tattooed on his upper right arm (his third such adornment); she had the good sense not to, but gave him gratitude in return ('I was thrilled when he got the tattoo. Wouldn't any woman be?'). He bought her a diamond solitaire engagement ring; she bought him his own star in the heavenly constellation. He washed the dishes; she dried. He exhibited a liking for cheroots and the 'grunge' look of ripped jeans; she... well, she preferred Chanel and Manolo Blahnik shoes. And so it went on. Nevertheless, the two had more in common than the mere facts that both were one of four children and shared the same opinion about *The Catcher in the Rye* and

Ennio Morricone's music for *The Mission* (1986), and the blossoming of young love weathered the initial storm of paparazzi attention which had been bound to focus upon it. 'I've never been one of those guys who goes out and wants to screw everything in front of him,' Depp told Dawn Bebe of *BIG!* 'When you're growing up you go through a series of misjudgements. Not bad choices, but wrong choices. People make mistakes. My previous relationships weren't as heavy as people think they were. But there's never been anything throughout my years that is comparable to the feeling I have with Winona.' The press could barely contain its enthusiasm: 'When they hug, they hug fiercely, in focused silence; their squeeze keeps regrouping. They seem to be lost in each other. She smokes his cigarettes, and she is not a smoker,' *Rolling Stone* revealed.

Ryder turned out to be more than friend and lover to Johnny Depp; she was also a good luck charm. When his love life took a turn for the better, so too did his career. He was now about to embark on another film, despite his ongoing commitment to *Jump Street*. Before he did so, he presented himself to a rapturous reception from his legions of teenage fans at the obligatory Baltimore premiere of *Cry-Baby*.

As *Cry-Baby* was a film by John Waters, it was always destined only to appeal to a minority audience already familiar with Waters' iconoclastic style when it opened in the USA on 6 April 1990, to limp reviews and correspondingly low returns. The same Rita Kempley said of it, '*Cry-Baby* is basically *Grease* without Divine inspiration, an agitated spoof of the leather-jacket genre from Baltimore's tacky John Waters. Set right next door in 1954, it is a mock-heroic medley of doo-wop, rockabilly, white bucks and bullet bras aimed not at camp followers, but at a mainstreamier audience of adolescents and nostalgic boomers.' But she had a good word to say for its star: 'This time around the kid stuff is Johnny Depp. Already knighted a "face of the '90s", the rock star-cum-teen idol has got bobby-sox appeal.' *Variety*'s staff writer was also underwhelmed: 'There's so much commotion in the pic … that one can't help but catch on that a story's missing.' The *Chicago Sun-Times*'s Roger Ebert missed the point of the film altogether: 'Today's teenagers will grow up to be tomorrow's adults and yet in every generation, teenagers and adults seem to have as little knowledge of that ancient fact as the caterpillar has of the butterfly. It is an additional irony that humans have learned little from the insects, and the butterflies turn into the worms.' Exactly. *Cry-Baby* was trounced at the box-office by *Teenage Mutant Ninja Turtles*, but Depp took it on the chin. 'There were people who thought *Cry-Baby* was a bad idea,' he reflected, 'but I've always admired people like John Waters, who's never compromised. The easy way is boring to me.'

The lukewarm reception notwithstanding, Johnny Depp had returned to the big screen in his first starring role since that of Jack in *Private Resort* and, this time, he had done things the right way around. He had just served a 15-hours-a-day, 9-months-a-year, three-year apprenticeship in television. He had learned his trade, and he had paid his dues. He was ready to make his mark. *Cry-Baby* was never going to be the film to do that for him, but Johnny Depp's 'breakthrough' film would not be far behind it. In the meanwhile, he remained philosophical: 'Given a certain amount of luck and opportunity, I think anybody could do movies and continue to play the same character and make tons of money and buy a big old house in Bel Air,' he breezed. 'But I'm not so much interested in that.'

Johnny Depp and Winona Ryder had officially become engaged in February, less than five months after their first date, but there are always some who are willing to spoil a party. A minor 'actress' named Tally Chanel soon revealed to the press that Depp had proposed to *her* at the premiere of *Die Hard 2* in July, where she was doing duty as a hostess: 'I helped him out of his limo,' she said. 'Our eyes locked, and he asked me to marry him.' The story went on that their subsequent dates consisted of quiet nights spent at Depp's home in the

Hollywood Hills, eating Chinese food. The premiere of Renny Harlin's *Die Hard 2: Die Harder* did indeed take place on 4 July 1990, but when Johnny Depp rented a house in Hollywood that year, it was Winona Ryder whom he chose to share it with him. Chanel was busy on her latest film: *Hollywood Hot Tubs 2: Educating Crystal*.

With his relationship with Ryder now well in its stride after those first months of initial uncertainty, Depp had signed to play the lead in *Beetlejuice* director Tim Burton's *Edward Scissorhands*, which coincidentally was filming on the same 20th Century Fox sound stages as had *Die Hard 2*. By now, he was past caring about Tom Hanson and *21 Jump Street*. His appearances in the show were becoming fewer with each passing episode and when he did condescend to show up, his hair looked invariably to have taken on a life of its own; on top of that, there were the hats and the wigs. Season Five went ahead without him, though he was nominally still on call.

A few weeks into the shooting of *Edward Scissorhands*, and Depp heard from his agent that he had finally been released from his *Jump Street* contract because of a technicality in the drafting. 'You're free,' he was informed. To say that he was elated at the news would be an understatement – 'My posture changed. Suddenly everything got bright' – but he was not entirely forgetful of the valuable training which the show had afforded him. 'I have to admit that my real schooling in acting was on *21 Jump Street*. During it, I could train five days a week for months and months. Television gave me the sort of self-assurance that nothing could replace.'

Depp chose to celebrate his new-found freedom in the land of liberté. 'When I broke my TV contract I immediately took the Concorde to Paris, following the writers I admired. It felt like a liberation. I could breathe again. But it wasn't a feeling of coming home; because of the way I was raised I had no conception of 'home'.' He stayed at the Plaza Athénée Hotel on the Avenue Montaigne – 'really beautiful, really old' – from where he set out to explore the sights. 'People recognised me,' he said. 'But I didn't really talk to anybody. I walked around, then I came home. That was before I met Winona. I did many things alone back then.' (Depp later elaborated this story to include the fact that he had slept in the bed in which Oscar Wilde died; Wilde died at the Hotel d'Alsace – now simply L'Hotel – at 13 rue des Beaux Arts.)

The very last episode of *21 Jump Street* was filmed during July 1990, but Johnny Depp had long since departed the fold. 'I'd rather pump gas,' was his last word on the series. 'I'd never do it again, ever – there's not enough money in Los Angeles.' That same month, the actor who had become a household name through playing a character called Tom Hanson in a prime-time television show was concluding his scenes in a film which was to redefine his image for a whole new audience.

3 THE GIELGUD OF GRUNGE

*One of the most incredible moments I've ever had was sitting in
Vincent's trailer ... I was showing him this first-edition book I
have of the complete works of Poe – with really amazing illustrations. Vincent was going nuts over the drawings, and he started talking about The Tomb of Ligeia. Then he closed the book and began
to recite it to me in this beautiful voice, filling the room with huge
sounds. Such passion! I looked in the book later, and it was verbatim. Word perfect. It was a great moment. I'll never forget that.*
JOHNNY DEPP, TALKING TO STEPHEN REBELLO IN *EMPIRE* (JUNE 1995)

IT WAS THROUGH Winona Ryder that Johnny Depp met his
alter ego. Director Tim Burton was nearly five years Depp's senior, but of a similar social caste and background. His childhood in
the Burbank suburbs is a matter of some conjecture, however,
shadowy and uncertain; his teen years were studious and intro-
verted, and given over to artistic pursuits. He was a prodigy who
had won a fellowship from Cal-Arts, which sent him to work at
Disney, though his dark vision found itself at odds with that of the
Mouse House. Whereas Depp had grown up with a minstrel's passion for nightclubs, Burton had inhabited a more interior world,
reclusively steeping himself in movies from an early age and
evincing a particular bent for fantasy and horror. But as the two
became better acquainted, Depp would find much of his own
thinking reflected in Burton's singular aesthetic while Burton,
likewise, would come to regard Depp as the perfect on-screen
expression of his inner self.

Depp had been sent the script of a film called *Edward
Scissorhands* late in 1989, which Burton had asked novelist
Caroline Thompson to develop from an idea of his own while he
was still hard at work on *Beetlejuice*. Twentieth Century Fox, the
backer of the film, had its corporate sights at the time set on Tom
Cruise for the role of Edward – an homunculus with scissors for

hands, who has been created by a mechanical genius in a magic castle. With the project due to commence production in the spring of 1990, Depp became convinced that the part was actually written for him.

Depp asked Ryder, who knew Burton through her role as raven-haired Goth-chick Lydia Deitz in *Beetlejuice* and who had herself been cast in the movie, to act as go-between, and a meeting was set up with Burton and *Scissorhands* producer, Denise De Novi. 'When I first met Tim, we talked for two or three hours,' Depp told Bob Thomas of the *Toronto Star*. 'I think we had similar images of the character. I saw Tim's drawings and everything just clicked.' Well, not quite. De Novi may have been convinced by Depp's evident enthusiasm, but Burton was initially sceptical of his ability to understate the character in the way that the screenplay envisaged him. Then there was the small matter of Tom Cruise. 'Who wouldn't want Tom Cruise in their movie? Automatic box-office,' Depp conceded ruefully. 'I was really disappointed to have to give up. From the minute I read the script, I knew that I had to play in it.'

Some months before, Depp had followed Ryder onto the set of Francis Ford Coppola's *The Godfather: Part III*, where a persistent sinus infection ended up removing her from her intended role as Mafia Don Michael Corleone's daughter Mary, and the pair had flown back to California after only 48 hours in Rome. (The part was taken by Coppola's daughter Sofia, to the universal dismay of the critics when the film eventually opened in December 1990.) It was as a result of having to pull out of *The Godfather: Part III* that Ryder had found herself free to re-team with Tim Burton for his Gothic fairy tale.

As designed by Burton and written by novelist Caroline Thompson, the story of *Edward Scissorhands* is unequivocally allegorical – a contemporary fantasy set in a suburban utopia overlooked by a castle on a hill, which draws its inspiration from Charles Perrault and Hans Anderson, but with a grain or two of the Grimm Brothers to add some spice.

On one of her field-trips to sell Avon cosmetics, Peg Boggs (a wonderful Dianne Wiest) ventures into the old mansion that sits on a hill at the edge of town, where she comes upon a lonely young man named Edward whose hands are formed entirely of scissors. Peg 'adopts' him and takes him back home to her family. At first, he is treated with curiosity and awe in the neighbourhood as his talents for topiary and haircutting are revealed, but suspicion and fear are eventually engendered through the misinterpretation of his motives, and he becomes an outcast. In the meanwhile, Peg's daughter Kim (Winona Ryder) and Edward have fallen in love, but hearts that are true are not enough to avert inevitable tragedy. Edward returns to the castle to live out his endless days in the carving of ice-sculptures – the frenzied shavings from which layer a blanket of snow over the community below.

Depp was still obsessed with the need to shake off his teen-idol image, and he knew that something more radical would probably be needed than *Cry-Baby* which, although a satire, was likely not to be seen that way by the less sophisticated of his teenage fans, who would remain oblivious to the irony in Waters' work. He persisted in his attempts to acquire the role of Edward, in spite of the fact that he believed it to be ear-marked for Cruise. 'It wasn't similar to anything I'd played before, to put it mildly,' he said to Glenn Collins of the *New York Times*. 'I thought, "No way that people would see me as Edward".' As it turned out, the whole Cruise thing was a blind; the studio had wanted a 'name' as insurance against the unpredictable nature of the subject, but neither Burton nor de Novi had seriously considered the star of *Top Gun*: 'We're creating a new character and didn't want an actor who carried baggage with him,' De Novi said. 'Johnny could do any movie he wants, yet he chooses to take risks on emotionally complex parts. The camera likes his cheekbones but it also likes what comes through in his eyes.'

To his surprise and delight, Depp was offered the part. Better still, he was now to play in the film opposite Ryder, who had already been cast in the role of Kim – a fact which was to send some tabloid flak flying Depp's way, with respect to this having been the 'real' reason why Ryder had upped sticks from *The Godfather: Part III*.

The character of *Edward Scissorhands* is undeniably one of the strangest ever to grace a film. Like Wade Walker in *Cry-Baby*, Edward was also required to be kitted out in leather, but his was a full body-suit of straitjacket constrictions. With his spiked hair and pasty, emaciated features, his liquid, expressive eyes and black gash for a mouth, he looked like a cross between Sex Pistols lead singer Johnny Rotten and Cesare, the somnambulist from *The Cabinet of Dr Caligari*, with more than a touch of Boris Karloff's Frankenstein monster thrown into the mix for good measure. Add a pair of hands with oversized scissor-blades for fingers, clack-clacking in constant agitation, and he could pass for the bastard offspring of Fred Krueger and Cruella De Vil. If Depp wanted to transform his image from glamorous to grotesque in one fell swoop, then *Edward Scissorhands* was the film to do it. To underscore the element of grotesque, the role of Edward's 'Inventor' was played by horror icon Vincent Price, in what would turn out to be his last-ever film.

> You know the mansion on top of the mountain? Well, a long time ago, an Inventor lived in that mansion. He made many things, I suppose. He also created a man. He gave him insides; a heart; a brain. Everything. Well, almost everything. You see, the Inventor was very old. He died before he got to finish the man he invented. So the man was left by himself, incomplete and all alone.
>
> Kim Boggs (Winona Ryder), Edward Scissorhands (1990)

Vincent Price represented the old guard of Hollywood; Johnny Depp, the new. By 1990, there were few actors of Price's generation still standing, let alone appearing in movies. In a screen career spanning more than 50 years, Price had been directed by Alfred Hitchcock, Otto Preminger, Cecil B DeMille and Joseph

Mankiewitz, as well as the Tim Burtons of his day – dark vision-
aries William Castle and Roger Corman. Burton and Depp were
respectful in his presence and appreciative of the fact that they
were working with a star of legendary status, albeit one with only
a fraction of his former power now at his command.

Price has few scenes, all of them shown in flashback. Their incorporation into the film as it stands has something of an air of contrivance about it, as though all of them together were originally
intended to form a prologue to the piece, rather than end up
being cut-and-pasted into the story at intervals. At the time, the
79-year-old actor was in thrall to the Parkinson's disease which
contributed to his final exit three years on; he is tragically frail,
walking with the aid of a stick, and the famous voice has finally
lost its timbre. It seems likely that he was unable to comply with
all that was asked of him on *Edward Scissorhands* and Burton
simply used the footage that he was able to obtain in the best way
that he could. 'His cameo had a real emotional context,' the director told *Starburst*'s Alan Jones. 'He was in the first film I ever
made [a Disney-funded cartoon called *Vincent*, 1982] and was so
supportive of it and me. He's an amazing guy and I got through
my childhood watching his horror movies. That he agreed to
appear in *Edward* gave it the strongest personal feeling for me.'

For all his obvious debility, Price still manages to inject a twin-
kle into his pained eyes as he gazes in awe upon his Pinocchio-like
creation. When he eventually expires in close-up, as though bid-
ding a silent farewell not only to his proxy son but to the audience
as well, Edward leans over him and caresses his face with his blad-
ed fingers, leaving a trail of blood across the old man's cheek. It is
an apt metaphor. (In addition to quoting him Poe's 'Ligeia', Price
advised Depp to 'buy art'. But as he was one of America's foremost art historians and had himself been an avid collector all his
life, he advised everyone to buy art!)

Edward Scissorhands owes its central image of a young man
with 'scissors' for hands to the wicked Tailor in Heinrich
Hoffman's *Struwwelpeter* (1845), a bogeyman who threatened to

snip the thumbs off little boys who insisted on sucking them. Hoffman's tale was meant to parody the political correctness of the children's fables of his day, though his creations soon joined the ranks of the very bogeys that he had sought to satirise when the ironies in them were lost on a readership which was less sophisticated than he was. The same lack of irony afflicts Burton's film, which is an uneasy mix of whimsy and dark fantasy, as emphasised by the real-life Tampa, Florida locations of Edward's adventures in Small-town, USA and the Gothic pile on the hill by which they are supposedly overlooked. That failing apart, *Edward Scissorhands* is a highly personal statement on the plight of the 'outsider' in society, who is at first greeted with indulgence by the community at large before ultimately being cast out, his eccentricity and general air of otherliness being viewed as too extreme to be tolerated by a populace whose communal sense of well-being is demarcated by passive acceptance and consensual mundanity.

The story makes a mawkish plea for tolerance, but its director's sympathies clearly lie within the brooding atmosphere of the castle, as he literally paints the sterile scenery below it as an anodyne picture-postcard landscape akin to the bland suburban nightmares depicted in the photographs of Robert Adams and reminiscent of the environment in which Depp had passed his troubled teenage years. Burton offers a cartoon-caricature of the commuter-belt, where husbands leave their pastel-coloured homes in pastel-coloured cars for their drive to the office while wives remain behind to gossip and shop and have their hair done, and make passes at tradesmen. 'His awareness of what we call reality is radically under-developed,' a psychologist says of Edward when he is arrested over a misapprehension. 'But will he be all right out *there*?' asks the policeman in charge. 'Oh yes. He'll be fine,' comes the reply.

The novice Thompson had written her script in three weeks, but with Burton's track record, Fox had budgeted their film at $20 million. '*Edward Scissorhands* was a unique situation,' she said.

'To the extent that when Tim Burton went to make the deal for it at 20th Century Fox, we both took very little money up front, relative to what we could have made at the time, in order to have a very short turnaround and to have the maximum of creative control. We developed it completely between ourselves.' Depp later reduced Edward's scripted dialogue to a minimum, in the way that Christopher Lee once did with the character of Dracula in a never-ending series of Hammer films. '[He] had a lot more dialogue in the script, but I personally felt that he was a little baby in the brain. A really small child.'

No birth is without some pain and for the role of Edward, Depp had to endure agonies of which Lon Chaney would have been proud: two hours spent in wardrobe and make-up, and trussed up like a chicken in a black leather body-suit in 110-degree Florida heat. 'I would freak out just thinking of how he must feel,' Ryder empathised. 'Like if he had an itch or if he had to go to the bathroom.' 'I had to just sort of deal with it,' Depp said.

Certainly, nothing could have been further from Tom Hanson – or any other red-blooded male, for that matter – than the mechanical marvel with black hair, pallid complexion, welts and scars and scissors for hands that notionally was created by Price's Inventor for this film. Sounds like the creature in Mary Shelley's classic *Frankenstein*? Looks like him, too. But the similarity goes beyond that: in the role of Edward, Depp turns in one of the great mime performances of all time, fit to stand alongside that of Karloff in the 1931 adaptation of the novel. 'I kept getting images of dogs that I'd had as a kid,' Depp said of his approach. 'The way that dog would look at me – this unconditional love – and it didn't matter; you scolded the dog and it went away, freaked out, and the minute you'd say come here, it'd come back, totally pure and full of love.'

Burton had nothing but praise for Depp's reading of the role; he even helped to exorcise one of his childhood demons by incorporating singer John Davidson into his film, in a small role as a talk-show host: 'Like Edward, Johnny really is perceived as something he is not,' he explained. 'Before we met, I'd certainly read about him as the Difficult Heart-throb. But you look at him and you get a feeling. There's a lot of pain and humour and darkness and light. It's just a very strong internal feeling of loneliness. It's not something he talks about or even can talk about, because it's sad.'

'I didn't know Tim very well,' Depp went on. 'He rehearsed everybody, the whole cast, except me. He didn't rehearse me. I think he was trying to keep me separate from everyone; to isolate me; to give me a feeling of loneliness – alone and excluded from the party. It was good for me, and it was good for the film. He rehearsed everyone, but he had no idea what I was going to do.'

Depp and Burton had found themselves in sympathy not only with regard to Edward, but in all sorts of other areas as well; they were kindred spirits. 'Punk music was very cathartic to me, the anger and the emotional immediacy,' Burton told Gavin Smith. 'It started when I was a teenager. I would go to clubs by myself and couldn't speak. It's rooted in depression, in having a lot of feelings inside that are very strong, and the very disturbing feeling of not being able to get those out to anybody.' It was an analysis of adolescent angst which Johnny Depp understood only too well. 'Edward is a total outsider,' he concurred. 'I really know how that feels.' As for Burton's 'dark' side: 'I'm fascinated by the dark and the absurd,' he said. 'I'm drawn to what's behind that. It fascinated me that Edward wasn't human, that he had the innocence and trust of a child but instead of hands, he had these long, lethal shears. What he loved, he couldn't touch. Winona was involved with the movie before I was, and I was thrilled that her character was the only one who doesn't see Edward as a freak and that she's the one he falls in love with.'

Vincent Price's last film role was a poignant affair, with his name well down the cast list as 'The Inventor' of a mechanical man with scissors for hands. But *Edward Scissorhands* is doubly poignant in that it captures on celluloid, and therefore for all time, the pangs of love which Depp and Ryder experienced for real only months before its making, like a dragonfly in amber. Given what was to happen to that love in the months ahead, it would also become something of a memento mori to their affair.

> *In beauty of face no maiden ever equalled her. It was the*
> *radiance of an Opium-dream-an airy and spirit-lifting vision more*
> *wildly divine than the phantasies which hovered about*
> *the slumbering souls of the daughters of Delos.*
> EDGAR ALLAN POE, 'LIGEIA' (1838)

Tim Burton's film does not so much tug at the heartstrings as to give them a good yank; in a finale which calls to mind that of William Wyler's 1939 *Wuthering Heights* – one of the greatest 'weepies' of them all (and one which Depp himself has shed a tear over more than once: 'I cry at the drop of a hat; I'm a real sap') – Edward is seen carving his ice-statues in memory of Kim, as Danny Elfman's lush score soars towards the end credits. 'It's a classic fable, a metaphor, like "Beauty and the Beast",' Depp said. 'It's my *Wizard of Oz.*'

Edward Scissorhands is more than a fairy tale for adults; it is a film for every Christmas. Required viewing for every hard heart that was ever broken, and for every old soul that was once young. It was too early in Depp's career to talk of it as his finest hour, but it was sure going to be a tough act to follow: 'I can remember when I finished *Edward Scissorhands*, looking in the mirror as the girl was doing my make-up for the last time and thinking, 'Wow, this is it. I'm saying goodbye to this guy – I'm saying goodbye to *Edward Scissorhands.*' It was kind of sad. But in fact, I think they're all still somehow in there.'

    Kim: Hold me.
    Edward: I can't...
    Edward Scissorhands (1990)

Depp had now rented a house in the Hollywood hills which he had furnished with clown paintings, Kerouac memorabilia, a television 'the size of a small car' and a nine-foot-tall, fibreglass model of a rooster, which he had bought in a junk shop called 'Off The Wall' and to which he could legitimately point when indulging his tongue-in-cheek tendency to advertise the fact in interview that he had the 'biggest cock in Hollywood'. To his automobile collection of cobalt blue '58 Chevy pick-up and black '51 Mercury, he had added a black Porsche 911 Carrera. His fascination with Hollywood's history was ever in evidence: he had already confided to *Rolling Stone*'s Bill Zehme that he wanted to buy Bela Lugosi's old house – 'or Errol Flynn's or Charlie Chaplin's' – and memorabilia from his own films was accruing by the month. His was an eclectic mix of styles and sensibilities, and the Hollywood press was fascinated by him: sophisticate and scoundrel, culture-vulture and vagabond. By this time, he had read Kerouac *and* Kafka, as well as the first unauthorised biography of his own life, which he dismissed out of hand for picture research which had turned up shots of someone else entirely.

No stone had been left unturned in the quest to turn up items of interest on the 26-year-old guitar player from Owensboro, Kentucky. Depp had been asked every question that there was to ask of a rising star: What was his favourite colour? (Black.) What was his fondest childhood memory? (Picking tobacco with Pawpaw.) How would he like to be remembered in five words? ('I really have no idea – there, that's five words!'; or simply 'Thank you'; alternatively, 'Give me a pig-foot and a bottle of beer; lay me 'cause I don't care'; or 'Give me a reefer and a gang of gin; slay me 'cause I'm in my sin' – lines from Blues-empress Bessie Smith's theme song.) The experiences of his early years had become a litany to be expounded, parrot-fashion, before an endless parade of interviewers that he never seemed to tire of or lose patience with: 'He was born in Kentucky. He's the youngest of four children. He moved to Miramar, Florida. His parents were divorced. He dropped out of school. He played in a band. He has tattoos…' Johnny Depp was nothing if not accessible, and willing and happy to engage his inquisitors on any topic they cared to mention, no matter how private or personal. In retrospect, this seems to have been a subconscious decision of his to ally himself to an army of fans and camp-followers whose future loyalty would stand him in good stead when it came to pursuing an artistic course, far from the mainstream of Hollywood movie-making. But all of it merely whetted the appetite for more and more minutiae from the young actor who had bucked the system which had tried to turn him into a teen icon. 'Johnny and I flew into LA from Tampa where we'd been working all day, and we were really tired,' Ryder explained to Michael Kaplan of *Sky*: 'We got off the plane, and about fifty paparazzi people jumped out and started taking our pictures. We couldn't see where we were going because the bulbs were popping. One guy stuck out his foot and tried to trip me! They were yelling at us, trying to get an 'interesting picture'. Finally, Johnny got so mad that he turned around and flipped them off. Now you'll see his picture in a magazine and he's going to look like some asshole.'

Not likely. Depp, like Coke, was perceived to be the real thing, not a product of spin and image-management.

As far as Depp was concerned, he and Ryder were made for each other: friends, partners and actors-in-arms, and he played the devoted suitor to the hilt: 'Johnny always makes me breakfast in bed. Eggs, hash browns, bacon, toast, and coffee. Lots of coffee,' Ryder cooed in *Seventeen*. It was love all right, and she and Depp had it real bad. 'In a perfect world, I'd just do movies with Winona, John Waters and Tim Burton, and live happily ever after,' he had confided to *Movieline* in May of 1990. Burton joked that to him, the pair seemed more like 'a kind of evil version of Tracy and Hepburn.' Or Gomez and Morticia, as others in the media less respectfully referred to them in an allusion to *The Addams Family*, but in reality sharpening their knives on Ryder's character in *Beetlejuice*. They were also offered films in which they could act together, as they had to such good effect in *Edward Scissorhands*, like *Mobsters* and the roles of Lucky Luciano and Mara Motes. In that instance, they deferred to Christian Slater

3 THE GIELGUD OF GRUNGE

and Lara Flynn Boyle, because neither of them wished to be one half of a tabloid 'double act' (or perhaps because Depp's co-star was to be Richard Grieco).

On 7 December, *Edward Scissorhands* opened on 1200 screens across the USA in time for Christmas 1990. The critics were unanimously in favour, with Janet Maslin of the *New York Times* calling Depp's character in the film 'a stunning creation'. '*Edward Scissorhands* isn't perfect. It's something better: pure magic,' Peter Travers echoed in *Rolling Stone*, singling out the ice-sculpting sequence for special mention: 'Depp and Ryder, a gifted actress, give the potentially sappy scene a potent intimacy.' Industry trade paper *Variety* called the film a 'delightful and delicate comedy fable,' and praised the 'former TV teen idol' for his reading of the role of Edward. 'I was worried that we'd get buried by all the other Christmas-week blockbusters,' Depp said, 'but word-of-mouth on the movie is great.' Not so well-received was the film which followed *Edward Scissorhands* into release on Christmas Day itself: *The Godfather: Part III*.

Edward Scissorhands grossed $33.8 million in its first four weeks, and its star was awarded a development deal with a grateful Fox: 'I have a production company with my brother Danny and we try to find material to do,' Depp enthused. 'If I find something I like and they say yes, I get to produce it and see what that side of things is like. I want to find something I feel good and passionate about.' (Fox felt 'good and passionate' about this arrangement only as far as the next 30 months, by which time Johnny and Dan Depp's inability to come up with ideas and the declining box-office status of his subsequent films brought things to a preemptive close.) Burton's film subsequently went on to take more than $80 million across the world.

Depp and Ryder were Hollywood's newest celebrity couple. They were young, spirited, dark, unorthodox and potentially dangerous: the epitome of cool (Ryder's godfather was the self-styled guru of 1960s drug culture, Timothy Leary). They were the latest celluloid prince and princess to walk the red-carpet in

Tinseltown's Hall of Fame and, in April 1991, *People* was to anoint them 'King and Queen of Young Hollywood', having previously catalogued a series of supposed bust-ups. 'Things like *People* magazine don't really bother me,' Depp had earlier retorted from the *Scissorhands* set. 'It's like the flies buzzing around this trailer. I can deal with their presence if I have to, but I'd much rather squash them like a pea.' He might better have quoted Kerouac, who was similarly put out by the adulation that greeted him after the critical success of *On the Road*: 'Wasn't there a time when American writers were let alone by personality-mongers and publicity monsters?' he had asked.

Behind the headlines, it was unarguably a serious romance – the most serious of both Depp's and Ryder's lives to date – but it was to be conducted almost entirely in the spotlight, with the inevitable consequence in the longer term. In the meanwhile, Depp took time out from 'courting' Ryder to appear in cameo alongside Roseanne Barr, husband Tom Arnold and rock star Alice Cooper in *Freddy's Dead: The Final Nightmare*, the sixth (and what most critics hoped would be an accurately titled) instalment of Wes Craven's *Elm Street* franchise. His 15-second appearance consisted solely of sending up the public service announcements which he had made at the end of episodes of *21 Jump Street* and which had become such a bone of contention to him during the last days of the series.

As Freddy victim Breckin Meyer awakes on the couch, the television bursts into life and Depp appears holding an egg: 'This is your brain,' he elucidates, before cracking same into a red-hot pan and adding 'This is your brain... on drugs.' A shot of the fried egg is followed by another of a smiling Depp, who urges, 'Question?' – at which point, Fred Krueger pops into frame, back-hands him in the face with the pan in the style of Tom and Jerry, and responds with, 'Yeah, what are *you* on... Looks like a frying-pan and some eggs to me.' It was half a day's work undertaken as a favour to Craven, but it appealed to Depp's sense of the absurd (he even refused a proper screen credit). 'You can say it's a subtle statement on my situation on *Jump Street*,' was his explanation to inquisitive journalists.

Subtle was not the word which sprang immediately to mind when *Freddy's Dead* opened in September 1991, and Kim Newman spoke for all when he opined in *Empire*, 'Freddy may or may not be finally dead, but he's looking pretty damn tired.' Depp could not have cared less; by then, he was back in the saddle on another high-concept project, and with a more stellar line-up of acting talent along for the ride.

Instead of cashing in on the commercial success of *Edward Scissorhands*, Depp reverted to *Jump Street* mode and exercised his artistic credentials by pulling in the opposite direction. He had seen a film called *Dom za vesanje* (*Time of the Gypsies*, 1988), directed by Bosnian émigré Emir Kusturica, and when the opportunity arose to star in a wistful fable set in the Midwest, he jumped at it. More confident than ever of his abilities as an actor and content, for the moment, in his blooming relationship with Ryder, one thing was certain: it was a new and more assertive Depp that emerged from the experience of *Edward Scissorhands*. Burton's film may have been Hollywood art-house, but Depp's stab at a genuine art-house movie came next, when he joined the cast of *The Arrowtooth Waltz*.

Now I ask you: what can be expected of man since he is a being endowed with strange qualities? Shower upon him every earthly blessing, drown him in a sea of happiness, so that nothing but bubbles of bliss can be seen on the surface; give him economic prosperity, such that he should have nothing else to do but sleep, eat cakes and busy himself with the continuation of his species, and even then out of sheer ingratitude, sheer spite, man would play you some nasty trick. He would even risk his cakes and would deliberately desire the most fatal rubbish, the most uneconomical absurdity, simply to introduce into all this positive good sense his fatal fantastic element.

FYODOR DOSTOEVSKY, *NOTES FROM UNDERGROUND* (1864)

Kusturica was a Bosnian Muslim who had been sent to film school by his parents while still in his teens; student success in Prague had led to plaudits on the international circuit for *Time of the Gypsies*, which in turn had bought him a ticket to Hollywood and a deal with Warners to develop a script called *The Arrowtooth Waltz* – itself the product of a degree thesis by a young screenwriter named David Atkins at Columbia University. While their joint venture was still in pre-production, the Bosnian War erupted in what is now the former Yugosalvia, when Slovenia and Croatia declared independence from Christian-Serbian dominance in June 1991. In spite of the precarious position in which his family now found themselves in his hometown of Sarajevo, Kusturica pressed on with *The Arrowtooth Waltz*, but it was to be at some cost both to himself and to the film as a whole.

Finally starring in his first feature for more than a year, Depp was cast as Axel Blackmar, a dreamy young fish-tagger for the New York Department of Fish and Game, who is whisked off by his friend Paul (Vincent Gallo) to act as best man at the wedding of Axel's Uncle Leo (Jerry Lewis), a Cadillac salesman in *The Last Picture Show* territory of a small town in Arizona (in reality, the town of Douglas in Cochise County). Once there, Axel falls prey to the attentions of the unbalanced Elaine (Faye Dunaway) and her neurotic stepdaughter, the suicidal Grace (Lili Taylor). Caught between the dreams and desires of the ménage into which he has stumbled and the harder-headed pragmatism of a career as a car-dealer, Axel undergoes a rite of passage which ends in tragedy and bitter-sweet awakening into adult life. Depp's casting as doe-eyed innocent abroad in a big bad world of sexual politics is a direct result of his having played Edward, and the scenes where he builds a series of flying contraptions to try to send Dunaway into the clear blue yonder are reminiscent of the frenzied bouts of topiary in which he was required to engage in Burton's film.

Good morning, Columbus: these were my mother's eternal words, reminding me that America was already discovered and that daydreaming was a long way from life's truths. But what's the point of breathing if somebody already tells you the difference between an apple and a bicycle? If I bite a bicycle and ride an apple, then I'll know the difference. But thinking about what to do made me more tired than the actual doing. I remember my father once said that if you ever wanted to look at someone's soul, you have to ask to look at their dreams – and that would allow you to have mercy for those that swim in bigger shit than your own.

Axel Blackmar (Johnny Depp), Arizona Dream (1991)

The Arrowtooth Waltz, which was less fittingly retitled *Arizona Dream* by Warners before its belated release, is a tragi-comedy – an elegant and elegiac fable on the human condition and the need for a dream-life to compensate for the mundanity of day-to-day existence. The passive Axel becomes the catalyst for some of these dreams: Elaine, who dreams of flying and whom he helps to build a flying machine; Leo, who dreams that his young nephew will one day join him in his auto-emporium; Grace, who is incapable of dreaming and whom he cannot help, and who kills herself at the climax for lack of them. Only Paul, whose dreams reside in movies all along, is free of this potentially destructive interdependency.

Comedy icon and Vegas habitué Jerry Lewis essays the role of Leo in an unshakeable echo of Buddy Love from his 1963 hit *The Nutty Professor*, while Dunaway retains the sassy style that she formulated originally for 1967's *Bonnie and Clyde*, but both of these seasoned performers in their well-turned routines seem a mite uncomfortable at times alongside the raw emotion on show on the part of 24-year-old Lili Taylor as Grace, not to mention the deceptively laid-back but gloriously funny turn of multi-faceted one-time Punk rocker Vincent Gallo as Paul. Depp as Axel is as much a foil for the others in the cast as he is a character in his own right, but he foils superlatively well. His ability to act with his eyes, honed to perfection in *Edward Scissorhands*, finds outlet here in the quiet interplay of characters, but specifically in a beautifully understated vignette in which he gradually comes to realise that Grace is about take her own life.

Kusturica's film is a rich confection of incident and imagery, which sometimes seems like a cross between the steamy sexual atmospherics of Tennessee Williams and the flighty fantasy of Robert Altman's *Brewster McCloud* (1970). Its languorous style and over-larding of visual metaphors were to prove too much for the American mainstream audience, as its poor box-office reception would testify, and its uneven emotional temperature ultimately works against its overall impact. But *The Arrowtooth Waltz* is a class act for all that, with Depp heading up a quintet of players who together showed that the concept of film as art was alive and well in the American cinema of the 1990s. (The 'Arrowtooth' of the original title is a flounder found in the seas off Alaska, which acts as a metaphor for dream in the script but which the film's prop men appear to confuse with a Pacific halibut throughout.)

Lewis's customary facial tics elicit the odd indulgent smile, but the film's funniest moments come via two elaborate set pieces. The first is a predatory dinner party at Elaine's house, which ends with Grace threatening to hang herself from the balcony by her tights; this she does, but as Axel springs to her rescue, Paul bangs his head in the mêlée and turns in an impression of Bert Lahr's Cowardly Lion in *The Wizard of Oz* ('What'd you do that for? I didn't bite 'im'), while Grace bounces up and down off the floor like a rag doll on elastic. (The shot in which Axel, having caught hold of her, then lets her go again to bounce out of frame is worth seeing the film for by itself.) This hilarious episode is followed by another at a local talent contest, in which Paul offers a rendition of the famous crop-dusting sequence from *North by Northwest* that consists of him staring into the middle distance and checking his watch (In the Hitchcock film, Cary Grant is awaiting a meeting with his pursuers when he is attacked by a plane). But, as though reflective of its director's own preoccupations during the revitalised period of the shoot, the slapstick elements of *Arizona Dream* very soon give way to dour and doomy meditations on death, against which the dream metaphor that is central to the theme of the piece begins to look increasingly pointless.

According to Gallo, Depp and Kusturica got along famously during the shooting of *Arizona Dream*. Both men had been guitarists in rock bands (Zabranjeno Pusenje or The 'No Smoking' Orchestra, in Kusturica's case) and Depp's sway with his director no doubt saw to it that Iggy Pop was hoist aboard the film to warble a Lou Reed-inspired song over its closing credits, 'In the Deathcar'. While making *Arizona Dream*, Depp had kept himself amused between takes by reading Dostoevsky's *Notes from Underground*, which prompted Kusturica to suggest to him that they should work together on an updated adaptation of the same author's *Crime and Punishment*, transposed to New York's Brighton Beach neighbourhood and with Raskolnikov as a bass player in a rock band. Depp was greatly impressed by Kusturica and would have done whatever was asked of him, but the negative reception which was accorded the film by Warners quickly put paid to the idea.

On this showing, Emir Kusturica had adapted well to the Midwestern milieu and the film betrays little if any European sensibility, but its narrative obliquities, underlying sense of tragedy and lack of a clear-cut resolution severely curtailed its commercial prospects. It was released in Europe in January 1993 but shelved in America until June 1995, more than three years after its completion.

Johnny Depp, screen actor, had clearly undergone something of a rebirth during *Edward Scissorhands*; in *Arizona Dream*, it is almost as though he has sprung fully formed from the star-speckled sea, like the 'Arrowtooth halibut' which sails surreally in and out of the story. If Burton's film had comprehensively bulldozed the image of Tom Hanson, then Kusturica's had erected a new model Depp in its place.

Don't you think maybe you should be with your sick uncle
instead of playing co-pilot with a nutcase here?
Paul Leger (Vincent Gallo), Arizona Dream (1991)

Notwithstanding the camaraderie on-set, *Arizona Dream* was a
troubled film; production was halted halfway through, when
Kusturica suffered something of a breakdown at the news that
Sarajevo was likely to be besieged by Bosnian-Serb forces, and
the uneven tone of the piece appears to reflect its director's
depressed state of mind. He later confessed that he had felt like a
'drowning man' during the shoot. When he was finally able to
return to the city in 1993, Kusturica challenged the leader of the
ultra-nationalist opposition party to a duel. The politician
declined, on the ground that he did not want the blood of an artist
on his hands.

On its European release, *Empire* called Depp's performance
'coolly understated' and the film itself 'a bizarre fusion of art and
stardom', though 'a joy to behold'. The director's cut was 142 minutes, but 23 of those (including a 12-minute dream sequence in
which Paul gets married) were excised by Warners prior to the
film's US opening. It made little difference: *Arizona Dream*
pulled in a meagre $100,000 at the American box office, barely
enough to have paid for the catering on-set. Against *Edward
Scissorhands'* $56 million plus, this was a bitter blow to Depp, and
his valiant attempt at a genuine art-house movie would continue
to stand as the least commercially successful of all of his films.

When production of *Arizona Dream* stalled at the turn of 1992,
Winona Ryder was set to play the role of Mina in Francis
Coppola's $40 million horror blockbuster for Columbia, *Bram
Stoker's Dracula*. The film had originally been planned as a TV
movie, to be directed by Michael Apted, but Ryder had taken the
screenplay to Coppola and sold him on the idea of turning it into
a feature film. In a reversal of what had transpired during *The
Godfather: Part III*, Depp had met with Coppola to discuss the
role of Jonathan Harker, Mina's fiancé. Before anything could be

agreed, filming was resumed and he felt duty-bound to honour his previous commitment to Kusturica; the role of Harker went to Keanu Reeves instead: 'The possibility came up just when *Arizona Dream* heated up again,' he said of what later turned out to be a major horror hit. 'So off I went to finish it.' To date, *Bram Stoker's Dracula* has taken more than \$190 million at the global box office.

Johnny Depp went straight from *Arizona Dream* into another of the same, *Benny & Joon*, where he was to play alongside Woody Harrelson (now famous for his role as 'Woody' the bartender in the long-running TV sitcom *Cheers*) and Laura Dern. Harrelson had agreed to play the Benny of the title and Dern his sister 'Joon' (Juniper), a mentally ill sibling whom Benny has cared for at home since the death of their parents in a car accident. Depp's role was that of Sam, the emotionally retarded cousin of one of their poker-playing friends, who comes on like a cross between Buster Keaton and Goofy and among whose more endearing traits is the ability to mash potatoes with a tennis racket.

Harrelson pulled out of the film at the last minute to play opposite Robert Redford and Demi Moore in the higher-profile *Indecent Proposal*, and Laura Dern quickly followed suit. 'I'd gone through the whole mess I usually go through when I'm about to start a movie, and then there was this strange thing with Woody,' Depp said. 'To be honest, I wasn't familiar with his work. I'd never seen *Cheers*. I was in France doing voice-overs for Emir and I'm hearing all this kind of weirdness, like "Woody's out", then "Laura's out because Woody's out". On and on. I was shocked by the whole thing.' Not as shocked as M-G-M, which sued Harrelson for breach of contract. The respective roles were filled by Aidan Quinn and Mary Stuart Masterson. 'Hearing it was to be Aidan Quinn in the part, not Woody, really made me happy,' Depp continued. 'I didn't know how happy until I started hanging out with the guy, who's so strong, smart, centred. The movie's kind of a weird triangle, so I'm falling in love with her and, in a way, I'm also falling in love with him, because he's this guy I can never be like.'

Benny & Joon was Depp once again back in *Scissorhands* territory, playing an eccentric outsider at odds with the world around him: Sam is first glimpsed sitting on a train, his head buried in a book entitled *The Look of Buster Keaton* by French film critic Robert Benayoun, just to make doubly sure that the viewer understands where exactly the character is coming from. Shot entirely on location in Spokane, Washington, and directed by Canadian Jeremiah S Chechik, the film is a slight and sugary affair, a twee and cutesy romance, with pretensions to something more profound. In its tale of love's awakening between Sam, Joon, Benny and local waitress Ruthie, it is formulaic enough stuff: boy gets girl; boy loses girl; boy gets girl again. Only in this instance, the formula is applied twice over.

For director Jeremiah Chechik, *Benny & Joon* represented an opportunity to break from the ribald inanities of his previous feature, *National Lampoon's Christmas Vacation*, but its quieter moments sit uneasily with its more over-the-top antics, such as Sam dangling precariously by a rope outside the window of Joon's room or dusting the ceiling in her home by trundling himself about in an armchair. 'Some cultures are defined by their relationship to cheese,' Joon observes, as Sam proceeds to make toasted sandwiches using a flat-iron. An attempt is made to contrast these amiable idiosyncrasies with the fact that Benny's poker-school chums gamble with items like 'soap-on-a-rope, slightly used' or bathroom-grouting, instead of money, but this is quickly revealed as a contrivance to allow Sam to be traded to Benny, after Joon loses a hand of cards.

For all its mawkishness, the film has its moments of ironic humour – Benny explains to Sam about his sister's mental illness while the latter sits in a bath, fully clothed – though not enough of them to offset a growing sense of nausea. Aidan Quinn maintains an admirable cool amid all the fruitcakes and saccharine that Chechik layers around him, and the developing relationship

between him and Ruthie (Julianne Moore) is often more enchanting than that between Sam and Joon, largely due to the eschewing of cloying sentimentality. Several ideas are left in the lurch at
the close, such as Joon's implied ability with oil paints, but *Benny
& Joon* is nicely directed, prettily photographed, and as highly
coloured as might be expected of a production emanating from
the studios of M-G-M. What it lacks is the harder edge of pain and
suffering that Burton was able to weave into his own fable of
childhood's end, and thus contain its sicklier elements. The tale
descends briefly into tragedy and pathos in the last reel, when
Joon is incarcerated for a spell after attempting to elope with Sam
and suffering a breakdown on a bus, but the sure-fire lure of the
happy ending soon puts everything to rights again.

Depp was becoming stuck in something of a rut by this time. His
wide-eyed innocence was beginning to falter in its appeal and, at
the age of 29, his expressive eyes were no longer able to disguise
the thought processes going on behind them. In *Edward
Scissorhands*, one believed in him as Edward, but his growing
sophistication, both as an actor and as a man, denies that belief to
Sam. Part of the problem is the unbelievability of the character
itself – child one minute and relative sophisticate the next – who
is imposed onto the action with little explanation of his odd
behaviour and nothing about his origins beside the fact that he is
'Mike's cousin'. It is a wholly unreal role, designed merely to meet
the dramatic needs of the story and, in this respect, Sam is a somewhat mystical figure, conjured, as in a fairy tale, to right wrongs
and to point up sins of omission in those around him.

Chechik was as ingenuous as the eponymous Sam when it came
to the allegorical aspects of the piece: 'I needed someone who
could play a character who is metaphorically an angel,' he said.
'Someone who could achieve a real naive innocence that would-
n't come off as foolish.' But the film in which Sam finds himself
has no fairy-tale qualities, and he comes across as just another
looney tune on the loose in a world which appears already to have
more than its fair share of them. It is only too apparent in *Benny*

& *Joon* that Depp is an intelligent man playing a fool; he is dextrous and one-dimensionally effective, but it remains a *performance* for all that, despite its passionate adherence to the technical adroitness of silent-screen comedians like Chaplin (whose 'dancing rolls' routine from *The Gold Rush* he mimics in the film) and Keaton: 'I liked the way he could communicate without using words,' Depp acknowledged. 'It's simple to say to someone that you love them; it's harder to express it *without* words.' His playing of Sam is attractive and self-deprecating, but something more demanding than *Benny & Joon* was now needed if Johnny Depp was to stretch himself as actor.

> Do you want to know why everyone laughs at you, Sam?
> Because you're an idiot. You're a first-class moron.
> Benny Pearl (Aidan Quinn), Benny & Joon (1992)

Benny & Joon had been given the green light on the back of Richard Attenborough's *Chaplin*, starring Robert Downey Jr, which moved into production some months before and whose large-scale celebration of the silent screen's greatest slapstick comedian undoubtedly helped to inspire a more modest stablemate, if not actively encourage an otherwise routine romantic comedy to incorporate its own Keatonesque character. As with Jonathan Harker in *Dracula*, Depp had found himself in the running for the Chaplin role, but somehow found it more daunting than the notion of playing a burlesque of Keaton. 'I met with Attenborough,' he revealed, 'knowing all the while that I was totally wrong to play Chaplin. I just wanted the chance to meet him – to say "Hi".' Downey Jr was nominated for a Best Actor Oscar for his performance as Charlie Chaplin, while Depp was nominated for a Golden Globe as Sam in *Benny & Joon*. Downey lost out to Al Pacino for *Scent of a Woman*, although he did gain a Best Actor Award from BAFTA. Depp won.

(Depp was later to reflect on *Benny & Joon* for a documentary made by Richard Schickel in 2002, called *Charlie: The Life and*

Art of Charles Chaplin, in which he shared a platform with the likes of Attenborough, Woody Allen, Martin Scorsese and *Independent* film critic David Thomsen to discuss the great man's life and career; he revealed that it took him three weeks to learn the famous 'roll dance' that Chaplin had concocted pretty much on the spur of the moment.)

Behind the smiles of *Benny & Joon* lurked a growing sense of sadness. Depp had begun to surround himself with something of a regular entourage: aside from his sister Christi as his personal assistant, make-up girl Cathy York and dresser Ken Smiley were now following him from film to film. None of them could do anything to protect him from the rumour mill, however, and word from the set of *Bram Stoker's Dracula* was that Winona Ryder had had an affair with her co-star Gary Oldman, who had recently split from Uma Thurman, his wife of less than two years. Depp's naivety in respect of his dealings with the press was coming back to haunt him: 'Initially, I tried to be open; I thought, I'll just say what I'm feeling right now; let them swallow that and then they'd leave me alone. That creates even more of a monster. You're walking around; you eat a piece of pizza; go visit the Collosseum – next thing you know, there's a guy with a lens as long as your leg taking pictures.'

There was no truth to the rumour, but its very existence had hinted at a deeper rift. Amid all the unwanted media interest in the Depp-Ryder relationship, it had become clear to both of them that they were falling out of love with each other; more precisely, that the 20-year-old Ryder was fast falling out of love with Depp.

With his private life thus thrown into tumult, confirmation that Johnny Depp was a force to be reckoned with in the screen-acting stakes would come in unlikely form: another small town, another dysfunctional family unit, and another mentally retarded character in the cast. But somewhere between the parochial preoccupations of screenwriter Peter Hedges and the new and harsher tomorrow which Depp now faced on a personal level, a lasting talent was about to be born. *What's Eating Gilbert Grape* would prove an ironic title in relation to the life of its star, but the film which bore it would take him to the limits of his profession and drag him kicking and screaming into the ranks of the greats.

> *Standing with my brother Arnie on the edge of town has become a yearly ritual.*
>
> *My brother Arnie is so excited because in minutes or hours or sometime today trucks upon trailers upon campers are going to drive into our home town of Endora, Iowa. One truck will carry the Octopus, another will carry the Tilt-a-Whirl with its blue and red cars, two trucks will bring the Ferris wheel, the games will be towed, and most important, the horses from the merry-go-round will arrive.*
>
> *For Arnie, this is better than Christmas. This beats the tooth fairy and the Easter bunny: all those stupid figures that only kids and retarded adults seem to stomach. Arnie is a retard. He's about to turn eighteen and my family is planning an enormous party. Doctors said we'd be lucky if he lived to be ten. Ten came and went and now the doctors are saying, 'Any time now, Arnie could go at any time.' So every night my sisters and me, and my mom too, go to bed wondering if he will wake up in the morning. Some days you want him to live, some days you don't. At this particular moment, I've a good mind to push him in front of the oncoming traffic.*
>
> PETER HEDGES, *WHAT'S EATING GILBERT GRAPE* (1993)

By the turn of 1993, the once-golden couple had begun to drift apart. Ryder's career was resolutely on the up, but Johnny Depp's had remained relatively static since his appearance in *Edward Scissorhands*. As had been the intention, his *Jump Street* persona had faded from collective memory in the interim but, since *Scissorhands*, nothing of substance had come his way to fill the vacuum and rumours of a fling between Ryder and Oldman had done little to stabilise their deteriorating relationship. Ryder, in the meanwhile, had also shot *Mermaids* (where co-star Cher handed out matronly advice to the prospective bride-to-be) and *The House of the Spirits*, was currently engaged with Martin Scorsese on *The Age of Innocence*, and planned to follow those up with *Reality Bites* and a remake of *Little Women*. After almost 30 months in which he had starred in only two films and spent the rest of his time doting on 'Noni', Depp accepted defeat and the title role in *What's Eating Gilbert Grape*.

The Paramount-produced feature was budgeted at $11 million and represented the third of Depp's 'Small-town Trilogy'. Based on the novel of the same name by Iowa indigent Peter Hedges, *What's Eating Gilbert Grape* was actually shot on location in Austin, Texas, over a ten-week period from February to April 1993. Depp played the eponymous Gilbert Grape, passive/submissive backbone of a close-knit but fundamentally dysfunctional family of two sisters, two more brothers (one permanently absent and the youngest mentally retarded) and a morbidly obese, housebound mother, around whom her four children swarm like obedient flies. This was not a good basis for a commercial movie and tragedy was in the air from the outset, but Swedish-born director Lasse Hallström, whose credits included *ABBA: The Movie* (1977) and *My Life As a Dog* (1985), managed to mould the arid and awkward material into something wondrous to behold, offering Depp the opportunity in the process to turn in what would unarguably be his most mature performance to date.

A few weeks into the shoot, Depp received a call from Vincent Price, with whom he had remained in touch after they had filmed *Edward Scissorhands* together. 'We lost Lillian this week,' Price told him, referring to silent-screen diva Lillian Gish, with whom he had starred in *The Whales of August* in 1987. 'I'm the only one left.'

Depp was consolatory. 'I've got a feeling you're going to outlast us all,' he said.

Price thought for a moment. 'Oh, *shit!*' he demurred.

'He was tired,' Depp said afterwards of the last time that he was to hear from filmland's former High Priest of Horror. 'He wanted to go somewhere else.' Vincent Price went there eight months later, on 25 October.

> Did you ever see a beached whale on television? – That's
> her. That's my mom.
>
> Gilbert Grape (Johnny Depp), What's Eating Gilbert Grape (1993)

Gilbert and his retarded brother Arnie (Leonardo DiCaprio) live in the town of Endora, Iowa – 'End(ora) of the Line', as one store-hoarding proclaims – where the highlight of their year is waiting by the side of the road for the annual wagon-train of camper-vans to pass, en route to more attractive pastures. His days are spent shelf-filling in a local grocery store that stands in the deepening shadow of an out-of-town supermarket called Foodland, delivering goods and sex to Mrs Carver (Mary Steenburgen) as a way of lightening his emotional load; his off-duty hours are spent chaperoning Arnie and sharing small talk with his two friends, a mortician and an odd-job man. He passes his evenings by pandering to his 'beached whale' of a mother, who has not been out of the house in seven years and whose closest attachment, other than Arnie, is the remote control that feeds her a TV diet of old Monty Clift movies.

Gilbert Grape is the stuff of William Faulkner and John Updike, and beautifully realised it is, too, in Hallström's hands: nothing ever happens in Endora, and nothing much happens in the film either, bar the imminent opening of a new 'Burger Barn' franchise (to the strains of The Drifters' 'This Magic Moment') and the arrival in town of a free spirit named Becky (Juliette Lewis) when her mother's camper-van breaks down along the way. Cue a tentative love affair between her and Gilbert, and his awakening to the possibility of a life outside of silent servitude to the needs of his nearest and dearest. Opportunities for romantic cliché are rife, but Hallström's manipulation of the viewer is subtle and affecting; his treatment of the material, touching and tender, while the vast, empty landscape in which Gilbert ploughs his daily furrow becomes another player in the drama through the impeccable lensing of Ingmar Bergman cinematographer Sven Nykvist.

Central to the story is the gross yet infinitely tragic figure of Gilbert's mother Bonnie, a widow of 17 years, whose mythical significance to the citizens of Endora has grown in direct proportion to her unfettered girth. Town and film both are inexorably subject to the immensity of her presence, even when she is absent from the screen, and much humour is affectionately extracted from clandestine attempts to reinforce the floor beneath her settee or prise the remote from her hand while she sleeps. Bonnie is played by the genuinely obese Darlene Cates, whose 500lb debut this was and who was discovered by Hedges himself, on a TV chat show. Her self-effacing turn is unique and heart-rending: 'I haven't always been like this,' she confesses self-consciously to Becky, after Gilbert has urged a meeting on the pair. 'I haven't always been like this either,' the astute girl empathetically replies.

The alert viewer can see the end coming, even if Gilbert himself cannot: his mother dies, after struggling up the stairs to bed for the first time in years, and her distraught children are left with the quandary of how to have her removed from the house for burial ('You'll need the National Guard,' the sheriff is tactlessly informed over his police radio). Gilbert comes up with the answer: with their possessions moved into the yard, Bonnie Grape is accorded a Viking funeral as the troubled homestead is torched. Freed by the flames from the drudgery of existence, Gilbert and his brother and sisters leave the ashes of their collective childhood behind them and embark on new lives, far removed from Endora.

As the emotionally repressed Gilbert, Depp's performance is gracious and engaging, and the film's director was effusive in his praise: 'It's not true, but I know he felt he was boring in the part,' he said. 'To me, this is his best performance. You see a little more of him. He doesn't hide behind his eccentricities.' Hallström's comments hit a nerve: 'Lasse thinks that I like to hide behind weird characters so that I'm not exposed, and that Gilbert is the most real thing that I've played; closer to reality and closer to me,' Depp responded in interview. 'It could be true. I don't know; I'm not in therapy.' But the role had resonated on a deeper level than those in his previous films. 'He shut down,' he said of Gilbert, 'and I can relate to that. I felt bad for the four months we shot. It was a very lonely time. Also, the movie had to do with family and growing up and, in a way, not growing up, and feeling responsible for your family. It struck some old memory chords.'

'I've got nowhere to go,' Gilbert confesses to Becky in a rare moment of self-revelation towards the end of the film. In his case, perhaps. But on this showing, it was patently untrue for the actor who had struggled to portray him. To the heights, Johnny. To the heights.

The whole cast is uniformly excellent, but the 18-year-old DiCaprio is nothing less than brilliant as the hyper-impulsive Arnie, imprisoned by a mental age which is stuck in single figures, but forever to be found perched precariously atop the local water-tower. (DiCaprio was deservedly nominated for a Golden Globe and an Academy Award for Best Supporting Actor; he won both.) Hallström observes the nuances of small-town existence with a keen and patient eye; his film is passionate in its admiration for the indomitability of the human spirit and his concern for his characters never falters, never bows to the temptation of cheap shots at their expense, and is never less than sympathetic to each of their individual plights. *What's Eating Gilbert Grape* is a movie of immense heart and endless charm, a 'feel-good' fable in the finest Hollywood tradition, a triumph for all who feature in it, and a great piece of American cinema, to boot.

Amy got a job-offer to manage a bakery in Des Moines. Ellen can't wait to switch schools. Arnie asked if we were going to go too and I said, well, we can go anywhere-if we

want. We can go anywhere.
Gilbert Grape (Johnny Depp), What's Eating Gilbert Grape (1993)

The experience of making *What's Eating Gilbert Grape* was as painful for Depp as life was for Gilbert in the story. Hallström said of him in the role: 'He's been forced to suppress his own feelings, his own emotions. It's a very tough part.' Tougher even than his director imagined, as it happened, as Depp embarked on a drink-and-drugs binge during shooting, to stave off the depths of melancholia that were inspired in him by the fact that his three-year affair with Ryder was now on the rocks. That Depp looks tired and washed out on occasion was not just the effect of make-up – he had returned to his old ways of 'medicating' himself into semi-consciousness, which only served to exacerbate the feeling of loneliness which he found well-nigh impossible to shake off. 'I just took to poisoning myself,' he said. 'There's an element of Johnny that's extremely nice and extremely cool but, at the same time, he's hard to figure out,' a bemused DiCaprio observed.

'I went through so many years where I medicated myself,' he later told Danny Leigh of the *Guardian*. 'But ultimately, all you're doing is postponing the inevitable. Which is that you're going to have to acknowledge your demons. But for years, the whole thing was, "Oh, fuck it, I'll deal with it tomorrow." And then you realise that you're hurting the people around you, and you're scaring the people around you, and it just seems... dumb. So you stop.'

Stop Depp eventually did, but not before experiencing a brush with mortality: 'At one point I was living on coffee and cigarettes; no food, no sleep. I was sitting around with some pals when my heart started running at 200 beats a minute. That's scary. You're mentally trying to slow down your heart, but you can't. It's like being on a plane when the bottom drops out-you drop a couple of thousand feet and one second turns into eternity. You really do get all those family pictures in your head. And you feel so totally fucking alone. I was thinking of my grandfather on my mom's side – a great man, whom I worshipped. His heart just exploded one day. When my heart started racing I hoped it was an anxiety attack, but when it went on for 45 minutes, I knew it wasn't anxiety: it was all the shit I'd done to my body. My friends got me to the hospital, where I got a shot – boom! A shot that basically stops your heart for a second. I could feel myself curling up, going foetal. Then it was over; I got to go home. Now, there's an experience that'll scare you into shape.'

Depp's family and friends used the opportunity to offer the prodigal some timely advice. He appeared to take it, and there was no recurrence of the incident. Thereafter, he set out to 'clean up his act'. He was later to reflect on this 'Damascene' event for Tom Shone: 'I don't particularly remember the moment of death and the moment of rebirth and everything. But I feel like I've gone through whatever I've gone through and then this other guy emerged.'

For a long time after, Depp could not bring himself to look at the result of his labours in *What's Eating Gilbert Grape*, yet his performance in the film is something of which he can be immensely proud. The reasons were personal, of course, and to do with his state of mind at the time of its production. But if troubled times can create troubled art, then they can also create great art: *Gilbert Grape* is Johnny Depp's *East of Eden*.

In May 1993, with shooting over, Depp and Ryder agreed to a parting of the ways. Depp had also resolved to cease decorating his person with assorted tattoos – make-up was having to be applied on a regular basis to the most visible of them, such as those on his fingers and knuckles, and he had come to realise how they could impede upon his future career. He was left with the problem of the now-notorious 'Winona Forever', however, though he chose to defer that for now: 'He was so desperately in love with Winona that when they broke up, he wouldn't admit it was over for the longest time,' an anonymous friend was quoted as saying in *People*.

Hanson: She was the one, Doug.

Penhall: What happened?

Hanson: I don't know. She blamed me; I blamed her. And now... she's with him.

'Eternal Flame', 21 Jump Street (1988)

Depp had consoled himself on the set of *Gilbert Grape* by hanging out with songwriter Bill Carter and raucous rock musician Gibby Haynes, front-man of the Butthole Surfers, whom he had met when he and others in the cast had gone on a sabbatical to see Neil Young play at a concert nearby. The three decided to form an 'occasional' band, with Haynes on vocals, Depp and Carter on guitar and Sal Jenco on drums. The four-piece outfit was christened 'P' (spelt 'u-r-i-n-e', Depp would explain, in his typically egregious way), and it played its first gig at the 1993 Austin Music Awards.

(The band jammed irregularly over the next two years, and Haynes eventually persuaded Capitol Records to cut a single entitled 'Michael Stipe' – after the lead singer of REM – and then an album, on which the four were joined by Chuck E Weiss, Flea of the Red Hot Chili Peppers and Steve Jones of The Sex Pistols. 'P' was released without fanfare in November 1995 and featured 11 tracks in a variety of styles, from psychedelic rock to reggae, of which the aforementioned 'Stipe', the hard-driving, Black Sabbath-inspired 'Oklahoma' and 'The Deal' are especially stand-out. Haynes returned to the Butthole Surfers when 'P' went nowhere, but the band remains informally in existence and its one album to date, while raw in places, is well worth seeking out – and not only for Depp's guitar-plucking.)

The notion of forming a band may have kept Depp occupied, but no amount of raunchy rock could drown out the sound of press hacks, sharpening their poison-pencils at the news that he and Ryder were soon to be no more. He was learning the hard way that the press was a Jekyll-and-Hyde monster with whom he had to tread very carefully: one minute fulsome in its praise; the next equally fulminating in its condemnation. 'I don't know what else they can come up with,' Ryder would plead in *Sky* magazine. 'I think they might even be running out of stories, so they'll try and create something new with someone that I probably don't even know.'

'They' were to have no need, as it turned out; stories have a way of creating themselves. Only six months later, Johnny Depp was to find himself subject to the duplicitous attentions of the tabloids over another affair entirely and the next one would prove to be a good deal more sordid than the last.

Johnny Depp as Officer Tom Hanson in *21 Jump Street*

With Ricki Lake and Traci Lords in *Cry-Baby* (1990)

With Winona Ryder at the premiere of *Edward Scissorhands* in December 1990

Depp as Sam and Mary Stuart Masterson as 'Joon' in *Benny & Joon* (1992)

Making an entrance in *Edward Scissorhands* (1990)

With a youthful Leonardo DiCaprio in
What's Eating Gilbert Grape (1993)

Depp and his mother Betty Sue (Palmer)
at a film premiere in New York, 1995

Martin Landau as Bela Lugosi and Johnny Depp
as Wood in *Ed Wood* (1993)

With director Tim Burton and co-star
Sarah Jessica Parker offset on *Ed Wood* (1993)

In iconic pose for *Don Juan DeMarco* (1994)

'Bill' Blake has intimations of
mortality in *Dead Man* (1994)

With Kate Moss at the premiere of
Donnie Brasco, 1997

Depp as Raoul, with Benicio Del Toro as Gonzo,
in *Fear and Loathing in Las Vegas* (1997)

Depp as Spencer Armacost, with Charlize
Theron as Jillian, in *The Astronaut's Wife* (1998)

'Even the paper sounds kosher' – Depp as
Dean Corso in *The Ninth Gate* (1998)

4 WIDE-EYED AND FECKLESS

FADE IN. HAUNTED MANSION PARLOUR – NIGHT.
We move through a spooky shrouded parlour, as a storm
rages outside. THUNDER roars, and lightning flashes in the
giant windows. In the centre of the room lies an oak coffin.
Suddenly the lid starts to creak open. A hand crawls past the
edge... and then the lid slams up! Famed psychic CRISWELL
pops out. Criswell, 40, peers at us intently, his gleaming eyes
framed under his striking pale blonde hair. He intones, with
absolute conviction:

> Criswell: Greetings, my friend. You are interested in the
> unknown, the mysterious, the unexplainable...that is why
> you are here. So now, for the first time, we are bringing
> you the full story of what happened... (extremely serious)
> We are giving you all the evidence, based only on the
> secret testimony of the miserable souls who survived this
> terrible ordeal. The incidents, the places, my friend, we
> cannot keep this a secret any longer. Can your hearts
> stand the shocking facts of the true story of Edward D
> Wood, Junior??
>
> from the screenplay of Ed Wood (1994)

SCREEN CAPTION:
*Valda Hansen: 'Ed said, 'Do you think I care if I'm a mil-
lionaire? No, Valda. What hurts me is the cruelty towards me.
The way they want to deride me. The way they want to put
me down and scoff at me. I'm only trying to do the best at
what I feel. All this garbage I see, they praise, and me – they
seem to love to deride me.'*
RUDOLPH GREY, *NIGHTMARE OF ECSTASY* (1991)

THE PRESS had a field day. According to the rumours, the three-
year Hollywood 'Camelot' of Depp and Ryder had finally

imploded. Eager gossip columnists had been looking for chinks in the armour of the relationship almost since the beginning, and their prurient patience had been rewarded by 1993, when word had crept out about Depp's morose behaviour on the set of *What's Eating Gilbert Grape* to supplement the earlier innuendoes that something more venal had gone on between Ryder and Oldman during the filming of *Bram Stoker's Dracula* than the fey attentions of a fictional vampire.

The title of Depp's latest film was in itself unfortunate. It was a punning opportunity too good to pass up for many headline writers, and 'What's Eating Johnny Depp?' soon became a byword for the actor's misfiring love life. *Benny & Joon* opened on 16 April 1993, earning high praise from *Empire* magazine's Matt Mueller, who called it 'a genuinely poetic love story … so captivating that only the most hardened cynic will fail to be enchanted', while among the 'immensely likeable performances', Depp's was singled out as 'appealing'. Less appealing for the film's young star was now the very real prospect of having to spend his life without Winona Ryder.

By June, the 'rebel love' (as *GQ* had called it) was most definitely at an end. 'I don't know how much the media had to do with it because we really had drifted apart a long time before the press found out that it had ended,' Ryder confessed in *Sky* the following January. By the time she talked to Jeff Giles of *Rolling Stone* two months later, however, she had removed the ambiguity that was present in her earlier account: 'I remember us desperately hating being hounded. It was horrible, and it certainly took its toll on our relationship. Every day, we heard that we were either cheating on each other or that we were broken up, when we weren't. It was like this constant mosquito buzzing around us.' Two years later, and Ryder was firmer still in her view of who, or what, had ultimately been to blame: 'We couldn't go a week without reading something that wasn't true or was only half true, or was taken out of context. I wouldn't want to go through that again. Looking back, I can see that it did affect our relationship,' she reaffirmed for *Vogue*. Within months of the split, Winona Ryder was on the arm of Dave Pirner, lead singer of Soul Asylum, whom she had met at an 'MTV Unplugged' awards ceremony; she followed this by abandoning grunge in favour of a more conservative lifestyle.

Depp was devastated; from the prospect of starring opposite 'Noni' in a new version of *The Three Musketeers* one minute – he as D'Artagnan, she as Milady de Winter – to a final parting of the ways the next. (In the event, the film went ahead without either of them.) He had unconsciously revealed in a recent interview that he felt Ryder might 'dump' him; now he protested in another that the famous tattoo of 'Winona Forever' had never actually read that way to begin with (despite photographic evidence to the contrary). As though to back up this contention, he underwent painful laser surgery to have the tattoo removed from his arm, managing only to have it foreshortened to a form which instead conjured up an image of self-pitying melancholy, as of one who feels the need to endlessly regurgitate his tale of lost love while slumped in an alcoholic stupor: 'Wino Forever'.

In a magazine article, Ryder had been referred to as 'Pre-Raphaelite' by a director with whom she had worked – if so, she had now become Millais' *Ophelia* in Depp's eyes: dead as earth and floating silently downstream, while Hamlet is left standing on the riverbank.

> *He did not love me living; but once dead*
> *He pitied me; and very sweet it is*
> *To know he still is warm though I am cold.*
> **CHRISTINA ROSSETTI, 'AFTER DEATH' (1862)**

In November 1980, two brothers named Harry and Michael Medved had published a book which they cleverly entitled *The Golden Turkey Awards*, and which is still best remembered for its nomination of the 1956 sci-fi thriller, *Plan 9 from Outer Space*, as the 'worst film of all time'. As with all such overnight fads, the Medveds' book became required reading and an immediate bestseller, thanks in part to brother Michael's enthusiastic promotion of it through a nationwide blitz of seminars and interviews, most of which were accompanied by appropriately dismal clips from the 50 film 'turkeys' in question.

The unfortunate recipient of the award for 'worst film' had a typical mid-1950s B-movie plot, in which aliens plan to conquer Earth using reanimated corpses (a concept made more explicit by the film's working title of *Grave-Robbers From Outer Space*). It was a theme which had cropped up many times before in the pulp magazines of the 1940s, and it would continue to surface in second-features like 1960's *The Day Mars Invaded Earth* – so *Plan 9*'s critical crucifixion at the pens of the Medveds was less to do with its storyline than it was with the severe lack of facilities available to those who had made it.

Plan 9 from Outer Space was actually the sixth feature of a 31-year-old director named Edward D(avis) Wood Junior, a self-confessed transvestite from Poughkeepsie, New York, and one of the many exploitation filmmakers who operated on the black-and-white B-movie fringes of Hollywood in the mid-1950s. Wood's cinematic outings were unique among those of his peers for betraying clear evidence of *no* budget, as opposed to a low budget, in their production, but the skid-row horrors for which he is best known nevertheless managed to achieve a measure of theatrical release on the strength of two important factors: iconic and easily marketable titles and the pseudo-'star presence' of one-time Hollywood legend and archetypal screen *Dracula*, Bela Lugosi. Filmed in August of 1956, *Plan 9* was the third of Wood's films to feature the ailing Lugosi.

Lugosi's career had itself been on the skids since 1952, when he was reduced to starring opposite music-hall comedian Arthur Lucan's 'Mother Riley' in *Mother Riley Meets the Vampire* (*Vampires Over London* in the USA). This was followed by a series of walk-ons as mad scientists or mute menservants in increasingly dire fare like *The Black Sleep* (1956), during which time the former 1920s matinee idol in his native Hungary also fell victim to morphine addiction. That same year, Lugosi's path crossed with that of Ed Wood, who was about to write, direct and star in his first full-length feature. Alert to the opportunity which had come within his grasp, Wood signed the impoverished actor for $500 and cast him in a nonsensical cameo role as the Spirit, which he then incorporated into *Glen or Glenda* (1957), a semi-autobiographical account of his own struggles with closet transvestism. The two went on to make one more feature together – *Bride of the Atom* (released as *Bride of the Monster* in the UK) – before Lugosi's death cut short their formative partnership. Not to be outdone by the Grim Reaper, Wood incorporated footage that he had earlier obtained of Lugosi into a film which he proposed to call *Grave Robbers From Outer Space* and matched it to shots of a chiropodist named Tom Mason, made up to look like the dead actor. The retitled *Plan 9 from Outer Space* was thus sold as 'starring' Bela Lugosi. Of such things are Hollywood legends made, no matter how poor the material from which they are spun.

One evening in May 1993, Johnny Depp was home alone, nursing the emotional wound that still pulsed red-raw from his as-yet unofficial split with Winona Ryder, when the phone rang. On the line was Tim Burton.

'Johnny?' Burton began. 'What are you doing?'

Depp was non-committal. He had passed up *Sliver* (in favour of William Baldwin), *Speed* (ditto Keanu Reeves) and perhaps significantly *Legends of the Fall* (Brad Pitt). Thirty was proving to be a dangerous age. 'Hanging out; sitting around,' he mumbled.

'Can you meet me somewhere?' Burton asked.

Depp thought for a moment. No, he had nothing better to do. 'Sure,' he said. 'Where?'

'How quickly can you get to the Formosa Cafe?'

'Twenty minutes.'

At that, Burton put down the phone.

The Formosa Cafe is a Hollywood diner perched on the corner of Formosa Avenue and Santa Monica Boulevard. A former railroad car, the Formosa had opened in 1925, directly opposite what were then the studios of United Artists, later to become the Goldwyn Studios, and now designated the Warner-Hollywood Studios. Something of a celebrity hang-out due to its unique location, the Formosa's car-park is mocked-up with spaces 'reserved' for stars and its interior walls are lined with more than 250 personally autographed photos of screen 'greats', from Jack Benny to James Dean.

When Depp arrived, Burton was seated at the bar. He ordered up two beers.

'I've got this project,' Burton began. 'It's going to happen and I really want to do it.'

Depp's ears pricked up. He was talking to the director with whom he had found himself most in tune and who had given him his biggest hit to date. 'What is it?' Depp asked.

'It's about Ed Wood.'

Depp was still none the wiser, but he could barely contain his enthusiasm. 'Whatever,' he consented. 'Whatever you want to do.'

When the meeting was over, Depp rang John Waters with the news. Waters was ecstatic; he had passed on the chance to make the film himself due to his current commitments with *Serial Mom*. 'I'm so happy for you,' he burbled. 'I'm *s-o-o-o* happy!'

Method-trained (though by no means convinced: 'Classes really bugged me out, people imitating lobsters and stuff') as he was, Depp's next move was to try to understand what it felt like to be a transvestite. To that end, he set about acquiring for himself a selection of female undergarments: 'I'd never worn a bra before,' he rather needlessly explained, 'so I couldn't understand that you're constantly bound and constrained and reminded by this thing. After wearing a slip and a bra, I have much more respect for women.'

If the Medveds' book had achieved anything of note, it was the fact that it inspired *Problem Child* screenwriters Scott Alexander and Larry Karaszewski to take a fresh look at Wood's life and career, free from the prejudices of self-serving cineastes. To do so, they turned instead to a book which had itself been sired by *The*

Golden Turkey Awards, but to more meritorious ends. Rudolph Grey's *Nightmare of Ecstasy* is not so much a biography of Wood in the conventional sense as a collage of (sometimes contra-dictory) reminiscences of the director, by anyone and everyone who ever met, married, mortgaged or made movies with him – an 'oral history', as its author describes the result of his ten-year trawl through the Hollywood trash-can. As such, it is excellent of its kind and astringently captures the seedy, down-at-heel, day-to-day experiences of talentless filmmaking wannabes in a dog-eat-dog world on the fringes of Hollywood hell.

Having mined Grey's book for its dramatic nuggets, the two writers took their screenplay to Michael Lehmann, who had directed *Heathers*, who in turn took it to producer Denise Di Novi and her partner Tim Burton. Burton floated the project with Columbia, who initially proposed a budget of $18 million but took fright and put it into turnaround when he said that he wanted to shoot the film in black-and-white; Burton, in response, pulled out of directing *Mary Reilly* and went with *Ed Wood* to Disney, who were only too happy to have the prodigal back in the fold.

> This is it! – This is the one I'll be remembered for!
> Ed Wood (Johnny Depp), Ed Wood (1994)

Ed Wood sensibly restricts the focus on its subject to what could loosely be termed 'the Lugosi years', opening with the production of *Glen or Glenda* and Wood's initial encounter with the ailing star, and closing with Lugosi's death and the premiere of *Plan 9 from Outer Space*. Between these two obvious biographical mark-ers, it sketches in Wood's transvestism with a series of camply humorous yet sympathetic vignettes and also recreates the hilari-ous shooting of *Bride of the Atom* and *Plan 9*, but it concentrates the greater part of its energies on the strange, interdependent relationship of Wood with Lugosi.

As the titular Ed Wood, Depp is on-screen for the whole of the film, but he finds himself faced with the scene-stealing antics of

Martin Landau as the tragic Lugosi for much of that time. It is Landau who provides *Ed Wood* with its memorable moments and, accordingly, he is given most of the script's best lines: '*Karloff!*' he snarls, when a sycophantic studio-hand inadvertently mentions the name of his co-star in *The Invisible Ray*, 'That cock-sucker isn't fit to smell my shit!' Landau gives a towering performance in the role – investing the faded star with a stature which, at this juncture, he surely lacked in life – and went deservedly on to collect a Best Supporting Actor Oscar for his pains (which were considerable). But it was Depp's gracious subservience, as compliant foil and willing fall guy to a craftily contrived cameo, which granted him both his head and his gong. Having said that, Lugosi was the role that Landau was born to play; the mark of great impersonation in this instance being the fact that to the mind's eye, he looks more like Lugosi than Lugosi did.

Depp's performance is a model of subtlety beneath the rictus grin of the ventriloquist's doll which he chooses to adopt for much of his pose as Wood: he never allows his playing of a deceptively difficult role to stray into the realms of outright farce – in spite of the often farcical nature of the situations to which his character naturally inclines – and even manages to elicit sympathy for Wood's erotic attachment to angora, which someone less sure of his ground might have felt obliged to reduce to the level of slapstick. So assured is his portrait of a sad and complex individual (but nonetheless one to be fleetingly admired) that Wood's presence in the film almost becomes sublimated into its textural air of wish-fulfilment, as though he were a sort of spiritual force, in the manner of Edward Scissorhands, to whom the other characters in the drama are desperately drawn and around whom they each revolve or die, like moths before a flame.

On this occasion, Depp took as his models for the character the host of 'American Top 40', deejay Casey Kasem, the Tin Man from *The Wizard of Oz* and Ronald Reagan, the former 40th President of the United States with a previous lifetime spent as an actor in 'B' movies. 'To me, Ed was a combination of Reagan, the Tin Man and Casey Kasem, mashed into one optimistic individual who also happened to be a transvestite,' he explained. (Depp had attended a 'Just Say No' anti-drugs bash at the Reagan White House during his stint on *Jump Street* and memories of the constantly smiling President 'wearing make-up' were still vividly etched into his mind.) 'I wanted to try and make a guy that was a ball of energy, but also so sickly optimistic, like Reagan.' It was Tim Burton who suggested Charlie McCarthy, the pre-war dummy of vaudevillian ventriloquist, Edgar Bergan.

At the time, Burton was a very static director, not much given to exotic camera angles or the tracking tricks that could be enabled by motion control; as such, he was ill-suited to the visual dynamic required of *Batman* (his previous feature) but perfectly in tune with the less mobile style required of *Ed Wood*, both consciously and unconsciously. The film unfolds as a series of tableaux, which allows the viewer to concentrate on the staging within the frame: the loving recreations of the period; the painstaking reconstructions of Wood's best-known films in the making.

Alexander and Karaszewski's script catches the essence of 'The Life and Art' (to quote the subtitle of Grey's book) of Edward D Wood to perfection, not an easy task with so many disparate recollections. Much of the truth shines through the fog of selective memory as a result: Wood's irrepressible optimism in the face of insurmountable obstacles; Lugosi's drug-addled unpredictability, coupled with genuine respect for Wood's cinematic abilities; the enduring loyalty of Wood's dysfunctional entourage; the sense of camaraderie, and of 'belonging'; his abiding passion for his craft, no matter how low it might be perceived by those around him; the sheer craziness of it all, a craziness which is manifest only in the fact that he was trying to make his movies for a buck-and-a-half, whereas those who put equally daft ideas on film for a million-and-a-half were allowed to pass without comment. It is also assiduous in extracting the salient points from Grey's communal narrative, like the fact that 1932's *White Zombie* was Lugosi's favourite among his own films, his dispensing candy to neighbourhood children, or his threatening Wood with a gun. The only significant falsehood in the otherwise faithful battery of anecdotes on display is an imaginary encounter between Wood and Orson Welles, in the style of General Gordon's fictitious meeting with Laurence Olivier's Mahdi in *Khartoum*. The real 'Vampira', Finnish-born Maila Nurmi, objected to Lugosi swearing in the script on the grounds that he never did so in life; others disagreed, and it seems likely that he confined his cussing to male company. Depp objected to Wood's swearing on the page, considering it out of character with the way that he was portraying him in the film. The one person who never swears in *Ed Wood* is therefore Wood himself.

> Ed: I'd seen him in a coffin so many times, I expected him to jump out...
> Kathy: Ed, you've got to snap out of this. Bela's dead-you're not!
> Ed: I might as well be. I made shitty movies that nobody wanted to see.
> (beat)
> I blew it. All he wanted was a comeback... That last glory...
> Kathy: Well you tried-
> Ed (angry): I was a fuckin' HACK! I let people recut the movies, cast their relatives...
> (beat)
> I let Bela down...
>
> (scene deleted) from the screenplay of Ed Wood (1994)

Wood had intended to use Lugosi for as long as his health would hold out. After *Plan 9*, he had planned to feature him in a film variously entitled *The Undead Masses* and *Ghouls from the Moon*; Lugosi barely even made it into *Plan 9*. What Wood eventually shot as the terminally strange *Night of the Ghouls* went ahead with the same motley crew who played in the preceding opus, but without Bela. It never saw release.

In fact, there was no difference between Wood and any number of journeyman directors working for the majors at the time that more money would not have blurred into invisibility. To underline the point, the script adds its fictional meeting between Wood and a creatively frustrated Welles, universally agreed to be one of the greatest film directors who ever lived, in which all that separates the two of them from their respective dreams is opportunity.

Wood himself was guilty of only a single forgivable sin: he seized the chance to hook up with a fading Hollywood star, whose marquee value still held enough potential to bankroll a low-budget horror movie. It is utterly unsurprising that Wood saw in the ailing Lugosi – still the screen's most famous personification of Bram Stoker's Count Dracula at the time – the chance to elevate his filmmaking ambitions beyond the poverty-row quickies in which, until then, he had been forced to submerge his doubtful talents. Nor was he as far removed from the bottom rung of the Hollywood ladder as the Medveds, popular opinion and Burton's film would have one believe. He co-wrote several exploitation features with Alex Gordon (with whom he shared an apartment for a time), who went on to become a major participant in American International with showbiz lawyer Sam Arkoff. *Bride of the Atom* was based on an Alex Gordon original story entitled 'The Atomic Monster', and Gordon received screen credit in recognition of the fact. It served the purpose of *Ed Wood* to paint him as an enthusiastic amateur, however, forever on the edge of acceptance; it also served Tim Burton's interior view of himself, despite the fact that he has since become one of the major wheeler-dealers on the Hollywood scene.

At its crudest, the horror film has always functioned at only one remove from pornography, sometimes crossing the line between the two: what this means in essence is that often it matters little who features in such films, so long as they deliver the requisite action. Horror and porn have acted as magnets for filmmaking wannabes since the beginning of cinema, and it is no surprise that Ed Wood's output soon came to incorporate elements of soft-core (later hardcore) pornography in their make-up, following the commercial failure of *Plan 9 from Outer Space*. Eventually, the horror was dropped altogether in favour of the sex. It is equally unsurprising that *Ed Wood*'s screenwriters should have chosen to leave this epilogue out of their version, preferring to exit the stage, in the manner of *42nd Street* and other musicals, with the feel-good fade-out of a 'premiere' for *Plan 9* (which was actually a single screening under its original title at LA's Carlton Theatre on 15 March 1957, before the film was shelved for two years).

Ed Wood is arguably the best film about filmmaking ever made, notwithstanding the fact that it cheerfully charts the career of a man who has been irreparably characterised as the worst director in the history of the movies. Burton's passion for his subject is stamped indelibly on every carefully composed frame, as it was on the soul of the poverty-row pioneer whose work he sought to reappraise, but it is Johnny Depp who brings the film so lovingly to life. His take on Wood is more psychological portrait than straight impersonation (though it brought him praise and genuine appreciation from Wood's widow, Kathy), but beneath the mimicry is a real feel for the pain and simple pleasures of the perennial outsider, which sparks incandescently of the stardust memories that (b)lighted the lives of *all* of Hollywood's legions of lost souls.

Depp had specialised in eccentric loners before *Ed Wood*, but all had been grounded in a recognisable reality. Wood was real enough himself, but director Tim Burton's exotic blend of fact and fiction, anchored by Landau's barnstorming turn as a profane Lugosi, had awakened in him a taste for the fantasy subjects to which he would now incline with more frequency as time went on. 'That role was the rocket ship that took me away from that horrible, black, bleak time,' he said. 'This guy needed to be the ultimate optimist, dreamer, idealist. It was like being in a completely different suit or skin. It felt very good.'

In what appears at first to be a one-dimensional portrait of little depth, Depp manages to capture the irrepressible optimism, feistiness and inviolate self-belief of the man. Many of those who knew Wood are in agreement about his ethereal qualities: Depp absorbs that and turns it into a beacon of hope for every star-struck wannabe, with a subtle and immensely sympathetic per-formance, while at the same time fostering a spirit of tolerance for his frailty and psycho-sexual weaknesses. *Ed Wood* is a feel-good movie in the great tradition of *It's a Wonderful Life*; one comes to the film to stare into the void of Wood's talent and laugh, but one leaves it in admiration for his resilience and indomitable drive. It is drawn from the life and allowing for the changes necessitated by the needs of drama, it never strays far from the truth. Although the real Ed Wood descended into hardcore sexploitation shorts and porno novels, there was still talent there: as a writer of pulp fiction, he was no worse than most and better than many. Booze and bad luck were his downfall, and the screenwriters under-standably left that less edifying epilogue out of their film. As biopics go, *Ed Wood* comes as close as any, and Depp's honest and heartfelt tribute to a director whose name has become synony-mous with ineptitude goes a long way to reversing the notion that he was simply another southern Californian jester, out to make a quick buck. Wood was passionate about his art; he may not have been much good at it but, through Ed Wood, Burton and Depp at least ensured that he could now be appreciated for trying.

> I'm just scared that it's not going to get any better than this.
>
> Ed Wood (Johnny Depp), Ed Wood (1994)

The announcement that the Depp-Ryder engagement was offi-cially off had been made to the world's media on 21 June, 1993. Though there are few signs of it in the film, the Wood 'mask' hid heartache on the set and Depp was sometimes given to shed tears openly for the loss of love's young dream – a fact which adds poignancy to the false hopes so eagerly pursued in *Ed Wood*. Independent writer-director Jim Jarmusch had been staying with Depp during the shoot, ostensibly to discuss a Western that he was planning but also to keep the disconsolate actor company. 'Sometimes I'd pick him up from the set and we'd get dinner,' Jarmusch recalled. 'It would take him three hours to stop being Ed Wood. I just wanted to slap him to get that stupid smile off his face! We'd be in this Thai restaurant and Johnny is going, "Hey, this Thai pad is fabulous!"'

'It took me a couple of months to not smile like Ed Wood,' Depp confirmed. He had been looking for something to take his mind off the break-up and Jarmusch's vision intrigued him enough to commit in principle to the lead in the proposed *Dead Man* but, by August, he had found an alternative therapy in West Hollywood, tucked disarmingly away on the world-famous Sunset 'Strip'.

While shooting progressed on *Ed Wood*, Depp was afforded the opportunity to return to his first love, music. Chuck E Weiss – singer, songwriter, drummer, front-man for the band Goddamn Liars and another of Depp's rock 'n' roll buddies (as well as the subject of Rickie Lee Jones's 1979 hit, 'Chuck E's in Love') – suggested to Depp that the pair of them could buy into a small nightclub. The once-popular but currently run-down venue in question was situated at 8852 Sunset Boulevard, its unassuming entrance in a side street named Larrabee, and Weiss had a soft spot for the place, as he had played there every Monday night for the previous 11 years. Club owner and general factotum Anthony Fox had been looking for new blood, *and* new money, to renovate this modest slice of Hollywood real estate, and Weiss's sentimental attachment to it had inspired him to turn to Depp. Owning an LA nightclub where he could canoodle and occasionally jam with his rock-star friends held considerable appeal for the disconsolate and downhearted Depp, but he was also attracted by the history and notoriety of the Central.

Depp needed little persuading. He bought 51 per cent of the company that owned the club for a reported $350,000, becoming chief executive of 'Safe in Heaven Dead' and beating off rival bids from Arnold Schwarzenegger and Frank Stallone (brother of

Sylvester) in the process, and renamed it the Viper Room – 'viper' being 1920s slang for a heroin addict, or as Depp preferred to explain it to *Playboy* magazine, 'After a group of musicians in the thirties who called themselves Vipers. They were reefer heads and they helped start modern music.' Fox took a salary of $800 a week and the post of vice-president and director, and Depp installed his friend Sal Jenco as the club's new general manager.

Depp's Viper Room had started life as a prohibition 'speakeasy', part-owned by Charles 'Lucky' Luciano (Salvatore Luciana), a one-time Sicilian émigré who had become the prime mover in establishing an Organised Crime Syndicate in America during the 1930s, and who had also founded Murder Incorporated as a means of maintaining order over his vast empire of extortion rackets, prostitution and drugs-trafficking. By the 1940s, the club was known as the Melody Room after it fell into the hands of Benjamin 'Bugsy' Siegel, a former Luciano hit-man who had since become a high-ranking Mafioso in his own right. A decade later and Siegel was dead from a bullet to the brain and the club had become the Central in an effort to rid itself of its former Mafia associations.

Depp's plans for the club were typically modest. 'I liked the idea of a sense of nostalgia for the twenties,' he told Chris Heard, 'so we built it in that style – an old speakeasy with viper music. When I thought of the club, the music of Fats Waller and Cab Calloway was playing in my head. Nobody plays that stuff anymore.'

The Viper Room was given a makeover which included a private booth for Depp and his agent Tracey Jacobs, complete with warning notice advising 'Don't Fuck With It', and was quickly reopened for business – but not before word had got out that the newest nightspot on Sunset was now co-owned by none other than Johnny Depp. 'The place became a scene instantly when we opened it,' he said. 'I never had any idea it was going to do that. I really thought it was going to be just be this cool little underground place. You can't even see the place,' he went on. 'There's no sign on Sunset.

It's just a black building, and the only sign is on Larrabee – a tiny little sign, real subtle. And I figured it'd be low-key.'

Within weeks of the Viper Room changing hands, record producer Rick Rubin, who at the time was best known for his association with the likes of Run DMC, LL Cool J and The Beastie Boys, chose it as the venue to inaugurate the 'comeback' of country legend Johnny Cash, who had signed up to Rubin's Def-American label following an unsuccessful six-year stint with Mercury Records after being dropped by Columbia in 1987. Cash was to try out a new acoustic sound at the club at Rubin's instigation, and ultimately to rapturous applause from what was, for him, an untypical audience of the cream of the Hollywood smart set, which included Sean Penn, Tom Petty and Juliette Lewis. Depp was also in attendance, and two of Cash's songs which were recorded during the performance – 'Thirteen' and 'The Man Who Couldn't Cry' – found their way onto the hugely successful album that Rubin cut as a result and which was released in March 1994, under the title of *American Recordings*.

The revamped profile of the club as the 'most consistently hip' in town, according to the *LA Times*, was to suffer a severe setback only a month later, though, when it was visited on the night of 30 October by another rising young star on the make and one-time Hollywood Brat-Packer, River Phoenix. What followed Phoenix's appearance at the Viper Room was to be recalled by Depp as 'Scary, devastating – just an absolute nightmare.'

River Jude Phoenix was one of five children born to Christian fundamentalists John and Arlyn Bottom (he changed his surname to Phoenix when he took up acting; his brother Leaf also changed his first name to Joaquin). Much of his childhood was spent in abject poverty, and when the family moved to South America at the behest of the Church of God, River was reduced to singing for his supper with his sister, Rain, on the streets of Caracas, Venezuela. The Bottoms' religious extremism had produced a son with equally extreme views about the subject of ecology: Phoenix grew up as a committed vegan, who refused to wear leather and gave financial and moral support to any number of charitable causes dedicated to saving the planet. His breakthrough movie had been *Stand By Me* in 1986, based on a story by Stephen King and made when he was 15 years old. From there, he had gone into *Running On Empty* (1988), *Indiana Jones and the Last Crusade* (1989), in which he played opposite Harrison Ford, and *My Own Private Idaho* (1991), where he was a male hustler alongside Keanu Reeves. There were numerous others in between. He was lined up to star in the screen version of Anne Rice's novel *Interview With the Vampire*.

In October, 1993, Phoenix was shooting a film called *Dark Blood* for Scala Pictures. He was domiciled in his usual LA haunt, the St James's Club and Hotel on Sunset Boulevard, and had become something of a regular at the nearby Viper Room. On the night of the 30th, clutching his guitar in readiness for an impromptu gig and in company with his girlfriend, Samantha Mathis, and his sister and brother, Rain and Leaf, he had decided to pay the club a late-night visit.

Phoenix had ingested a 'speedball' of heroin and cocaine prior to his arrival at the club, the same combination of drugs which had killed John Belushi at the Chateau Marmont more than ten years before, and he promptly went for another snort in the club's toilet once he was inside. It was this last intake of 'Persian Brown' which proved fatal; on returning to his seat, he was overtaken by violent seizures and began to slip in and out of consciousness. He asked to be taken outside, where he collapsed and eventually died on the sidewalk, only feet from the door. He had arrived at the Viper Room a few minutes after midnight; by 1.41 am, he was in cardiac arrest, and he was officially pronounced dead at the Cedars Sinai Medical Centre a mere ten minutes later. He had just turned 23. The cause of his death was recorded as acute multiple drug intoxication. In other words, a lethal mix of heroin, cocaine, Valium, marijuana and ephedrine (known as crystal meth).

The film community expressed collective outrage at the news, bleating in disbelief at the very idea that such a clean-living young 'new-ager' could have acquired a heroin habit. But when the medical facts were shown to be incontestable, there was little for it but to confess all: Iris Burton, Phoenix's agent, revealed that she had suspected her client of hard-drug use for some time, while Peter Bogdanovich, who now had the dubious distinction of directing the actor in the last film that he was able to complete before his death – the same year's *The Thing Called Love* – said that Phoenix's drug habit had been the talk of the set.

The unfortunate Phoenix was himself a mass of contradictions – or just another product of the Hollywood publicity machine, whichever is nearer the truth. He was a vocal campaigner on 'green' issues but his death showed him to be an enthusiastic ingester of chemicals. Like Depp, he was anti-Hollywood, played guitar (in a band called Aleka's Attic, in his case) and tended to choose films which were creatively challenging. He, too, had sought to play off his looks after featuring on the covers of teeny-bopper magazines like *Tiger Beat*, much to his dismay. His choice of roles was adventurous and eclectic and looked likely to continue that way. Unlike Depp, however, he never made an *Edward Scissorhands* or an *Ed Wood*, and his death in early adulthood was eerily predicted in that of his character in what remains his most famous film next to *My Own Private Idaho*: *Stand By Me*.

When he died, Phoenix had been passed over by Robert Redford for the sought-after role of Paul Maclean in *A River Runs Through It* (the part went to Brad Pitt) and was instead shooting *Dark Blood* with Judy Davis and Jonathan Pryce; by all accounts, the production had not been a happy one, with palpable tensions between director George Sluizer (of *The Vanishing*) and his stars. Producer Stephen Woolley recalled Phoenix's erratic behaviour on-set: 'He was very animated and off-the-wall, and prone to do almost anything – skittish, like a hyperactive kid. One minute, he'd be sitting there quietly; the next, he'd be jumping up and doing embarrassing things.' There were four weeks of shooting still to go; the film had to be abandoned. The same year, John Candy had died while shooting *Wagons East* and Brandon Lee during the filming of *The Crow*. 1993 was not a good year for the insurers.

Phoenix was laid to rest in a blue coffin on 4 November at a Quaker-style funeral in which those in attendance were encouraged to shout their thoughts aloud about his passing. 'Why did he have to take all those drugs?' director John Boorman was moved rhetorically to inquire. 'To dull the pain,' Samantha Mathis self-consciously replied – though it prompted the question often asked of celebrities: what pain? River Phoenix had a cult following, but *he* was no James Dean either; he did not die a 'hero's' death in a speeding Porsche; rather, it was an ignominious one, choking on his own vomit while convulsed on an LA sidewalk and removing, at a stroke, all the romantic notions about recreational drug use to which Hollywood's Brat Packers had become so fatally attached. Instead of being remembered for his acting, Phoenix found himself listed in the *Guinness Book of Records* as the youngest celebrity ever to die of a drugs overdose.

The sudden, sordid demise of River Phoenix did not function as a wake-up call for Johnny Depp (who was at the bar of the club on the night in question); he had experienced that already on a more personal level. But it vindicated the stance which his friends and family had taken in seeking to protect him from continuing on down the same lost highway. He closed the doors of the Viper Room for two weeks as a mark of respect, and to prevent it from becoming a morbid attraction on the Hollywood sight-seeing trail. He then chose to stay away from the venue until the dust had begun to settle on the media frenzy which naturally erupted in the wake of such a high-profile drug-death. 'I closed the club for a few nights,' he told *Playboy*. 'To get out of the way so River's fans could bring messages; bring flowers. And I got angry. I made a statement to the press: "Fuck you. I will not be disrespectful to River's memory. I will not participate in your fucking circus".'

For one who only months before the Phoenix incident was still admitting amiably to his own intake of recreational chemicals, Depp's attitude on finding the results of such a course of action on his own doorstep was less than libertarian. He decided to shoot the messenger, rather than have to tackle the message head-on: 'When River passed away, it happened to be at my club. Now that's very tragic, very sad, but they made it a fiasco of lies to sell fuck-ing magazines,' he ranted in *Playboy*: 'They said he was doing drugs in my club – that I *allow* people to do drugs in my club. What a ridiculous fucking thought! Hey, I'm going to spend a lot of money on this night-club so everyone can come here and do drugs. I think that's a good idea, don't you? We'll never get found out. It's not like this place is high profile or anything, right? That lie was ridiculous and disrespectful to River... It was awful for my nieces and nephews to read that stuff; to have every two-bit pseudo-journalist speculating viciously... viciously. And it hurt.'

Despite the toll which the tragedy took on him personally, the 30-year-old Depp was still of an age where he refused to forswear the practice in principle which so dramatically had cost the life of one of his peers. 'If you're talking about drugs, you're talking about America. People die from drug overdoses every single day,' he protested: 'You can't say specifically Hollywood or Sunset Boulevard. The problem is everywhere, and it's been going on for 30 years at least. And the people benefiting from the drugs are very rich and it's a huge business. So let's not pretend. The prob-lem is not necessarily on the streets with the kids. Though there's a lot of curious kids who will try this and try that. The real prob-lem is way up there. And you can't own a night-club where you shake down every single person who walks in the room. You can't do a body search and check their pockets.'

The death of Phoenix had caught Depp off-guard: his back-cata-logue of press statements on his youthful excesses no longer car-ried the same edge-of-danger element of rock rebellion. His drug-taking heroes no longer resonated with the same air of impervious artistic detachment. Future public pronouncements in the wake of the affair were to undergo a subtle change, on the advice of his agent and in measured response to the more experienced words of wisdom that he would glean from the actor with whom he was about to work on his next film. 'Do people think I'm insane? Do they think I'm ignorant? To open a night-club and allow people to do drugs, even in the bathroom? That I'm going to throw everything away so that some people can get high in a night-club?'

Under the circumstances, it was clear that Depp did 'protest too much'. His own history of substance abuse was well documented and self-confessed: 'Cocaine is a strange one – a really strange one. I mean, I hated it,' he told Danny Leigh of the *Guardian*. 'You get this synthetic happiness and then you're just panicking and grinding your teeth.' To suggest that a club which was set up as a venue for rock musicians to hang out and jam was free of drugs was either naive or disingenuous, to say the least. Free of *known* dealers, it may have been, but drug use was subsequently shown to have been endemic among many of the Viper Room's more celebrated habitués, while rumour had it at the time that the club was a place where they could buy or use drugs in private, in a room set aside especially for the purpose. Nevertheless, Depp and his club managed somehow to survive all the bad press that resulted from the death of River Phoenix. Drugs have always been the way of life in Hollywood, and any stigma which occasionally attaches to them tends never to last too long. Other fracas would come along at intervals to temporarily dent the reputation of the club: in September 1996, Motley Crue's Tommy Lee was sentenced to two years probation for assaulting a man who tried to film his then-wife Pamela Anderson; a similar incident took place a month later, which involved Rolling Stone Mick Jagger, a photographer and Uma Thurman (Jagger settled out of court, but the plaintiff was also awarded $600,000 in damages against the Viper Room). None of them would match the gravitas of the events of 31 October 1993, until millennium year had come and gone.

Depp consoled himself in the meanwhile by purchasing a 29-roomed mansion on Laurel Canyon Drive, in the Hollywood Hills, for $2.3 million, the renovation of which provided him with an excuse to steer clear of the Viper Room in the process. Supposedly the former home of Bela Lugosi and scene of

Munchkin orgies during the filming of *The Wizard of Oz*, the house had previously belonged to divorce lawyer Michael Mitchelson, before being lost to him in a bankruptcy suit. Depp had finally bought himself the piece of Hollywood history (and notional memento of *Ed Wood* to boot) that he had expressed a desire to do some years before, and he now had a place to call home. It had not necessarily been Lugosi's, as he was soon inclined to claim; that idea is disputed as myth by historian Laurie Jacobsen in the book *Hollywood Haunted*, in which is documented a different history for the property whose gated portals open onto North Sweetzer Avenue and whose California Gothic facade is thought merely to *look* like it should have been owned by the star of *Dracula*. But it was the 'big old house in Bel Air' which he had previously disdained.

What's Eating Gilbert Grape opened in America on Christmas Day 1993, to some less than inviting reviews and little financial return, its prospects not helped by the imposition of a PG-13 certificate. As a result, the film failed to recover its quoted production budget of $11 million. The critics in general were taken with Depp's performance: 'He brings a quiet, gentle sweetness that suffuses the whole film,' said Roger Ebert in the *Chicago Sun-Times*, while *Empire* thought it 'vastly charming' and the film itself 'enchanting and disarming'. They were, however, even more impressed with DiCaprio, although they felt in the main that Lasse Hallström's approach to the material was synthetic and formulaic.

At 4.31 am on the morning of 17 January 1994, before Depp could avail himself of the opportunity to set foot inside his castle aerie overlooking Sunset, the Northridge section of the San Fernando Valley was hit by an earthquake measuring a 'modest' 6.7 on the Richter scale. His 'Lugosi' house suffered structural damage in the so-called Northridge quake, and he suddenly found himself once more in residence in his hotel.

It was not a promising start for the New Year, but brighter things lay on the horizon. If a 'rolling stone' proverbially gathers no moss, the same could not be said about Johnny Depp. By the end of that month, he was dining in the newly opened Café Tabac, on New York's East Ninth Street, in company with other celebrities who had chosen to adopt the chic Manhattan bistro as a home-from-home, when he chanced upon some friends whom he instinctively invited to join him. Among their number was Calvin Klein supermodel Kate Moss, who was herself on the rebound from a three-year relationship, in her case with photographer Mario Sorrenti. Depp had been intent on dinner alone; by the end of the evening, he had become one of a couple again. 'I knew from the first moment we talked that we were going to be together,' Moss said. 'I've never had that before.'

The following weeks inaugurated the new love in Johnny Depp's life, and introduced her to the eagerly waiting media – though the former Katherine Moss of Croydon, in the English county of Surrey, was already better known to the press than her film-star beau.

The 20-year-old Moss had begun her modelling career six years before, at the tender age of 14, after being talent-spotted while on vacation with her family in the Bahamas. Since then, she had appeared on the covers of almost every fashion magazine of note in the world, from *Vogue* to *Harper's Bazaar*, and in innumerable adverts aimed at the conspicuously super-rich and paid for by the crème de la crème of agency wish-lists: Dolce & Gabbana, Versace and Yves Saint Laurent to name but some. Charging an estimated fee of $10,000 a day, her earnings at the time that she met up with Depp were more than $2 million per annum. In 1994, she was (and still is) best known for being the perfumery 'face' of fashion giant Calvin Klein, specifically in relation to 'Obsession' and 'cKone'; one Klein contract had paid her $4 million for three months' work. In common with her latest flame, her parents had divorced when she was 15.

The spring of 1994 saw Depp and Moss become fully engaged in the predictable rounds of the celebrity social scene: In February, they were in Los Angeles for an anti-drugs benefit on behalf of Drug Abuse Resistance Education, at which Depp premiered an eight-minute short called *Banter* that he had directed himself. It was the couple's first appearance in public as a couple after tabloid speculation had placed them in New York's Royalton Hotel together, where they waited out a snowstorm earlier in the month. In March, they were photographed clandestinely on the West Indian island of St Barts. By April, they were back in New York, where they attended the premiere of Waters' *Serial Mom*, while May saw them at a fashion show at Mann's Chinese Theatre in Hollywood, with Moss taking to the catwalk in support of an AIDS foundation; later the same month, they turned up in London for the launch party of sister-supermodel Naomi Campbell's autobiography *Swan*, at Tramp's nightclub.

Moss was a tough cookie, as might be expected of anyone who had made it to the top of the high-fashion tree while still in their teens, and Depp's relationship with her would turn out to be fierier than were his three years with Ryder. The first crack in the carefully cultivated facade of romantic harmony appeared in June, at the same Royalton Hotel, when fellow-diners in the swish 44 restaurant were stunned to see the lovebirds engaged in a shouting-match over dinner. Peer pressure may already have come to play its insidious part: Moss was much in demand and led a hectic international existence; Johnny Depp, on the other hand, was still intent on turning down commercial properties like *Speed* (the part went to Keanu Reeves) and *Mobsters* (ditto Christian Slater) right, left and centre. And with *Ed Wood* not due for release until September and *Arizona Dream* on hold, his last big-screen outing had proved a resounding flop.

If a break was required to dampen down any heat which might have accrued in the short but reportedly intense relationship between the two, it was imminent anyway: Depp had signed for a film to be called *Don Juan DeMarco and the Centrefold*, on condition that the one actor in the world whom he most admired – Marlon Brando – play the role of the psychiatrist in its tale of a young man who believes himself to be Sevillian nobleman Don Juan, mythical hero of Byron's epic poem of the same name and ostensibly the world's greatest lover. Brando had not appeared on-screen since providing a cameo as Tomás de Torquemada for 1992's *Christopher Columbus: The Discovery*, after which his only son Christian had been sentenced to ten years in prison for shooting Dag Drollet, the Tahitian-born lover of his stepsister Cheyenne. But much to the surprise of all concerned in the production, the reclusive Brando had accepted, and Depp was now due on-set.

In Seville he was born, a pleasant city,
Famous for oranges and women — he
Who has not seen it will be much to pity,
So says the proverb — and I quite agree;
LORD BYRON, DON JUAN, CANTO THE FIRST, VIII (1819)

Don Juan DeMarco and the Centrefold was both written and directed by first-timer Jeremy Leven, and produced by Francis Coppola's American Zoetrope. In addition to fielding dialogue with Brando, Depp was reunited with Faye Dunaway in the role of Brando's screen wife – she and Depp shared the set, but no scenes on this occasion. The supporting cast was conventional, but on the level of a TV sitcom, although 250 semi-nude starlets stood poised in the wings and *Vanishing Point* director Richard Sarafian had been requisitioned to supply a brief walk-on as a police detective. Its star was typically upbeat about the virtues of the film: 'A great screenplay, profound. Some of the things that were in it were beautiful, poetry,' he enthused.

Brando plays Dr Jack Mickler, a clinical psychologist on the verge of retirement, who takes up the case of the suicidal John DeMarco (Depp), a young man who has deluded himself into believing that he is the legendary Don Juan. Mickler finds himself succumbing to the spell that DeMarco seems able to exert over those around him – particularly women – and determines to establish the truth: is his patient the mixed-up son of a New York 'dance king' named Tony DeMarco, or really a reincarnation of the spirit of love-god Don Juan? Despite all his training and accumulation of evidence to the contrary, Mickler settles for the latter on the grounds that if the fantasy is preferable to the facts, live the fantasy. The 'Centrefold' of the title is the ambiguous 'ideal woman' whom Don Juan craves and John DeMarco merely idolises from a distance; she was dispensed with during production to leave the snappier *Don Juan DeMarco*.

Either way, *Don Juan DeMarco* is a dud, a florid, flaccid, pop-psychological panjandrum of a film, full of sound and fury, ultimately signifying nothing of note. The role gave Depp his first chance to try out a genuine accent – Spanish, in this case, and worthy of Frank Sinatra in *The Pride and the Passion* (1957) – though his most poignant scene has him revert to his native tongue, when he feigns confession of his delusion before a judge, in order to secure his release from Woodhaven State Hospital. Despite the almost unanimous accord that he was now one of the best-looking men on-screen, his effect on the women who fall for his Sevillian small-talk is largely unconvincing. Part of this is due to Leven's preference for smarm over charm – some of Juan's verbal allusions descend to the soft-porn level of a phone-sex call – but some of it has to do with charisma, and the sheer animal magnetism which enabled the dowdy Casanova to boast of 122 conquests in his own autobiography. Handsome though Depp undoubtedly is in the part, his testosterone is complemented in the script by the implied suggestion that the size of Juan's 'manhood' is the killer argument, rather than the efficiency of his technique. The reason for this is that Don Juan's seductions are concerned only with sex, and not at all with love or romance, despite his philosophical entreaties to the contrary. In this, Leven is true to his Byronic source, but his story aspires to a different reading.

Depp is consummately professional but too serious by half for a role which required a light, romantic air of devil-may-care, a reflection, perhaps, of the wars behind the scenes in both his public and private lives; he never quite manages to regain the sense of calculating charm which he employs to sweep his initial conquest off her feet during a fleeting encounter in a restaurant. More often than not, his reading of Don Juan is as heavy-handed as Leven's direction: a leaden, by-the-numbers approach, which elicits admiration for its technical accomplishments but leaves the viewer cold on an emotional level – the opposite of what is intended. There is a steel in his eyes that was absent before, which aids the impression of an amoral seducer. If this is the great lover, then the love of Don Juan must have been a very mechanical affair indeed.

> My name is Don Juan DeMarco. I am the son of the great swordsman, Antonio Garibaldi DeMarco, who was tragically killed defending the honour of my mother, the beautiful Doña Inez Santiago De St Martin. I am the world's greatest lover.
>
> Don Juan DeMarco (Johnny Depp), Don Juan DeMarco (1994)

The film was the directorial debut of its screenwriter, Jeremy Leven, himself a psychologist. Whatever his clinical skills, his ability as a director is sadly lacking: *Don Juan DeMarco* is staged entirely in set-ups from an apprentice's handbook. In a story that cries out for flair and flourish, his approach to his material is obdurately flat and monotonous, devoid of mobility and lacking even the most basic of stylistic tricks. Editing is similarly rudimentary. Given the film's accredited budget of $25 million, its evident disdain of cinematic device in the telling of its tale can only be attributed to its director's limited vision. DeMarco's story is less about dream-life than it is about one man's mission to convert those around him to his personal point of view; in that, it is a veritable hymn to hubris.

Brando makes a passable psychiatrist but an unlikely rejuvenate lover. He is self-conscious and ill-at-ease in the film – unsurprisingly, given his weight problems, as well as the strain of the court-case involving his wayward son and the emotional and financial toll it had exacted on him – and appears happy to defer to Depp for much of the proceedings. Brando is still Brando, but the magic is long gone. The psychiatric episodes themselves are a psychobabble of clichés ('obsessive/compulsive disorder' and so on); Mickler's assessment of his patient is simplistic to the point of caricature, but it is obscured by Brando's characteristic nasal mumble, its missing syllables making it sound more authentic than it actually is. Less convincing is his conversion to Don Juan's philosophical outlook and rediscovery of *joie de vivre*. There is no magic bullet; no light on the road to Eros; no profound revelation of the truth. Instead, there is homily, delivered by Juan with admirably straight-faced gravitas: 'There are only four questions of value in life,' he confides. 'What is sacred; of what is the spirit made; what is worth living for, and what is worth dying for. The answer to each is the same – only love.' So there you have it: love makes the world go round.

Conversely, the film's funniest line comes when the initially cynical Mickler is apprised of the first of Don Juan's tall tales about his fanciful upbringing down Mexico way. 'There was a lot of sword-fighting going on when you were growing up?' he queries, figuring that the events being described must have taken place a mere decade before. 'Well, it was a small and isolated town. It resisted foreign technology,' Juan replies.

The kernel of a good idea lies at the heart of *Don Juan DeMarco*, but Leven has neither the wit nor the sophistication to see it through. As it stands, the film is crudely drawn and clumsily executed, its philosophical insights drowned in a sea of puerile profundity: 'What makes you think that Dr Mickler is Don Octavio de Flores?' Juan is asked of his habit of incorporating the psychiatrist into his delusion. 'What makes you think Don Octavio is Dr Mickler?' comes the reply. It sounds deep and meaningful, but the answer is simple: proof. They can each be put to the test, and one will be found wanting. Mickler barely even considers this obvious route to the truth, because he chooses delusion over enlightenment and thus becomes as mad as his patient, instead of liberated by a heightened consciousness.

Ambivalence should have been sewn more assuredly into the story, but none of the participants are up to the task. What remains is a clever concept reduced by peculiarly American sensibility to simple platitude: embrace fantasy and all will be right with the world. If the going gets tough, take a trip to Disneyland, in effect.

> Sadly, I must report that the last patient I ever treated – the great lover, Don Juan DeMarco – suffered from a romanticism which was completely incurable... and even worse, highly contagious.
> Dr Jack Mickler (Marlon Brando), Don Juan DeMarco (1994)

Don Juan DeMarco was a vanity project for Johnny Depp, but vanity had come in the form of a blinkered desire to work with screen legend Marlon Brando. Brando had famously played Mark Antony to Louis Calhern's Julius Caesar back in 1953, and he advised his young protégé to enrol in RADA. 'He spoke so passionately about Hamlet,' Depp said, echoing his education in Poe at the feet of Vincent Price on the set of *Edward Scissorhands*. 'He planted the seed that made me pick it up again and really read it.' But the call of Shakespeare was not enough, even with Brando acting as salesman for the bard; what Depp wanted more was a commercial hit on the scale of his Burton film, and he already knew that his latest attempt was unlikely to provide it. 'Of course I'm retiring, but I think this would make a hell of a swan-song,' Brando had said in his role as Mickler in *Don Juan DeMarco*. Close, but no cigar.

If working with Brando proved an uplifting experience for Depp, working with first- (and only) time director Jeremy Leven was exactly the opposite. Leven had sold his screenplay on the condition that he would also direct the film, having directed for the stage off Broadway. Despite the presence of method-maestro Marlon Brando in the cast line-up, Leven adjudged his credentials as novelist and professor of psychology to be more than adequate for the task in hand and he soon found himself overstepping the mark, so far as second-billed Depp was concerned: 'He refused to admit that he didn't know what he was doing and he wouldn't take advice from people. He just forged ahead and it was awful,' he said, of the patronising attitude to which he was subject on-set.

After the mutually collaborative working relationships that he had recently enjoyed with Kusturica and Burton, and a raft of rave reviews for his performance in *Ed Wood*, Depp had found his feet at last; buoyed by the fact that he was also sharing a film-set with Brando, he decided that he would have none of it: 'We hit a point in that film where I actually had to tell the guy, "You can say action and cut and print, if you like, but don't say anything else to me because I'd really like to have my hands around your throat…" He didn't bother me any more; just stayed away. He said "action", "cut", "print", "wrap" – and that was it.' 'I think Johnny is far and away the most talented of today's young actors,' Leven later acknowledged. 'He is very much like Marlon on many fronts: they both have a 100 per cent "bull" detector.'

Leven's exercise of 'control' even extended to the novelisation that was to be based on his own screenplay. He nominated Maryland poet and fellow Rye High School alumnus Jean Blake White for the task, insisting that she write a 'real' novel, and collaborating on the project from inception to completion via phone calls and faxes. His enthusiasm to be at the centre of things quite ran away with him when he was questioned in interview about the experience of working with his stars, however: 'We were shooting this scene where Depp and Brando are standing on scaffolding 80 feet in the air, and there was no question what was really going on up there,' he gushed. 'I was standing next to the director of photography, and we looked at each other at the same time and recognised what was happening: Marlon was passing the torch to Johnny… You could feel it in your bones; it was so obvious. Marlon was giving Johnny the room to be the next Marlon Brando. And you know something? – I think Johnny can handle it.'

Johnny Depp may still turn out to be the 'next Marlon Brando', but Tim Burton could have said the same thing about Vincent Price offering him the real hands in *Edward Scissorhands*. If Depp should move into horror films in his forties, as Price did, then this second contention will prove the more accurate of the two – but such self-aggrandising predictions are mere ballyhoo of the moment, designed to reflect favourably on the intuitive abilities of the observer. Leven is a psychologist; he must have known that.

(Depp's version of the incident was more mundane: 'After the scene, he [Marlon] came to me and he grabbed my hand, and he came up real close to my ear, and he went, "You nailed it." You just float after that… I just floated away.')

Depp and Moss were together again in August, though, going by the press reports, one could have been forgiven for thinking that peace appeared not to have broken out in the interim. The London *Evening Standard* wrote of a brawl in a pub which involved Depp, a photographer and an over-zealous bodyguard, during a visit to see Moss that the actor had made in the first week of September. One week later, and the pair were once more in New York, cosily ensconced in the luxurious Mark Hotel on East 77th Street, off Madison Avenue, when an incident took place which was to find itself enshrined in Depp legend.

The premiere of *Ed Wood* was due to take place at the New York Film Festival on the 24th of the month, and Depp was in town to promote his movie. He and Moss had booked into room 1410 at the Mark. On the night of the 13th, they returned to their room in the early hours, after an obligatory bout of merrymaking. Within minutes, crashing sounds from inside the suite sent a night security guard named Jim Keegan scurrying to Depp and Moss's door, outside which, a picture frame lay smashed and discarded on the floor. Assuming the room either was already, or was now about to be, comprehensively trashed by a malicious movie star with more money than sense, Keegan felt duty-bound to ask Depp to leave. Depp protested and offered to pay for the damage. Not good enough. Either he vacated the premises, or Keegan would call the police. The predictable stand-off followed, which was brought to an end at 5.30 am when three officers from New York's 19th Precinct arrived to escort the crestfallen star from the premises.

The New York news-hounds having been alerted to the incident even more quickly than the cops, Depp was photographed being led out of the Mark in green woolly hat and handcuffs, to spend the next few hours in custody on a charge of causing criminal mischief. Later that same morning, all charges were dropped on condition that he reimburse the Mark and agree to stay out of trouble for six months. 'Maybe it's time Depp got a serious wake-up call,' wrote Shelley Levitt in *People*. 'These days the chain-smoking, tattoo-festooned, Viper Room-owning movie star seems to be dancing on the edge of danger.' In relation to the fact that Kate Moss had been present in the room at the time, it was not allowed to go unnoticed that he had recently directed and featured in a video with Shane MacGowan of The Pogues, called 'This Woman's Got Me Drinking', on behalf of which he had also appeared on BBC TV's *Top of the Pops* (the song was one of two solo releases by MacGowan, neither of which made it into the charts).

In explanation of the affair, Depp said that he had had what he termed as a 'bad day', which had ended with him letting off steam by smashing a picture frame and committing sundry other acts of rock 'n' roll mayhem in the room. The Mark levied a bill for $9,767.12, which Depp's lawyer David Breitbart vehemently protested, suggesting that not all of the damage supposedly incurred – such as a cigarette burn on the carpet – was necessarily of his client's doing and that like many an insurance claim before this one, pre-existent breakages had been added to the list, or further damage perpetrated after the event. Given Depp's own pleadings about the incidental nature of the 'fracas', this seems eminently plausible. Notwithstanding, he dutifully paid up and considered the episode closed. Not so the tabloids, who not only continued to pose rhetorical questions about his few moments of impotent rage for years afterwards, but had them laminated and stapled to Depp's CV. Thus a relatively insignificant incident for which ample recompense was made freely and without hesitation became another badge of dishonour for an actor whose nose a hypocritical media took much pleasure in rubbing in the dirt.

When the press looked to be having a field day with the affair, Depp's friends were quick to defend him: 'The room service must have been bad,' John Waters said acidly, while Marlon Brando called Depp's lawyer to express his support. 'He said he was very concerned about Johnny's well-being,' Breitbart explained, 'and if there was anything he could do to help, he would like to.' 'Surely it's time to take stock when you're eligible for counselling from Marlon Brando,' Levitt later bitched at this development.

There was nothing that Brando could do: by the time his call had been made, Depp was out of the slammer and partying at Babyland, a Lower East Side bar adorned with the paraphernalia of motherhood. A new charge was levelled against him as a result, when a Manhattan plumber complained that after bumping into the actor, he was beaten to a pulp by a group of heavy-duty bikers in his company. 'Depp, Pals in Lower East Side Brawl' ran the headline in the *New York Post* – 'It didn't take long for Johnny Depp-lorable to show his wild side again following his hotel hi-jinks the other night,' the report went on. Breitbart was again forced to defend his client publicly, but coming hot on the heels of the Mark incident, the alleged brawl smacked of little more than opportunism.

David Blum penned a deft piece on the Mark incident for the April 1995 issue of *Esquire*, to which Depp subsequently took humourless exception. As a satire on celebrity foibles, it was priceless, but there was no denying the irony which underpinned its tongue-in-cheek dissection of the ruckus and it is worthwhile quoting the opening passage in full: 'Fuck you, okay? Just – Jesus, what a week. You know, you're staying at this hotel, the Mark. It's not your regular place, but come on – you're paying twenty-two hundred goddam dollars a night for the presidential suite, you think at least they wouldn't look at you funny when you cross the lobby. Is that too much to ask? Every time… especially this one guy who works there. You can just tell he doesn't like you, he doesn't like you at all. And why? Because you didn't change your jeans or wash your hair? So it's five in the morning and a couple of million cups of coffee later, and you punch their stupid couch. So what? Technically speaking, you're paying for this couch. Right now, you own this couch. And the lamps and the coffee table – oh, sorry, was that an antique? Bummer. But, you know, for the first time, you're really enjoying yourself here at the Mark hotel.'

One constant which had began to appear in every interview was a Depp complaint about his maltreatment in the media. The ploy was designed to elicit sympathy for the complainant in anyone to whom such information was divulged, and Depp utilised it at every opportunity in an attempt to win the press-pack over to his point of view, rather than its own. In fact, he had never been treated unduly harshly by the press and any innuendo that may occasionally have surfaced about his love life, his temper tantrums or his recreational peccadilloes had been more than recompensed by articles which had kept his name and his face in the public eye, while at the same time promising greater things from one of Hollywood's fastest-rising and most fascinating young stars. Be that as it may, Depp's blood pressure had been raised to boiling point by the intrusive nature of the coverage during his time with Winona Ryder, as well as the treatment which was meted out to him over his tangential association with the death of River Phoenix. Regardless of the huge amount of positive coverage which weighed in his favour, he had determined not to leave himself so open to such attacks in the future.

The self-destruct button which is possessed by even the most fastidious of public figures was still there waiting to be pressed, however, and press it Depp had at the Mark. Again, he railed against the kind of coverage which the incident had naturally attracted, viewing it as 'not particularly newsworthy': 'I didn't think it deserved equal billing to the invasion of Haiti!' he said.

On a scale of one to ten in the rock 'n' roll roster of room-trash-ings, it barely registered, but actions speak louder than words and it was made apparent to the world's media that this was a stormi-er coupling than that with Ryder, even if the fundamental diffi-culty between the two remained the same: Johnny Depp still lacked a universally acclaimed hit movie, while Kate Moss was earning $2.2 million for a single ad campaign with *Vogue*.

Two months after Depp was escorted out of the Mark by three of New York's finest, actor Mickey Rourke was summarily eject-ed from the Plaza Hotel, on Fifth Avenue, for trashing *his* suite: 'Mickey's Plaza Rampage' headlined the *New York Post*, though in terms of newspaper coverage as a whole, the incident paled by comparison to the column inches which had earlier been devoted to Depp's stay at the Mark. Nicolas Cage put Rourke's behaviour in perspective when he declared, 'Who's he trying to be – Johnny Depp?' (Depp had thrown a birthday party for Rourke at the Metronome on Broadway, following the premiere of *Ed Wood*.)

'Of course, not everyone feels the need to trash a hotel room at any point in their lives,' the pilloried Depp was sanctimoniously informed by TV chat-show host David Letterman when he tried to put the incident down to a single aberrant moment, and his varying attempts to quantify the event were to be endured in the US media for almost as long as US President Bill Clinton's upcoming apologies for his sexual misdemeanours in the Oval Office. The harassed actor took it all with professional stoicism and eventually came to embrace the benefits to his image which continued to accrue in fan circles in respect of his roguish behav-iour. Protest turned to amused acceptance, and acceptance to humorous reflection about his night at the Mark and his brief spell in the 'Tombs'. But it was not to be the last time that Johnny Depp would find himself behind bars of the custodial variety.

The other side of Johnny 'Depp-lorable' provided less interest-ing copy, but it was there for anyone willing to see: he had now bought his mother and stepfather a three-bedroom house on the outskirts of Los Angeles at a cost of $294,000, and Betty Sue's waitressing days were long over. 'She doesn't talk much about my movies,' Depp told *Playboy*, 'though she knows when I'm real, when it's me at my most honest. She can sift through whatever horseshit I might have thrown in there and find that. Sometimes she still looks at me and says, "God! Can you believe your life? Going from living in a motel to all of this?" She's still a little shocked. So am I. I'm probably more shocked than anyone.'

Ed Wood opened nationwide in the US on 28 September to unanimous critical praise but doubtful commercial prospects, as *Variety* explained: 'Tim Burton pays elaborate tribute to the maverick creative spirit in *Ed Wood*, a fanciful, sweet-tempered biopic about the man often described as the worst film director of all time ... Result is beguiling rather than thrilling, oddly charming instead of transporting, meaning that Disney will have its work cut out for it with what is at heart a cult movie and a film buff's dream.' On its UK release, Mark Salisbury wrote: 'Depp himself gives a truly mesmerising performance, both in and out of drag, notching up another distinctly oddball role that again reveals the measure of the young actor's talents.' Despite the lack of discordant voices and Tim Burton's name on the marquee alongside that of Johnny 'Scissorhands' Depp, the Touchstone release recouped barely one third of its $18 million production cost. It turned out to be a significant commercial failure, but it put Depp back on the Hollywood map. This time, he was there to stay.

Ed Wood did more than make a star out of Johnny Depp. After eight films in a decade, all of which had been chosen by him for their theme, their director, or the appeal of the role itself (or simply because they had been offered), he at last had found one which exemplified what the 30-year-old actor now seemed best suited to represent on-screen. To the camera's eye, the teen idol looks of his early years had finally divested themselves of Punk pouting and puppy fat and matured to reveal the delicate features and wide-eyed vulnerability of the aesthete. The new Depp perfectly typified the disenfranchised outsider; the romantic loner (in the Byronic sense); the social misfit with the proverbial heart of gold. *Ed Wood* had bestowed a screen persona on the actor who portrayed him which resonated beyond the confines of the character. The film's Wood was a tragic figure, but one whose implacable optimism in the face of adversity – up to and including his own insurmountable lack of talent – nevertheless won through in the end. *Ed Wood* may not have been biography, but it was moral fable and the part had fitted Depp like a glove. The quirks of characterisation which he had brought to the role gave him something to aim for in his craft; it showed him a road down which he could travel. It had also garnered him his best critical notices. It was a lesson that Johnny Depp was not likely to forget.

The benefits of Burton's film aside, Depp had reportedly regarded *Don Juan DeMarco* as a transition to more adult roles (even though, at one point, the script had required him to play DeMarco aged 16) after the string of angst-ridden teens that he had essayed in his 'Small-town Trilogy' and which had led to him adopting a more innocent approach to the character of Wood. He must therefore have taken heart at the fact that the word 'Man' featured prominently in the title of his next outing for the cameras.

If the fool would persist in his folly he would become wise.
WILLIAM BLAKE, 'THE PROVERBS OF HELL'/ *THE MARRIAGE OF HEAVEN AND HELL* (1790)

Dead Man returned Depp to territory which he had previously come to regard as his own: a high-concept project with a filmmaker of integrity and vision. This was the revisionist Western that writer-director Jim Jarmusch had spent time discussing with Depp during the production of *Ed Wood*, now finally come to fruition under the auspices of Miramax. Like *Ed Wood*, it was also to be shot in black and white.

Ohio-born Jarmusch was a graduate of the film school at New York University. His first feature had been *Permanent Vacation* (1980) and his most recent was *Somewhere in California* (1993). At varying intervals between the two had come *Stranger Than*

Paradise (1983), *Down By Law* (1986), *Mystery Train* (1989) and *Night On Earth* (1991), and what most of them had in common – aside from their preoccupation with looking at American culture through foreign eyes – was a string of awards to their names.

Jarmusch was ten years older than Depp, but they shared the same Punk sensibility: he, too, had played in a rock band (named the Del-Byzanteens) in the early 1980s, and he had directed music videos for Tom Waits, Talking Heads and Big Audio Dynamite; he was equally fond of casting musicians in his films. In 1994, he was still the critics' darling: after *Mystery Train*, the *New York Times* had called him 'the most adventurous and arresting filmmaker to surface in the American cinema in this decade'. 'I had Johnny Depp in my head for the character of Blake and Gary Farmer in my head for the part of Nobody,' Jarmusch has said of the genesis of *Dead Man*. 'If either one of them had refused or had not been interested, I'm not sure I would have made the film.' Awards he had a-plenty, but little or no commercial track record. Nevertheless, Jarmusch had acquired some influence. His last student feature, *Permanent Vacation*, had cost $15,000 to make; *Dead Man* was budgeted at close to $9 million.

The plot of *Dead Man* is minimalist in the extreme. William Blake (Depp) is an accountant from Cleveland who is travelling to the far west to take up a post at Dickinson's metalworks in the town of Machine – 'the end of the line' – after the death of his parents. When he arrives, the job is already gone and he takes solace in the arms of Thel (Mili Avital), a one-time whore who now makes her living selling paper roses. Their tryst is interrupted by Charlie (Gabriel Byrne), Thel's ex-fiancée, who shoots her dead in the heat of the moment. Blake responds instinctively and shoots him dead also, but the bullet that killed Thel passed through her body and now rests next to his own heart. He flees the town and is found and nursed back to a semblance of health by a nomadic Indian named Nobody (Farmer). However, the 'Charlie' that Blake killed was the son of

John Dickinson (Robert Mitchum), owner of the metalworks and the most powerful man for miles around. Dickinson places a bounty on Blake's head, and a trio of hired killers sets out in pursuit. All of this happens in the first two reels, and the remainder of the film's 121 minutes is taken up with Blake's sombre and soulful journey to the 'land of the spirits', in the company of his Indian guide.

> Last night, my youngest son Charlie, God bless his soul, was gunned down in cold blood right here in our own hotel. The gutless murderer, one Mister Bill Blake, also shot to death Miss Thel Russell, the fiancée of my beloved son. Not only that, but he stole a very spirited and valuable horse, a beautiful young pinto, that belonged to my personal family stable...
>
> I want him brought here to me – alive or dead don't matter, though I reckon dead would be easier. I'm hiring you boys on an exclusive basis, and I'm willing to pay more money than you've ever seen before. Boys – the hunt is on!
>
> John Dickinson (Robert Mitchum), Dead Man (1994)

Dead Man opens on a quote by twentieth-century Belgian poet Henri Michaux: 'It is preferable not to travel with a dead man.' Jarmusch consciously set out to impose a poetic sensibility on his story, not only by naming his protagonist after the eighteenth-century poet, painter and visionary William Blake, but also by investing 'Nobody' with an anachronistic appreciation of the real Blake's life and work (in his teenage years, Jarmusch was himself influenced by the writings of Blake, as was Allen Ginsberg). Taking its lead from Michaux, who was a minor celebrity in the ranks of the Beat poets for his spiritual pessimism and ten-year employment of transcendental drugs, the film is one long, slow, gruelling and ultimately inexorable descent into the inferno, a theme which nowhere is better realised than in its pre-credits sequence, as Blake rides the train which takes him from

Cleveland to the outpost town of Machine: through a series of fades, he watches with increasing apprehension as the ever-changing contingent of passengers with whom he has to share his carriage slides subtly down the evolutionary scale, the further west that he travels. The point is underscored by the train's stoker, his face blackened by the heat of the boiler, who questions the accountant on the reasons for his trip: 'That doesn't explain why you've come all the way out here – all the way out here to Hell!' Later in the film, Blake shoots the racist owner of a far-flung trading-post (Alfred Molina). 'God damn your soul to the fires of Hell,' he cries, before dropping dead. 'He already has,' Blake replies.

Blake is a 'dead man' almost from the outset, with a bullet lodged next to his heart after his encounter with Charlie, and the film charts his path to understanding and ultimately to Valhalla. This is alluded to when Nobody eventually relieves him of his spectacles. 'Perhaps you will see more clearly without them,' he notions. The more removed that Blake becomes from the moral and spiritual certainties of so-called civilisation, the more his preconceptions are stripped away from him until, at last, he stands before a barren tree on the edge of a different understanding of life and death. With his transformation from William Blake to 'Billy the Kid' complete, he is confronted by a pair of lawmen. 'Are you William Blake?' asks one. 'Yes I am,' he says; 'Do you know my poetry?' Without further ado, he kills the marshal. His 'poetry' is now a hymn to death; a bow of burning gold, carried on a chariot of fire. 'What amazed me about Johnny was his ability to go through a lot of very subtle but big changes in his character, out of sequence but without ever telegraphing that character development,' Jarmusch enthused. 'He was much more precise than I thought he would be. He was also very inventive.'

The film's cast of sundry characters is colourfully grotesque. Blake's Indian spirit-guide is named Nobody (a beautifully timed performance by Canadian Gary Farmer), which predictably allows him to claim, when asked with whom he is travelling by a trio of homosexual trappers, 'I'm with Nobody.' The cold-eyed, brutal-featured Lance Henriksen is a bounty hunter named Wilson after the hired killer played by Jack Palance in Shane (1953). And there are the in-jokes that might be expected of a project that was initiated among friends: Iggy Pop plays a transvestite trapper named Salvatore 'Sally' Jenko, while the marshals that Blake guns down go by the names of Lee and Marvin. Not that the script is otherwise lacking in humour: a running gag about tobacco (or the lack of it) is particularly adroit in context.

One critic referred to *Dead Man* as an 'acid western', presumably in reference to Michaux. If so, it is a very concise and controlled vision, almost mystical in its purity. It is certainly a post-modern Western, in that it takes a bleak, dystopian view of landscape and human nature, freed from the inherited clichés and mythical overtones of the genre as perpetuated in the films of John Ford *et al.*: asked why she keeps a six-gun under her pillow, Thel replies, 'Because this is America.' The violence is random and casual and ever-present people almost stand in wait to be hit by bullets, knowing how inaccurate are the weapons to be used against them. In this respect, the film is also realistically graphic, if a little over the top on occasion: Wilson crushes the head of a dead marshal underfoot, cracking it open like an egg; it is a striking and repellent image, but wholly unfeasible all the same.

The film is riddled with symbolism and ritual, from Thel's paper roses lying scattered in the mud as Blake flees the scene of his crime to the aforementioned crushing of the head. But *Dead Man* is more than simply a metaphorical journey through a philosophical landscape; it is about how society as a whole creates outcasts, through incomprehension or sheer bloody-mindedness. Blake and Nobody are kindred spirits, having suffered similar fates at the hands and prejudices of their fellow men. Jarmusch cites many influences upon his work, but the film which perhaps comes closest to the mood of *Dead Man* is actor Charles Laughton's directorial debut of 1955, *The Night of the Hunter*, with its strik-ing monochrome photography by Stanley Cortez.

Cinema audiences have become so accustomed to the stylised and fanciful depictions of the Old West which Hollywood has evoked since its inception (and which reached its zenith in the slow-motion mythologising of Sam Peckinpah) that when pre-sented with something akin to the real thing, they view that as stylisation instead. When the intellectual critic sees *Dead Man*, he sees Art; artistic it certainly is, but not self-consciously so. Jarmusch's film goes out of its way to be as realistic as possible and any who have seen photographs of frontier towns in the 1880s, pioneers in their wagon trains, or tribes of Plains Indians in their natural habitat will recognise the authenticity of the piece. Jarmusch intentionally leaves aside the sense of community, sense of purpose and spirit of hope and adventure which must surely have featured in the exploration and establishment of a new land, preferring a narrower focus on the idea of lost souls inhabiting a lawless and alien landscape, but his film's depiction of period is spot on.

Dead Man was largely filmed in national parks, in Arizona and Nevada. It is never less than absorbing and often spellbinding in its effect. Neil Young's expressive score, conducted mainly in the form of a guitar solo (as well as a haunting piano rendition of 'Billy Boy' in a saloon-bar scene at the beginning of the film), will remain in the memory of many after Jarmusch's images have faded from view. 'This is one of those films where you walk away with a spider-web on your brain. It doesn't just leave you; it sticks with you,' Gary Farmer remarked. 'Whatever you get from it is different for the individual. I think it's a great movie that way.' Of his co-star, he observed more flippantly, 'He's pretty much half dead for most of the movie. It takes a lot of patience to be half dead – especially for someone like Johnny.'

Patience was becoming a trademark of Depp's. The patience to wait for the right project to arrive, and then to make the absolute most of it once it had done so.

Every night and every morn,
Some to misery are born.
Every morn and every night
Some are born to sweet delight.
Some are born to sweet delight,
Some are born to endless night.

WILLIAM BLAKE, 'AUGURIES OF INNOCENCE' (1803)

'I hope this is the last of these innocents that I play,' Depp said in reference to *Dead Man*. It certainly marked the end of his apprenticeship as an actor. It was now ten years since he had been sucked into a bed in *A Nightmare on Elm Street* and into a new way of life as a result. He had not been found wanting. In that time, he had carved a unique niche for himself in the annals of American cinema. He had a long way still to go, but he had finally paid his dues.

During the filming of *Dead Man*, Depp kept some lines from William Saroyan taped to his dressing-room mirror: 'In the time of your life, live – so that in the wondrous time you shall not add to the misery and sorrow of the world, but shall smile to the infinite delight and mystery of it.' The desiderata-style homily is from the preface to the Californian author and playwright's Broadway hit of 1939, *The Time of Your Life*, for which he was honoured with a Pulitzer Prize; Saroyan declined the award on the grounds that 'commerce should not patronise art'.

With another incident like that at the Mark an ever-present possibility, the massed ranks of the world's media trailed doggedly after Depp and Moss wherever they went. During Christmas 1994, the couple holidayed in the Colorado ski resort of Aspen, where they were photographed 'walking arm-in-arm through the streets, window-shopping'. On 16 January 1995, Depp threw a surprise party at the Viper Room to celebrate his girlfriend's 21st birthday, at which she was serenaded by Gloria Gaynor and Thelma Houston. 'They opened the curtains and there was my mum and my dad, and everyone had flown in from London and New York.

It was amazing. I was like, shaking-you know when you start to dance and your legs don't work? I had to go into the office for ten minutes till I'd calmed down,' a clearly delighted Moss later revealed to *Elle*. By 21 January, they were to be seen among the invited guests at the Beverley Hilton Hotel in Los Angeles for the Golden Globe Awards, alongside Tim Burton and Martin Landau; Depp and Landau were each nominated for awards as Best Actor and Best Support respectively, but only Landau won (again).

If things looked more settled on the private front, with rumours abroad that Depp had begun to think not only in terms of marrying Moss but of having a child with her as well, they were a good deal less rosy on the business side of the Viper Room. Amid increasing friction between the Depp contingent and the club's former owner Anthony Fox, acting manager Sal Jenco was given the onerous task of informing Fox that his agreed salary was no longer to be paid to him. This helped only to make matters worse, but Fox decided to bide his time.

Depp himself had a more pressing engagement with his most overtly commercial project to date, at a reported salary of some $4 million. The film was called *Nick of Time*, and it was to be directed by John Badham, forever remembered as the man who made *Saturday Night Fever*. In the film, Depp was to play a typical John Doe named Gene Watson, a single-parent accountant who becomes embroiled in a plot to assassinate the Governor of California; the cutting edge of experimental cinema it was not. He explained his reasons for taking the film to *Playboy*: 'I'm interested in story and character and doing things that haven't been done a zillion times. When I read *Nick of Time*, I could see the guy mowing the grass, watering his lawn, putting out the Water Wiggle in the backyard for his kid and I liked the challenge of playing him. He's nothing like me. It gives me a chance to play a straight, normal, suit-and-tie guy.'

Depp denied that commercial considerations were a factor in choosing to act in a thriller for the director of *Blue Thunder* (1983), *Stakeout* (1987) and *Bird On a Wire* (1990): 'It's not a conscious attempt to be commercial at all,' he told Brendan Lemon. 'I read the screenplay and liked it a lot. I was on the edge of my seat when I read this thing. It reminded me a lot of the old Hitchcock films. I wanted to do it, and I wanted to work with John Badham; I was a big fan of *Saturday Night Fever*, which he directed – it's a great movie. I also wanted to work with Christopher Walken, whom I've always admired.' When Badham was introduced to the young actor who was to play a conservatively dressed executive in his film, he did a double-take: 'He looked like one of those identikit police drawings,' he demurred.

If the money was a factor, Depp had good reason, and his magnanimity was not confined to Moss. Later that same year, he paid a reported $950,000 for a 43-acre horse-farm in Lexington, Kentucky, for his mother and stepfather, where the couple then lived until February 2000, when they decided to return to Florida; the property was subsequently sold on for $1 million.

Don Juan DeMarco premiered on 7 April, with Depp and Moss in attendance. 'The movie itself is never as good as it should be, owing to Leven's lifeless staging,' Peter Travers wrote in *Rolling Stone* – though he praised the performances of its two stars: 'All the vital signs are due to Depp and Brando. Following Edward Scissorhands, *What's Eating Gilbert Grape* and *Ed Wood*, Depp ranks with the best actors of his generation.' *Variety* thought likewise: '*Don Juan DeMarco* isn't particularly well directed; the story often drags and the transition from one bizarre tale to another (all of which are narrated and presented in flashback) is at times rough … Perfectly cast in a role that brings to mind *Edward Scissorhands*, *Benny & Joon* and *Ed Wood*, heavily accented Depp is delightfully fetching as a young Casanova.' The *Sun-Times*'s Roger Ebert merely begged to differ on the subject of Brando: 'Brando doesn't so much walk through this movie as coast, in a gassy, self-indulgent performance no one else could have gotten away with. Having long since proved he can be one of the best actors in movie history, he now proves he can be one of the worst.'

Given that the premise of the film was based on the universal male fantasy of the irresistible lover, it was to no one's surprise that male reviewers found generally in favour of it; the female of the species, however, was less convinced. After its UK opening 12 days later, *Empire*'s Mark Salisbury lauded the choice of Depp for the role of Don Juan as 'one of the most inspired pieces of casting in many a year', while he thought the film itself to be 'slight but undoubtedly sweet' and 'a comic confection of innocence and charm'. There is nothing on record as to how Depp squared his casting as the devilishly handsome Don Juan with his much-touted desire to play against his looks, other than the fact that the part had offered him the opportunity to work with Brando and he spent some of his time in a mask. But his relations with the press had hit an all-time low at this point in his career, so the absence of the usual chummy insights was only to be expected. Positive reviews aside, *Don Juan DeMarco* also failed to recover its costs. Mark that down as three in a row.

His commercial standing may have taken something of a beating, but Depp could still look to his résumé: from *Arizona Dream* to *Ed Wood*, it was a fascinating body of work for a young actor to have accumulated in so short a time; even *Don Juan DeMarco* could hardly be classed as run-of-the-mill. Ever since *Cry-Baby* broke the mould, there had barely been a formula film among them. But that was now about to change. 'I understand that you have to have a balance in this town, between commercial hits and smaller roles, and that balance is tricky to maintain,' he said. 'But I like to experiment and try new things and my agents have been very supportive of my choices. I thought it was a good time to make a change. I figured I'd do something else after being accused by everybody of playing weirdos.'

For all his protestations, *Nick of Time* was precisely the kind of action-thriller which Depp had repeatedly turned down in the past. If he was influenced in his decisions by those to whom he currently felt closest, then Kate Moss was possessed of a wholly different sensibility to that of Winona Ryder.

An ordinary man... Chosen by chance... Driven by fear.

from the trailer to Nick of Time (1995)

Nick of Time is a Hitchcock-style thriller in the mould of *The 39 Steps* (1935) or 1959's *North by Northwest*, inasmuch as it focuses on an individual who is isolated and in peril, and who must achieve a specific goal by a specific time or dire consequences will result. Here, the individual concerned is Gene Watson (Depp), a young widower newly arrived at LA's Union Station from San Diego with his young daughter. Unbeknown to him, Watson is being observed by Mr Smith and Ms Jones (Christopher Walken and Roma Maffia), as Cary Grant was similarly observed in the lobby of New York's Plaza Hotel, before being kidnapped and pursued across America by communist spies in Hitchcock's 1959 classic. Watson's fate is not so wide ranging; he and his daughter are snatched by the pair and he is given a gun, six bullets and an ultimatum: shoot the governor of California (Marsha Mason) during a campaign stopover at the nearby Bonaventure Hotel within the next ninety minutes or his daughter will die. Thus, in one quick-fire sequence, is established the premise of the film. For the remainder of its 'real-time' running time, Watson has to wrestle with the conundrum of how to avoid killing the governor, simultaneously save his child and bring the bad guys to justice. Does he succeed? – You bet he does. 'If Hitchcock were making this picture, he'd have wanted Jimmy Stewart,' Badham said about the casting of Depp. 'Who's the Jimmy Stewart of the nineties? Nice, unassuming, unpretentious? Johnny has a basic sweetness to him. He's a classic movie actor: minimalist in approach, but extremely honest. He has this great ability to be in a scene where he may do nothing and yet he establishes his presence on the screen.'

John Badham is a dab hand at slick action fare, and nothing about *Nick of Time* in any way diminishes his reputation in that regard. But he is no Hitchcock. And the difference between the two lies not in the way in which the film's suspense sequences are handled – although there *are* differences – but in the fact that Hitchcock respected writers (insofar as they provided him with his stories). *Nick of Time* screenwriters Patrick Sheane Duncan and (an uncredited) Ebbe Roe Smith came up with a great 'hook', which one can envisage being pitched to backers Paramount in the requisite two sentences: 'The small daughter of an ordinary, unassuming guy is kidnapped; he's given a gun and told to shoot the governor in 90 minutes or his daughter will die'. But the logic of the plan collapses almost as soon as it has been imparted to Watson and audience alike. When it eventually transpires that almost everyone *but* Depp is in on the plot, one wonders why they could not simply have done the deed themselves and provided each other with alibis.

Nick of Time glosses over elements which Hitchcock would have taken the time to ensure made logical sense, both for his characters and for the viewer, such as the fact that Watson is chosen at random, which makes the entire process more difficult from the outset. He is also chosen for his initiative, which is the one characteristic that would not have been required of a man picked to carry out an onerous task without question. 'You're out of your mind' Depp says to Walken, to which the latter replies, 'What's your point?'

> Well, this is a nightmare. This was supposed to be clean and simple, remember? A high-powered rifle and it's over. But no, you've got to get creative. Drag some jerk in off the street. Stick a gun in his hand and what? – I mean, what the hell were you thinking of?
>
> Brendan Grant (Peter Strauss), Nick of Time (1995)

Watson's nemesis is Mr Smith, the psychopathic Head of Security who has engineered the plan to deploy a patsy for the attempted assassination. 'Smitty' is played by Walken with his usual full head of steam (not to mention hair) and fund of facial tics as a myopic madman, fuelled by fundamentalist zeal; he is everywhere that

Watson turns, to coax, cajole or simply kick him into submission. It is fascinating to watch Walken and Depp interact, coming as they do from completely different schools in the profession: whereas Depp chooses to immerse himself in his characters through study and research (not quite method but close), Walken's is a bravura turn who prefers to rely on natural poise – he used to be a dancer – and a reading of any script which is peculiar to him alone. His Smitty is, as always, right over the top, whereas Depp's Watson is a study in naturalism. Do they strike sparks off each other? Well, not quite. And the fact that Watson has inevitably to turn the tables on Walken's crazed killer at the climax is one of the script's major failings. Walken is best equipped to fling obstacles into the paths of superheroes; Depp might have been better complemented in *Nick of Time* by a more authentically nasty bad guy.

Hitchcock might also have avoided the irritating anomaly of Walken's character becoming so closely attached to Watson as the story progresses that he pops up like a jack-in-the-box at every twist and turn, to such a degree that he might as well have pulled the trigger himself. As it is, his presence beside the alleged assassin would have been picked up by every security camera in the building. As questions are raised in the viewer's mind over Smitty's ability to organise a tea party in a kindergarten, so one starts to ask similarly why he did not give the gun to Watson a mere five minutes before the appointed time, instead of the full hour and a half. The climax is equally contrived, with a squad of hotel staff press-ganged by Thomas C Dutton's 'shoeshine boy' into conducting what amounts to a highly organised campaign of sabotage against the conspirators, in order to prevent the assassination.

Badham pulls a trick on his audience at the midway point, to liven things up for those who had figured already that in a supposed real-time film, nothing of substance was likely to happen until the final few minutes. Trapped in the plotters' executive suite, Watson grabs Smitty's gun and shoots him, before blasting his way from the room. But the wounded Smitty revives to grab hold of Watson and hurl him from an internal balcony to the floor of the lobby, several hundred feet below. As he is about to hit the marble, he wakes from an earlier faint. The sequence helped to supply a little ancillary action to the trailer, but it served only to underline its deficit in the film. Depp thought this fall important enough to tackle it himself: 'I wanted to do the stunt because only if I did it could the camera get close enough to see that it was really me. But it was a little much. It was a 97 per cent free-fall. They had a rope, or whatever, around me, but when you're falling, it didn't feel as if anything was there. I looked over and the stunt-man was eating a doughnut and saying, "You're doing fine, Johnny. You're doing good. Just go ahead." Sure, that's easy for him to say.'

As an action flick, *Nick of Time* is as good as any in spite of the flaws in its plot. The rigour of its self-enforced timescale carries the willing viewer along, although it never quite succeeds in going beyond the kind of formula affair which almost seems to beg an audience to debate its inadequacies immediately upon leaving the theatre.

Depp is thoroughly convincing as the John Doe terrified both for himself and his daughter, and *Nick of Time* offered him the opportunity him to play a doting parent for the first time on-screen. Never work with kids or animals, they say; in the case of seven-year-old Courtney Chase, what was happening off-set gave Depp his most cause for concern. 'This was a great kid,' he said. 'She won a lot of money off me. We'd bet on how many takes a scene would require; the bet was $20 each time out. She won about $60... A pretty sharp kid.' His approach to Gene Watson was typically unorthodox; he had been asked to play an 'ordinary' guy and that was exactly what he did: 'If I look at the average macho film heroes, I see characteristics that in daily life you only find in aggressive bastards. I have no problem playing a bastard, but not with the intent that he gets cheered at the cinema.' Unfortunately in the case of *Nick of Time*, there was to be no fear of that.

After *Nick of Time* wrapped, *Dead Man* was shown in competition at the 48th International Cannes Film Festival on 28 May 1995, but the prestigious Palme d'Or was awarded instead to Emir Kusturica's *Underground*. Jarmusch's Western was less well received than earlier films in his oeuvre, the result of which was that a US release was deferred by distributors Miramax until its editors could take another look at it.

During their stay in Cannes, Depp and Jarmusch jumped at an opportunity to poke some fun at the movie business when they were approached to appear as themselves in Richard Martini's semi-professional *Cannes Man*, shot entirely in and around the Festival. The film is basically a one-note symphony at the expense of the industry; a candid-camera piece which is built around the old ploy of a double-dealing Hollywood producer by name of Sy Lerner (Seymour Cassel) who takes a bet that he can turn a complete unknown into a celebrity by bullshit alone. Spotting a gormless gopher (Francesco Quinn, son of Anthony, with whom Depp had shared a jungle in *Platoon*), Lerner reinvents him as a fictitious screenwriter named Frank Rhino and proceeds to prey on the vanity and greed of industry 'players' in order to raise funds for a equally fictitious script called 'Cannes Man'. The remainder is too easily imagined: a script, and film, which no one has heard of at the outset suddenly becomes the talk of the circuit, with everyone and their agents wanting to be in on the act. It would be funny if it were not so true-to-life.

Depp and Jarmusch act out a parody of what they perceived to be the industry's perception of them both after *Dead Man*: Lerner comes upon them transcendentally meditating on a lawn, surrounded by bodyguards. He feeds them his line and in minutes, they end up tussling between themselves about which of them will direct the proposed feature. In the end, they agree to go to bat together. Jarmusch coolly sends up himself and his film by informing Lerner that tobacco is a 'religious sacrament' to the Native Americans, to which the producer replies ingratiatingly, 'I used to smoke Peyote. I didn't like that bitter taste and the throwing up.

That's why I switched to cigars.' Depp follows up by injecting a joke at the expense of Harvey Weinstein, the boss of Miramax, to the effect that he would want Weinstein to re-cut his movie (which is exactly what he now planned to do to *Dead Man*). 'He can re-cut your half,' Lerner says.

Much of the dialogue in *Cannes Man* is ad-libbed, which makes for a few longeurs; some of the celebrities who find themselves buttonholed by Lerner and Rhino are in on the gag (such as Jarmusch and Depp), while others clearly are not. The film is intermittently funny – but only to those who are able to ferret out the satire, much of which is too obscure for a lay audience.

In June, *Premiere* set aside two whole pages to knock *Ed Wood* off its critically acclaimed pedestal, despite its having won two Oscars in the interim. 'Depp,' Ryan Gilbey opined, 'looks petrified with glee throughout the entire film. You'll groan with relief when he finally has a tantrum some ninety minutes in.' He finished his piece by querying the raison d'être behind its making – 'You'll realise the movie has no intention of addressing the one question it seems implicitly to suggest: can irrepressible enthusiasm compensate for talent, and should that in itself be celebrated?' – forgetting, in the process, that 'irrepressible enthusiasm' is what makes the movie-world go round, whereas talent is considered to be something of a bonus. However, Angie Errigo, in the same issue, wrote that *Don Juan DeMarco* was both 'a joyous fable' and 'an original and delicious comedy of delusion'.

(That same June, Warners finally gave *Arizona Dream* a belated US release on the strength of Kusturica's Cannes success, but no one turned out to see it. Some years later, Depp summed up the experience for Chiara Mastroianni in an interview that was broadcast on Canal+: 'They [Warners] didn't care about the story; they didn't care about the shots; they didn't care about how beautiful the cinematography was, or the poetry of Kusturica's ideas … I think they didn't give a damn.')

Whether or not Marlon Brando did see anything of the spiritual son in Johnny Depp is open to question, but he lost no time in returning the favour which Depp had accorded him on *Don Juan DeMarco*. In July, the man whom critics the world over cate-gorised as the greatest screen actor of his generation – if not the greatest ever – invited Depp to join him in the cast of a film called *Divine Rapture*, which was to shoot at Ballycotton in the Republic of Ireland.

For Brando, *Divine Rapture* was to have represented escape from the latest in a long line of personal tragedies: two months before, on 16 April, his daughter Cheyenne had hanged herself in her mother's house on the island of Tahiti. Consequently, he was chipper at the prospect of a new film role to take his mind off things. 'Come over and join me in Ireland,' Depp was urged. 'We'll do this thing. It'll be fun.'

It was an offer that Depp could hardly refuse; on his arrival in Eire, he joined Debra Winger and *Dead Man* co-star John Hurt on the set of a whimsical comedy about the Catholic Church's attitude to miracles. The film lasted three weeks. 'We started shooting and we're having a great time. Everything was real good. The next thing we knew, they were saying, "It's over." And that was it,' he said of the experience.

Due to the sudden circumstance of the film's collapse, many of the cast and crew of *Divine Rapture* ultimately went unpaid, including the voluble Hurt.

Got up and dressed up and went out & got laid
Then died and got buried in a coffin in a grave, Man –
Yet everything is perfect, Because it is empty,
Because it is perfect with emptiness,
Because it's not even happening.
JOHNNY DEPP READING FROM 'MEXICO CITY BLUES, CHORUS 113' BY JACK KEROUAC, IN *THE UNITED STATES OF POETRY* (1995)

Depp filled the unexpected gap in his schedule by agreeing to guest in a two-hour television special for the PBS network, called *The United States of Poetry*. The show examined the work of

American poets and lyricists through visualisations of pre-record-ed readings, and Depp had been chosen to perform some lines of Kerouac's; among those with whom he shared the literary stage were Allen Ginsberg and ex-US President Jimmy Carter, who read from one of his own compositions.

As Depp worked on 'Mexico City Blues' prior to the recording, he suddenly became aware of the gaze of an observer. Out of the corner of his eye, he saw that Allen Ginsberg himself was watch-ing him. When he finished rehearsing, he was introduced to Ginsberg, who promptly launched into a version of the same chorus, assuring Depp in the process that his own rendition was 'how Jack would have done it'.

'But I'm not reading it as him; I'm reading it as *me*,' Depp replied. 'It's *my* interpretation of his piece.'

There was a long silence, broken only by Depp's nervous inhala-tion of cigarette smoke, as director and crew waited for the poet to come back with an appropriate riposte. Instead of that, he smiled what Depp regarded as 'a mystic smile' and invited him back for tea at his apartment on New York's Lower East Side. It was the beginning of a beautiful, if occasional, friendship, broken only by Ginsberg's death in April 1997. 'I felt as though God him-self had forgiven me a dreadful sin,' Depp said of the incident. (He added to his occasional poetry readings later in the same year by contributing some verses from William Blake to Neil Young's soundtrack album of *Dead Man*.)

Asked in August if marriage to Depp was now a real possibility, Moss was coy: 'He's just my boyfriend. That's all,' she said, but during the last quarter of the year, the pair continued to wade knee-deep in the kind of celebrity froth which did little to damp-en speculation in the tabloids about the prospect of forthcoming nuptials. In September, Moss launched the glossy, coffee-table *Kate Moss Book* at the Danziger Gallery in New York, with Depp at her side and a fashionable line in political statement at the ready, to enhance her street-cred: opposition to the resumption by the French government of nuclear testing in the South Pacific.

(On 5 September, France had detonated a 20-kiloton bomb on Mururoa atoll in French Polynesia.) Depp held a poster aloft in protest and Moss urged attendees not to buy French goods, while quite failing to notice that she was sipping champagne at the time.

The couple's new-found radical consciousness continued into New York's Fashion Week in November, before transferring its opportunistic populism to London. France conducted a total of six tests in all, before President Jacques Chirac called a halt to the process in January 1996, clearly piqued by the disapproval of someone so closely associated with the House of Chanel.

Nick of Time opened on 22 November, but found itself up against Pixar's *Toy Story*, a film which eventually went on to gross close to $200 million at the world box office. *GoldenEye* had opened five days before. Thoroughly overshadowed by such heavyweight competition, the film returned a poor $8 million, or twice what Depp had been paid to star in it. The competition for ticket sales was not the only factor, however, and the review in *Rolling Stone* was typical: 'The gimmick in the script by Patrick Duncan and Ebbe Roe Smith is that the film will take place in the actual time, 90 minutes, that Gene has to complete his mission. Alfred Hitchcock played a similar time trick in *Rope* in 1948. Director John Badham can't even cut it as a hack Hitchcock. A movie in which time is of the essence is really a botch job when you don't believe a minute of it.' *Variety* was less dismissive of the lead actor – 'After a string of impressively quirky roles in *Edward Scissorhands*, *What's Eating Gilbert Grape* and *Benny & Joon*, Depp tries his hand at an everyday Joe with solid results, limited by the fact that we know virtually nothing about him other than that he loves his daughter' – but *Nick of Time* did not turn out to be the success that either he or its production company had hoped for, although it was to lead him directly into another potential hit: *Donnie Brasco*.

Christmas 1995 again found Depp and Moss at Aspen, this time in the company of Moss's mother and brother Nick. During their stay, they visited the famous Woody Creek Tavern, local watering hole of none other than Hunter S Thompson, whose heavily fortified Owl Farm home was situated nearby and whose *Fear and Loathing in Las Vegas* had been devoured by Depp as a teenager, alongside *On the Road*. The visit proved fortuitous: the foursome did not have long to wait before the tavern's most famous customer put in a customarily eccentric appearance.

'In walks Hunter wielding two cattle prods, with serious voltage going up and down,' Depp told *Rolling Stone*'s Chris Heath. 'A wand of electricity. You could see it crackling up.' Since the inaugural publication of his most celebrated work in the same magazine in November 1971, Thompson had become as famous for his behavioural excess as he was for his ground-breaking journalism, and the next few hours were to be no exception. Introductions were made and Depp was informed by the writer that he had seen *Cry-Baby* – though not through to the end, because he had partaken of 'a little acid.' Nevertheless, Thompson offered a critique: 'It seemed like watching *Oklahoma* go on for three years.'

The two men found themselves on common ground – the 'dark and bloody ground' of Old Kentucky, in fact – and Thompson invited the party back to Owl Farm, where he and Depp then rounded out the evening by constructing home-made bombs and using them for target practice, much to the dismay of Moss's mother. 'She just thought Hunter was a madman and horribly dangerous, and that we should escape as soon as possible,' Depp said.

Escape they eventually did, but Depp was to hear from Hunter Thompson again.

5 HEROES AND VILLAINS

There was madness in any direction, at any hour. If not across the
Bay, then up to the Golden Gate or down 101 to Los Altos or
La Honda...You could strike sparks anywhere. There was a
fantastic universal sense that whatever we were doing was right,
that we were winning...

And that, I think, was the handle — that sense of inevitable
victory over the forces of Old and Evil. Not in any mean or
military sense; we didn't need that. Our energy would simply
prevail. There was no point in fighting-on our side or theirs. We
had all the momentum; we were riding the crest of a high and
beautiful wave...

So now, less than five years later, you can go up on a steep hill
in Las Vegas, and with the right kind of eyes you can almost see
the high-water mark-that place where the wave broke and rolled
back.

JOHNNY DEPP, READING FROM *FEAR AND LOATHING IN LAS VEGAS,*
HUNTER S THOMPSON TRIBUTE CONCERT (DECEMBER, 1996)

IN MANY WAYS, 1995 had been Johnny Depp's year: following
the out-of-sync openings of *Don Juan DeMarco* and *Ed Wood* in
the UK (19 May and 26 May respectively), *Empire* and *Premiere*
had both run major interviews with the star of the films within a
month of each other. *Premiere*'s was the more revealing of the
two. Holly Millea said of him: 'Depp pulls odd but entertaining
answers from the air, all the while willing to let you check up his
sleeves.' By this juncture, even Depp's agent, Tracey Jacobs, had
been moved to comment on his artistic ethic, quoting American
poet Robert Frost to describe her client's idiosyncratic approach
to his work: '"I have taken the road less travelled and that has
made all the difference." That would be the quote that I would use
to describe him in general,' she said. ('I took the one less travelled
by/And that has made all the difference' – 'Mountain Interval',

1916.) 'This is a great time for me – one of the best times I've had,' Depp confirmed on BBC TV's *Live and Kicking*. 'I have a girl who I'm in love with; we have a good, solid relationship and we're having a great time. My family's alive; everyone's OK. This is definitely a very good time!'

Due to the closing-down of *Divine Rapture*, Depp had managed to feature in only one film during the previous 12 months, though it had been high profile and was at least accorded a premiere (at the Samuel Goldwyn Theatre in Beverly Hills, which he attended with his mother); unlike *Nick of Time*, Jim Jarmusch's *Dead Man* was still awaiting release more than six months after its screening at Cannes because the distributors, Miramax, had asked its director to cut it by 14 minutes. However, the media were less interested in an experimental Western than they were in the fact that Depp was now booked to play the lead in a $35 million gangster epic for the man who had given the world the sleeper success of *Four Weddings and a Funeral*.

It's funny. All you have to do is say something nobody understands and they'll do practically anything you want them to.
J D SALINGER, *THE CATCHER IN THE RYE* (1951)

After the trauma of his break-up with Ryder and later involvement in the River Phoenix affair, it was clear from the interviews to which he graciously continued to submit that Depp had finally learned to play the press at its own game. Gone was his openness of personality and willingness to express forthright opinions, and in their place had come reticence, a more defensive posture in general, a multiplicity of self-invented personae to suit each and every instance (and inquisitor), as well as a miscellany of carefully calculated sound bites of pure gobbledegook. Some of this studied laissez-faire could be apportioned to sloppy journalism and the very misrepresentations which he had previously complained about so consistently, but press interviews from 1995 on nevertheless began to reveal a rigidity of tone that hinted at the emergence of a new and more politicised Johnny. He was also in his early thirties by this time, without much more than personal heartache and a few good movies to show for it, and there were signs that he was starting to mature with age. Ex-fiancée Winona Ryder, now in her mid-twenties, had already absorbed the same lesson herself: 'It's really interesting to see how I changed in terms of talking about my relationships,' she said in *US* magazine. 'I learned a lot from that – from being so open, and from being stupid.'

Depp was an actor, after all, and he had merely taken to acting off-camera as much as he did on, in order to protect himself from any further invasions of his privacy. But he was also a Hollywood actor and, as such, he was perfectly placed to benefit from the advice of others of the same ilk who had trod this particular path before him and who had emerged from the experience to be more circumspect in their dealings with the media. In this particular, Depp had now been mentored by Marlon Brando, an actor who had suffered the slings and arrows of a hostile press more than most and whose friendship and admiration he had retained after they had worked together on *Arizona Dream* (and almost on *Divine Rapture*). Brando was a past master at fielding questions, and his personal philosophy was to give as few interviews as possible and to say as little as practicable when the necessity for public utterance became unavoidable. Depp could hardly subscribe to the first of these tenets – Brando's career had since gone into one of its habitual declines and he could afford to keep his head below the parapet, but Depp's was just beginning and the fuel of publicity was an essential to forward progress. But he could easily sign up to the second: don't be drawn on contentious subjects and always try to stay on message. Accordingly, it was a more self-assured but significantly less forthcoming Johnny Depp who gifted *Time Out* with a summary of the story so far: 'Five years ago, I was doing my best to numb myself – feelings, thoughts, things from my past, my childhood – all those clichéd things. I wasn't the happiest guy in the world. But I don't think I'm much different, really. I'm happy, but I was happy then. I'm angry, but I was angry then. I think my heart is in the right place. I'm not a bad guy. You know, I don't want to get old in the sense that I don't want to get jaded; I don't want to get complacent or lazy. I still feel 17. I think I stopped growing at a certain point in my brain. Everything else ages, but I still feel 17, like that kid who was playing rock 'n' roll clubs.

Press interest in Depp's private life continued unabated. By the mid-1990s, film journals had moved from inquiring about the kind of the choices that Depp was making in terms of the roles that he picked to play to whether or not he was happy with the size of his penis and, in the same self-consciously hip interview for *Empire*, what was his most embarrassing moment when putting on a condom. Depp's responses had, in the interim, conversely become more sanguine and sophisticated as well as prophetically Thompsonesque: to the former, he replied, 'I haven't up till now. *Should* I start pondering? Nah, it's been a good friend to me. I'd certainly miss him if he were gone'; while to the latter, he relayed a tale about an armadillo in his New York hotel room. 'Were you alone at the time?' asked Stephen Rebello (neglecting the armadillo). 'Yes,' Depp confirmed, 'I was alone.' 'So you were going to put on a condom for the hell of it?' his questioner pursued. 'Just because you never know, you know? So you want to be ready,' Depp replied, deadpan.

This was Rebello's third version of his 'Depp interview', so a new take on his subject was getting harder to come by. 'By the way, is this interview about penises now?' Depp queried at length. 'Is this National Penis Month?' In magazines like *Empire* and *Premiere*, every month was National Penis Month.

> Bela – those people are parasites. They just want to exploit you.
>
> Ed Wood (Johnny Depp), Ed Wood (1994)

It was all par for the course now, and noticeably absent were the vitriolic diatribes of only a year before against perceived outrages perpetrated by the media. Depp at last was able to treat the press with the amiable contempt that much of it justly deserved. He was also in the middle of a new romance and his career was on the up. For the moment, the darkness had lifted – though it was soon to return.

In January 1996, Depp and Moss were dancing the night away at a party on Florida's South Beach in honour of Chris Blackwell, the boss of Island Records, but, by February, more reports had surfaced concerning the imminent end of the affair. Depp was now literally 'in training' for his next role, for which he was required to put on some 20lbs in weight. TriStar Pictures had bought the rights to a book called *Donnie Brasco: My Undercover Life in the Mafia* by Joseph D Pistone. Pistone had become an agent for the FBI in 1969 and, in September 1976, he inveigled himself into the Colombo and then the Bonanno crime families of New York, the object being to gather incriminating evidence against members of the syndicate. What started out as a modest 'sting' operation against local hoods developed into something much more substantial as Pistone went deeper undercover into the ranks of the Mafia, including the Santo Trafficante organisation in Florida. His minders were two 'wise guys' who went by the names of Dominick 'Sonny Black' Napolitano, a local *capo* (boss), and Benjamin 'Lefty Guns' Ruggiero, a small-time bookmaker and thief. After a full six years of subterfuge, the operation was terminated and Pistone testified against his former associates in a number of criminal trials. Sonny Black was assassinated as a direct result of the ruse being uncovered, but Ruggiero was picked up by the FBI before he too could be hit. Pistone's Mob-name had been *Donnie Brasco*, thus the title of his book. This was the role that Depp had been hired to play, from a script by ex-*Washington Post* critic and writer of *Quiz Show*, Paul Attanasio, and principal photography got underway in March.

My real name was not revealed until the first day I testified, when I walked into the courtroom, raised my right hand,

*and swore to tell the truth. Then I was asked to give my name,
and I gave it, for the first time publicly in six years: Joseph D
Pistone.*

*All those years undercover in the mob, I had been lying
every day, living a lie. I was lying for what I believed was a
high moral purpose: to help the United States government
destroy the Mafia.*

JOSEPH D PISTONE, *DONNIE BRASCO: MY UNDERCOVER LIFE IN
THE MAFIA* (1987)

During the first week of shooting on *Donnie Brasco*, Depp
received a phone call on-set. On the other end of the line was
Hunter S Thompson.

'Listen,' Thompson said, 'They're talking of making a movie of
Vegas. What do you think about playing me?'

Depp was intrigued. Prospective movies 'of *Vegas*' had come
and gone with the regularity of the seasons, ever since the piece
was first published in book form. Director Martin Scorsese had
been interested in casting a post-*Easy Rider* Jack Nicholson in the
Thompson role, and *The Last Picture Show*'s Larry McMurtry
had also tried his hand at an adaptation. John Belushi and Dan
Aykroyd's names had been mentioned in connection with it from
time to time. The nearest that anyone had come to putting
Thompson's zonked-out world-view onto a screen was director
Art Linden, in a 1980 film called *Where the Buffalo Roam*, starring Bill Murray and Peter Boyle. It was not best remembered.

Nevertheless, Depp was up for it. 'Absolutely,' he said.
Thompson put the phone down.

By 1996, the template for gangster movies was no longer
The Godfather in any of its three incarnations, but Martin
Scorsese's *GoodFellas* (1990). Any film which attempted to deal
with the activities of the Mafia had now to look over its shoulder
at Scorsese's frenziedly paced and foul-mouthed epic of Mob
disloyalty – not least because it starred Robert De Niro, Ray
Liotta and Joe Pesci. Scorsese had stripped the genre of its

romanticism; not for him the lyrical strains of Nino Rota, sepia-tinted images of turn-of-the-century New York, or gambols in the fields of Sicily: Martin's wise guys were devious, duplicitous and deadly, meaner than the mean streets that bred them, and they observed no rules and gave no quarter. Now top that.

Donnie Brasco had decided to go another way – after all, what choice did it have. The clue was in Pistone's testimony before a Senate hearing in 1988: boredom. The sheer mind-numbing monotony of men without a future, who while away the present by dreaming up get-rich-quick schemes that exhibit all the flair of a parking meter hit with a claw hammer. A fine supporting cast was assembled to counter the anticipated tedium: in addition to Johnny Depp, gangster *par excellence* Al Pacino (*The Godfather; Scarface*) was brought on board to play the pivotal role of Lelly Ruggiero, with *Reservoir Dogs'* Michael Madsen as Sonny Black.

The film received much critical praise for its supposedly realistic portrayal of the mundane lives and nickel-and-dime criminality of minor Mafiosi; The *GoodFellas* gangsters were equally engaging as characters in their own right, but Scorsese ensured early in the film that the viewer was made privy to what such men were actually capable of. No matter how chipper they might appear to be on the surface, his gangsters were congenitally psychotic underneath – which was not a long way down. Consequently, the narrative of *GoodFellas* fairly bristled with tension due to its very unpredictability. Scorsese understands violence – the psychology, as well as the brutality of it – but Hertfordshire-born, Cambridge-educated *Donnie Brasco* director Mike Newell (of *Four Weddings and a Funeral*) goes about his film as though he has never encountered it in his life, not, at least, outside of the make-believe variety which is dispensed in television series like *The Young Indiana Jones Chronicles*, for which Newell directed several episodes. *Donnie Brasco*'s gangsters are merely good-time fellas with small-time criminal habits, which makes their persecution at the hands of agent Pistone increasingly questionable as the story slowly unfolds.

In Newell's hands, the film not only becomes obsessed with the minutiae of the day-to-day lives of two-bit hoods on the bottom-rung of the Mafia ladder but with the idiomatic intricacies of their native Bronx patois as well. In this unfortunate regard, it all too often assumes the air of an anthropology lesson; an outsider's eye-view of an alien culture:

> 'Fuhgedaboudit'... It's like, uh, if you agree with someone, you know, like Raquel Welch is one great piece of ass... Fuhgedaboudit... But then, if you disagree, like a Lincoln is better than a Cadillac – Fuhgedaboudit! But then, it's also like if something is the greatest thing in the world like mingia those peppers: Fuhgedaboudit. But it's also like saying 'go to hell' too, like, you know, like, uh – 'Hey Paulie, you got a one-inch pecker!' and Paulie says, 'Fuhgedaboudit!' Sometimes it just means... forget about it.
>
> Donnie Brasco (Johnny Depp), Donnie Brasco (1996)

One is hard-pressed to imagine Scorsese halting *GoodFellas* midstream in order to deliver a dissertation on semantics but this is exactly what Newell does in *Donnie Brasco*, and though he and screenwriter Paul Attanasio might have been fascinated by the jargon, the average viewer can get a handle on its meaning simply by observing its usage in context. Pistone, on the other hand, probably elaborated on some of these details simply for the sake of padding (he has so far managed to expand his time with the Mafia into some half dozen assorted books).

Michael Madsen's Sonny Black aside (though ironically, Pistone is on record as saying that the real Black cut quite an amiable figure), the Mafiosi in the film are not the kind of men who might cut each other's throats to settle a gambling debt or repay some sleight against their good names. Lazy, parasitic and amoral they may be, but the threat which their real-life counterparts must surely have posed to the well-being of Pistone's *Donnie Brasco* goes largely unrealised in Attanasio's screenplay. The real surprise about *Donnie Brasco* is how little violence it actually contains: only the late-addition assassination of three gang bosses comes close to conveying the terrifying reality of a business where boardroom battles are fought out in dark basements, with sawn-off shotguns and chainsaws (and even then, the supposedly graphic dismemberment of a corpse is visualised by somebody rather incongruously cutting through a *boot*). Other than this one bloody interlude, the most ferocious explosion of violence in the story comes from Brasco himself, a curiosity which is made all the more confounding by the fact that he directs it against a third-party innocent in order to ingratiate himself with Ruggiero. 'I've got twenty-six fucking hits under my belt, and *you're* the one he's scared of,' Ruggiero says, perplexed.

For *Donnie Brasco* to have worked more effectively, the members of the Mafia gang which Pistone infiltrates required to be less sympathetically portrayed and treated more in accordance with the way that their kind are rightly perceived by the majority of American police officers, including the real Joe Pistone. In a film that essentially centres on a 'Judas' figure, it is vital to make sure that a protagonist's actions are for the greater good and conducted against clear-cut villainy, or 'stone-cold gangsters' as Pistone himself referred to his quarry. The modus of *Jump Street*, in which storylines were blatantly biased in favour of the police so that their undercover activities would appear less unsavoury, might have been usefully employed in *Donnie Brasco*. Ambivalence is not a quality best suited to a film in which the audience is asked to side with a participant who knowingly sends men to their deaths for the needs of his own self-preservation, even if the men in question are mobsters. In humanising his subjects to the point of banality, Newell undercuts this essential and makes Pistone/Brasco a much more dubious figure in the narrative. In the end, Pistone's undoubted heroism is seriously tempered by the cruel fate which is meted out to the one man who trusted and protected him, and who welcomed him into the bosom of his family. The viewer waits in vain for Pistone to cut a deal with the authorities which will let Ruggiero off the hook, but it never comes. The real Ruggiero went to prison for 18 years when the sting was shut down, but *Donnie Brasco* sends him to his death by ritual execution.

Ruggiero's eventual fate is telegraphed to the audience earlier in the film, when he receives a telephone call from Sonny Black requesting a meet. Along the way, he reveals his suspicions to Brasco: 'In our thing, you get sent for. You go in alive. You come out dead. And it's your best friend that does it.' It so happens that this particular appointment is merely to impart the news that Black has been made up to a local boss, and to give Ruggiero a lion (yes, a *lion*) as a consolation prize. A similar call is made at the end, although ostensibly to a different outcome; the Mafia must therefore be filled with people who respond to phone calls thinking that they're about to be whacked, only to find themselves at a surprise birthday party – and vice versa. One can only assume that it keeps them on their toes.

Despite a professed '26 hits' to his credit, Al Pacino invests Ruggiero with tragic humanity, and the penultimate scene of the film – which sees him disposing of his personal possessions in a bureau drawer where his wife can find them, in the certain knowledge that he will not return from the meeting to which he has now been summoned – is carried off to poignant effect. But then *Donnie Brasco* is Al Pacino's film, not Johnny Depp's – Ruggiero's, not Brasco's – and Pacino is an actor who can engender sympathy for the Devil (as he was indeed to do the following year by playing Old Nick himself in *The Devil's Advocate*). The decision to concentrate effort on the relationship between Brasco and Ruggiero inevitably moved the centre of empathy away from the film's nominal hero and onto his burnt-out prey who, in Pacino's expert hands, consciously evokes memories of Brando's Oscar-winning turn as Terry Malloy in *On the Waterfront*, with his plaintive refrain, 'I could've been a contender.' Lefty is the ultimate loser, passed over for years within the ranks of the Mob, then betrayed by his own protégé and climactically whacked in consequence. In Pacino's take on the man, he is typically full of streetwise bluff and bluster (intermittently accompanied by bouts of naked aggression), but beneath it all is a world-weary Mafia gopher, watching disconsolately on as his life passes before his tired eyes.

Yet the switch of emphasis is a miscalculation at the expense of the film as a whole: Lefty is shown performing his own last rites as Pistone is given a medal of honour and token cheque for services rendered to law enforcement, which merely compounds the suspicion that both writer and director have actually been on Pacino's side, rather than Depp's, all along-and regardless of the fact that their story is notionally that of 'Donnie Brasco'. Depp does little to counter the growing sense of audience alienation with the title character. He cohabited for a while with the real Joseph Pistone, prior to production, in order to get down his speech patterns and physical mannerisms, but his time might have been better spent in closer examination of the direction in which Attanasio's script was gravitating. Pistone's climactic close-up is intended to be one of moral confusion over the outcome of his undercover mission; in context, it looks more like he is left to wonder how exactly he failed to end up as the *hero* of *Donnie Brasco*.

Much else is left unresolved – such as the fate of Ruggiero's junkie son – and the climax is rushed and unsatisfactory: it might have been preferable to have been informed of the fate of some of the characters whom one has just spent two hours observing (and even coming to like, as Brasco ostensibly does), not just that of Pistone himself, but such a resolution would have undermined the ambiguity in the finale, so a cursory screen caption tells us only of the number of Mafiosi tried and convicted as a consequence of the operation.

In fairness to Depp, it has to be said that his generosity as an actor is second to none. He is always more than willing to allow others to take centre stage, often to his own detriment; so it is with Pacino, with whom he makes little attempt to compete and thus affords him the opportunity to steal the film completely away. His own performance is one of some subtlety in part, and his studied air of subservience towards his Mob mentor – nodding, agreeing or feigning misunderstanding in turn – perfectly captures the strain of a man who is at pains to comprehend the psychology of one from a different cultural milieu altogether, even if only at face value. Depp is at his best when he is at his most deferential, letting Pacino's bravura turn carry the day, but the script misses a vital trick in not contrasting Brasco's ingratiating manner with what must have been a more constant fear of discovery. Only in one sequence in a Japanese restaurant is he shown to be in danger of having his real identity revealed, but that, too, is muffed, as the clearly psychotic Sonny Black calmly accepts Brasco's contrived explanation for not removing his shoes as requested (one of which contains a tape recorder) and beats the hell out of the restaurateur instead; at the very least, a timely word in Brasco's ear about his earlier insubordination was required to make the scene ring more true, but this lack of cohesion is painted over by the violence of the subsequent assault.

> He's right in the line of fire. Not because he's one of us. Because he's one of them.
>
> Dean Blandford (Gerry Becker), Donnie Brasco (1996)

The sub-text of the piece is Pistone's gradual loss of his own identity, the more that he takes on the mantle of *Donnie Brasco*, and the knock-on effect on his wife and family. Depp seems to have been wrong-footed by the supposed evolution of Joe Pistone from special agent of the FBI to Mafia foot-soldier over the period of the required six years, and it has to be left to occasional snatches of dialogue to convey the notion that he has been 'taken over' by his Mob personality in the process. As the screenplay fails to facilitate a glimpse of Pistone as he was prior to 1976 (even in flashback), no sense of change in his character subsequently is allowed to come across, struggle as Depp might to suggest one.

Unlike his mostly American predecessors, British director Mike Newell was less reserved in his opinions when it came to discussing the experience of working with the Jekyll-and-Hyde character that Johnny Depp could on occasion be. 'He bit my ass a couple of times and, to this day, I don't know what I did,' Newell revealed. 'He suddenly fell completely out of love and was vile. The reason it was disconcerting is that he's so sweet the rest of the time; he's so hard working, so sensitive, with all the right vibrations. And just a couple of times, he comes on like the blood-beast terror and you don't know where you are.' Depp was playing the role of a man under stress and living a double life, and an element of method technique may have come to the fore in his outbursts against his director. But Newell's account paints a different picture of the actor to the studiedly rose-tinted version which had been given to the world at large by those with whom he had worked previously. While he was making *Donnie Brasco*, Depp's two-year relationship with Kate Moss had been getting into difficulties, which might also have had some bearing: 'There's a great deal more going on underneath than the sweet boy your mother would like,' Newell concluded. 'Somewhere along the line, that sort of rackety life on the wrong side of the tracks has left a big mark, which, because he's so strong a character and so intelligent, he has disciplined, but once in a while, when he's not looking, something jumps out that is ancient and atavistic. But it's a mark of how decent a person he is that it's over almost instantaneously. You don't carry any resentment about it. I didn't.'

What lingers in the mind with the character of the Tramp is that sweetness, that innocence, that purity. But at the same time, there is that other side, that rascal. I remember watching The Immigrant again recently, and for a second being really stunned. Chaplin's playing cards. He loans the guy money and the guy gives him his pistol as collateral. And when Chaplin wins, the guy gets violent. I remember being stunned when Chaplin pulls the gun on him and gives him this look. Hey... You know? Just for that second. And

then he immediately goes back to this pure being, this innocent thing.
JOHNNY DEPP, TALKING ABOUT CHARLIE CHAPLIN, *CHARLIE: THE LIFE AND ART OF CHARLES CHAPLIN* (2003)

Joe Pistone also throws a moody at the close, when presented with a departmental medal and a cheque for $500, but it is hardly enough to compensate for the fate of the unfortunate Ruggiero, let alone wash the blood off his hands. One is left to wonder why Lefty himself was not offered an immunity deal at Pistone's request, which would have left the agent with honour intact, and the lack of such an obvious (and authentic) resolution is more explicable of Pistone's guilt at the climax than the notion of regret that he has been forced to abandon Ruggiero to his fate, as the film has one believe. Pacino had played a similar role himself in 1973's *Serpico*, but he did so with more sympathy for a central character who sets out to betray his comrades than Johnny Depp was able to contrive for *Donnie Brasco*.

Joe Pistone and a former wise guy named Rocco Musacchia both acted as technical advisers to the film, in which Musacchia also played one of Santo Trafficante's henchmen. No love was apparently lost between them. During production, makers TriStar let it be known that Pistone had a $500,000 bounty on his head, to engender media interest. Musacchia pooh-poohed the very idea: 'Those guys wouldn't pay a half a dollar for him,' he said. 'They don't whack cops. Plus if they wanted him they knew he was on the set. That's just publicity hype.'

For all of its notional realism, *Donnie Brasco* is tinged with the kind of romanticism which Scorsese rigorously eschews, from anachronistic sequences of mobsters frolicking like children in the theme parks of Florida, to its obsession with 'codes of honour' and Lefty's mock-heroic date with destiny at its close. In its rose-tinted approach to its Mafia material, *Donnie Brasco* is closer in mood to *The Untouchables* than it is to *GoodFellas*; there are touches of Clintonesque liberalism about it, coincident with when it was made, but its heart and its message belong to a different era, that of the age in which it is set: "'John Wayne Dead – Nation

Mourns'. How can John Wayne die?' Sonny Black asks, after digesting a newspaper headline from 11 June 1979. The right-wing agenda which Wayne embodied has much more to do with the ethos of *Donnie Brasco* than some commentators seemed to appreciate at the time. Perhaps they do now.

With Kate Moss playing footloose, Depp had looked to his old pal Sal to provide some much-needed moral support during the making of *Donnie Brasco*, and a brief role as a timid bartender had been found for Jenco in the opening sequence. He had been cast to type, as he was currently running the Viper Room on behalf of his friend. When Jenco returned to LA after shooting his scenes, he carried with him an offer from Depp to Viper Room co-owner Anthony Fox, to buy out Fox's remaining 49 per cent stake in the club's holding company, Safe in Heaven. Aggrieved by the loss of his salary, Fox refused. He had other plans.

On 10 May, an abridged version of *Dead Man* was put into release, a year after its premiere at Cannes. It barely managed to scrape $1 million at the box office. Jim Jarmusch was already working on a documentary about Neil Young and his band Crazy Horse, but it was to take him the best part of another three years before he made his next film, the more overtly commercial *Ghost Dog: Way of the Samurai*. In June, another rumour surfaced to the effect that Depp and Moss had split, until they were spotted together on the Caribbean island of Mustique with Noel Gallagher of Oasis and his girlfriend (later wife) Meg Matthews. Gallagher was reported to be working on songs for the band's new album, which saw release in 1997 as *Be Here Now*, while Depp was busy putting the final touches to a project of his own.

> Depp: I'd like to direct. If I could, you know?
> Lerner: Sure. I'm sure you could direct. I'm sure you'd be a damn good director. I hadn't thought – You want to direct and act too?
> Depp: I mean, why not? Why not?
> Cannes Man (1995)

In August 1996, Johnny Depp embarked on what would turn out to be the most arduous and courageous endeavour of his career to date. He was finally to take his directorial bow in a film called *The Brave*; not only that, but he had co-written the screenplay and was himself intent on playing the starring role. He had been nurturing the project for some time, but to the interest of few so far. With funding now secured through Majestic Films and enter-prising British producer Jeremy Thomas, *The Brave* was at last ready to go before the cameras.

The author believes the third chapter of The Brave, *Chapter c, is an integral part of the story, that exactly what transpired between 'the uncle' and Rafael in that second story loft must be reported fully.*

However, the author realises that this chapter is particularly strong and repulsive as it has to do with both immediate, and planned, prolonged human cruelty.

He wishes he could have avoided writing that particular chapter.

The author also believes The Brave *justifies the events and cir-cumstances depicted in Chapter c and throughout the narrative generally.*

Therefore the reader is advised that not all will find it desirable or perhaps absolutely necessary to include Chapter c in their read-ing of this work.

GREGORY MCDONALD, 'FOREWORD', *THE BRAVE* (1991)

The Brave was adapted from a 1991 novel by mystery writer Gregory McDonald, creator of 'Fletch'; McDonald's original title for his story was *Rafael, Last Days*, and it was published as such in France (as *Rafael, derniers jours*). The rights to an untypical work which the *New York Times* described as 'a resourceful young man negotiating a malignant dystopian landscape' and a EuroArts Channel documentary labelled 'one of the two or three greatest novels ever written' were purchased by Aziz Ghazal, a one-time film student and producer of *Zombie High* (1987), who then hired LA-based Paul McCudden to produce a screenplay. McCudden's script was as irreducibly dark in tone as its source, with a stark undertow of NC-17 brutality which put it on the same level as Wes Craven's *Last House On the Left.*

McCudden's script had accurately reflected the novel: The metaphorical and literal 'Brave' of the title is Raphael, a Native American drifter who squats with his wife and two children in a shanty town on the edge of a town dump. Acutely aware of the hopelessness of this situation, he offers his services to a local thug named McCarthy, whose seedy speciality is the production of 'snuff' movies in which an innocent victim is tortured to death; in return, his family will receive $50,000 ($30,000 in the novel). Having signed up to this Faustian pact, Raphael has seven days in which to make his peace with the world. In the time left to him, he rediscovers the love of his family but remains honour-bound to fulfil his part of the bargain. After the requisite time is up, he sets out to face the slow and painful death which was gleefully promised him.

McDonald's 'Chapter c', in which Raphael is informed in detail of what exactly will happen to him during the course of his torture, is the stuff of nightmare. Only David Lynch, of directors working today, has the visual sensibility – and stomach – to contemplate such material. It made *The Brave* a contentious project from the word go. It was to remain a contentious project to the bitter end.

In 1993, Ghazal committed suicide after shooting dead his wife and daughter and the script, felt by those in the industry to be a jinxed property as a result, fell into the hands of producers Carroll Kemp and Robert Evans Jnr. Depp's agent was one of many with whom it subsequently 'did the rounds', but its intended recipient was less than impressed. 'I hated it immediately,' he recalled. 'It was full of clichés'; a sort of Christ-like allegory that was like a long funeral march without the slightest humour.' Nevertheless, there was something about *The Brave* which stuck in his mind. 'In spite of everything, I found the idea very interesting – could you sacrifice your life for love?'

Uncommercial was not the word for this story, and Depp immediately thought to revise the script in collaboration with his brother Dan. What they did, in essence, was to turn McDonald's polemic about the plight of a people on the edge of the abyss into one man's journey through a dark night of the soul. But the key change came at the climax: Raphael could not be allowed to die in the film – instead, he returns to McCarthy's warehouse to tell him of his change of heart. According to author Christopher Heard, the Depp brothers' shooting script has McCarthy try to bribe Raphael with more money before revealing himself to be a white supremacist and racially abusing him, at which point, Raphael shoots him with his own gun. Satisfied with *his* version of *The Brave*, Johnny Depp took his crew to Ridgecrest, a small town to the north of Los Angeles on the edge of the Death Valley National Park.

During the shooting, Gregory McDonald visited the set and met with Depp. In terms of the finished film, their opening salvo was a significant one. In spite of years of publicity which had taken pains to advance the notion of Depp as a voracious reader, he somehow had managed to avoid the novel on which *The Brave* had been based when he set out with his brother to revise McCudden's script.

Depp apologised to McDonald for the omission, and then reversed the roles:

'Have you read the screenplay?' he asked the author.

McDonald smiled indulgently. 'No,' he replied, 'I haven't been offered one.'

Depp nodded his head. 'Good,' he said. 'Let me make my movie. Then if you don't like it, you can come beat me up.'

McDonald acquiesced to the request but has declined to see the film, and so has never been in a position to take its director up on his offer. Not that he had any need; there were soon to be plenty of others only too willing do it for him.

'I came about the job.'

*The blue eyes of the heavy young man sitting with his feet
propped on the desk first studied Rafael's eyes, then scanned
Rafael's thin body.*
'Why?'
Rafael shrugged and looked away.
GREGORY MCDONALD, *THE BRAVE* (1991)

The Brave offered Depp the opportunity to work with Marlon
Brando again. Having got to know Brando on *Don Juan
DeMarco* and then been reacquainted with him during the deba-
cle of *Divine Rapture*, Depp still had the great man's phone number. He had thought to offer him the pivotal role of McCarthy, but
the character required some enlargement to make it worthy of
consideration, let alone their prospective star's ever-expanding
girth. To this end, Depp and his brother reconstituted and expanded upon two key sequences, at the beginning and the very end of
the film, to accommodate the potential change in the casting.
Depp had discussed the project with Brando but had fought shy
of asking him outright, for fear of rejection; he need not have worried: Brando offered to play the part off his own bat, and to waive
his fee in the process.

Twenty-two years before, Marlon Brando had won his second
Oscar for his performance as Don Vito Corleone in Francis
Coppola's *The Godfather* (his first had come in 1955 for *On the
Waterfront*) and his on-screen appearances since then had been
few and far between. For every *Last Tango in Paris* there was a
Superman; for every *Apocalypse Now*, an *Island of Lost Souls*.
Critics in general were all too aware of the predilection for honourable artistic failure in which Brando indulged; as a result, his
presence in a film was rarely treated with neutrality: invariably it
augured either something very good or something very, very bad,
so particular was he about the roles that he chose to accept and
so eccentric could be his taste with regard to those which did
appeal. Brando had now offered to participate in *The Brave* and
Depp accepted gratefully, but in doing so, he had set his sights on

an albatross whose powers were capable of sinking the entire ship without trace.

> I regard death as now a sort of necessary metamorphosis.
> Perhaps the more painful the death, the more...
> Well, it's a kind of refinement. You know in some ways,
> Raphael, I feel a kinship with you... that we are of the
> same mind. Watching painful death can be a great
> inspiration for those who are not dying, so that they
> can see how brave we can be when it's time to go. It is
> the final measure of bravery to stand up to death. An
> exquisite anguish.
> Marlon Brando (McCarthy), The Brave (1996)

With Brando on board, the film underwent something of a transformation in retrospect. The great actor remoulded the role of McCarthy, eschewing all references to the character's original motivation as a purveyor of snuff movies (despite the adjacent presence of a torture chair and a camera as he delivers his maiden speech), and created instead a unique cameo of a man trapped in a twilight of unspecified mental anguish, who finds some form of sadomasochistic catharsis through experiencing the ultimate dread by proxy; he establishes an explicit psychic bond with Raphael, but refers only implicitly to the real reason for their unholy alliance: 'You know, it's always really insulting to put a price on life, but if we have to render unto Caesar the things that are Caesar's and render unto God the things that are God's, then I'd say $50,000.'

Brando's McCarthy is on a par with his Colonel Kurtz in *Apocalypse Now*: strange, intense and ethereal, some of which can be put down to the fact that much of his dialogue is ad-libbed (and soliloquised from his own familial experiences) and some because he had developed the habit of having his lines read to him through an earpiece before he uttered them. The net effect is to produce a character in polar opposition to the scripted

McCarthy (who in the novel is little more than a Mafia thug): a mystical and oddly sympathetic messenger of death, whose oblique philosophical musings shift the film onto a higher plane. Brando invests the man with an entire résumé, without uttering a single word to the effect or having anything to work with beyond the immediate requirements of the plot. Small wonder that Depp was entranced by the performance to the degree that he eventually allowed it to send his film teetering out of control. 'You don't direct Marlon Brando,' he stated. 'With him, I feel like a student facing a great teacher. I have total confidence in him.'

It is a captivating star-turn, to be sure, but it had little or nothing to do with *The Brave* as it initially was designed and had now been shot. As Brando's scenes were the last to be filmed (in an abandoned warehouse in downtown Los Angeles), this change of tack presented Depp with something of a dilemma; in essence, it had made a mockery of the ending in which McCarthy's actions were meant to have precipitated an exchange with Raphael which, in turn, was to have provided him with an 'out'. But a violent conclusion no longer seemed feasible. The pair went into a huddle to try to reach a compromise, and Brando's scheduled time on-set went from two days to six, but no solution was forthcoming. So it would remain.

The Brave opens on what Hollywood terms a 'possessory credit': 'A Film by Johnny Depp' looms enigmatically onto the screen after which the film's star lists himself third in the cast. An evocative and sometimes disturbingly discordant score by Iggy Pop sets the tone for what is to follow: a thoughtful muse on the human condition, filled with colour and rhythm, hardship and pain, and played at the slow and sombre tempo of a New Orleans funeral march.

Depp's direction runs the gamut from the professionally inventive, through to the tediously expedient (too many interminable tracking shots) and virginally self-indulgent, but the film as a whole has a resonant quality which rewards repeated viewing. It is by no means a tyro work; on the contrary, it is richly atmospheric and often transcends the material from which it weaves its strange magic. In addition to Brando, Depp found room for his old *Jump Street* buddy Frederic Forrest in the cast, but the former Coppola protégé had lost both his looks and his pizzazz since his days in Chapel, and his role here is little more than token. Depp's own performance as the 'three-time loser – habitual' (as Larry demarcates him) is quite stunning, particularly given the fact that he was directing himself. One is aware of his every thought and emotion, so expressive is his face, even in repose. Raphael is far and away Johnny Depp's best performance to date; if the character lacks something, it is any trace of the back story which ostensibly has him as an alcoholic ex-jailbird and petty criminal. In the film, that has to be taken as read, for the sainted Depp betrays little evidence of such a sordid past.

The Brave is a strange mix of nightmare and nocturne. If a film reflects its maker, as auteur theorists like to claim, then Johnny Depp is a creature of vivid extremes. 'What we have here is a little bit of shadow-play,' Brando says at the start. What we have here is a dark and disturbed psychopathology, but married to a poetic imagination capable of great flights of romanticism and transcendent moments of lyrical beauty. Of course, Depp pulls in influences from wherever he can find them. The pacing is that of Jarmusch, the moments of humour and surrealism those of Kusturica, and the entrance of Marlon Brando into the torture chamber echoes the coming of the mad monster in any number of horror films, but *The Mystery of the Wax Museum* would be a strong contender. (He even cheekily pinches a line for Larry which comes straight out of the mouth of Christopher Walken's Smitty in *Nick of Time*: 'I'm really a nice guy, when you get to know me.') The tale's contemplative elements – of which there are many – are all Depp's own, however. As is the soul of *The Brave*.

Besides the films of Jarmusch or Kusturica, the most striking influence on *The Brave* is that of director David Lynch, especially the implied violence and nightmarish coterie of hoods from his dark thriller *Blue Velvet* (1986). Lynchian motifs feature throughout, from Raphael's initial encounter with McCarthy's infernal bureaucrat – an ultra-creepy turn by Marshall Bell – in an ominous warehouse straight out of Alan Parker's *Angel Heart*, through the shuddersome torture chair perched high on its symbolic altar, to Larry's subsequent Mephistophelean persecution of Raphael and the mystical graffito which the latter sees scrawled on walls at intervals. These hellish allusions are more resonant in the film as a whole than its occasional allegorical nods to the suffering of Christ, such as the wound which Larry inflicts on the palm of Raphael's hand, or a brief shot of him stumbling under the weight of a 'cross' of water pitchers. So redolent is the atmosphere of doom which pervades the piece that it almost justifies Depp's last-minute imposition of a more fatalistic finale: Luciferian contracts cannot be revoked, no matter how sincere the penitence of their signatories. 'See you in the movies, Tonto,' Larry jocularly affirms.

> Larry: Mr McCarthy sent me out here to check on you. Thought you might be getting cold feet. My advice to you is: don't.
> Raphael: I'll be there.
> Larry: It's my function to make sure you are.
> Raphael: I said I'll be there.
> Larry: Well, that's good. 'Cause unless you plan on putting that pretty little wife and kids of yours on a plane to fucking Bora-Bora, not to mention old gimp Dad and whoever else you may care for out here in this shit-hole, I'm going to find 'em. And then I'm going to kill 'em... and then I'm going to fuck 'em... and then I'm going to eat 'em...
> The Brave (1996)

(The parting threat in this exchange was derived by the Depps from what the bounty hunter Wilson was alleged to have done to his parents in Jim Jarmusch's *Dead Man*.)

This undertow of good and evil battling it out on an Old Testament plane in Death Valley is further evoked during Raphael's introduction to McCarthy. 'My God,' the old man exclaims in surprise, as though recognising the sacrificial victim who stands meekly before him, but refuses to elaborate the reaction. The enigmatic exchange remains unexplained. (In Christian tradition, Raphael is an 'angel of healing'.) That such elements required fuller exploration than Depp was able to give them is clear, but *The Brave*'s financial backers pressured him to prepare a cut for screening at the 1997 Cannes Film Festival. In his haste to complete, he altered the climax with Brando and reverted to that of the novel, in an expedient montage of cross-cuts which sewed together pre-existent footage, partly to comply but mostly because he had grown frustrated with the whole process of editing: 'I hate seeing myself on the screen: I get the feeling of seeing by turns my father and my mother.' The good ship *Brave* was in danger of having been spoiled for a ha'p'orth of tar, but Depp was exhausted. 'I never imagined how difficult it would be to act and direct at the same time. It requires two opposite attitudes: when you direct, you have to be able to control everything down to the last detail. When you act, you have to forget everything, even lose control of yourself. It's hard to go from one to the other.' Whether he had succeeded or failed would now be for the critics to decide. Like Raphael in the film's final cut, he was to find himself damned for his pains, in any event.

> Tomorrow morning, father, I'm going to walk into a room and some men are going to kill me. They're going to torture me, and then they're going to kill me. And for this service, I'll be paid – my family will be paid $50,000. Which isn't enough, really, but it might be just enough to get everybody out of here forever.
>
> Raphael (Johnny Depp), The Brave (1996)

The novel's Rafael is a stupid drunk Indian – so stupid that he not only allows himself to be exploited literally to death but comes to see it as affirmative action, and willingly engages with those who plan to kill him and then rip him off. (The last page of the story reveals the contract to be completely bogus.) McDonald left it to his readers to make the connection to the evils of the capitalist system, and avoided all the obvious dramatic devices which might have helped to convince swing voters along the way. In this respect, the book is an abstract, lacking in a point of focus for the reader. Depp's script alters that (as well as the spelling of Rafael) by making Raphael fully aware of the course of action that he is about to take but thinking of it as an act of desperation. Thus, the focus is shifted from the ills of society in general to the plight of a single individual at the end of his tether. This gave the drama two possible endings, whereas the novel could only allow for one: Raphael could submit and die, or fight and survive.

Depp had resolved this classic dichotomy to his own satisfaction prior to the shooting, and in true Hollywood style: Raphael would see the light during his 'last days', and the light would open his eyes to the truth. That was the plan, but 'the best-laid schemes of mice and men...'

'I'd say that 70 per cent of what we've shot wasn't written like that in the script,' Depp told *Studio* magazine when the production wrapped. That 70 per cent had included the ending, but even the revised version failed to find its way into the completed film.

Until its nihilistic last scene, the whole mood of *The Brave* is one of redemption, rather than sacrifice. There is much in the film that echoes Brando's Western masterpiece, *One-Eyed Jacks* (1960), on which its star had inherited the director's chair from a disgruntled Stanley Kubrick (as did Kirk Douglas on *Spartacus*). In *One-Eyed Jacks*, Brando plays an outlaw named Rio, who is betrayed by a duplicitous partner after a bank robbery. Years later, 'Dad' (Karl Malden) has used the proceeds of the robbery to turn legitimate and now represents the law in the town of Monterey. After a series of reversals and humiliations, including a public whipping and the smashing of his gun-hand with a rifle-butt, Rio rehabilitates himself and takes his revenge on his erstwhile friend, killing him in a shoot-out. What *The Brave* shares with *One-Eyed Jacks* is its leisurely pace and loving interaction with landscape (as well as a single, sudden eruption of brutal violence), but more than that, it shares the notion of rite of passage which is absent from both the original script and the novel on which it was based; it is easy to see the initial appeal for Depp in the physical and psychological masochism of Raphael's plight, but it is tantalising to speculate that Brando's influence on the production might have extended beyond his few moments on-screen and persuaded his director to recast the film as moral fable, instead of a dialectic about despair. Brando's Rio and Depp's Raphael have much in common: both are driven by an all-consuming passion and are prepared to sacrifice themselves to that single end, but both are redeemed by a renewed sense of purpose and find true meaning to life in the love of others. At least, Rio does. But Raphael was meant to also.

There are clues in *The Brave* which point to its intended ending: when McCarthy reaches into his desk drawer to fetch Raphael's advance, he first pushes a revolver out of his way – the same revolver which was to have been used by Raphael at the climax to shoot his tormentor but which in the extant print is now anomalous. But of more significance is the exchange between Raphael and his son, after his wife has been assaulted by his dope-peddling brother, Luis. In a heart-rending performance by Cody Lawrence, Frankie apologises to his father for not having been able to prevent the attack, given that with Raphael absent, he considered himself the 'man of the house'. It is clear at this point, from Depp's extraordinary ability to convey his innermost thoughts in his eyes, that Raphael realises his family need *him* more than they need the money, especially when their ramshackle home is about to be torn down around their heads. It is here that he finds the truth and resolves not to go through with his plan. He goes to the warehouse as intended, even giving Father Stratton the contract in case things go wrong, but now he intends to tell McCarthy that he is not going through with their deal.

Unfortunately, things did not work out quite that way. Brando and Depp could not agree on a suitable ending and, under pressure to complete, Depp wrapped his film without resolution, reverting it to the ending of the novel as a way out of the impasse. (The extant climax, in which shots of the shanty town being demolished are intercut with scenes of Raphael going to his fate and overlaid by glimpses of McCarthy culled from shots taken during the epilogue, was clearly contrived in the cutting-room, makes no sense, and was to blame for the film's eventual critical mauling.) But novel and film were set on a different course to begin with, of which Depp might have been more aware had he read it. McDonald's story is a polemic about the treatment of the underclass, specifically but not exclusively Native Americans; Depp's film is about one man's desire to provide for his family. Much has been written on *The Brave* which points to its motif of self-sacrifice, and the Christ-like allusions which it embraces to that end. But what purpose is served by Raphael's death if no one is saved? As the film stands, his death is a futile gesture, not even certain to guarantee the beneficiaries the balance of the 50 grand, as he would not be around to conclude the transaction. No – it was never meant to be thus.

The Brave is incomplete and fatally flawed, but it is a magnificent mistake all the same. The passion of its creator burns in its every frame. It is a work of great beauty, both inside and out, which deserves to be rediscovered, if no longer recut. If only Depp had not deferred to Brando so, or had found a way around his mentor's objections, his debut as a director could have been greeted by cheers instead of cries of derision. As things stand, it is still a movie of considerable grandeur, which plumbs the depths of the soul but also soars to the heights of the spirit. A great film, certainly, and it represented Depp's coming of age as an actor and as an artist. From here on in, he could walk tall with the best of them-even though his elevation was not immediately apparent to many, and the world at large was to take seven more years to catch on.

Johnny Depp had kept in irregular touch with Hunter S Thompson since that first meeting at Aspen more than two years earlier had led to him and Moss being invited back to Owl Farm for Budweiser, and an impromptu shotgun session on Thompson's private firing range. A party in Thompson's honour in New York in November therefore included them among the guests and later the following month, Depp gave a reading from *Fear and Loathing in Las Vegas* in front of a 2,000-strong audience at a tribute concert for the author, which was held at the Memorial Auditorium in his hometown of Louisville. The grand finale of the evening was a performance of 'My Old Kentucky Home', during which Warren Zevon played piano and Depp played slide guitar. But there was no mention of the prospective film of *Fear and Loathing* at either venue, any more than there had been six months before, when Thompson had performed a monologue at Depp's Viper Room.

If Kate Moss's public appearances on the arm of Johnny Depp seemed confined to parties, film premieres, fashion shows and charity gigs, then the opportunity for a timely photo shoot to once more prove their 'togetherness' arose on 28 February 1997, with the premiere of *Donnie Brasco*. It was only three months since *Nick of Time* had been given less than a warm welcome in theatres and with pressure building on him to deliver a print of *The Brave* to Cannes in time for the Festival, Depp was atypically on edge. He need not have worried; the balance of critical opinion on *Donnie Brasco* was to find in his favour. 'Depp moves through the film with a brand-new hard-boiled grace to give it heat, and a more familiar conscience-stricken sensitivity to keep it interesting,' wrote Janet Maslin in the *New York Times*. 'Despite the Mafia theme (we've been there) and the casting of Al Pacino as a mobster (boy, has this godfather ever been there), *Donnie Brasco* is one terrific movie … Depp digs deeply into his role, finding sweetness and unsettling stealth in this agent who chooses to work undercover. The delicate balance of Depp's performance ranks him with the acting elite', said Peter Travers in *Rolling Stone*. 'A bit overlong, [Brasco's] story on-screen doesn't have the sweep of *GoodFellas* or the grandeur of *The Godfather*, but this ironic last gasp of the genre is a compelling examination of honour, betrayal and trust,' agreed Jane Sumner of the *Dallas*

Morning News. 'The true soul of the New York mob is portrayed in *Donnie Brasco*, a first-class Mafia thriller that is also in its way a love story – perhaps director Mike Newell's best', confirmed the *San Francisco Chronicle*'s Mike La Salle.

Perhaps predictably, the *Sun-Times*'s Roger Ebert stood outside the crowd: '*Donnie Brasco* is frustrating, because it's literate, smartly made and maybe only a couple of scenes away from greatness … There's a beautiful epiphany when Depp shows us Brasco realising that he takes better care of his mob "family" than of his own family. The problem is that the movie does exactly the same thing.' The film went on eventually to turn a small profit – $42 million against a stated budget of $35 million – which was at least on the right side of the line for a change, though not really reflective of the consensus among the national critics. Nor was there any real competition in the week in question, in the commercial sense, at any rate: David Lynch's *Lost Highway* also opened on 28 February, leaving reviewers thoroughly perplexed and a gaping hole of some $7 million in its profit-and-loss account.

Increasingly, it was becoming a numbers game. *Donnie Brasco* did make a profit, but it was the first film of Depp's out of his last seven to do so. If ever he wanted to direct again, then he would have to do much better than that to stand any chance of raising the necessary capital.

At the beginning of April, Depp received another telephone call out of the blue, but it was not from Thompson; it was from Allen Ginsberg, who had called to tell him that he was dying. Depp was severely shaken, and he promised Ginsberg that he would fly out to New York to see him for what was probably the last time, just as soon as he could. He never made it. Ginsberg died in his apartment in East Village on 5 April from a heart attack brought about by liver cancer. Depp paid his own tribute in *Rolling Stone*'s 'Book of the Beats': 'Ginsberg was a great man, like his old pals,' he wrote, 'who had paved the way for Many, and many more to come.'

The Brave had its inaugural screening in competition at the 50th International Film Festival du Cannes at 8.30 am on the morning of Saturday 10 May. The reception that was accorded the film was 'mixed' to say the least, and word soon spread that Johnny Depp's *magnum opus* had been booed off the screen. Cannes thrives on controversy, and controversy was what *The Brave* brought to it – as well as the opportunity to rub an upstart star's nose in the dirt. *Screen* called *The Brave* 'narratively inept and dramatically empty' while in *Variety*, Godfrey Cheshire wrote that it was 'a turgid and unbelievable neo-Western' before going on to complain that 'Johnny Depp offers further proof that Hollywood stars who attempt to extend their range are apt to exceed it. In this case, the main fault lies with the writing. Lacking both a realistic grounding and compelling internal momentum, *The Brave* wastes its handsome mounting and capable cast on a plodding tale that eludes either psychological or allegorical sense'. Then he delivered the knockout blow: 'Overlong and unexciting, it will be a tough sell in all areas except epicentres of Depp devotion.'

Cheshire showed himself to be more perceptive when it came to the anomaly that had been thrown up by the film's last-minute revision, however: 'Even given the premise's waftiness, little is done to develop it in logical dramatic ways. If a man sold his own suicide to benefit his family, would he not face a crisis over whether death might hurt his loved ones more than poverty ever could? Not in *The Brave*, where basic human emotions stand little chance against the script's laboured contrivances.' Still, this was damning stuff, and at a festival which many of the critics present decried as 'the dullest in living memory', it made the headlines.

'I've never felt anything quite like that before,' Depp said later of the experience. 'It's like you're walking into battle. I've walked up the steps before, the carpet or whatever, as an actor. But you walk up as a filmmaker, you're so exposed. You feel that there's at least two or three snipers in trees somewhere, that are going to take a pot shot at you and get you.' In truth, there had been an entire army of them. Sentence was passed by Lisa Schwarzbaum in *Entertainment Weekly*: life! 'With any luck, it will never be released and nobody will ever have to see it, and I mean that for him as well as the audience.' Its director was crestfallen: 'I was cutting the film with the Cannes Film Festival in mind,' he said. 'It's not a proper motivation. If I'd had more time to edit the movie, it would have been a different film.'

The coveted Palm d'Or was eventually shared by films from Iran and Japan, both of which concerned themselves with suicide. Despite having shared the billing with Depp in *Dead Man*, John Hurt protested the inclusion of *The Brave* in the competition line-up, citing the fact of its stars being present as the only justification for its entry in a Festival where famous names were conspicuous by their absence; Hurt, it seems, was still smarting over the treatment meted out to him by the producers of *Divine Rapture*.

Depp did not take the critical hammering well, a situation that was exacerbated by having to tolerate it with Kate Moss by his side throughout. 'It was such an attack – such a vicious, vindictive move for my throat and parts below. They really went for me, all out, so it was kind of difficult to avoid,' he said. 'I definitely felt they'd written the reviews before they saw the film. They don't want you to think. They don't want to even begin to think that you might have some semblance of a brain, some shreds of creativity inside you. They don't want that. They prefer a puppet.'

Depp's film had cost $7 million to make, a large amount of which had come out of his own pocket. After its hostile reception at Cannes, *The Brave* was denied a US opening (a situation that remains unchanged to this day) and so was unable even to compete with *Arizona Dream* for the title of his least successful movie ever.

Commenting on the 'snuff movie' element of the plot, Depp ventured: 'I thought it sort of paralleled what happened to the American Indians one hundred or more years ago. US troops and government officials such as 19th-century President Andrew Jackson – the one featured on the $20 bill – were 'murderers' who conducted acts of genocide. Now people turn a blind eye as the 20th-century survivors often live in miserable conditions. A lot of people live exactly as these people do, or some in conditions that are much worse. So the American Dream – I don't think it exists at all. I think it's propaganda.'

Whether he was subconsciously alluding to the role in his next film for which he was currently preparing and ignoring, for the moment, the fact that he was himself a product of the very 'Dream' which he now chose to castigate, his cinematic chance for an all-out assault on the American Dream was waiting just around the corner, under the zany eye of Python collaborator Terry Gilliam.

In due course, Depp tried to put a brave face on things: 'One of the most important things I learned in the couple of times I worked with Marlon Brando is that it's okay to have a ball. It's okay to have fun and fuck up because, after all, it's only a film.' But he had commemorated the occasion by hastily adding another tattoo – 'The Brave' – to his right forearm.

I'm with you in Rockland
in my dreams you walk dripping from a sea-journey on the highway across America in tears to the door of my cottage in the Western night
ALLEN GINSBERG, 'HOWL' (1956)

Depp's cinematic career was becoming polarised: from the self-consciously arty extremes of *Dead Man* and *The Brave* to the conspicuously commercial overtures of *Nick of Time* (from the director of *Saturday Night Fever*) and *Donnie Brasco* (from the director of *Four Weddings and a Funeral*). Not only his career, but his life as well. Right from the start of his relationship with Kate Moss, the tabloids had portrayed it as a torrid on-off affair, typified by public spats, high-profile exhibitions of togetherness and long periods of separation in between. In celebrity circles, there is rarely smoke without fire and behind the publicists' spin, the unalloyed facts of a fractious and temperamental teaming had begun to speak for themselves: the pair had put on a public display of unity for the Cannes premiere of *The Brave* in May but, according to the *New York Post*, they had needed to rent separate villas to do so. By June, the *Sun* had had enough of the innuendo and had decided to go for broke: 'Supermodel Kate Moss has finally split with Hollywood hell-raiser Johnny Depp' ran its headline, which sparked follow-up stories in other newspapers on both sides of the Atlantic. 'Moss wants to continue to date Depp, but Depp isn't into open relationships,' *People* qualified, while the *Post* spoke of Moss two-timing Depp with Tarka Cordell, the musician son of Moody Blues producer Denny Cordell. *New York* magazine added its tuppence-worth to the gossip with 'According to fashion-world insiders, Kate has told friends that she called it quits with the hot-tempered heart-throb last week because they were having too many fights' and, on *El-Gossip*, Janet Charlton spoke of the pair taking a sabbatical while Depp worked to improve *The Brave*. In fact, Depp had given up all hopes for *The Brave* (which after its critical mauling at Cannes was thought to be beyond commercial redemption, in any event) and had begun instead to immerse himself in a project which he felt might bridge the growing gap in his film work between art and commerce.

While he was still editing *The Brave*, Depp had at last been approached to play the lead in a screen adaptation of *Fear and Loathing in Las Vegas*, the semi-autobiographical account of an acid-trip to Las Vegas in 1971, by the same Hunter S Thompson who had coined its title phrase in relation to the Kennedy assassination in 1963. Depp's explosive encounter with the literary wild-man during that Christmas in Aspen had finally paid off.

Thompson's *Fear and Loathing* was the literary culmination of his fractious friendship with an excitable Chicano (Mexican-American) civil rights lawyer named Oscar Zeta Acosta, known affectionately as 'the Brown Buffalo'. The two had known each other since 1967 but, in 1971, Thompson was working on a story about the death of journalist Ruben Salazar at the hands of the Los Angeles police during an anti-war demonstration in the east of the city. (Salazar was hit in the head with a tear-gas canister fired at point-blank range.) Acosta was active on the same case, and the paranoid Thompson, who had himself been pummelled by police during rioting at the 1968 Democratic Convention in Chicago, suggested to Acosta that he should join him on an assignment to Las Vegas to cover the 'Mint 400' motorcycle race. Both men were activists and acid-heads, though not necessarily in that order. The rest became gonzo history, if not quite the real thing: a bilious blend of fact and fantasy, wistful-thinking and unreliable reminiscence, and all of it paraded before the reader in a self-serving, high-octane haze of hallucinogenic imagery and scatological prose.

In fact, Thompson and Acosta undertook two such trips into what the subtitle of the book called the 'savage heart of the American Dream', one that covered the off-road race and a second, more satirical stab at a District Attorneys' convention; Thompson combined these for the sake of narrative clarity. 'I wrote the book as an experiment, trying to teach myself how to write cinematically,' Thompson later explained. 'But I forgot the interior monologues and the hallucinations.' Readers of the book might dispute the second of these so-called omissions.

Thompson had employed an alias ('Raoul Duke') when the piece was first serialised in *Rolling Stone*, as he was then in the process of applying for White House press affiliation in the run-up to the 1972 presidential election. By the time of its publication in book form, he had received his accreditation; despite this, the character names in *Fear and Loathing in Las Vegas* were left as Duke and Gonzo, instead of Thompson and Acosta.

> The race was definitely underway. I'd witnessed the start, I was sure of that much. But what now? – What comes next?
>
> Raoul Duke (Johnny Depp), Fear and Loathing in Las Vegas (1997)

When Depp signed up to the project, *Fear and Loathing in Las Vegas* was to be directed by Alex Cox, the 32-year-old Liverpool-born director of *Repo Man* (1984) and *Sid & Nancy* (a fiction-alised account of the murderous affair between Sex Pistol Sid Vicious and his girlfriend Nancy Spungen, made in 1986), who was primarily known to British television viewers for his sardonic introductions to several series of 'cult' movies on late-night BBC2 in *Moviedrome*. The script for the film had been written by Cox's collaborator (and later wife) Tod Davies, and she and Cox met with Thompson at his Aspen retreat to discuss their more cartoonish approach to the book. As meetings go, it was not good; in fact, it could hardly have been worse: Thompson threw them out of the house. 'It's a classic example of how not to work, as a director, with writers,' he recalled. 'First, [Cox] hated football – he refused to watch football. And then I cooked really good sausage, which I prize, and he disdained that: vegetarian. Here in my house comes this adder, this asp. And he just persisted to insult and soil the best parts of the book. It's a miracle I didn't fucking stab him with a fork.' (The episode was captured in its entirety by documentary filmmaker Wayne Ewing, who incorporated it into his *Breakfast With Hunter*, in which Depp is featured and which belatedly saw release in 2003.)

Exit Cox and Davies; enter Terry Gilliam of the Monty Python troupe, *Life of Brian* (1979), *Brazil* (1985) and a dozen other satirical flights of fantasy, and *his* collaborator Tony Grisoni. Gilliam and Grisoni wrote a new screenplay in ten days, which met with Thompson's approval, although Davies and Cox retained partial screen credit after arbitration by the Writers' Guild of America. (Gilliam resigned the Guild and publicly burned his membership card when an initial hearing denied him any credit at all.) Shooting on the film was originally due to have begun in April 1997 but, with all the upheavals, the start date was pushed back to June. Then July. *Fear and Loathing* finally got underway on 3 August.

Meanwhile, Depp had ingratiated himself into Thompson's basement at Owl Farm for the purposes of observation and character study, as he had done with Joe Pistone. 'Johnny was like some kind of vampire,' Gilliam told *Elle*'s Elizabeth McCracken.

'Each time he'd come back with more of Hunter's clothes and things. He was stealing Hunter's soul, really, secretly, which Hunter was apparently quite happy to go along with.' But Depp did more than bunk with Thompson, he also followed him around (including acting as his 'roadie' on a book tour of San Francisco), 'watching his mannerisms, the way he rocked back and forth, the way he talked, his expressions. It's weird with Hunter,' he said at the time. 'It's more sort of watching the way he thinks. You can see the wheels turning and you can see an idea coming. That was really the key for me because he's thinking constantly. He's very, very quick and there are no lulls.' The man himself was more sanguine: 'He worries too much,' Thompson said. 'He couldn't possibly do an accurate job. He's too short.'

Whatever genius Hunter Thompson had once possessed was much in remission by the time that Depp met up with him. Depp was his usual indulgent self when it came to the literary icons whom he had revered from his youth; the less reverent Alex Cox had been more abrasive: 'His head is just one big bucket of alcohol,' he declared. 'Even though he has all these pilgrims and admirers going over to tell him how great he is, the guy needed to check into a hospital. He's an alcoholic, and he needs to get better.' Terry Gilliam steered a middle course on the writer, acknowledging Thompson's erstwhile talent and place in American letters but pragmatic when it came to the question of what the years of drugs and booze had evidently done to him and how involved he wanted him to be in the making of his film: 'Hunter was on the end of the phone quite a bit,' he said. 'The most useful thing was that Johnny spent a lot of time with him and basically stole a lot of his clothing and his car, which were then used in the movie!'

As Duke's troglodytic travelling companion Dr Gonzo, Puerto Rican Benicio Del Toro was less respectful of the (long-dead) source when it came to modelling his character, and he had no qualms about turning him into something of a walking drugs laboratory. The 30-year-old Del Toro was on familiar territory, having played numerous drugs barons in the past, in addition to popping up as a heavy in movies as disparate as *Licence to Kill* (1989) and *The Usual Suspects* (1995). He was also coincidentally the son of a lawyer and had trained as a Method actor under Stella Adler. Depp's way with Thompson had been more than method, however. 'He's not like a Method actor,' Gilliam said. 'Osmosis is what he uses.'

As had been the case with Ed Wood's smile, Depp's repertoire of Thompson mannerisms and affectations began to creep into promotional interviews for *Fear and Loathing in Las Vegas*, such as when the private diaries which he had kept throughout most of his career came suddenly to be referred to as 'brain vomit'. 'You put so much of them into your system, it's like there's residue when you're done,' he said. 'It took me a while to stop being Hunter.'

Terry Gilliam's most recent feature had been the commercially successful *Twelve Monkeys*, starring Bruce Willis, so with his name attached to *Fear and Loathing in Las Vegas*, the budget for the independently produced (but Universal-released) Rhino film had risen from a modest $5 million to a stately $18.5. This elevated the project onto an altogether different plane from that which originally had been envisaged by Davies and Cox. 'With Gilliam directing, we'll see the bats,' Cox notioned dismissively, and in reference to the book's opening scene. He was proved to be correct. The trouble was, we were to see little else besides.

BLACK SCREEN.
A desert wind moans sadly. From somewhere within the wind comes the tinkly, syrupy sweet sounds of the Lennon Sisters singing 'My Favourite Things'. A series of sepia images of anti-war protests from the mid-sixties appear one after another on the screen.
In the violently scrawled style of Ralph Steadman, the title FEAR AND LOATHING IN LAS VEGAS splashes onto the screen. A beat, and then it runs down and off revealing:
 TITLE: 'He who makes a beast of himself
 Gets rid of the pain

Of being a Man.' – Dr Johnson

The VOICE of HUNTER S THOMPSON – aka RAOUL DUKE:

Duke (V/O): We were somewhere around Barstow on the edge of the desert when the drugs began to take hold.

from the screenplay of Fear and Loathing in Las Vegas (1997)

If the character of Donnie Brasco had been a hero in the guise of a villain, then Raoul Duke (aka Hunter Thompson) was both, at one and the same time: hero to the counter-culturalists to whom he represented free-thinking radicalism; villain to conservatives who damned him as a thinly veiled advertisement for the liberalisation of drugs.

OK. The plot. Raoul Duke is a sports journalist and dope fiend who is despatched to Las Vegas in the company of his equally addled lawyer Dr Gonzo to cover the $50,000 'Mint 400' motorcycle race. Faced with the gaudy excesses of the 'American Dream' for real, they retreat increasingly to the cover of their hotel suite and unbridled indulgence in illegal substances until the difference between dream and reality blurs into invisibility. Whoa. Mishap and mayhem are the result, punctuated by occasional flashes of socio-political comment: Vegas and Vietnam are crazier than anything that their frazzled brains can conjure up from the narcotics. Cool. Sounds neat, yeah? Should make required viewing with that Python guy mixing the meds; a no-brainer. Sweet Jesus! What are these things? Bats?

Gilliam and Grisoni's script is effectively a collage of Thompson's novel and unarguably a faithful adaptation because of that. It is incisive in extracting not only all of the key sequences from the book but its most important philosophical passages, as well. These are conveyed in a voice-over narration from Depp which apes Thompson's first-person narrative.

As always with Gilliam's films, there is much rib-tickling hilarity to be savoured and black humour to be reflected upon. One standout, which is a compression of separate incidents in the novel, has Duke tripping on some adrenochrome in the foreground while Gonzo grapples with an invisible opponent behind him in an attempt to convince the girl to whom he is talking on the phone that a fight has erupted in the room. But there is simply no getting away from the fact that the novel is a qualified argument in favour of drugs. What was considered tolerable in the cultural climate of the 1970s had become anathema to the majority of media commentators by the 1990s and, while the screen version of *Fear and Loathing in Las Vegas* is not so much pro-drugs as it is anti-hypocrisy, it was to find itself vilified on release, with some US television networks refusing to carry ads for the movie in prime time.

In an unhappy reflection of the book itself, Gilliam was both the right and the wrong man to direct the film. Right, inasmuch as his warped, psychedelic visual sense is nearer in tone to the sheer craziness that permeates the printed page than anyone else could have achieved; wrong, because he finds it more difficult than Thompson did to cut through that craziness and deliver a salient lesson at the finish. Watching *Fear and Loathing in Las Vegas* is like being waylaid in the street by a one-man band wearing a clown's outfit, who then attempts to deliver a lecture on global warming above a din of his own making.

Thompson's novel is a paean to the 'hippie dream', but beneath his self-aggrandising prose and scattershot style is a serious commentary about the loss of innocence which he perceived to have taken place in American society through its ever-deeper involvement in the Vietnam War. 'You've got to remember,' he told the film's director, 'we were serious people. I was a serious journalist; he was a serious lawyer. And this book was only one weekend.' (It was two, in fact.) Gilliam gives due weight to this in the film, with shots inserted from newsreel footage and one late-entry scene of Duke watching the war on TV, but he spends more time watching clips from Universal's 1955 *Tarantula*. And there lies the rub. Film is a visual medium, and Gilliam is a director of great visual intensity. In adapting the book's gonzo idiom into a linear structure for the screen, many of these voice-overs are juxtaposed on scenes of drug-induced delirium, with the result that their point is often lost. *Fear and Loathing in Las Vegas* is a film which demands to be watched through once, then watched again immediately afterwards, so that the overwhelming impact of its drug scenes becomes more muted through familiarity. Like the onset of sobriety, only then does it become clear that Gilliam not only had a handle on his film but the measure of Hunter Thompson, as well. In many ways, the visual excess for which Gilliam is known and for which *Fear and Loathing* offers ample opportunity, is the movie's undoing. The socio-political sub-text of the novel is utterly swamped by the arbitrary antics of Duke and Gonzo, and while it is possible to catch a passing glimpse of Thompson's nostalgia for a lost dream that never was, that, too, is largely submerged by a succession of sequences which wallow increasingly in the depths of degradation to which these two bombed-out bozos sink. A subsequent viewing shows up an altogether different argument and Gilliam's corrective to Thompson's thesis is ultimately revealed, like air molecules during an acid trip.

Gilliam does little to make the consequences of drug use appear attractive. The opposite, in fact: he uses every means at his disposal to highlight the results of addiction as unattractively as possible, even thrusting his lens down a toilet bowl as Gonzo lets rip with the seafood contents of his over-distended stomach. A hotel suite which is callously defaced in Thompson's novel is comprehensively destroyed by the time that Gilliam has finished with it, and the implicit threat of violence from people who no longer have any intellectual control of their faculties is always bubbling just below the surface spin, at first in comedic encounters like that with a naive young hitch-hiker (Tobey Maguire, famous nowadays as *Spiderman*) but later, terrifyingly real in the film's most powerful sequence in a run-down diner.

Two sequences in particular are specifically deployed to point up the paradox at the heart of Thompson's book. The first is a flashback to a San Francisco disco *circa* 1965, in which Grace Slick and the Jefferson Airplane anachronistically crank out

'Somebody to Love' (not released on disc until 1967, although the band was formed two years earlier) while Depp's Raoul Duke stumbles upon his alter ego in the shape of the real Hunter Thompson seated at table, a glass of Chivas Regal in hand. This terrifically evocative and technically tight vignette of acid haze and lazy days of 'love and peace' beautifully illustrates the 'wave' speech from the novel that Depp had rendered at the tribute concert for Thompson on the previous December, and it magically realises the false dawn on which the author's nostalgic meanderings are predicated. The second is a highly charged encounter with a mouthy waitress (Ellen Barkin), which positively reeks of menace. It comes near the end of the film (although not the novel): Duke and Gonzo are seated by themselves in a late-night diner when Gonzo passes a note to the lone waitress which poses the question, 'Back Door Beauty?' Stung by the innuendo, the waitress calls him a 'spic pimp' and demands that they leave. Gonzo pulls out his Gerber Mini-Magnum – a hunting knife – and taps it threateningly on the counter, sending the woman into paroxysms of fear. He negotiates a price for a lemon meringue pie, shoves five dollars down the front of her blouse, and exits the diner. After some reflection, Duke follows suit. That is all there is to it. But this edgy encounter is Gilliam's corrective to Thompson's acid-coloured advocacy of drug-culture, and it makes the point of *Fear and Loathing in Las Vegas*: junkies may on occasion be funny and anarchic, but they are dangerous as well. Duke says it all with his eyes as he watches the actions of his friend and the effect that they have on his victim; his wordless response speaks volumes. (It's worth recalling at this point that Depp's mother was a waitress.) The laughter dies on the lips; the air of devil-may-care is no more; the fun-house has closed its doors. In this one scene is Brian Jones and Janis Joplin, the Stones at Altamont – even the Manson gang. It is the dystopian reality of the hippie ideal, stripped of romantic aura and the selective memory of hazy days in Haight-Ashbury. The Dream was over.

> One of the things you learn after years of dealing with
> drug people is that you can turn your back on a person,
> but never turn your back on a drug – especially when it's
> waving a razor-sharp hunting-knife in your eye.
>
> Raoul Duke (Johnny Depp), Fear and Loathing in Las Vegas (1997)
>
> (In adapting this line, Gilliam and Grisoni unfortunately saw fit
> to delete Thompson's trenchant observation that to the drug
> person, 'everything is serious'.)

This single sequence literalises the undertow of the novel, in which Thompson is strident in railing against the illusory certainties of the drug-culture, while contrarily clinging to its ethos. Also expertly evoked is the all-pervasive paranoia of the addict, and the latent sense of danger which lies in wait for the unwitting after one pill too many, or one too few. But for all Gilliam's obvious comprehension of the subject in question, he does not do enough, in the final analysis, to counteract the cumulative effect of all the clowning around.

(Gilliam chose to end his film with a scene in which Duke is offered the 'granddaughter' of the owner in his Hardware Barn. In a world where everything is for sale, he instinctively adopts the pose of a district attorney from the convention that he has just attended, frightening the man away. In doing so, he becomes the very thing which he despises the most: repressive authority. Realising his mistake, he slinks back to his car and pops open a capsule of amyl-nitrate to blot out the memory. The scene was cut from the release print.)

Thompson's employment of Vegas materialism as a metaphor for the American Dream was weak to begin with; it does not take copious quantities of LSD to comprehend the hollow sham at the atavistic heart of Nevada's most famous temple to greed, and the film finds it as difficult as Thompson does in the book to exaggerate its Moloch-like excess into pertinent parable, even through the distorting lens of hallucinogens. On the other side of the philosophical coin are the drugs, here assumed to represent personal freedom. The problem with Thompson's novel, aside from its obvious flaw of appearing to condone and condemn its thematic preoccupation at one and the same time, is that it offers no substantive alternative to the situation to which regretfully it alludes in its most sober passage, and neither does Gilliam's film:

We are all wired into a survival trip now. No more of the speed that fuelled the Sixties. Uppers are going out of style. This was the fatal flaw in Tim Leary's trip. He crashed around America selling 'consciousness expansion' without ever giving a thought to the grim meat-hook realities that were lying in wait for all the people who took him too seriously. After West Point and the Priesthood, LSD must have seemed entirely logical to him ... but there is not much satisfaction in knowing that he blew It very badly for himself, because he took too many others down with him.

Not that they didn't deserve it: No Doubt they all Got What Was Coming To Them. All those pathetically eager acid freaks who thought they could buy Peace and Understanding for three bucks a hit. But their loss and failure is ours, too. What Leary took down with him was the central illusion of a whole life-style that he helped to create ... and a generation of permanent cripples, failed seekers, who never understood the essential old-mystic fallacy of the Acid Culture: the desperate assumption that somebody-at least some force-is tending that Light at the end of the tunnel.

Drug-use was never intended to be an end in itself, in other words-but a means to that end. And if Leary fucked up, then Thompson fucked up too. These lines, which are employed pretty much verbatim in Gilliam and Grisoni's script, must have played particularly ironically with Depp, given the fact that the aforementioned Leary was godfather to his former fiancée.

Depp's bald-headed, bow-legged, bug-eyed Duke is Thompson to the life, a caricature of a man who is really a caricature of himself, and his many months of painstaking study paid off in spades. It stands in the same league as his Ed Wood: a brilliant impersonation of the genie that can be summoned up from a bottle of Chivas Regal. 'Hunter was the deepest I've ever got into a character,' he noted. 'I really wanted to get him down right.' Del Toro's turn, if anything, is even more convincing in its drug-ravaged depravity, but in his quest for quasi-realism, the actor loses many a pertinent line to incomprehensibility, and thus he exacerbates the superficial sense of pointlessness which pervades the piece.

The period is well captured, from Duke and Gonzo's arrival in Las Vegas to the vocal vibe of Tom Jones, to the antiquated anti-drugs documentary that is shown at the DA's convention: 'Know your dope fiend. Your life may depend upon it! You will not be able to see his eyes because of Tea-shades, but his knuckles will be white from inner tension and his pants will be crusted with semen from constantly jacking-off when he can't find a rape victim'. If it lacks in this regard, it is only in the breadth of the predominately West Coast soundtrack, but copyright issues had proved inhibiting.

Nicola Pecorini's cinematography is stunning in its depiction of the eye-popping neon-glitz and horde of high-rolling human flotsam that encouraged Thompson to opine about Vegas that 'This was not a good town for psychedelic drugs. Reality itself is too twisted' – although a visual gag on 'lounge lizards' stretches metaphor a little too far. Gilliam's own predilection for quirky cameo is satisfied by two non-Thompson interludes, featuring Gary Busey as a lonely Highway Patrolman and Christopher Meloni as a worm of a hotel clerk who is given his chance to 'turn' when confronted by an obstreperous police chief with a late reservation.

That Duke is rarely seen in reporting mode in the film can partly be forgiven in light of the theory behind gonzo journalism, whose purpose was to capture an *impression* of a scene, or the impressions of the *observer* of a scene, even if those impressions were entirely unrelated to the scene in question; thus occasionally he is shown wielding a gun-mike in his attempts to capture the moment before him, or tapping vainly at the keys of his portable typewriter as though he were trying to type his name backwards. ('All play and no work makes Duke a dull boy.') But such cavalier contempt for the processes involved in producing a work like *Fear and Loathing* militates against the value of the very source from which the movie springs; Thompson may not have turned in an article about the Mint 400 road-race, but he did produce a 70,000 word essay on his recollections of the trip which, for all its exercises in fantasy, tends to negate the notion that he was out of his brains for the whole of the time. Only in its final few frames does the film bow to any such possibility.

Thompson's 'gonzo' journalism was more carefully crafted than he often liked to make out, although initially he confessed to having been influenced by William Faulkner. His editors may have been driven to print up his scribbled notes and garbled faxes verbatim, due to his terminal inability to hit deadlines (or even care, for that matter) but the subtly disciplined product of this journalistic so-called anarchy could only have come from someone with a shrewd bent for wry observation and a natural way with words. The notion of writing 'on the run' was largely a con, meticulously enshrined in legend by its practitioner, but *Fear and Loathing in Las Vegas* is still a compelling read and a work of considerable literary worth. No such notion finds its way into Gilliam's film.

Even in 1997, *Fear and Loathing in Las Vegas* was at least two decades out of time. Had a film of Thompson's novel been made when its point was still relevant, it might have been one of the greatest cult movies of them all, with Alex Cox singing its praises on *Moviedrome*. As it stands, that accolade is justified by its manic style and unique subject-matter, but no longer by its outmoded message. If 'the medium is the message', as Marshall McLuhan once decreed it to be, then Gilliam's film triumphs on all fronts. But McLuhan's diktat was as wrong-headed in its overview of counter-culture as Thompson is in his.

In his years with Kate Moss, Johnny Depp's social life had become almost as hectic as that depicted in *Fear and Loathing in Las Vegas*. Her catwalk commitments meant that one or other of them often had to jet halfway around the world, just so that they could be together for a short while. It had been recipe for disaster, and now that disaster was looming. Moss, for one, had already found a way to deal with the pressures involved, but it entailed an habitual intake of champagne, vodka and pot. After nearly a decade at the top of her profession, the strain was starting to take its toll. As was the alcohol.

By December, it was Oscar season, and the publicists at TriStar distributed tissue-boxes which played Depp's 'fuhgedaboudit' speech from *Donnie Brasco* as a promotional gimmick to journalists. In the event, the film caught a cold and found itself nominated for but a single Oscar, that for Best Adapted Screenplay. It lost out to Matt Damon and Ben Affleck's script for *Good Will Hunting*, a film which Depp had been offered and turned down earlier in the year. Be that as it may, he had another project lined up for the end of January which promised a much bigger pay-day. Moss's capitalist sentiments had begun to rub off on him, and their jet-setting lifestyle had whetted an appetite for more entrepreneurial activity. As his relations with Anthony Fox at the Viper Room had shown no signs of improvement, he and Jenco had clandestinely formed a subsidiary company called Trouser Trumpet, Inc., in which they had registered the Viper Room trademarks and merchandising rights with a view to franchising. The idea had been inspired by the success of Planet Hollywood, the burger-chain fronted and partly co-owned by Sylvester Stallone, Arnold Schwarzenegger and Bruce Willis. Depp had had talks with Planet Hollywood President Brian Woods about his participating in the business, but the idea had come to naught; instead, he joined with fellow celebrities Mick Hucknell, Sean Penn and John Malkovich in the purchase of a small restaurant-bar at 31 rue Marboeuf on the Champs-Elysées in Paris, which they named 'Man Ray', after the Philadelphia-born surrealist photographer Emmanuel Radnitsky, who had based himself in the city between the wars.

Prior to embarking on his new film, the science fiction nature of which already was causing raised eyebrows among his fans, Depp joined Moss in New York on Friday 16 January 1998, to celebrate her 24th birthday. The pair started out their evening by attending a performance of the Rolling Stones' *Bridges to Babylon* concert at Madison Square Gardens, in company with Uma Thurman and Ethan Hawke, but they ended it in Stones' guitarist Ronnie Wood's suite at the Palace Hotel, where they partied till the early hours. The following morning, Moss grabbed a commercial flight to Kingston, Jamaica, from where she hired a helicopter to fly her to Chris Blackwell's Strawberry Hill hideaway and the opening of his Aveda spa. Four hours later, she was back in New York. 'She looked like she'd been through Hell,' Blackwell said, 'but I was impressed that she kept her word and decided to show.' The previous evening, the Stones had kicked off their obligatory encore with a soulful rendition of 'You Can't Always Get What You Want'. Kate Moss had everything that she could ever have wanted, except the simple ability to get along with a man that she loved. In that one particular, Hell was exactly what she was now going through.

After the party, the New York *Daily News* had reported that she and Depp 'appeared to be back together'. Appearances can be deceiving, however, and the *News* had found itself alone in its assumptions. To most other observers of these things, the end was imminent.

Depp's publicists fought tooth-and-nail to contain the rumours. It is embarrassing enough to lose a girl under any circumstance, but to do so in the full glare of the world's media is nothing short of traumatic. His love affair with Moss may not yet officially have been over, but director Gilliam effectively confirmed its crumbling status at the time when he spoke subsequently of Depp's temper tantrums on the periphery of the *Fear and Loathing in Las Vegas* set: 'I've never seen him lose his temper, but I've seen the results of it,' he recalled. 'Broken doors and things. I've seen his trailer roughed up a bit. It's interesting, because he's a gentleman and he's very considerate and very intelligent and if people take advantage of it, or if things build up, they have to find an outlet-like a piece of furniture. He wouldn't do it to a human being; he'll take it out on inanimate things. Like paparazzi.'

Until now, Depp had acted for some of the most respected directors in the business. Among the illustrious names with whom he had worked were Oliver Stone, Tim Burton, John Badham, Mike Newell and Terry Gilliam, all of whom would have featured on anyone's current A-list. But any such list compiled in 1998 was unlikely to have included writer-director Rand Ravich, whose previous film was an 18-minute Sundance short called *Oink* (1995). Nevertheless, it was he in whom Depp had decided to place his trust after being sent the script for a science fiction thriller called *The Astronaut's Wife*. Ravich, and an $8 million pay cheque.

> Spencer: I'm resigning from the service.
> Jillian: Because of what happened?
> Spencer: I'm done up there, Jillian. I got an offer, from an
> aerospace firm, an executive position. Lots of money,
> Jillian, bucket loads.
> from the screenplay of The Astronaut's Wife (1998)

Astronaut Spencer Armacost (Depp) returns to earth from a shuttle mission during which he and a fellow crew member had lost contact with NASA for two minutes. Something about him has changed, but it remains relatively unnoticed until his wife finds herself pregnant with twins. When Armacost is offered a job in the aerospace industry to help design an 'airborne electronic warfare platform', Jillian (Charlize Theron) is confronted by Reese (Joe Morton), an ex-NASA technician, who confirms her worst fears: 'He's not your husband, Mrs Armacost – he's not!' Pretty soon, Reese winds up dead, as does Jillian's sister. Not knowing what to believe, she tries to abort the babies but is prevented from doing so by Armacost, with whom they now have telepathic communication. Jillian manages eventually to lay a trap for Armacost and electrocute him, but the alien entity inside of him transfers to her own body as he dies. Much later, she has changed her name and remarried; she has twin sons, both of whom want to be pilots like their (step)father. Seen it all before? You betcha.

Critical opinion subsequently decreed *The Astronaut's Wife* to be a cross between *Alien* and *Rosemary's Baby* (1968). In the handling of its theme, it certainly recalls the second, but its story of an astronaut whose body and mind are taken over by an organism from outer space derives much further back than *Alien* – to *The Quatermass Experiment*, in fact, a BBC TV serial written by Nigel Kneale in 1953 and adapted into a feature by Britain's Hammer Films in 1955. In *The Quatermass Experiment*, an astronaut returns to earth having unwittingly been infected by an invisible force while in orbit; his behaviour appears increasingly strange to those around him until, at last, he begins to mutate into a cosmic creature capable of ingesting the entire planet. The threat of alien invasion was a staple ingredient of the paranoid science fiction films of the cold war 1950s, but the post-cold war 1990s demanded a more internalised psychology. The revision which writer-director Rand Ravich applied to Kneale's original premise is revealed in the title of the film, which switches its focus to the impact that the elusive transformation has on the protagonist's wife – especially when the threat is transferred to her own body in the form of her impregnation with 'alien' seed. Another analogy would be a remake of *Rosemary's Baby* in which John Cassavetes' husband-figure was the centre of attention, rather than Mia Farrow's possessed Rosemary.

Film theorists might be tempted to praise the ambiguity that results as a layered approach to the text, which allows *The Astronaut's Wife* to be read as the pre-natal delusions of a suburban housewife. The audience at large is more likely to consider it a leaden way with narrative, and Charlize Theron's increasingly hysterical attitude towards the marginally unsettling behaviour of her 'all-American hero' of a husband rapidly becomes grating in the extreme.

The extraordinary thing about Depp's acting ability is how effectively he is able to convey a character's inner thoughts through his eyes. It is a rare talent, and one which sets him apart from his peers. Slight of stature – well short of six feet – he was never going to be a physical actor; on the contrary, he is a passive, reactive player, who relies (often to the benefit of his co-stars) on a range of facial expressions and big, expressive eyes. And that is the problem with Depp's role in *The Astronaut's Wife*. The eyes are dead.

Depp plays astronaut Spencer Armacost as a swaggering Southern 'good ol' boy' in a blond crew-cut; he is cold, cocksure and intellectually unattractive from the off, which denies the tale its built-in sub-text of Jillian watching in growing bewilderment as the man she loves turns into someone she no longer recognises. Thus *The Astronaut's Wife* fails to register even on a simple metaphorical level. Redneck impersonation notwithstanding, what Depp is actually enacting in *The Astronaut's Wife* is the role of the typical Hollywood movie star; what he might have come to had he not stood his ground and gone his own way. His chameleon-like ability to embody the persona of a character astonishes all the more in how far Armacost is removed from his Hunter Thompson of only months before. In Depp's hard-eyed, chisel-jawed astronaut can be seen the ruins of another lost love affair. Moss on the rocks. Can't live with you; can't live without you. It is not a pretty sight.

> Have you noticed any change in your husband's behaviour since the shuttle-mission, because I've been going through these files and there are some... peculiarities.
> Sherman Reese (Joe Morton), The Astronaut's Wife (1998)

Like Armacost himself, the film is essentially an empty vessel. It sets up a premise which it cannot sustain, due to a consummate lack of imagination. Take away the technical trickery and Jillian's anguish about the nature of the life inside of her and what do we have: an alien plot to conquer earth through the 'transmission' into all human life of an extraterrestrial intelligence, by means of the advanced warplane which Armacost has been hired to help build. (That is more than can be garnered from the film itself, as most of the explanation in the script was jettisoned during shooting, especially in the final scenes.) They used to churn these things out at a rate of one a week in the 1950s. And they did them better. *Invasion of the Body Snatchers*, this is not. *The Astronaut's Wife* is nothing more than a B-movie writ large and the lowest point of Depp's career so far. It is almost as though he had lost interest. With Moss gone in all-but press release and his own hopes for a baby put on hold as a result, perhaps he had. His input into the film as a whole appears to have been limited to the inclusion of The Sex Pistols' version of 'My Way' into his character's NASA leaving party.

Violence is kept to an absolute minimum, further emasculating the supposed threat. The only murder shown on-screen is that of Jillian's sister Nan (Clea DuVall), whom Armacost somehow 'whispers' to death. His true character is finally revealed in his angry reaction to his wife when he discovers her attempting a chemical abortion in order to thwart the alien's plan of planetary domination: he slaps her hard and allows her to tumble down the stairs of their home. As these actions would more likely have induced the abortion than Jillian's pills, the question is begged as to why he might have been concerned over her intentions in the first place. 'I don't know what I'd do if anything ever happened to you and the babies,' he smarms, after standing by and watched as she took the fall. Samantha Eggar's strange German obstetrician also adds an unwelcome edge of Nazi eugenics to the piece.

With Depp playing an out-and-out villain, his slip into callous brutality at his wife's expense is neither shocking nor surprising; for Jekyll and Hyde to work effectively, there must first have been a Jekyll. The climax contrives to have Jillian kill her erstwhile husband in the most preposterous electrocution sequence that it is possible to imagine. She saturates the entire flat in water to the degree that it even seeps through the ceiling, and then plugs in a radio that is floating nearby. Armacost fries, but she avoids his fate simply by sitting prettily on a stool and raising her feet off the floor. The alien still manages to body-hop into her at the critical moment (in the manner of *Fallen, et al.*), so it seems that she was not that smart, after all.

The intense performance which Theron affords to the piece is far more than it is worth. The viewer does indeed end up feeling sorry for this particular astronaut's wife, but not because she is an incubator for alien babies.

Depp was to be saved from an ignominy worse than death by the timely intervention of the man responsible for the very *Rosemary's Baby* to which Rand Ravich's film owed so much, but his credibility in the meanwhile was taking something of a knock.

> Thou shalt not be such a shit you don't know you are one.
> William S Burroughs, The Source (1998)

When he had finished with *The Astronaut's Wife*, Depp was finally given the chance to play Jack Kerouac – not in a screen version of *On the Road*, as he always had wanted to do, but in a documentary about the history and influence of the Beats, called *The Source*. Along with John Turturro and Dennis Hopper as Allen Ginsberg and William S Burroughs respectively, Depp contributed a cameo to the piece in the guise of Kerouac, reading extracts from *On the Road*. In doing so, he shared a stage with some of the best-known 'rebels' of the age, including Dean, Brando, Dylan, Leary, the *Grateful Dead*'s Jerry Garcia and, of course, Hopper himself.

The three writers are dealt with in order against a congratulatory overview of the movement which their collective muse inspired, and Chuck Workman's film makes good use of an eclectic mix of rare archive material interspersed with contemporary interviews. The result is a collage in sound and vision of the social revolution which came eventually to touch every teenage life during the 1960s. *The Source* is not without fault: its conspicuously informal structure makes it difficult to determine at times whether the emphasis is on the writers themselves or the Beat generation in general (some might say that they were indistinguishable anyway), and Workman loses focus by switching continually between these twin tracks. An example is the way in which footage of Kerouac and Ginsberg is featured even after the individual segments have informed the viewer of their respective deaths; another is a piece to-camera by Timothy Leary in which he reflects on his advocacy of drugs in the 1960s, before a voice-over reveals that the story has now reached the end of the 1950s. A jarring musical note is also struck in the anachronistic use of the Stones' 'Sympathy for the Devil' in the section on Burroughs.

For all of its 'kickwriting' incongruities, *The Source* contains many interesting insights into the birth of Beat. Extracts from television shows of the late 1950s, as well as satirical digs from the likes of Alfred Hitchcock, Steve Martin and Bob Hope, aptly convey the air of incoherence on both sides of the divide about the meaning of a movement which no one among its founders was actually aware of having started – a situation not helped by the fact that they seemed to be singularly incapable of expressing themselves and their far-reaching ideas in any way other than through poetry or prose. There clearly was as much dissonance as dissidence in the early years, and Kerouac's subsequent alcoholism, uncomfortably evoked through archive footage of some incomprehensible performances on patronising chat shows, did little to improve matters. Most striking is the impression that the originators of Beat were an odd triumvirate of social outcasts, from the morose Kerouac and the intense Ginsberg to the psychologically disturbed Burroughs. Yet each had something to say about freedom and the human spirit, which struck a chord in the consciousness of a generation and has resonated philosophically ever since.

Workman's narrative is at its most incisive when it shows how mainstream society sought to tame the rebellion in its midst by satirising it; put simply, the Beat writers were made to look like fools, which resulted in Kerouac's descent into drink, and

Ginsberg and Burroughs making a temporary exit to the more sympathetic climes of Paris and Tangiers. But the best critique of the conformist America of Lyndon Johnson, which the resultant counter-culture movement later sought to challenge, is delivered by Chicago Mayor Richard Daley, in true Sam Goldwyn style, when he attempts to defend the brutal tactics of his city's police by telling a news crew, 'The policeman isn't there to create disorder; the policeman is there to preserve disorder.'

Depp pops up more frequently in the 88-minute film than do his acting compatriots, largely because of Kerouac's loftier position in the hierarchy of Beatdom. Sporting the crew-cut that he had adopted for *The Astronaut's Wife*, he acts out the last of his soliloquies in a tweed coat that had once belonged to Kerouac himself. He had bought the coat for $10,000 in 1990, as part of a job-lot that comprised two coats, a hat and a letter from Kerouac to Neal Cassady, all of which cost him $35,000 in total. The sale had been arranged through Alan Horowitz, Winona Ryder's father, and he had purchased the items from book-dealer Jeffrey Weinberg, who acquired them in turn from the executor of Kerouac's bitterly contested estate. The sale had been conducted in good faith all round, but a question mark remains to this day as to whether the memorabilia was actually available for sale to begin with.

The Source was released in July the following year. The title had been drawn from a remark made by Burroughs, which features in the documentary. 'We're the source,' he says.

> *What is that feeling when you're driving away from people and they recede on the plain till you see their specks dispersing? — it's the too-huge world vaulting us, and it's good-by. But we lean forward to the next crazy adventure beneath the skies.*
> JOHNNY DEPP, READING FROM *ON THE ROAD*, *THE SOURCE* (1998)

By April, it was finally over. Finished, done, kaput. Moss and Depp were no more. Official. 'Kate is somebody I care about deeply,' he explained. 'Distance is very difficult when you're trying to maintain a relationship, when you're thousands of miles apart for a lot of time. We still see each other, hang out, talk on the phone. We're close, but I'm not with anybody.' The relationship had lasted a full four years, but it had come to the end of the road.

Fuhgedaboudit.

Gallant to a fault, Depp shouldered the entire blame for the long-predicted break-up: 'I was an horrific pain in the butt to live with. I can be a total moron at times. I let my work get in the way, which made me difficult to get along with.' It echoed uncannily the situation in which he had found himself in *The Astronaut's Wife*. A case of art copying life. 'I got tired of feeling like Dracula,' Moss declared. 'I wanted to see some daylight, and not just at six o'clock in the morning.' The press thought that there was more to it than that: that almost five years of high living had also taken its toll on Depp. 'I want to have children,' he had confessed in an unguarded moment. 'I'd really like to become a parent now, but finding the right woman to share that with is proving difficult.' The staunchly independent, high-earning Moss had clearly not been the right woman, and Depp consoled himself by listening to the gospel Blues of Blind Willie Johnson, among whose legacy of original recordings from the late 1920s lay a personal favourite: 'Keep Your Lamp Trimmed and Burning'.

The couple were 'just good friends' by the time they turned up hand-in-hand at the Cannes Festival in May for the premiere of *Fear and Loathing in Las Vegas*, then again at the opening on 22 May; both occasions were merely for the sake of appearance and neither turned out to be a pleasant experience. The critics were decidedly unimpressed.

Roger Ebert weighed in: 'The result is a horrible mess of a movie, without shape, trajectory or purpose – a one joke movie, if it had one joke … Johnny Depp has been a gifted and inventive actor in films like *Benny and Joon* and *Ed Wood*. Here he's given a character with no nuances, a man whose only variable is the current degree he's out of it … What was he thinking when he made this movie? He was once in trouble for trashing a New York hotel room, just like the heroes of *Fear and Loathing in Las Vegas*. What was that? Research? After River Phoenix died of an overdose outside Depp's club, you wouldn't think Depp would see much humour in this story – but then, of course, there *isn't* much humour in this story.'

Gilliam's film fared little better from a more moderated Stephen Holden in the *New York Times*: 'In refusing to cling to the book's quaint cocksure attitude, the film really has no attitude at all. For all of Thompson's intimations of the failure of the drug culture to save the world, his book still promoted a righteously hip us-against-them agenda in which the Rolling Stones, Buffalo Springfield and Janis Joplin were the cheerleaders for the good guys. And the Las Vegas version of the American dream ... was the enemy. As we all know now, it was never that simple.'

Cold turkey came in the form of Todd McCarthy in *Variety*, however: '*Fear and Loathing in Las Vegas* is a bad trip. Long-gestating adaptation of Hunter S Thompson's hallucinatory 1971 gonzo tome has become an over-elaborate gross-out under Terry Gilliam's direction, a visualisation of a flash-point in the history of trendy pharmaceuticals without a story or detectable point of view. Johnny Depp's impersonation of the Thompson figure is effective up to a point, but it's hard to imagine any segment of the public embracing this off-putting, unrewarding slog through the depths of the drug culture. Beyond whatever draw Depp and Gilliam provide for the opening round, the pic's commercial ride will be a bummer.'

Fear and Loathing premiered in US theatres only two days after Roland Emmerich's $125 million remake of *Godzilla*. 'I hope it makes a noise,' Gilliam had said of it. 'I don't want it to go unnoticed.' It was noticed all right, by a 400-foot-tall prehistoric monster; it got stomped.

The film took a little over $4 million on its opening weekend, and hit its ceiling at a paltry $10 million. 'I'm a master of movies that have life in video,' Del Toro said later. 'They come out, they don't work, and eventually in video everyone goes, "Oh yeah, it's good." Like *Fear and Loathing* which, little by little, has picked up a crowd.'

Leaving aside the modest profit turned by *Donnie Brasco* in its first year of release (though it would go on to take more than $120 million worldwide), Depp had now made nine flops in a row, from *What's Eating Gilbert Grape* to *Fear and Loathing in Las Vegas*. Marlon Brando had advised him that in order to make one artistic movie, an actor should make two commercial ones; he had chosen to ignore that at the time, seeing no need to follow such advice so long as the offers kept coming his way. But things were now beginning to look a little shaky in terms of his ongoing bankability. Johnny Depp was badly in need of a hit if he was to have any chance of holding onto his artistic independence in the future. If the adage about only being as good as one's last success were in any way true, then Depp's last success was looking a long time past.

While Depp had been shooting *The Astronaut's Wife*, two other projects had come and gone. He had been tipped to play Christopher Marlowe opposite Jude Law, in a $12 million film about the Elizabethan playwright's life which was to be produced by Natural Nylon for Alliance Pictures. The film found itself up against two more Marlowe projects, the first of which was *Vainglory* starring Rufus Sewell. Natural Nylon's title was a simple *Marlowe* (despite its unwanted connection to Dashiell Hammett's private detective of similar name), but the most apt of the trio, in terms of Depp's past career, had already been appropriated by the third contender for the Marlowe stakes: *Dead Man in Deptford*. Three proved too much of a crowd, however, and none of these productions were to make it to the screen. One that did was *L.A. Without a Map*, a romantic indie comedy by Mika Kaurismäki, brother of Aki, in which Depp performed a literal 'walk-on'.

There also had been speculation about an acting 'reunion' for Depp and Winona Ryder on Michelangelo Antonioni's *Just to Be Together*, but Ryder's current boyfriend and star of *Good Will*

Hunting, Matt Damon, reportedly put the kibosh on that. The bittersweet re-teaming of Depp and Ryder was therefore not to be, though the project remains on Antonioni's prospectus. Instead, Ryder went into *Girl Interrupted* after a brief cameo for Woody Allen in *Celebrity*.

Not that Depp was left hanging out to dry in the process. During his stay at Cannes, he had been introduced to Roman Polanski, the controversial 63-year-old director of numerous critical and commercial successes, including *Cul-de-sac* (1966) and *Chinatown* (1974), as well as 1968's timeless horror classic: *Rosemary's Baby*. Polanski's last feature film at that point had been the highly acclaimed *Death and the Maiden* (1994), but word was out that he was about to start on another. Interviewed by journalist Jenny Peters for the Australian edition of *GQ*, Depp was asked what was next for him.

'*The Ninth Gate* with Roman Polanski,' Depp informed her.

'Out of the US, I'd guess?' Peters asked, in respect of the fact that there was an outstanding arrest warrant for Polanski on a charge of statutory rape should he ever again set foot inside the United States of America.

'Oh, yeah,' Depp said. 'We'll be in Paris.'

'Is it a thriller?'

'Yeah. It's very interesting,' Depp replied. Then, after a pause. 'Well... a little dark.'

Johnny Depp's Raphael had encountered a metaphorical Devil in *The Brave*, and his Raoul Duke had met an hallucinogenic one in a seedy hotel room in *Fear and Loathing in Las Vegas*, but his next character for the big screen was to come up against the real thing.

FADE TO BLACK

6 ROMANCING THE DARK

FADE IN. PARIS, FRANCE. 1998.
'Who are you?'
'The Devil,' she said. 'The Devil in love.'
And she laughed. The book by Cazotte was on the sideboard, next to the Memoirs of Saint-Helena and some papers. The girl looked at it but didn't touch it. Then she laid one finger on it and looked at Corso.
'Do you believe in the Devil?'
'I'm paid to believe in him. On this job anyway.'
ARTURO PÉREZ-REVERTE, *EL CLUB DUMAS* (1993)

Anything I've done up till 27 May, 1999, was kind of an illusion, existing without living. My daughter – the birth of my daughter – gave me life.
JOHNNY DEPP, SPEAKING IN 1999

IN 1992, Johnny Depp had been forced to pass up the role of Jonathan Harker in Francis Ford Coppola's *Bram Stoker's Dracula*. Early in 1993, his name had been mentioned in connection with the long-deferred film adaptation of Anne Rice's *Interview With the Vampire* (though not in relation to her vampire Lestat, for which hotly contested audition he would have had to stand in a long line behind Rutger Hauer, John Travolta, Mick Jagger, Richard Gere, Jeremy Irons, Daniel Day-Lewis, Rufus Sewell and, of course, Tom Cruise). Depp's career may have been set in motion by *A Nightmare on Elm Street*, but aside from the indirect nod to the genre that was *Ed Wood*, he had otherwise managed to steer clear of the darker side of cinema for more than a dozen years. With the horror film regaining its appeal as the millennium approached, due partly to the supposed mystical significance of the date, it became almost inevitable that Depp would eventually feature in another of his own. In the final few years before that fateful transition, he found himself starring in two of them.

Not that he was especially averse to horror. 'I can remember being totally fascinated with Bela Lugosi and the Dracula films when I was five years old,' Depp told one interviewer. 'And I can remember sitting in class in first grade and drawing pictures of Dracula and Frankenstein. When I was a kid, in about 1968, I was completely and utterly obsessed with a television show called *Dark Shadows*. I wanted to be Barnabas Collins, and I wanted the cane with the wolf's head on it.' But it was rare for the average horror film to attract the kind of filmmaking talent on the other side of the lens for whom Depp might express an affinity. As with all film genres, there are notable exceptions: Tim Burton was one; Roman Polanski, another.

It seems fair to say that *The Astronaut's Wife* might have been categorised as a horror film by some, though its proper classification is science fiction thriller. The true horror film requires an element of the supernatural, not mere lashings of gore, and it was with the supernatural that Depp now sought to concern himself.

1993 had not been a good year for the literary novel – or for much else, come to that. What had begun for Depp in the bitter-sweet spring of *What's Eating Gilbert Grape* and the heartache of parting from Winona Ryder had ended with the death of River Phoenix. The arts in general had fared little better. On one side of the cinematic coin had come *El Mariachi*, Robert Rodriguez's inventive low-budget homage to the Spaghetti Westerns of Sergio Leone, while on the other was the low-common-denominator spectacle of *Jurassic Park* and the fully fledged inauguration of CGI, which was to prove both a blessing and a curse to fantasy films thereafter. *Jurassic Park* had been adapted from the book of the same name by sci-fi populist Michael Crichton; in 1993, he had turned his pen to the sexual politics of *Disclosure*, but that could hardly be counted as literature. The one ray of literary light in an otherwise dull and soundless year had been a novel by Spanish author Arturo Pérez-Reverte called *El club Dumas*, or *The*

Dumas Club as it is was known in its 1996 English translation by Sonia Soto, and from it had come the 'dark' project to which Depp had referred (although two non-fiction works which had stood out from the crowd in the same period – *Before Night Falls* and *Blow* – would soon feature in his oeuvre as well).

Pérez-Reverte's novel is a brilliantly realised literary puzzle, which is designed to play a clever trick on the reader's perception in the same way that its protagonist, rare book-dealer Lucas Corso, is wrong-footed by his own reading of the mysterious events to which he finds himself party in the course of the narrative. Corso is hired by one Varo Borja, the owner of a treatise on demonology called 'The Nine Doors to the Kingdom of Shadows', to seek out the other two copies of the book which are known to exist. At the same time, Corso is trying to authenticate a manuscript which purports to be a missing chapter from Alexandre Dumas' *The Three Musketeers*. These two plots imperceptibly become interwoven, to the extent that Corso thinks himself pursued by devilish agents in the form of well-known characters from Dumas' renowned adventure serial. But straddling these strands is a third, which involves a strange girl who believes that she is one of the angels fallen from Heaven in Lucifer's battle with God; this last supplies the tale with its conclusion, although much of the black-magical chicanery which has preceded it is merely a blind to mask the main plot, the secret of which gives the novel its title.

Despite its evident complexity and reputation as 'difficult' novel, it was *El club Dumas* which Roman Polanski had now chosen to film as *The Ninth Gate*. 'It's all very convoluted, one of those rambling books; enjoyable and literary, with clever observations; very erudite,' Polanski told Cynthia Fuchs. 'The problem was how to make a movie out of it, because at first glance, it really doesn't look like it's possible. We had to abandon a lot of elements, because a movie must be much more rigorous. But I had no hesitation, because I knew it would be fun to do.'

The genesis of *The Ninth Gate* dates back to Cannes 1997, when Depp was in competition with *The Brave* and had met the director during the course of the festival. Polanski had been sent a screenplay by Enrique Urbizu which was based on Pérez-Reverte's novel. He had been intrigued enough to want to read the novel himself and, with regular collaborator John Brownjohn, he had set about redrafting Urbizu's script. 'We did quite extensive work on the script,' he told Caroline Vie. 'The story was very complex and we were obliged to simplify it a lot for the screen version. Even if the avid reader in me is sorry we had to cut parts from the book, I knew as a director that it was unavoidable.'

Essentially, what Polanski and Brownjohn did was to jettison the major thread of the novel, that of the missing chapter from *The Three Musketeers*, and enlarge on the minor, that of 'The Nine Doors'; they then employed the action from the first to provide a narrative for the second. The strange girl was retained, in all her ambiguous, otherworldly glory. Thus their retitled *The Ninth Gate* became a supernatural thriller, in which the renamed Dean Corso is pursued across Europe by Devil-worshippers while he searches for the elusive grimoires. 'I'm not interested at all in witchcraft and demonology, as a philosophy – the Devil makes me laugh,' Polanski said. But the hope was that he would have a different effect on an audience.

He took off his glasses, breathed on the lenses, and set about cleaning them with a very crumpled handkerchief which he pulled out from one of the bottomless pockets of his coat. However fragile the over-sized coat made him appear, with his rodent-like incisors and calm expression, Corso was as solid as a concrete block. His features were sharp and precise, full of angles. They framed alert eyes always ready to express an innocence which was dangerous for anyone who was taken in by it. At times, particularly when still, he seemed slower and more clumsy than he really was. He looked vulnerable and defenceless: barmen gave him an extra drink on the house, men offered him cigarettes, and women wanted to adopt him on the spot. Later, when you realised what had happened, it was

too late to catch him. He was disappearing into the distance,
having notched up another victory.
ARTURO PÉREZ-REVERTE, *EL CLUB DUMAS* (1993)

Polanski had hesitated when it came to considering Depp for
the role of Corso, even though the latter had expressed considerable interest in working with him as a director, no matter what the
subject. When finally Depp was given the script for *The Ninth
Gate*, he promptly set out to persuade Polanski that he was right
for the part. 'He convinced me that age didn't matter that much,'
the director explained. 'I came to understand that people like
Corso tend to mature very young. Their character and reputation
are formed when they're in their thirties.'

To play the shrewd and cynical Corso, Depp adopted a guise of
goatee and glasses, as well as greying his hair a little at the tem-
ples and functioning with a marked economy of movement; all of
Corso's agility is of the mental variety. 'Johnny has an extraordinary and spontaneous way of giving his own rhythm to a character,' Polanski said. 'It seems quite natural for him and you never
feel like he's making any effort whatsoever. His work was brilliant. The Corso that you see on the screen is exactly the one I had
in mind before hiring Johnny.'

The excellent but undervalued Frank Langella was cast as vil-
lain-in-chief Boris Balkan (who is actually the amiable narrator of
the novel, but whose alliterative name was felt more suitable for
the film), a millionaire dealer in antiquarian texts, who hires
Corso to prove the provenance of the pride of his private collection: the arcane text entitled 'The Nine Gates to the Kingdom of
Shadows', which reputedly enables its owner to summon the
Devil himself. The role of the Devil – referred to only as 'The Girl'
in the film's credits – was given to Polanski's wife, the ethereal-
looking Emmanuelle Seigner.

Another actress originally had auditioned for the part: Vanessa
Paradis. The 25-year-old chanteuse of 1988's 'Joe le Taxi' fame,
had been building a new career for herself in films, and she was

presently in Paris shooting the low-budget *La Fille sur le pont* (*The Girl on the Bridge*) for director Patrice Leconte – her first since recovering from the broken leg that she had acquired in a snowmobile accident in Canada five months before. The former nymphet, whom songwriter Serge Gainsbourg had once christened his Lolycéenne (Lolita schoolgirl), was also a successful recording artist and model; ex-boyfriend Lenny Kravitz had produced her last studio album, *Vanessa Paradis*, while, in 1991, she had been paid three million francs by the House of Chanel to become the face of 'Coco' perfume for a controversial but commercially disastrous ad campaign, which had sat her in a gilded cage adorned only with feathers. (Director Jean-Paul Goude was reported to have come up with the idea because she was 'the image of Tweety Pie'.) Paradis may have failed to impress Roman Polanski enough to be cast in *The Ninth Gate*, but she was to have the opposite effect on Johnny Depp.

As Depp and his director dined out amid the marble-and-glass opulence of the exclusive Hotel Costes K, at 81 Avenue Kleber in the heart of Paris, he noticed Paradis seated nearby. He invited her to join them, and a new and beautiful friendship was born. In fact, the two of them had met before, but each had been in the company of another. On this occasion, both of them were free agents. The press-pack was quickly alerted to the news: 'He would come to work shattered sometimes, because the photographers would make his and Vanessa's life miserable,' Polanski recalled. But despite the now-inevitable gauntlet which required to be run by any female on Depp's arm, the blossoming relationship was set to endure.

> BALKAN BUILDING: COLLECTION. INT/NIGHT.
>   Balkan: Ever heard of the 'Delomelanicon'?
>   Corso: Heard of it, yes. A myth, isn't it? Some horrific book reputed to have been written by Satan himself.
>   Balkan: No myth. That book existed. Torchia actually acquired it.

He returns to the window overlooking the sheer drop. Gazing down, he goes on:

Balkan (cont.): The engravings you're now admiring were adapted by Torchia from the 'Delomelanicon'. They're a form of satanic riddle. Correctly interpreted with the aid of the original text and sufficient inside information, they're reputed to conjure up the Prince of Darkness in person.

FROM THE SCREENPLAY OF *THE NINTH GATE* (1998)

The premise of *The Ninth Gate* is conventional enough: Balkan has tried out the invocation which he thought was contained in his copy of 'The Nine Gates' but has failed in his efforts to raise the Devil. Surmising something to be amiss, he hires Corso to find and examine the other two copies, to see if there are discrepancies between them. The story then devolves to Corso's pan-European search for the remaining books, and the resultant game of spot-the-difference as he finds that only *three* out of nine illustrations in each copy are genuine, inasmuch as they are signed 'LCF' – Lucifer himself. But Balkan has followed closely behind, and he now steals the other two books after murdering their owners: his plan is to combine the three sets of genuine woodcuts into an entirety, and make the magic spell complete. His ultimate aim is power, of the kind which only Satan can provide.

The incidentals of this plot are exceedingly convoluted, though. Do try to pay attention...

Corso's search for the various copies of 'The Nine Gates' takes him first to Toledo, where twin brothers named Ceniza reveal the secret of how to spot the genuine engravings. But Liana Telfer (Lina Olin), the leader of a satanic coven called the Order of the Silver Serpent, is also on his tail; Telfer originally was the owner of Balkan's copy of 'The Nine Gates', which Corso carries with him, and she wants it back. Throughout, Corso is helped by a mysterious girl who appears to have supernatural powers. Events come to a head when Balkan gatecrashes a Black Mass and strangles Telfer, who by this time has recovered her own copy. With all three books finally in his possession, Balkan retreats to the Devil's Tower, his castle in Portugal, to invoke his dark master. But the spell goes awry and as Balkan inadvertently sets himself ablaze, Corso delivers a *coup de grâce* by shooting him dead. It transpires that the ninth engraving was a fake engineered by the Cenizas; Corso obtains the real one, and *the Ninth Gate* opens up to him.

> I'm convinced there'll be a third one in here somewhere. Three variations in three copies makes nine. Coincidence- or something more? Maybe Torchia hid the secret of the Ninth Gate in three books, not one.
>
> Dean Corso (Johnny Depp), The Ninth Gate (1998)

The woodcuts which are seen in the film appear in the published version of *El club Dumas*, but they also incorporate some subtle differences. 'I kept part of the illustrations shown in *The Dumas Club*,' Polanski explained. 'But I had the characters' faces altered for some of them, to look a bit like the actors in the film.' Some of this authorial addenda was contributed late in the day, as shooting progressed, and it brings an unwelcome element of confusion into the finished piece. *Balkan* is the killer of three out of the story's four murder victims (the first murder, that of Corso's bookseller buddy, has no logical explanation whatsoever) and confesses as much in the original script, yet the etching that Corso is working on when he is knocked unconscious in the library of Baroness Kessler (owner of the third book), and which depicts that self-same act, shows Telfer's henchman committing the deed. Whether Polanski chose consciously to muddy the waters along the way is a matter of conjecture, but his final cut differs markedly from what he intended prior to shooting. 'I'm starting to see things,' Corso says, early in the proceedings. In the script, it was a casual statement of fact concerning his sudden rash of pursuers but, in the extant film, it assumes an altogether different tenor.

The major alteration comes at the climax, however. The screen-play has only the revelation that the old forgers who put Corso on the track of the Nine Gates had long been dead before he appar-ently spoke to them, and that the Girl was the Devil all along. In other words, there *was* a supernatural element to the story, but Corso only realised it in the closing scene, when the final engrav-ing of the Whore of Babylon sitting astride the seven-headed beast is in his hands and he is startled to note her resemblance to the Girl who has helped him to obtain it. He walks away, his cyn-ical belief system shattered forever.

This rather feeble ending was subject to drastic revision when the film was on the floor: one which brought it more in line with the closing passages of the novel. Corso has sex with the Girl as the Devil's Tower burns behind them, during which her face 'morphs' almost imperceptibly, but quite chillingly, between a demon persona and that of Liana Telfer. The pact is thus sealed, and Corso retrieves the last engraving of the Whore from the Cenizas's bookshop, which is now revealed to have been a front for other agents of the Devil (the original brothers are replaced by two workmen, and all four are played by the same Jóse López Rodero who was also production manager on the film). He returns to the castle and walks through the Ninth Gate in a white-out of light, where the Devil waits to greet him.

Few reviewers were to grasp the significance of this finale, which contributed considerably to the hostile reception which *The Ninth Gate* was later to receive. A cinematic trickster to the last, Polanski made his film too oblique for its own commercial good by removing the scripted reference to Balkan's culpability for the murders (thus positing a number of suspects; there are *no* murders in the novel), and adding ambiguities which encourage an alternative reading of the plot; several scenes now invite the possibility that Corso is himself the Devil, even though this is shown to be erroneous by internal logic. But it provides for a fas-cinating collage of hints and allusions, all the same, and produces an exercise in satanic game-play that turns *The Ninth Gate* into a worthy addition to the *ars diavoli*, as Boris Balkan might have put it.

To remove any doubt about who the Devil actually is in *The Ninth Gate*, the clue was meant to have been the book which the Girl was to have been reading in the lobby of Corso's hotel in Sintra, Portugal. Novel and original screenplay both have this as *The Devil in Love* (*Le Diable amoureux*), a Gothic fantasy by French author Jacques Cazotte, dating from 1772, in which the hero falls in love with the Devil in his *female* form, under the name of Biondetta. ('The truth is that the Devil is very cunning. The truth is that he is not always as ugly as they say.') Polanski substituted Dale Carnegie's much less obvious *How to Make Friends and Influence People* for the film. It won him few admirers.

> There have been men who have been burned alive, or disembowelled, for just a glimpse of what you are about to witness.
> Boris Balkan (Frank Langella), The Ninth Gate (1998)

Contrary to critical expectation, which was still suffused with fond memories of *Rosemary's Baby* more than 30 years before, *The Ninth Gate* is not so much a horror film as an homage to Hitchcock with supernatural overtones. The film has more in common with Polanski's earlier Hitchcockian thriller *Frantic* (1988), starring Harrison Ford and also featuring Seigner, than it does with his adaptation of Ira Levin's seminal satanic novel of 1967, even though the director himself referred to it as a cross between that and his Oscar-winning *Chinatown*. There are other influences as well, as *Se7en* cinematographer Darius Khondji recalled: 'Roman kept reminding me about *Touch of Evil* by Orson Welles. We watched that film together, and we both liked its sense of darkness; we decided that feeling was one side of *The Ninth Gate*.' The other side was exotic location-shooting in Spain, Portugal and France, where Polanski found Balkan's *tour de Diable* in the fourteenth-century Puivert Castle at Aude, in the French Pyrenees. But not New York, because of Polanski's outstanding arrest warrant. The scenes in the Big Apple were all created at the Epinay Studios in Paris, including that of Balkan's library aerie at the top of his personal skyscraper. As Corso examines 'The Nine Gates', Balkan stands before a window that stretches from floor to ceiling and gazes down on the world of men from on high, as did Satan in the Old Testament. 'Don't you get dizzy standing there?' Corso asks him. No reply.

Depp plays Corso with the imperturbability of Cary Grant for the most part, reacting to the disturbing events in which he finds himself embroiled with contained concern and a nice line in dry wit: 'I had thought about it, yes' he says, a faintly hysterical edge to his voice, when asked by the Girl if he would like to gain entry to a house whose owner he has discovered dead in a fishpond. Khondji also had input into the characterisation of Corso: 'I had to take into account that Johnny was playing a character with two sides,' he said. 'We present the Dean Corso character as very ambiguous. He definitely has a dark, cold side, but at the same time there's a side of him we don't know about, so it was a simple decision to half-light him throughout.' Depp turns in a deceptively understated but typically thorough performance as the book world's equivalent of a gun for hire, even if his lack of involvement in the creative side of the endeavour inhibited him from discussing it in his usual voluminous manner when the shooting was over.

There is one aspect of the film which stands out uniquely. An enormous number of process shots were required in post-production, from the early scenes in New York City through to the fiery skies which frame the 'Devil's Tower' at the climax, but *The Ninth Gate* is that rare beast of a fantasy film in that few of them are detectable, so well-integrated are they into the tapestry of the piece as a whole. The most blatant are two brief shots in which the Girl appears to 'fly', and the occasional use of demonic eyes of the now-you-see-it, now-you-don't variety. But even the fact that no less than *two* pairs of two characters in the story are played by the same actor in the same shot (one of whose voices was dubbed by Polanski himself) is likely to pass unnoticed before the eyes of the casual viewer. There is a lesson in this for Hollywood, whose love affair with CGI still shows no signs of dimming. Polanski is story-driven: he sets up projects like a precisian, and he affords the written word as much respect as anything else on-screen – the perfect instrument to film *El club Dumas*.

The Ninth Gate has a nice, old-fashioned feel to it, and is none the worse for that. The pace is measured and stately, as befitting its subject: rare and expensive old books. 'I loved the idea of a book being the hero of a movie,' Polanski said. 'I don't believe it's ever been done before. That's one of the reasons why the script appealed to me.' The plot's reverence for the mystical reputation of the fictitious 'Nine Gates of the Kingdom of Shadows' extended to the director's treatment of it in the film: 'I really considered the book as a whole character,' he continued. 'I designed the pentacle for the cover, and chose its colour and size as I would have done for an actor.' Polanski's single-minded desire to exercise such a measure of control over all elements of a production was not to everyone's taste, however – including that of Johnny Depp.

'It was not an easy film to make. Roman is pretty set in his ways. I'd heard things about his methods but I decided to see for myself,' Depp explained. Polanski's 'methods' were much the same as Alfred Hitchcock's: actors are 'cattle', and should be treated as such. 'Acting is a very unhealthy profession. Actors go mad. Sometimes they are not in contact with themselves,' the director has stated. To make his point more forcefully, he once referred to *Chinatown* star Faye Dunaway (whom Depp had played opposite in *Arizona Dream*) as 'neurotic and argumentative, irritable and unprepared'. 'He didn't tell me how to say my lines,' Depp responded. 'If he had, I'd probably be in some French jail – but he's definitely out there in his own world.' At least Depp finished *The Ninth Gate*, which is more than can be said for John Travolta, who worked with Polanski on *The Double* in 1996. Travolta walked out, which led to him being sued by the film's producers for $50 million; the case was settled out of court.

Having lived in Paris since 1978 after fleeing the USA before his trial on a charge of sex with a minor (but after undergoing psychiatric evaluation in a Federal penitentiary), Polanski shared Depp's distaste of the press – particularly the British tabloids – but not his way of dealing with it. 'He should grow up a little,' he commented. Darius Khondji leaned towards Depp's view of his director, though: 'It's difficult to make him alter his ideas completely, because he has such a measured way of seeing things. He doesn't film things just for aesthetic purposes,' he said of Polanski in *American Cinematographer*. 'You can sometimes get him to change shots a little bit but never drastically, or else you'll make him unhappy!'

Questioned about his recent detours into science fiction and horror, Depp responded by saying, 'I've probably seen *Dracula* one too many times.' If it were not true before, it was by the time that he was finished with *The Ninth Gate*: Depp co-star Frank Langella was still best known for his performance as the count in John Badham's 1979 remake of Universal's vampire classic, and Polanski had nothing but good words to say about him after hiring him from seeing his performance in Adrian Lyne's *Lolita* the previous year: 'Frank is charming and disturbing at the same time,' he said. 'He was a great sport. We almost burned him one time, when his character was on fire. And I love his voice, which was extremely important since he exists in this movie over the telephone, for most of it.'

A notable cameo in the film is provided by Barbara Jefford OBE, as the wheelchair-bound Baroness Kessler, whose particular area of expertise is Old Nick: 'I saw him one day,' she tells Corso. 'I was fifteen years old, and I saw him as plain as I see you now.' *The Ninth Gate* was a welcome return to fear films for Jefford, who is best-known to fans of Hammer Horror for her role as the countess in Jimmy Sangster's *Lust for a Vampire* (1970). If any Hammer connection nevertheless remained somewhat tenuous in *The Ninth Gate*, it was to be much more to the fore in Johnny Depp's next foray into supernatural cinema.

The Girl: What do you plan to do if you see them?
Corso: Probably hide behind you.
The Ninth Gate (1998)

Throughout the production, Depp took solace in the company of Vanessa Paradis. Within a few days of that initial meeting at the Hotel Costes K, the two had become inseparable, and no sooner was shooting complete on *The Ninth Gate* than Paradis found herself pregnant, though official confirmation was not to be forthcoming till later in the year. 'We didn't plan anything,' Depp confessed. 'I don't believe that you have an influence on what happens to you. Life is a ride with someone else behind the wheel.' Nonetheless, he was overjoyed at the possibility that his world could soon be filled with new meaning: 'I've been in love before – less often then the tabloids suggest – but for the first time I found someone who wanted a child with me. Luckily, Vanessa comes from a good family, otherwise I wouldn't have dared to do it. I never learned how to raise a child, I only saw how you don't do it.'

Over the next few months, Depp arranged for Paradis to move back to her parental home, to ensure her a safe and stable pregnancy. 'They say you realise only afterwards that you have been happy, but during Vanessa's pregnancy, I was very consciously very happy,' he purred. By November, he was happier still: he was now due to fly in to Britain's Shepperton Studios to reunite with his cinematic sparring-partner, Tim Burton. Notwithstanding the lack of an official announcement as yet as to the nature of Paradis' delicate condition, news – like 'the dead' in a Bram Stoker novel – travels fast.

In the second week of November, tabloid headlines were full of the fact that Kate Moss had booked herself into the exclusive Priory Hospital at Roehampton, in South West London, for a two-month bout of rehab, at a cost of £300 a day. 'Nervous exhaustion' was given as the reason for her sudden stay, but Moss had previously engaged with Alcoholics Anonymous and, by her own admission, apparently had been drunk more times than she had

With Vanessa Paradis at the premiere of
Sleepy Hollow, November 1999

Ichabod Crane brings technology to bear on the
Headless Horseman in *Sleepy Hollow* (1999)

Depp as Cesar, with Christina Ricci as Susie,
in *The Man Who Cried* (1999)

Roux (Johnny Depp) and Vianne (Juliette Binoche) cosy up
for a cup of hot *Chocolat* (2000)

George Jung (Depp) samples the high life
with Mirtha (Penelope Cruz) in *Blow* (2000)

With Albert and Allen Hughes, on location
for *From Hell* (2000)

Captain Jack Sparrow cuts a memorable
dash in *Pirates of the Caribbean* (2002)

With Keira Knightley and Orlando Bloom in a
publicity shot for *Pirates of the Caribbean* (2002)

Meeting Keith Richards backstage at a Stones
gig in Hollywood, November 2002

Shades of Oedipus: Agent Sands is blind-sided in *Once Upon a Time in Mexico* (2001)

Mort Rainey has words with
himself in *Secret Window* (2003)

J M Barrie (Depp) confers with Charles Frohman
(Dustin Hoffman) in *Finding Neverland* (2002)

A more conservative
Johnny Depp
attends the Venice
Film Festival in
September, 2004

been sober while strutting her high-fashion stuff on the catwalks of the world over the preceding decade. To add insult to psychological injury, her eight-year, £1 million-per-annum contract with Calvin Klein had been dissolved in September. The real reason for her fractious and volatile relationship with Johnny Depp was now somewhat clearer. 'I've been doing a lot of work and too much partying,' Moss told the *Daily Mirror*. 'I wasn't happy with the way my life was going, so I decided to take a step back. I want to be totally responsible for myself, and this is the place where I can get the peace and quiet I need to start the process,' she added, in reference to the Priory. However, the *Mirror* also reported that Moss had been upset by the death from a heroin overdose of fashion photographer Mario Sorrenti, whom she had dated for three years before Depp; in fact, it was Sorrenti's brother Davide who had died, aged 20 – a tragedy which had inspired President Bill Clinton himself to speak out against the culture of 'heroin chic' in the fashion industry.

More than ever convinced that he was at last making the right moves in his life, and pleased to be working with a kindred spirit again after the constrictions of his experience with Polanski, Depp set about preparing for the starring role in Burton's latest effects-laden extravaganza: a big-budget adaptation of 'The Legend of Sleepy Hollow'. 'It's just amazing for me, going back to work with Tim. It's like returning home after a war,' he said, in reference to Polanski. 'He's a dream for an actor. He's not totally rigid.'

The dominant spirit, however, that haunts this enchanted region, and seems to be commander in chief of all the powers of the air, is the apparition of a figure on horseback without a head. It is said by some to be the ghost of a Hessian trooper, whose head had been carried away by a cannonball, in some nameless battle during the revolutionary war, and who is ever and anon seen by the country folk, hurrying along in the gloom of night, as if on the wings of the wind.
WASHINGTON IRVING, 'THE LEGEND OF SLEEPY HOLLOW', *THE SKETCH BOOK OF GEOFFREY CRAYON, GENT.* (1819)

Tim Burton's *Sleepy Hollow* was planned as a $65 million horror spectacular, adapted from a 180-year-old novella by revered American author Washington Irving. For a change, no one in the press corps had to be enlightened about the plot. Everyone in the western world was surely *au fait* with some aspect of Irving's famous tale of a love-struck schoolmaster named Ichabod Crane who is sent scurrying off with his tail between his legs after coming face-to-face with the fearsome Headless Horseman of Sleepy Hollow. Generations of children had grown up having been spoon-fed on the story of Brom Bones and the callous trick that he plays on poor Ichabod to discourage him from paying court to the pretty Katrina Van Tassel. Tim Burton and Johnny Depp certainly were. 'I loved it as a kid,' Depp told Mark Salisbury of the *Guardian*. 'I was probably not too dissimilar to Tim in the sense that I was drawing Frankenstein and Dracula at a very early age – too early. It was very early that I went to this dark... I always loved that image of the Headless Horseman.' And if some details are forgotten (and many forget the most telling detail of all, that the tale is actually concerned with a practical joke), the image of the phantom horseman, riding helter-skelter through the woods of Sleepy Hollow, head in hand, is not. It has become a Gothic icon, fondly recalled at each Hallowe'en by the hollowed-out pumpkin which the cunning Brom had employed in place of a head.

The first screen Ichabod of any real note was a cartoon characterisation of him in a Disney animation of 1949 in which 'The Legend of Sleepy Hollow' formed one half of *The Adventures of Ichabod and Mr Toad*, the remainder of the film being taken up by an adaptation of Kenneth Grahame's *The Wind In the Willows*. The animated version was made in the Golden Age of the Walt Disney Studios – between *Song of the South* and *Cinderella* – and was a faithful rendition of Irving's tale which, by its very nature, lent itself to the Hallowe'en whimsicalities of the studio's 'Silly Symphonies' shorts of the early 1930s, like *The Skeleton Dance* and *Hell's*

Bells (both 1929); an added plus was an evocative voice-over by crooner Bing Crosby. True to form, Disney's Ichabod was a caricatured grotesque, complete with beaked nose and gangling limbs, but even this kept faith with the description of the fastidious schoolmaster which was given by Washington Irving in his story: 'He was tall, but exceedingly lank, with narrow shoulders, long arms and legs, hands that dangled a mile out of his sleeves, feet that might have served for shovels, and his whole frame most loosely hung together. His head was small, and flat on top, with huge ears, large green glassy eyes, and a long snipe nose, so that it looked like a weathercock perched upon his spindle neck, to tell which way the wind blew. To see him striding along the profile of a hill on a windy day, with his clothes bagging and fluttering about him, one might have mistaken him for the genius of famine descending upon the earth, or some scarecrow eloped from a cornfield.'

Presented with such an outlandish creature, Depp suggested to his director that they should follow the Disney route and ply him with prosthetic nose and ears, all suitably elongated. Even Tim Burton was taken aback by the idea of his star being made up to look like Count Orlock in *Nosferatu*. 'Basically, we said no,' Burton explained. 'Although we tried to be respectful of Ichabod's eccentricities, his squeamishness, his sort of odd behaviour.' 'I thought I could wear a nose, and the big ears, and stuff like that,' Depp said. 'The Paramount people weren't very enthusiastic about it.' Instead, a more psychological approach to the character was agreed upon, in place of Depp's preference for a physical one, which nevertheless emphasised his excessive prissiness. Accordingly, Depp immediately thought of Angela Lansbury, veteran star of films like *The Picture of Dorian Gray* and *Samson and Delilah*, and mainstay of television's long-running *Murder She Wrote* during the 1980s: 'I thought of Ichabod as a very delicate, fragile person who was maybe a little *too* in touch with his feminine side, like a frightened little girl,' he said – a concept which encouraged producer Scott Rudin to refer to him on-set as 'Ichabod Crane, *Girl* Detective'. 'He wanted to make Ichabod Crane the first action hero to act like a 13-year-old,' Burton remarked. For good measure, Depp also added a smidgen of actor Roddy McDowell to the androgynously elaborate goulash. 'He's really a transformer,' Burton elaborated. 'He doesn't really care how he looks and he's willing to try anything. It just makes the process exciting and easier for me.'

The original idea for *Sleepy Hollow* had come from Kevin Yagher, the make-up effects artist responsible for two of the *Elm Street* sequels, *Child's Play* and *Tales from the Crypt*, as well as the brother of actor Jeff Yagher, whom Depp had replaced on *21 Jump Street*. Yagher brought in Andrew Kevin Walker, writer of *Se7en*, and a screenplay was commissioned by Scott Rudin and sold to Paramount in 1994. From there, the project had stalled until 1998, when Rudin sent Walker's script to Tim Burton, whose own *Superman Lives* (with Nicolas Cage) had just been cancelled by Warners after a year in pre-production. Burton was in need of a film and he liked the idea, but he thought Walker's take on the story was too dark and lacking in humour; his star agreed with him and Burton, in turn, asked playwright Tom Stoppard to give it a polish.

'The initial script was very good – very solid,' Depp recalled. 'But Tim and I talked about this early on, and we knew we were going to throw in as much humour as possible. There were opportunities that had been missed.' Stoppard dutifully provided them, in the form of comedic interludes which saw Ichabod faint no less than five times during the course of the action, and a more overtly romanticised 'love interest' for Depp and co-star Christina Ricci, whom he had known since she was nine years old, having first met her on the set of *Mermaids* in 1989.

> Burgomaster: There is a town upstate, two days journey to the north in the Hudson Highlands. It is a place called Sleepy Hollow. Have you heard of it?

Crane: I have not.

Burgomaster: An isolated farming community, mainly Dutch, Three persons have been murdered there – all within a fortnight. Each one found with the heads lopped off.

Crane: Lopped off?

Burgomaster: Clean as dandelion-heads, apparently. You will take these experimentations of yours to Sleepy Hollow, and there you will detect the murderer.

Sleepy Hollow (1999)

In Walker's draft(s), Ichabod Crane had been turned from a superstitious schoolmaster into a post-colonial police detective and scientific rationalist, of a kind which was not to be seen in fiction until 50 years after the story was meant to take place (in 1799), when Edgar Allan Poe created Auguste Dupin. He was also transformed into a man of action, in the style of Stoker's Van Helsing, who finds himself pitted against a force of supernatural evil. These two facets of the lead character, combined with the Dracula-like onslaughts of the Horseman and the script's propensity for playing up the fearful murmurings of rhubarbing villagers, had reminded Burton of the Hammer horror films which he had watched in his youth. So it was that he began to think of *Sleepy Hollow* as a kind of 'homage' to Hammer, an idea which was soon perpetuated by his willingness to discuss it as such – even after the film was finished and subsequently deemed to have little in common with the well-known product of Bray Studios.

'One of the reasons I wanted to do this was to capture the beautiful, lurid atmosphere of the old Hammer films,' Burton was quoted as saying in *Cinefex*, before adding a more eclectic mix of influences for *Premiere*'s benefit: 'We really wanted to evoke the spirit of the old Hammer horror films, Vincent Price movies, Roger Corman's work.' Emmanuel Lubezki, his director of photography, surprisingly sought to differ. 'I don't think *Sleepy Hollow* resembles the Hammer films, except in the way it was made. We did a lot of work on sound-stages. The Hammer films were made that way because the filmmakers on those pictures didn't have a lot of money. Our biggest frame of reference was *Black Sunday*,' he informed *American Cinematographer*, citing the stylised chiaroscuro of director Mario Bava's 1960 mono-chrome classic (*La Maschera del demonio*, in its native Italy) as his own model in context. Depp was encouraged to toe the party line and follow his director's lead, as was Christina Ricci. From co-star Michael Gough, whom Burton had persuaded out of retirement to make the film (and who was the one member of the cast other than Hammer habitué Christopher Lee who had actu-ally *worked* for Hammer Films, more than 40 years before), there was only diplomatic silence on the issue, however. 'I think Michael thought I was always laughing at him because of the cos-tume, but I was just looking at him thinking, "He was in *Horrors of the Black Museum* and *Konga* – these are my favourite films!"' Burton told Mark Kermode.

The notion that *Sleepy Hollow* was to be Tim Burton's 'Hammer' film became set in stone with the casting of Christopher Lee as Ichabod's superior, and press interviews were conducted accordingly. When *Empire*'s Simon Braund caught up with Depp on the village set which had been constructed in fields near the town of Marlow in Buckinghamshire, he already had set-tled into promotional mode with the film's Hammer connection high on his agenda: 'Tim gave me a couple of Hammer tapes ini-tially and we talked about the style,' he explained. 'There's a style of acting that's borderline bad, but it's so borderline that it's actu-ally brilliant. I find that very interesting. I think Peter Cushing was a master craftsman, and Christopher Lee definitely is.' This last remark having no doubt been injected because he was now required to act with Lee in the prologue to the story, Depp was moved to expand on his admiration for Hammer's veteran vam-pire to Mark Salisbury in the *Guardian*: 'Christopher Lee is just legendary,' he said. 'He was just so on the money every take. It was inspiring. He's probably had to deal with every petty bullshit thing in life and in this business and he's survived with integrity.

He's a very graceful man – as Vincent was – gracious, humble, wise, a survivor. He's done hundreds and hundreds of films. He's just an amazing presence; an amazing man.' Enough, already. But no, there was more: 'When you're in a scene with the guy and he's leaning down into you, his voice booming, and you look in those eyes – I mean, it's *Dracula*!'

Sleepy Hollow's affinity to Hammer Horror is no more than skin deep. The plot of Walker's take on Washington Irving owes something to Hammer's 1959 version of *The Mummy* (as well as several earlier Universal entries in the same series), where a long-dead creature is revived by the black art of magic and dispatched to murder those who have perpetrated an ancient wrong; the Hessian in *Sleepy Hollow* may sweep all before him with the unstoppability of a juggernaut, sword and axe in either hand, but he is Hammer's Mummy in post-colonial disguise (making it all the more appropriate that Christopher Lee, who had played Kharis the Mummy in the film, should have been cast as the High Constable who despatches Ichabod Crane to Sleepy Hollow to investigate the gory goings-on; typically, Lee complained about the weight of the cloak that he had to wear during shooting). This much, Burton had gleaned from Walker's original but, in spite of his and Depp's insistence on a connection, none of the obvious nods to Hammer which might have been incorporated into the story are anywhere in evidence. Burton's desaturation of the photographic image divorces the film completely from the highly saturated Eastmancolor of Hammer's early horrors, and what tenuous links there are to be found – a character named Van *Ripper* (after Hammer actor Michael Ripper?); Martin Landau's resemblance to Peter Cushing in the film's opening scenes; a fight in a windmill which echoes that at the end of *The Brides of Dracula* – are entirely coincidental: the character of Van Ripper appears in the story; Landau's role was appended to the film after principal photography was complete; while the scene in the windmill, by Burton's own admission, pays lip-service to that at the climax of Universal's 1931 *Frankenstein*, rather than Hammer's *Brides*.

It might have seemed to some like an expedient sales pitch to tie *Sleepy Hollow* to Hammer Horror, but anything more substantive than its vaguely Gothic atmosphere remained dormant in Tim Burton's imagination, or was party to the popular shibboleth that all Gothic must somehow be Hammer Gothic. In fact, the Gothic element in Washington Irving's 'The Legend of Sleepy Hollow' is peculiar to its native land (notwithstanding Irving's Celtic ancestry: his father was a Scot), as American literature had divested itself, through emigration, of the folklore which had fed its European counterpart; the 'Headless Horseman' was one of the first of a new and more indigenous breed of monster, which had to be invented from scratch to infest the nightmares of those who chose to settle in the New World. Irving's Hessian mercenary, whose provenance is dated only as far back as the revolutionary war of 1776, was a spectre possessed of as short a history when the story was written as have Freddy, or Jason, or *Halloween*'s Michael Myers to the cinemagoers of the new millennium. *Sleepy Hollow* is a distinctively American tale, which happened to be shot in the English counties of Buckinghamshire and Middlesex (at Shepperton Studios) with a cast that was mainly comprised of Britons, but Hammer Horror is the last thing to which anyone with a proper Gothic sensibility might justifiably compare it.

> You're a long way from New York, Constable.
> Baltus Van Tassel (Michael Gambon), Sleepy Hollow (1999)

Nevertheless, the notional imposition of a spurious Hammer motif persuaded Tim Burton to invest his *Sleepy Hollow* landscape with an artificial history in kind, as though it were the wilds of Transylvania, where bloodstained deeds spread back a thousand years. Thus he transposes a mock-European vernacular onto a uniquely American idiom where all, in truth, was relatively fresh and new, the itinerant nature of these early communities afforded little time for ghostly legends to develop (as Irving makes plain in the story) and the closest that anyone could come to a sense of supernatural horror was to hollow out a raw pumpkin into the semblance of a skull and place a lighted candle within it. Irving's tale is actually predicated upon the unwillingness of the pragmatic Dutch inhabitants of Sleepy Hollow to indulge in the silly superstitious beliefs to which Ichabod, a native of Connecticut, appears particularly prone, due to his unquestioning acceptance of the idea of an 'invisible world', as set down by Cotton Mather in *A History of New England Witchcraft.* This premise is reversed in the film, in which Ichabod is portrayed as an incredulous man of science, although his 'simple credulity' in the story finds literal outlet in a screenplay which sees fit to supply him with a mother who was a witch, and a father who was, ironically, a witch-finder. (The Puritan father-figure in *Sleepy Hollow* may have been imported into upstate New York directly from nearby Salem, but his personal Iron Maiden is unlikely to have made a similar journey from Nuremburg.)

To Ricci, Lee and Gough was added some stellar support in the shape of Michael Gambon, Ian McDiarmid, Christopher Walken and Miranda Richardson (as the real villain of the piece), as well as Burton regulars Jeffrey Jones and Lisa Marie. 19-year-old Christina Ricci, with a full ten years of film roles already behind her, had so much in common with Johnny Depp that they could almost have been twins: she was also the youngest of four children, and her parents were divorced when she was just 13; she read Dostoevsky, chain-smoked and wore tattoos, as a child, she could not stand the sight of herself. Ricci's father was a psychiatrist whose speciality was so-called 'primal scream' therapy, but he somehow managed to raise a damaged daughter who suffered from anorexia and indulged in bouts of self-harm. She had nevertheless grown up to be as controversial and outspoken as her co-star, in contradiction of the image of vulnerability that went hand-in-hand with her diminutive five-foot frame. Before she came to *Sleepy Hollow*, she had just directed her first film; after she finished with it, Depp was to find himself supporting *her*.

FLASHBACK-AMERICAN BATTLEFIELD (WINTER)-DAY.
The HESSIAN HORSEMAN rides his black steed into a gory,
close-quarters clash, his cloaked uniform adorned with edged
weapons. He cuts down Americans left and right.

> Baltus (VOICE OVER): He rode a giant black steed named
> Daredevil. He was infamous for taking his horse hard into
> battle... Chopping off heads at full gallop.

The HORSEMAN dismounts, hoists a battle axe. With sword
and axe, he annihilates. Blood gushes. Bones crack.

> Baltus (cont'd; VOICE OVER): To look upon him made
> your blood run cold, for he had filed down his teeth to
> sharp points... to add to the ferocity of his appearance.

The HORSEMAN lets out a war-cry. Jagged teeth. Grotesque.

from the screenplay of Sleepy Hollow (1999)

Burton was also right 'on the money' in deducing that a tale about beheading should feature the most convincing (and often blackly humorous) decapitations' ever committed to film, with CGI wizardry enabling most of them to be perpetrated full-frontally and therefore, to all intents and purposes, to the unfortunate actors themselves. The results are stunning, as is the realism of the Horseman himself in 'headless' guise – a blue-screen composite which caused problems for Jim Mitchell of effects house Industrial Light & Magic when it came to scenes of hand-to-hand combat with Johnny Depp or Casper Van Dien: 'Once we erased the Horseman's head, we also erased Johnny or Casper's face, and we had to replace that,' he said. 'I would have Johnny or Casper go through the same actions without the Horseman in there, and we'd just put their head into any frames where the Horseman's head was blocking theirs. It's a tricky process, but it was actually pretty effective.'

In these days of digital magic, the idea of a Headless Horseman being played by a short actor in a suit with built-up shoulders seems pretty remote, but there were occasions in *Sleepy Hollow* when even that old trick was brought into play: 'If the Horseman's

. coming straight at you, the guy's got his head back and there's a portion of the torso and shoulders that are built up to hide it,' Kevin Yagher explained. (As well as co-producing, Yagher supervised the special make-up effects for the film.) 'When they shot the reverse angle, we had a different piece where he was bending his head forward. We also did a torso that we used at one point for a close-up in which Ichabod looks down into the horseman's neck and sees a mass of worms and insects crawling around.' When not in the form of Christopher Walken, the Hessian was played by Ray Inch on horseback and by Ray Park on foot (Park's sword-fighting skills were more famously put to use when he was cast as Darth Maul in *Star Wars: Episode I – The Phantom Menace*, 1999).

Understandably for a story which includes the line 'It was the very witching time of night…', Washington Irving's 'The Legend of Sleepy Hollow' is an iconic spook-fest, ideal for campfire or candlelight, but with no real sense of dread beyond the temporal *frisson* which is engendered by its bogus bogeyman. The sequence in the Disney animation in which Ichabod and his gallant steed Gunpowder move warily through the woods on the outskirts of Sleepy Hollow is a classic of mounting suspense and comedic contrivance, and Burton chooses wisely not to imitate it in his version, although he does nod to it in Depp's first encounter with the Horseman in the film, which turns out to be similarly bogus. Having acknowledged their debt to Irving and to Disney, Burton and his screenwriters then sweep away such impedimenta to pursue a narrative entirely of their own crafting. The actual storyline of the film is far too complex to bear repeating in detail; suffice it to say that it all boils down to a plot by Lady Van Tassel (Richardson), wife of the town's patriarch, to regain the inheritance that was stolen from her as a child and which she is executing by means of witchcraft, raising the dead Hessian from his grave on the pretext that his missing skull (which she has secreted away) will be returned to him on the completion of his mission of murder. Even this précis sounds ridiculously overblown.

Uncredited script 'doctor' Tom Stoppard did more than simply give the screenplay a polish, unfortunately; he also radically overhauled the motive for murder which, in Walker's draft, had come down to land-grabbing greed. (Stoppard exemplified his disdain for the murder-for-profit scenario by verbalising it in the form of a remark made to Ichabod in passing by his adopted assistant, Young Masbath (Marc Pickering): 'All these murders ... just so that Baltus Van Tassel should inherit yet more land and property?') He overlaid it with a more primal one of revenge but, in doing so, he was forced to alter the existing back story, as well. This meant introducing new scenes which hinted at Lady Van Tassel's prior history, including one in which, as a young girl, she watches the Hessian die, and others between Ichabod and Katrina which take place in her childhood home, now ruined and deserted. A new sub-plot also had to be introduced, which linked all of the murder victims to something other than property. Thus a grand conspiracy was devised, where the legally sanctioned theft of her family's land drew other residents of Sleepy Hollow into the web of deceit, until the Horseman's blade had to be notched with kills from all parts of the town and for a number of different (but still associated) reasons. This was too much weight of plot for the story to bear, and Burton disposes of it, rapid-fire, as the film approaches its effects-heavy climax: evidently tiring of repetitively picking off his victims one-by-one, the Horseman launches an all-out assault on the town, at which juncture, the carefully contrived air of mystery comes crashing down around the heads of all concerned, while Ichabod and Kristina (Ricci) are left with no alternative but to run screaming from a screenplay which has just blown up in their faces. 'The original image that I had in my mind is a character who lives in his head versus a character with no head, which I always thought was a wonderful symbol,' Burton said of his film. Wonderful it may have been, but meaningless all the same when a movie monster is riding roughshod over symbol and storyline alike.

This enforced nod to horror convention quite diminishes the power of the second half of the film, and the tortuous explanation which the screenplay eventually provides for the Horseman's mission of revenge on behalf of wicked Lady Van Tassel becomes utterly incomprehensible in its disjointed delivery at intervals during the blitzkrieg of beheadings which dominates *Sleepy Hollow*'s final half hour. Narrative clarity is self-confessedly not one of Burton's strong points, and a little more tinkering with the script prior to production could easily have straightened out some of the unnecessary plot twists which convolutedly connect all the victims in the laboured manner of an Agatha Christie mystery. Depp's Ichabod is climactically reduced to a befuddled bystander, variously fighting or fleeing by turns, as Tim Burton's rampaging ghost rider cuts a bloody swathe through the teasing air of unspoken terrors and carefully wrought atmospherics which earlier he had been at pains to build.

> There is a conspiracy here, and I will seek it out!
> Baltus Van Tassel (Michael Gambon), Sleepy Hollow (1999)

Irving's tale is a simple one of a clever practical joke played on a man who is susceptible to scary stories; Andrew Kevin Walker gave his Horseman a methodology, and his puppet-master a simple reason to kill; Stoppard and Burton, between them, cluttered up the clean efficiency of narrative which Hammer, for instance, would happily have settled for, with a complex weave of conspiratorial claptrap which would not have seemed out of place in *JFK* – and all of it so that Ichabod can be presented with a superior mystery to solve, while wrestling with demons of his own in the form of childhood memories of a pagan mother tortured to death by a Puritan father (a sub-plot which serves no purpose in *Sleepy Hollow* whatsoever, other than to provide a role for Burton's long-time companion Lisa Marie and nod anachronistically to the movies of Roger Corman). Phew. No wonder audiences were to be perplexed about who had done what to whom, after the last drop of blood had been spilled on-screen.

Like the arm that juts incongruously out of the Tree of the Dead after the Hessian has taken his last victim to Hell, niggling details remain. The revision to the storyline which altered the murderer's schema from greed to revenge could barely be accommodated by the script's extant timeline: we are told that the Hessian was killed in 'the winter of '79' (repeated as 'a legend told for twenty years') – an incident which is witnessed in flashback by the young Lady Van Tassel and her sister, both of whom are under ten years old at the time. The film takes place in 1799, which meant that the 40-year-old Miranda Richardson ostensibly was playing a character who, according to the story, was still under 30 and had inveigled her way into the marriage bed of Baltus Van Tassel only two years earlier. In the welter of action on display, this point passes virtually unnoticed (along with much else besides) but, in avoiding the episode of the sisters, the original script needed to be less specific about Lady Van Tassel's age. Richardson was cast on the basis of Walker's drafts, otherwise a younger and more seductive actress might better have suited the change – even though such a move might have given the game away more quickly to an audience. The other question mark which all of this raises is that given her history, and their complicity in it, would the town's elders not have come to suspect Van Tassel right away?

So muddied had the rancid waters of *Sleepy Hollow* become that Burton was forced to take remedial action after the film was complete. He devised a new prologue, the purpose of which was to show the death of Peter Van Garrett and thereby place the person ultimately responsible for the chain of events into the action. After putting in an emergency call to *Ed Wood*'s Martin Landau to play the role of Van Garrett, Burton shot the scene in a warehouse in New York. 'In two and a half days, we did the entire prologue,' Landau told Jim Smith and J Clive Matthews for their book *Tim Burton*. 'On the last day, Danny Elfman came on the set because the score had already been finished, but he had to score this piece. Within a week he and Tim went to London with the orchestra there, scored the prologue, and then four weeks later the movie was in 2,500 theatres in America. Four weeks from the day we finished.' The fine details of the plot had already been plugged by a montage of will-signings which ran behind the opening titles (not that anyone was going to notice those at the time of their unveiling, but at least it could be said that they were there). Why Lady Van Tassel goes to the trouble of faking her own death as the climax approaches remains a mystery, however, beyond the contrivance that were she not to have done so, the departing Ichabod (who has previously arrived at the wrong conclusion as to the identity of the real killer) would have been deprived of the opportunity to spot the anomaly and return belatedly to *Sleepy Hollow* to solve the rest of the puzzle.

> The Van Garretts, the Widow Winship, your father, Jonathan Masbath, and now Philipse. Something must connect them...
>
> Ichabod Crane (Johnny Depp), Sleepy Hollow (1999)

Depp's performance as Ichabod Crane, for all its inventive physical tics and psychological traits of character, is ultimately overwhelmed by the digital dynamics of the hideous Horseman. His predisposition to squirm, shy away or faint at much of the proceedings tends to remove him from the nucleus of the action, and the resultant vacuum is invariably filled by others of the cast who happen to be in the vicinity at the time: it is left to Casper Van Dien, as Brom Van Brunt, to engage in the most ferocious bout of hand-to-hand combat with the phantom Horseman, Van Helsing-style, before being cleft in two. Consequently, Depp is less of a star presence here than in his two previous outings for Burton, and what must at first have seemed a thankless role for a non-speaking Christopher Walken as Ichabod's night-riding nemesis turned out in the end to be the engine which powered the film to box-office gold. Like Burton's earlier, fun-filled (but commercially unsuccessful) *Mars Attacks!*, *Sleepy Hollow* is another special-effects spectacle; a Gothic fairy tale of mythic proportions, to which Depp's contribution was neither central nor critical, partly of his own making. It is an ensemble piece, and he is but one of the many players in the drama. As with the many versions of *The Phantom of the Opera*, its 'phantom' is actually the star, and Depp's Ichabod Crane is not even a catalyst in a dark narrative which is content to wend its predestined way, largely oblivious to his presence.

The notion of pitting a rationalist detective against a supposed supernatural enemy is hardly a new one; one need only recall Sherlock Holmes and *The Hound of the Baskervilles* to arrive at the model for Walker's script. But Holmes was able to solve that case because the enemy in question was not supernatural at all. Screenwriter Jimmy Sangster was faced with a different dilemma when he had to pit Van Helsing's man of science against Count Dracula in Hammer's *Dracula* (1958); he overcame the problem by grounding his vampire in a 'reality' of sorts, and jettisoning the supernatural elements of the novel which science would have found itself unable to combat. Burton's *Sleepy Hollow*, on the other hand, sets up two oppositional forces with no common ground between them, and one of them has therefore to abandon its stated position for resolution to be forthcoming. Faced with a genuine ghost, Ichabod swaps his rational approach for a logical one, reasoning that if the Horseman is singling out particular individuals for death, then human agency is somehow behind his actions. But the supernatural is an irrational concept and its rules, if rules there are, must be beyond logic. There is no logic to such an assumption; it is merely a stab in the dark – but like so much of *Sleepy Hollow*, it passes without murmur in the confused context of the film as a whole.

Reviewers were to put the film's aesthetic failure down to its uneasy conflation of detective story and supernatural yarn, the latter being a misreading of the original and the former having been grafted onto the tale by its screenwriter. The problem is not so much the conjunction of these two elements – which have a long and honourable history of playing off one another in fiction

– as it is the *collision* of them: Burton proves himself unable to make the combination gel, and the film's initial concentration on Ichabod's investigation of the mystery is deliberately sidestepped in favour of some incongruous Gothic imagery and strident scenes of sword-wielding butchery. Which is not to say that the last half hour of *Sleepy Hollow* is not fast-paced, full-blooded and thoroughly invigorating; it is. But for all of the impact that Depp's character makes on a climax which, by this point, has been comprehensively commandeered by the digitally enhanced figure of the Headless Horseman on a killing spree, he might just as well have been featured wearing that rubber nose.

> The Horseman comes ... and tonight, he comes for you!
> Lady Van Tassel (Miranda Richardson), Sleepy Hollow (1999)

Leaving aside the flaws in its plotting, *Sleepy Hollow* is Halloween hokum of a high order, and it went on to be nominated for three Oscars, though none of them were to acknowledge the input that was provided by Johnny Depp. (The nominations were for Best Art Direction and Set Design, Cinematography and Costumes; Rick Heinrichs and Peter Young were joint recipients of the award for the film's overall production design.) For the most part, it thunders through the sensibilities of its audience at a breakneck pace, rarely pausing to catch its breath and barely at all to elucidate on the mechanics of its over-complex exposition. Without a synopsis to hand, it is virtually impossible for the viewer to discern how the various threads of the plot fit together, but in the mêlée of mangled corpses and hyperventilating action, no one seemed to care. With *Sleepy Hollow*, Tim Burton had come a long way from the funereal tempo and stilted staging of his *Batman* films, and the new spring in his directorial step was to be reflected in the eventual returns for his 'Hammer' horror on speed.

'Working with Tim Burton on *Sleepy Hollow* was like an exorcism. It was a cleansing from my *Ninth Gate* experience,' Depp said after the event. In addition to listening to the anecdotes of Christopher Lee, he doubtless enjoyed the company of (Sir) Michael Gambon, the Irish-born actor noted, like Depp, for the unusual choices that he has made in his 40-year career. During the shooting, Christina Ricci found herself the butt of the dust-dry Gambon's wry wit, when he regaled her with elaborate tales about the clubs which he had visited on previous evenings, and all the drugs that he had ingested in the process.

Gambon's tales were pure blarney, but Johnny Depp's latest adventures on the social circuit were calling all too easily to mind the hot-headed image of his days with Kate Moss. On 30 January, taking a break from filming *Sleepy Hollow* to celebrate the news that his girlfriend of six months was pregnant, he and Paradis dined with friends at celebrity chef Marco Pierre-White's recently reopened Mirabelle, a French bistro in Curzon Street, in the heart of London's Mayfair district, which has been a favoured haunt of the rich and famous since the so-called 'swinging' sixties. Before sitting down to eat, Depp and Paradis had posed for the gaggle of photographers who had gathered outside the restaurant and then asked them to refrain from taking any further pictures, as they wished to spend a quiet evening together. Wapping's finest would not take no for an answer, apparently, and continued to camp out on the doorstep of number 56.

Having downed a bottle of 1978 Romanée Conti burgundy at a cost of some £11,000, Depp decided to use the Mirabelle's wooden door-prop as a makeshift club in order to put his request more convincingly. One hapless snapper received a set of bruised knuckles as a result, and the police were called by the big, brave boys of the press. Once again, Depp found himself arrested for breach of the peace. He spent several hours in the cells before being released under caution. No charges were brought as a result of the fracas. 'He reacts viscerally, and that's what they're waiting for,' Roman Polanski remarked. 'He falls into their trap. That's his teenager reaction. He should shake that off.' (One trap that he was able gleefully to avoid was paparazzi attention surrounding the imminent birth; the couple had announced that their baby was due in *June*.)

When it comes to famous faces eating in London restaurants, enterprising news-hounds can always be relied upon to slip the accommodating maitre d' a wad of cash, so as to be apprised of the cost of a meal as well as the content. Thus Depp was duly reported to have forked out a total of £17,000 on his evening out. The cost to his reputation as a reformed character remained to be audited.

On 27 May, Vanessa Paradis gave birth to a baby girl at the American Hospital of Paris, on rue Chauveau in Neuilly-sur-Seine, and the upcoming summer of '99 now looked set to be the best of Johnny Depp's life. He was 35 and she was 26, and their child was christened Lily-Rose Melody – an enchanting name, full of the promise of spring. Depp had already let it be known to his agent that he wanted to scale back his film work for the time being, so that he could play the doting dad in the Montmartre apartment which he and Paradis had purchased between them the year before. 'Vanessa and I agreed never to work simultaneously,' he explained. 'So small parts that allowed me not to be away for long were welcome. Evidently, the rumour spread and all at once, there were a lot of small parts.' The first call came from Julian Schnabel; the second was from Sally Potter.

Schnabel was a New York painter and conceptual artist in the Andy Warhol mode, who had risen to fame in the 1980s, had since made one feature film (1996's *Basquiat*, about the graffiti artist Jean-Michel Basquiat, in which David Bowie had played Warhol) and who now planned to make another about the Cuban writer and dissident Reinaldo Arenas. Arenas was a writer of great poetic promise, but he was also promiscuously gay and he found himself persecuted when Cuba's US-backed Batista regime fell to Castro's revolutionary army in January of 1959 and its new rulers embarked on a programme of cultural cleansing to rid Cuban society of corrupt and immoral influences. According to gay-rights campaigner Peter Tatchell, homosexuals were routinely denounced as 'sexual deviants' and 'agents of imperialism' in

Castro's Cuba. As a result, Arenas spent several years in jail, smuggling his manuscripts abroad, before finally fleeing into exile in the USA in 1980, along with 125,000 other 'unwanted elements' in a mass boat-lift from the port of Mariel.

The anticipated 'promised land' turned out to be something of an illusion, however. Arenas thought Miami was a caricature of 'the worst of Cuba', which did little to endear him to the rest of the exile community with whom he was sharing a political bed, and he quickly moved on to New York. After another decade spent struggling for recognition, and diagnosed with AIDS, he took his own life on 7 December 1990, at the age of 47, in an apartment on 44th Street. Raised in abject poverty and forced to flee from tyranny and persecution, Reinaldo Arenas ended as he began, having, in his words, merely exchanged 'political repression for economic injustice'.

I think the splendour of my childhood was unique because it was absolute poverty but also absolute freedom; out in the open, surrounded by trees, animals, apparitions, and people who were indifferent towards me. My existence was not even justified, nobody cared.

REINALDO ARENAS, *BEFORE NIGHT FALLS* (1993)

Arenas revisited his experiences in pre- and post-revolutionary Cuba for an autobiography which he entitled *Before Night Falls*, and he committed suicide only after he had completed the book. Written under the debilitating influence of AIDS, its account of the consequences of the Cuban revolution is questionable, if not bitter and openly biased. Nevertheless, Julian Schnabel and scriptwriters Cunningham O'Keefe and Lázaro Gómez Carriles (Arenas's partner at the time of his death) adapted it chapter-and-verse for the screen. Schnabel the director then thought to add some 'liberal cred' to his $12 million self-financed production, and what better way than a couple of high-profile cameos from known Hollywood rebels. Sean Penn had already agreed to throw his hat into the ring; not surprisingly, Johnny Depp was also attracted to a project about a young artist struggling against oppression. 'It depends on the director whether I play them,' he said. 'I'd known Julian Schnabel for years from New York – a witty guy, even if all his droll stories are about himself. He called and asked if I wanted to play a small part as a transvestite in *Before Night Falls*. I thought, easy enough, I only need to wear a bra and a dress; nice of him to ask me.' His view of Julian Schnabel was not one that was widely shared in the world of art, however. 'Schnabel's work is to painting what Stallone's is to acting: a lurching display of oily pectorals, except that Schnabel makes bigger public claims for himself,' wrote *Time* magazine art critic Robert Hughes.

Depp maintained his radical chic by accepting two cameo roles to Sean Penn's one of an unlikely Cuban farmer in *Before Night Falls*, both of which turned out to be jaw-droppingly extreme and in neither of which is he really recognisable or any more than a token presence. The first is something of an 'isn't that…?' in-joke, as he sashays around Havana harbour's El Morro castle in high-heels and headscarf, his eyes mascara'd and his lips brightly rouged as 'Bon-Bon', an outrageous transvestite who smuggles Arenas's manuscript out of the fortress by secreting it in his rectum, a hiding-place which Cuban officials were evidently loathe to search (although Customs officers suffer from no such qualms). 'I went deeply into the real Bon-Bon and found that he looked exactly like Sophia Loren!' Depp said. So he does, circa 1957 and Stanley Kramer's *The Pride and the Passion* again. For sheer audacity on the part of a major American star, this buttock-clenching cameo takes some beating. Beat it, he tried to, however, and in the same film. As a slick-haired apparatchik of Cuba's communist state named Lieutenant Victor, he forces Arenas to renounce both his sexuality and his art while taunting him by fondling his own crotch and having him fellate his automatic weapon. Depp plays Victor as though he were a Gestapo officer, which was the idea; his scenes were shot in Veracruz, Mexico.

I will close my eyes now, and you will be gone... You're gone.
Lieutenant Victor (Johnny Depp), Before Night Falls (1999)

Much of *Before Night Falls* is a rant of the Cuban-American right, pandering to predictable anti-Castro prejudice and preaching to the converted while playing fast and loose with history, including Arenas's own, and propagandising to the unaligned. Spanish-born Javier Bardem, last seen in Pedro Almodóvar's *Live Flesh* (1997), is outstanding as Arenas, playing it rigorously 'straight' and refusing to tug unnecessarily on any emotional heartstrings. But Arenas's profligate sexual adventuring is conveniently sidestepped; there is no mention of his self-confessed 5,000 sexual partners, and his arrest and imprisonment on a charge of molestation of a minor is presented as a frame-up (despite Arenas's own admission to the contrary). Nor is any weight given to the fact that he was himself an ardent Castrist until the late 1960s, only abandoning the revolution when its ideology turned against all forms of sexual 'deviation'. (Author Peter Marshall's 1988 *Cuba Libre* makes it clear that many gay artists and intellectuals of the time saw the rebellion against the capitalist dictatorship of Fulgencio Batista as paving the way to sexual liberation, as well as social justice.)

Its omissions notwithstanding, Schnabel's film is chiefly concerned with censorship and the suppression of human rights, and Arenas experienced both, though he felt that his subsequent treatment in the USA was not much of an improvement over that in Cuba, only different. *Before Night Falls* was included in a *New York Times* list of the Ten Best Books of the Year in 1993, but that was a full three years after Arenas died. The screen version is a moving document, shot in pseudo-documentary style, but it presents only one side of the argument, and prejudicially at that. As with so many causes taken up by the fashionable on the spur of the moment, its take on the history of the Cuban revolution is as partisan as was Arenas's revisionist view of his own life in *Before Night Falls*.

The last week in August saw the Spanish premiere of *The Ninth Gate* (as *La novena porta*) as well as the US release of *The Astronaut's Wife*. The latter was denied a press screening and rushed straight into theatres, though some critics caught up with it anyway. Ebert thought Depp had a 'thankless role', while the *San Francisco Chronicle*'s Mick La Salle was left up in the air facing an onslaught of imponderables: 'The script needs something more – I'm not pretending to know what it is. But the ending leaves the audience with an empty feeling and a few nagging questions: Who is this alien? Where is he from? What does he want?' *Sight and Sound* saw virtue in these enigmas: 'Ravich's script keeps all alien elements to an elegant minimum: no reason is ever given for the mysterious entity's presence on Earth', which is to suggest that a black hole where a plot should be can henceforth be construed as 'elegant' minimalism. Peter Bradshaw in the *Guardian* was less easily fooled: 'Depp lumbers through on autopilot with a clichéd good-ol'-boy accent derived from Kevin Bacon in *Apollo 13*. Houston, do we ever have a problem here.'

Most commentators on *The Astronaut's Wife* were left in little doubt that money rather than art had been the reason for Depp's choosing it as a vehicle. This was big-budget sci-fi schlock, in which the concept of characterisation came a very poor second to special effects and spooky atmosphere. It was also highly derivative, with the Depp role of astronaut Spencer Armacost in play only to provide a host body for the monster which actually supplies the requisite threat. In accepting a part as a man possessed by alien intelligence, he had been preceded by Richard Wordsworth and Marshall Thompson (*The Quatermass Experiment* and *First Man Into Space*, respectively), neither of them known for discrimination in terms of the roles that they elected to play. Johnny Depp now appeared to be in some danger of undermining the artistic integrity on which the public's perception of him as an actor had largely been built, despite a belated plea to the effect that the project was 'one of those things that looked better on paper'. Had the film turned out a success, that might have been seen as some justification. But *The Astronaut's Wife* bombed big-time, recouping only one third of its $34 million cost.

Still, the offers kept coming. It was next announced that Depp had been approached to play eighteenth-century Scottish poet Robert ('Rabbie') Burns in *Clarinda*, which was being produced by actor James Cosmo for Alloway Productions. Just as the entire population of Scotland appeared ready to take up arms over the prospect of their national poet being portrayed in a $28 million film by an *American* actor, it was revealed that Eric Rowan, a director of Alloway, had served time as a convicted fraudster; apparently, Rowan had been jailed for five years on fraud charges in 1983, followed by three more in 1995 for conspiracy to steal cars. Investors suddenly turned into wee, sleekit, cow'rin', tim'rous beasties at the news and promptly bade him farewell with a chorus of Auld Lang Syne. The project then went the same way as *Marlowe*.

Fear and Loathing's Terry Gilliam had also wanted Depp for *his* new film, the story of which was based loosely on Cervantes' *Don Quixote* and had been developing in his mind for more than a decade, but the project had unexpectedly gone onto the back-burner due to lack of funds, and Depp had been forced to cry off for the time being in favour of *The Man Who Cried*. 'We were desperately trying to keep Johnny on board and he was committed to the film, but he was being offered $2m for three weeks' work while we were expecting him to do 17 weeks for the same fee,' Gilliam sobbed, before adding with tongue in cheek, 'All he does is talk about the baby. He's become an incredibly boring human being. He's no longer a great actor – just one of hundreds of millions of fathers.'

A search for one out of hundreds of millions of fathers was central to Sally Potter's *The Man Who Cried*, a tale of a young Jewess named Fegele, whose own father decides to leave their impoverished Russian village and carve out a new life for them both in America. When contact with him is lost, Fegele sets out to find him, travelling first to England, where she is invested with the anglicised name of Suzie, and then on to Paris on the eve of the Second World War. There, she teams up with Lola, a gold-digging Russian chorus girl with her eye on Dante, an Italian opera singer who also has roots in the back-streets. Suzie finds herself attracted to an enigmatic Gypsy named Cesar, to whom she surrenders her virginity. When the advancing German army finally occupies France, she flees the country to continue her quest.

The Man Who Cried was a mere three weeks' work for Depp at Epinay Studios in Paris, where he had shot *The Ninth Gate*. In a complete reversal of the situation on *Sleepy Hollow* only six months before, he found himself playing support to Christina Ricci, whose film this effectively was: Ricci was Suzie to Depp's gypsy, but the film's flashiest roles were allotted to Cate Blanchett as the well-meaning Lola and John Turturro as the egotistical Dante, sold on the idea of ethnic cleansing. The always watchable Harry Dean Stanton was also on hand to provide a considerate cameo as Dante's long-suffering producer.

London-born 52-year-old Sally Potter was dancer, choreographer and composer first and foremost, film director a poor fourth; consequently, *The Man Who Cried* is orchestrated like a silent film, in which its operatic score does most of the talking. (Dante belts out 'Torna a Sorrento' as the Nazis make a sweep of the gypsy camp, killing a young boy.) A context for this approach was given on the blurb to Faber & Faber's published version of Potter's script: '*The Man Who Cried* is a young woman's coming-of-age story set in the dangerous maelstrom of Nazi-occupied Paris. The film charts a journey that begins in the lost world of old Jewry and ends in the new world of Hollywood: a journey in which a seven-year-old girl's name and native tongue are stripped from her, causing her to retreat into silence even as she discovers her family gift for song.'

That may have been the original plan, but the promise of an intriguing premise is dashed by turgid stylisation and terminal lack of focus. The result is intellectually void, and Potter seems incapable of extracting anything more from the ambitious canvas on which she paints than a series of pretty pictures. Every opportunity to advance an ethical argument is fluffed, every conceptual Big Idea half-formed, every dramatic highlight detoured down a dead-end street. The scene in which Suzie finally 'finds her voice' and confronts Dante's prejudices comes off as little more than mild rebuke; Cesar mumbles impotently about the need to stay and fight; Dante petulantly betrays Suzie's racial origins to the Germans and promptly exits stage-left. Not even that brings any tension into the story. She makes her escape on a cruise ship at a leisurely pace, while the storm clouds of Belsen and Auschwitz supposedly gather overhead. Reaching Hollywood with little difficulty (beyond her ship being torpedoed along the way), she finds that her father has remarried, raised a new family and suffered a nervous breakdown as a result of making one too many Busby Berkeley-style musicals. She arrives at his hospital bedside, where recognition (just about) flickers into his tired eyes, and sings to him in Yiddish. A tear rolls down his cheek – hence the film's title; then again, it could be a reference to Cesar on their last night together before she had to leave for the States. Nothing is resolved, and two hours of one's life have just evaporated before one's very eyes.

The characters are as stereotypical as the storyline, from John Turturro's mother-fixated, Mussolini-supporting, temperamental tenor, to Depp's sullen, scar-faced, gypsy horseman, a romantic ideal that comes straight out of a pop video by way of Rudolf Valentino. Ricci has to play impassively throughout, but the part of Cesar is virtually a mime-role for Depp; he is never less than interesting, though, and he invests the man with a tangible history through his demeanour alone, despite being given little to work from in the script and having even less dialogue to back it up. Needless to say, he is wasted here but, like the greats of old, how the camera loves him! Only six months had elapsed since *Sleepy Hollow*, and yet he appears to have aged six years, from insipid investigator into sensual gypsy king.

The most satisfying element in a film so given over to unspoken thought is the sense that the coming war was bringing with it the opportunity to settle old scores with ethnic groups, be they Jew or gypsy, while its most cinematic sequence sees three of the principals become aware of a sound like distant thunder, growing louder: it is actually the marching jackboots of the German army entering Paris. There is also an interesting sex scene, in which the focus is rigorously on Suzie as Cesar deflowers her in a coldly mechanical way; that, and the price which Lola knows that she has to pay for a life of security with Dante reveals a refreshingly feminist perspective on the part of the film's director. As more sex scenes choreographed to operatic arias soon come thick and fast, however, *The Man Who Cried* is quickly reduced to the level of a soft-porn glossy: *Playboy* edited by Jean-Paul Gaultier.

The Man Who Cried is posh tosh, saturated in fake period flavour and spooned over with a Sunday-supplement sauce of social awareness. It is as shallow as Turturro's opera-singer; as satisfying as nouvelle cuisine – pretty to look at but wholly devoid of sustenance.

The late 1990s had witnessed something of a revival of the New Romantic movement of the early 1980s, epitomised originally by the likes of Adam Ant and bands such as Spandau Ballet and ABC. Johnny Depp had always been a fashion junkie – albeit that it was usually a fashion of his own contrivance – and in his public outings, he was soon to discard the ripped jeans and incongruous tuxedo of earlier incarnations and replace them with a fedora, pin-stripe suit and wild, flowing locks. It was a logical move to extend this image into the films that he was choosing to do. The fact that he consciously had opted to accept more cameo roles in order to reduce his workload since the birth of Lily-Rose meant also that the type of roles which would be offered him were going to play to his looks; the film business being what it is, casting agents requiring a derelict or a clean-cut, guy-next-door type were unlikely to suggest Johnny Depp – unless the guy next door was meant to be a pin-up.

In terms of Depp's screen image, the unashamedly romantic *The Man Who Cried* had been blatant typecasting of a sort not seen since the earliest days of *Jump Street*. This was 'chocolate box' artifice at its most overt, paraded as social commentary but photographed in the style of a fashion-shoot for *Vogue*. The only thing required of Depp was his sultry good looks, an act of calculated pimping that was underscored by the fact that throughout the film's 100 minutes, he utters a mere half a dozen lines. Sally Potter's feature may have feigned concern for the kind of subject matter which Depp had always professed so dear to him as an artist, but even he could not deny that his own part in the film represented little more than the male-model fantasy figure of the average Mills and Boon novel – there not only to flutter the heart of the female lead but, by association, those of the female members of the audience, as well.

Yet Depp continued to talk in the press of his disdain for this aspect of his screen persona, with a vehemence which at times almost bordered on self-loathing. Quoting the case of French singer-songwriter Serge Gainsbourg, one-time mentor of Vanessa Paradis, he said: 'His whole life, the press wrote: good singer, good actor but God, he's so ugly! This troubled him, until at a given moment he said, "Okay, it's true – but it's better to be ugly than beautiful; ugliness lasts." Sooner or later, gravity will get us all anyway, and if you ground your life on appearance, you are fooled beforehand. If I had a choice, I'd prefer my head to be a mask that I could take off at the end of each day of shooting.'

Despite all his previous remarks to the contrary, Depp's next two films were to see him play to his looks more than he ever had before, as though the birth of his daughter had endowed him with a new sense of machismo and, for now at least, he was intent on flaunting it on-screen.

> For you, at this moment, running is good. It is better to run and live than stay and die. It's not the same for me. I am not alone; I have my family. I must fight for my family.
> Cesar (Johnny Depp), The Man Who Cried (1999)

If Depp's career appeared to the industry insiders to have gone suddenly on the slide, given that his involvement in his last two films had been little more than cursory, he could not have cared less: he had a daughter now, and there were more important things in life than mere movies. He could hardly contain the joy of father-hood; it had been a long time coming. But he felt the need to explain what looked increasingly like his permanent relocation to France: 'The life we lead now looks like a normal life, as far as that is possible in our profession. I don't hate America; I nurse a beau-tiful feeling for what it once was or could have been – people in the Midwest who simply work and try to survive. But I hate the ambitions, the short-sightedness, the needless pain and violence in families. I feel an aversion to what America has become. I almost became crazy there myself. I certainly won't expose my girl to it.'

Johnny Depp had now starred in 17 feature films over ten years (excluding his brief appearance in *Freddy's Dead*) – from *Cry-Baby* in 1989 to *The Man Who Cried* in 1999 – only three of which had so far turned a profit. By November 1999, *The Ninth Gate* was still awaiting release, but advance screenings did not bode well for its chances. When it did eventually open in the USA on Christmas Eve and in the UK the following March, reviews were uniformly downbeat and its performance at the box office fol-lowed the pattern that had been set by its predecessors. 'The end is neither frightening nor funny, pure Eurotosh,' Peter Preston wrote in the *Observer*. 'No wonder Depp, toiling quietly away, looks dazed and confused'.

Depp's integrity as a performer may have been restored by working with Polanski, but he was sorely in need of another hit if his star status and corresponding salary demands were to contin-ue to be met. Before his track record of commercial failure was returned to normal by the erratic releases of both *Before Night Falls* and *The Man Who Cried*, the 19 November opening of *Sleepy Hollow* provided it.

Tim Burton's film took $30 million on its opening weekend, and it went on to cover its estimated costs of $65 million inside two weeks; in six months, it was to double that figure. Its current worldwide gross stands at some $202 million. The review in *Rolling Stone* was typical: 'Even when the narrative stalls from too many detours and decapitations, *Sleepy Hollow* is gorgeous filmmaking that brims over with fun-house thrills and ravishing romance.'

Depp and Paradis had flown to Los Angeles for the 17 November world premiere of *Sleepy Hollow* at Mann's Chinese Theatre and, on the day before the event, he had been honoured with a star on Hollywood Boulevard's famous Walk of Fame – the 2,149th. The unveiling had taken place outside the Hollywood Roosevelt Hotel, in a ceremony presided over by Honorary Mayor of Hollywood, Johnny Grant. Also present were Tim Burton and Martin Landau, both of whom gave speeches about Depp's achievements as an actor. This being Tinseltown, little Lily-Rose later found herself the recipient of an 'Ichabod Crane' action figure in the likeness of her father and manufactured by McFarlane Toys.

British critics were more reserved in their opinions when the movie opened in the UK three weeks later, with most of them honing in on Depp: 'Johnny Depp's Ichabod Crane is a man of many parts, never conclusively adding up to a whole. Depp's willingness to push his characters in unsympathetic directions is always engaging, and he plays Crane as a Clouseau-like incompetent, his face a mask of involuntary tics and twitches,' Andrew O'Hehir wrote in *Sight and Sound*. 'With his sharp mind, his gallantry and his nervous fainting fits, Depp's Ichabod is an attractive hero but the detective story element doesn't quite gel with the fairy tale or supernatural aspects … But it's an engaging entertainment, both handsome and scary, with excellent special effects,' Philip French agreed in the *Observer*. 'Eventually it gets tiring, and if anything in this camp Goth extravaganza scares you, you must be a real wuss. But it's worth it for Johnny Depp's feathery, nervy performance as Crane,' Peter Bradshaw contradicted in the *Guardian*. But if *Sleepy Hollow* was the least effective of

Depp's three collaborations with Tim Burton in terms of his contribution as an actor, it was far and away the most commercially
successful: Depp had a hit on his hands – his first since *Donnie
Brasco* – and the question now was how to follow it up.

During press junkets for Burton's film, Depp had been inclined
to apologise for the fact that some of the cinematic allusions that
he was calling to mind in answer to questions were either too
obscure or 'before the time' of the younger members of his audiences. He was now 36, and though resolutely still a young man
himself, he had begun to be aware that the cultural icons to whom
he previously adhered were fast fading into history as the millennium approached. More than half a century had passed since Jack
Kerouac took to the road by hitching lifts or stealing cars; almost
30 years since Hunter Thompson did the same in his famous 'Red
Shark' Chevy convertible. And it was over a decade since he had
strutted his own teen-idol stuff astride a Harley Davidson in
Vancouver. After his parting from Kate Moss, he had started to
take fresh stock of his life and career. His deep-seated yearning
for a more settled domestic situation had been met by Paradis
and Lily-Rose, but roles which better expressed his growing sense
of maturity were also to be part of the plan.

With a new and more permanent partner in Vanessa Paradis, a
six-month-old daughter, a hit film and a star on the Hollywood
Walk of Fame, the 1990s ended on a high for Johnny Depp. It
remained to be seen what the new millennium would bring.

7 DREAMS AND NIGHTMARES

Ken: Good morning, sir. And how are we today, sir?
Johnny: Fine. I'm fine, thank you. Radiant! – Radiant,
as you ... English people like to say. I was looking for
something in a very traditional British suit.
Ken: You're an American, aren't you, sir?
Johnny: Yes.
Ken: Have you been here long?
Johnny: Couple of days.
Ken: Have you boned anyone yet, sir?

Paul Whitehouse and Johnny Depp, The Last Fast Show Ever (2000)

DRUGS HAVE been a feature of Johnny Depp's appearances on-screen since the very earliest days, whether he was indulging in them in *Platoon* or railing against them on *Jump Street*. They have been a running sore in his personal life, as well, most recently with Kate Moss checking herself into rehab at the Priory clinic, from which she had now been discharged. He had cleaned up his own act long before the birth of his daughter and had since settled on a glass or two of red wine or vodka to mask his insecurities, in addition to his habitual intake of nicotine.

Depp's attitude to smoking has always been refreshingly libertarian; he has never made any bones about the fact that he has chain-smoked since his teens, and he has for years been one of the few remaining champions of the weed in a climate of growing political correctness on both sides of the Atlantic: California's state-wide ban on smoking had figured among his reasons for settling permanently in France: 'I'd like to say I moved to France so I could smoke in peace; it's a crime to light up in LA,' he stated. 'But it's more than that. I find Europe more civilised, more sophisticated. It has older culture – a stronger foundation.' An exception is usually made for him, and an ashtray provided, whenever he is interviewed on television, which goes to show that if one is famous or eccentric enough, one can get away with any-thing, especially if those in the position to indulge are desirous of an autograph.

In the rheumy eyes of the press, Depp and drugs have always appeared to go hand-in-hand. Perhaps because of his own experi-ences, he has never shied away from dealing with them in his films, one of the few actors to do so with such abandon. The most obvious example is *Fear and Loathing in Las Vegas* but, in February 2000, Depp and New York-born director Ted Demme (nephew of Jonathan, director of *The Silence of the Lambs*, 1991) set out to explore the darker side of the *Fear and Loathing* ethos: the hard-nosed, amoral, money-laundering realities of the Colombian drug-cartels which, in the 1970s, cashed in big-time on the flower-powered dreams of the likes of Hunter Thompson by flooding a burgeoning American market with a drug which had been banned from sale since 1914: cocaine. By 1982, 5.6 per cent of the population claimed to be using cocaine. This was tanta-mount to an epidemic, and one man more than any other was responsible for 85 per cent of all the cocaine which was now being consumed by high-rollers or low-lifers throughout the USA. His name was George Jung.

> Danbury wasn't a prison, it was a crime school. I went in with a Bachelor of Marijuana; came out with a Doctorate of Cocaine. And after sixteen months, I was once again a free man...
>
> George Jung (Johnny Depp), Blow (2000)

Cocaine, or 'snow' or 'blow', is a derivative of the coca plant and its attraction as a drug of choice for so-called recreational users in the 1980s was due to its ability to supply an instant 'buzz', like an adrenaline rush, as well as the various methods by which it could be ingested – the favoured one being 'snorting' through the nose. The effect is short-lived, however, and repeated hits are required to maintain equilibrium. By 1982, there were some 10 million cocaine-users in the USA alone, which rose to 22 million by 1985, while a kilo of blow could rise in value from $20,000 dollars at source to half a billion retail, by the time it was cut with amphetamines or turned into 'crack' and sold on the streets of American cities.

Ted Demme's film is adapted from *Blow: How a Small-Town Boy Made $100 Million with the Medellin Cocaine Cartel and Lost It All*, the 1993 bestselling biography of drug-smuggler George Jung by Bruce Porter. As a savage indictment of the American Dream, *Blow* is nearer the mark than *Fear and Loathing in Las Vegas*. Jung was a young guy on the make, looking for an easy way to the top; drugs provided it. A life of luxury beyond his wildest dreams ensued for the best part of two decades, until one drugs bust too many ultimately cost him his freedom, as well as the love of his wife and child.

Demme bought the rights to Porter's book on publication, but only when he became a father himself in 1996 did he find the key to turn the material into a workable screenplay. Interviewed by Cynthia Fuchs, he gave a succinct appraisal of his take on *Blow*: 'It's about what happens to children when they're brought up in a bad household. They grow up to become their parents. And that's something I can relate to now. I have a responsibility that I didn't have when I first got the book. Then I met co-writer Nick Cassavetes; he has kids and his dad (John Cassavetes) passed away at an early age. And we both have kids, so then we found out what the core of the movie was, which was that responsibility. Then I got jazzed, because I knew that if I told that story, everything else would fall into place, and we could have fun with Escobar and the sixties and blow it out, and not be self-conscious about what message we're giving.'

Aside from opening at the point in the story where he is about to be sold down the river for the last time and then flashing backwards, *Blow* moves through the events of Jung's life in strict chronological order. He starts off as the gauche only son of humble and hardworking (but poor) Massachusetts parents, before leaving for California in 1968 where he soon becomes known as 'Boston George' from selling pot on California's Manhatten Beach. By 1969, he has graduated to importing it from Mexico by the kilo-load. In another decade, after serving time in prison on a first drugs bust, he is in Medellin, Columbia, dealing directly with Pablo Escobar, and flying cocaine into the States by the tonne. When he then tries to 'quit' the business, he has made $60 million in cash, half of which he stashes (and eventually loses) in a Panamanian bank owned by Manuel Noriega. From there on, it is all downhill. He loses his partner, his contact on the West Coast, his loot, his liberty, his wife and, ultimately, his daughter in a custody suit. 'Everything I love in my life goes away,' he says in sad reflection. He does not, however, lose his life, as did so many of those whose drug habits he not only supplied, but helped to create. Instead of $100 million, he winds up with 60 years in Otisville Federal Correctional Institute, at which juncture a screen caption informs the viewer that he will be eligible for parole in 2015, and that Kristina Sunshine Jung (the daughter) has not yet visited her father. An American tragedy.

With a budget of $30 million from New Line, producer-director Demme had his sights set on Johnny Depp to play the part from the very beginning. 'When I finally got a script that I was happy with, I went and tracked him down in Europe,' he explained. 'I wanted an actor to give me George Jung. I didn't want a movie star to come in and star in *Blow*. I really wanted the guy to be George. Johnny has done that on every film. You put *Edward Scissorhands*, *Ed Wood*, *Donnie Brasco* and George in the same room, and they don't look alike at all. I needed someone who was also sexy – someone who would walk into a room and everyone would be, like, "wow – who is that guy?"'

Depp spent two days in prison with George Jacob Jung 'trying to steal a part of his life, his soul', as he put it. 'At first, you tend to see him as a major drug-dealer, who's abandoned his family, and not at all as a sympathetic figure,' Depp said. 'When I met him and read the book, I realised that the whole thing was not that simple. He was doing what he knew best. What he got from his upbringing. He became exactly what he didn't want to be: a greedy person who doesn't think of anything other than money, just like his mother. I figured that my goal would be to take what seemed to be nothing but a party-boy and turn him into a real man that you can relate to.' Depp could certainly relate to him: Jung had read Kerouac.

Depp defended his take on Jung on the grounds that *Blow* was one man's tragic story, rather than a commentary on the drugs trade of the 1980s: 'It would have been easy to present him as an odious person, much more difficult was to show his humanity without judging him. He's really a classic victim of the American Dream: get the most that you can. That's what we've all been taught.' But his immensely sympathetic portrait does blind the viewer to the grim realities of the business which provided Boston George with his livelihood.

The film treads very softly over Jung's Colombian cohorts: the Medellin cartel was actually a joint venture between Escobar, José Gacha, the Ochoa organisation and Carlos Lehder Rivas, a notorious drugs lord who operated his Miami run out of a forti-fied Bahamian compound, and who is represented in *Blow* by the character of Diego Delgado (Jordi Mollà), Jung's fictitious part-ner-in-crime. By 1982, Panamanian President Manuel Noriega had also been brought in on their act, but the covert connection to the US government, and the CIA in particular, was better dealt with in Roger Spottiswoode's TV movie of 2000, *Noriega: God's Favorite*, than it is in *Blow*. Jung was small fry in comparison to the thoroughly reprehensible characters with whom he did busi-ness, which is how he managed to get stuck with 60 years; Lehder was extradited to stand trial in the USA in 1986 and received life plus 135 years with no possibility for parole, but he cut a deal with the authorities and was released by the Clinton administration in 1995. Jung cut a similar deal which halved his sentence, but his 'ratting' never made it into the film:

Calibanos: Mr Jung, don't you have an agreement or understanding with the United States Government in connection with your testimony in this case?
George: I'm doing sixty years at Otisville, no chance of parole. Even if they cut my sentence in half I'll be seventy-three years old. That's some fucking deal. I don't know if the parole board, the judge, the Pope or Jesus Christ himself can get me out of here. I have a really bad record, I'm not sure what's going to happen.
Calibanos: So you do have an agreement with the United States Government, Mr Jung, correct?
George can't respond. Looks to Diego. Looks from the jury, the judge, George is on the spotlight and it's uncomfortable. He feels suddenly sleazy.
Calibanos: I thought so. No more questions.
(scene deleted) from the screenplay of Blow (2000)

Depp makes it too easy to forget that *Blow* is a Hollywood biopic, with the emphasis on the Hollywood, and that the word 'loosely' should have been inserted between the first two in its opening screen caption: 'Based on a true story'. No wonder Jung cried when Depp showed him a tape of the completed film in prison – he could no doubt see how well it was bound to play to some future parole board; either that, or he is a sucker for sad endings. 'After seeing the movie, he accused me of being a witch, because I'd been able to absorb so much of his life in only two days,' the actor said.

Blow is heavily biased in Jung's favour, presenting him as basically honest (at least, when it comes to his dealings with his various partners and associates), monogamous, personable, naive and ultimately unlucky. It takes no account whatsoever of the larger consequences of his actions, or the damage that they caused to western society as a whole. We are shown no dead teenagers, their bodies ravaged and aged by the switch from Jung's cocaine to crack or heroin. Nor do we see much evidence of the mobsters and the muscle behind the drugs trade; even Pablo Escobar is depicted as essentially honourable, ordering an underling to be shot in the head only because the man was about to betray the cartel for money. Jung's weak father (an excellent Ray Liotta) passively tolerates his son's illegal activities, although the situation sends him to an early grave, and his mother disowns him – but she is portrayed as a reactionary harridan in the process. The former multi-millionaire drug runner's failure to provide for his daughter financially is glossed over in a brief exchange with his wife, but Depp's infinitely sympathetic performance turns her into the villain of the piece for asking.

Jung's attempt to rectify this situation is blamed for his capture in a 'sting' operation, where his remaining friends betray him for promises of amnesty. Set up like the 'Last Supper', this is where Demme's film begins and effectively ends. Jung has kept faith with all of his compatriots throughout, but those around him are only human, and weaker than he. The Christ-like allusion of sacrifice at the close takes things a little too far; the real George Jung could hardly have been so gullible, or even so simple. Greedy and stupid, more like. But greedy, stupid people tend not to make for attractive protagonists in Hollywood biographies; Demme cut the courtroom scene which led to Jung's lengthy prison sentence at the climax, in order that the violin strings could continue uninterrupted.

What makes *Blow* stand out from the crowd of crime films dealing with the cocaine trade is the towering performance of Johnny Depp. In the course of the story, Jung has to go from being a brash teenager who lectures a judge by quoting Bob Dylan lyrics ('It ain't me, babe, it ain't me') to a broken-hearted 'lifer' who tapes moving goodbyes to a dying father and strolls in the grounds of the prison with only an imaginary daughter for company. Many actors have played the ageing prisoner role – perhaps most famously Burt Lancaster in *Birdman of Alcatraz* (1962) – but none quite like this. Depp's recent paternity adds extra dimension to the scenes with his screen daughter, and depth to the sense of loss which he evinces at the thought of not seeing her again, but that is to sell him and his talent short; his George Jung is pure craftsmanship.

> I'm great at what I do, Dad. I mean, I'm really great at what I do.
>
> George Jung (Johnny Depp), Blow (2000)

It has been luxuriantly present throughout most his career but in *Blow*, Depp's hair takes on a starring role of its own, from youthful blond mop-top to prison-grey ponytail and all forms in between, it is his single best physical asset as an actor next to his eyes; a personal prop which is ever at his disposal to aid and abet characterisation. Despite the assistance from Barnett, the transformation from nervous teenager to world-weary old lag over the course of the film's 124-minute running-time is imperceptible and utterly convincing. It is not just the physical change, but the emotional and psychological one, as well. If silent-screen star Lon Chaney was the Man of a Thousand Faces, then Johnny Depp is the man of a thousand personalities. Demme's film provides him with the opportunity to turn in a virtuoso performance, for almost the first time in his career; it supplies the expected quota of sterling support, but none of his co-stars are placed on equal footing with him. *Blow* is Depp's film, and his alone, and he does not shrink from the challenge. He grabs it with both hands and runs with it, as Jung is shown to do when offered his fortune (and fateful future) by Pablo Escobar. The role is an absolute triumph for the actor who himself came to California in search of wealth and fame, all those years before. A magnificent performance in every respect, bar one: it is only a pity that the subject in question was not more worthy of it.

> So in the end, was it worth it? Jesus Christ ... How irreparably changed my life has become. It's always the last day of summer and I've been left out in the cold with

> no door to get back in. I'll grant you I've had more than
> my share of poignant moments. Life passes most people by
> when they're making grand plans for it. Throughout my
> lifetime, I've left pieces of my heart here and there, and
> now there's almost not enough to stay alive. But I force a
> smile, knowing that my ambition far exceeded my talent.
> There are no more white horses, or pretty ladies at my
> door.
>
> George Jung (Johnny Depp), Blow (2000)

The film closes on the self-pitying apologia from Jung that his ambition exceeded his talent. In Johnny Depp's case, *Blow* showed once and for all that exactly the opposite was true. In the case of director Ted Demme, however, no one was to know either way.

Demme had come to *Blow* with an agenda, though not the traditional one of 'crime doesn't pay'; to its director, *Blow* was a love story – strange and warped and lived in a haze of toxins, but a love story, nonetheless. Demme was the father of a three-year-old daughter, and what he had taken from *his* prison visits to Jung (as well as his conversations with Jung's wife and daughter) was the inequity of incarcerating not only drug users but dealers as well, for lengthy periods of time, because of the knock-on effect on the families left behind. His film was never intended to take a stand about drugs, one way or the other (although he supported the legalisation of cannabis); it was intended to take a stand about the penalties that were currently being imposed for possession. Johnny Depp picked up on the same vibe during the shoot and became vocal in interviews in support of Jung's release. 'He's paid his debt to society,' he said. 'He should be able to go out and teach kids about the dangers of drugs.'

But herein lieth the salutary lesson which none of these liberal thinkers quite seem to dig at the end of the day: 20 months after close of shooting on *Blow*, Ted Demme died of a heart attack while playing basketball. He had just turned 38. The inquest found an amount of cocaine in his system – small, but sufficient to be considered a contributory cause. By then, Demme had left behind a five-year-old daughter and a two-month-old son, in addition to a grieving widow.

Depp had been accompanied by Paradis and his daughter during the production of *Blow*, in California and Mexico, but his next role placed all of them closer to home. Demme's film had wrapped at the end of April; only one month later, Depp was in the quaint, tenth-century village of Flavigny, in the Dauphine region of the South of France, on the set of *Chocolat*.

Chocolat was to be directed by Lasse Hallström, with whom Depp had made *What's Eating Gilbert Grape* back in 1993. 'When Lasse came to me with the idea of doing *Chocolat*, I was very surprised,' he said. 'We had a good experience on *Gilbert Grape* but it was also difficult. I was surprised that he'd want to go through something with me again, thinking that I was some kind of moody, brooding, horrible shit-head.' Two years previously, on *The Ninth Gate*, he had made love on-screen to Hallström's wife, Lena Olin, in her role as Liana Telfer; the same film had required him to make love to Emmanuelle Seigner, the wife of *Ninth Gate* director, Roman Polanski. He had found that experience a little unsettling, with Polanski peering at him from the other side of the camera, and here he was being asked to play opposite Olin again. 'Hopefully, he won't ask me to play the lover of his wife, because I wouldn't make it,' he conceded. In the event, he had nothing to fear; for *Chocolat*, Depp was to play the lover of Juliette Binoche.

> Once upon a time there was a quiet little village in the French countryside, whose people believed in tranquilité – tranquillity. If you lived in this village, you understood what was expected of you; you knew your place in the scheme of things. And if you happened to forget, someone would help remind you.
>
> Vianne Rocher (Juliette Binoche), Chocolat (2000)

Chocolat was the third novel of Leeds Grammar School teacher and part-time writer Joanne Harris, but it turned into her first international bestseller. Published in the UK in 1999, its setting of a *chocolaterie* in a small village in rural France was a result of Harris's mixed blood: her mother was French. A critique of the novel which asked 'Is this the best book ever written?' put veteran producer David Brown (husband of *Cosmopolitan*'s Helen Gurley Brown) onto its trail, and Miramax snapped up the rights almost before the ink was dry on the paper. The tale is a classic one of a battle of wills between the free-spirited female proprietor of the *chocolaterie* and the austere local priest who views her devotion to the sins of the flesh – in the metaphorical form of chocolate – as a threat to the spiritual well-being of his flock. In order not to offend any religious sensibilities in the USA or Europe, Robert Nelson Jacobs' screenplay opted to swap the priest for an equally austere town mayor, and to up the layers of sugar-coating:

A long, long time ago (1959, to be precise), a Good Fairy alights on a sleepy French village and makes Dreams come true by feeding its inhabitants Magic sweetmeats. The Bad Fairy, who holds sway in the village, is won over to the path of Goodness by accidentally eating the Magic candy himself. With no more disharmony, Prince Charming sails into view in a golden boat and sweeps the Good Fairy off her feet, and everyone lives Happily Ever After...

Alternatively – Vianne Rocher (Binoche) and her daughter decide to settle in Lansquenet, a Breton hamlet ruled over with Catholic efficiency by town mayor and Gallic equivalent to lord of the manor, the Comte De Reynaud (Alfred Molina). Reynaud is an oily aristocrat of the old school who keeps his flock in line with an iron hand tucked snugly inside a velvet glove, and he is discomfited by Vianne's plan to open a *chocolaterie* in the town over Lent. Sensing the devil of Temptation in their midst, Reynaud sets his face against the seductive trifles and siren wiles of the attractive newcomer. As Vianne faces defeat after the obligatory series of mishaps, help arrives in the form of Roux (Depp), a wandering Gypsy minstrel and kindred spirit, who, along with other newly liberated souls, gives her the emotional support that she needs to recover the courage of her convictions and ultimately win the day.

The part of Roux was another token one for Depp. He first arrives quite late in the film, repairs a door, throws a party on his barge and sails into the sunset, returning in the closing moments to provide the obligatory happy ending. He does what is asked of him in *Chocolat*, combining faintly roguish charm with underlying strength of character, but he is given little chance to shine on his own account and the key confrontations between the characters all take place without him. Aside from the obvious convenience of shooting in France and England (the latter so that *Chocolat* could qualify for tax breaks as a British production), few actors of his status at this stage in their careers would have contemplated such an unrewarding and underwritten role, but he seems content to let his co-stars take the glory while he dallies on the periphery of the story; his *presence* is felt throughout the second half, where the sense of expectation that he will arrive on a white charger and take the heroine in his arms becomes almost tangible, but this never comes to pass and the feel-good factor for which the film has been aiming is undercut by its refusal to resort to such familiar romantic cliché. Then again, perhaps *The Man Who Cried* was still too fresh in everyone's mind.

Taking his inspiration – and his accent – on this occasion from Pogues lead singer Shane MacGowan, Depp started out in typically self-denigrating fashion by adorning the character of Roux with a wild mane of curly hair that cascaded down either side of his face; this was amended early in shooting to a tightly swept-back style that braided into a ponytail and thus revealed more of his features. He was, after all, the romantic lead in *Chocolat* and, whether he liked it or not, romantic leads need to have their features *seen*. His performance in the film is that of a man who is well aware of his sexual attractiveness and plays upon it. Depp offsets this by investing the character with a strong sense of moral rectitude and, ultimately, a soft heart. But it is a confusing turn: the

Irish accent is passably acceptable in an itinerant, albeit one who cruises around the rivers and canals of France, but less in keeping is the mix of Blues and Django Reinhardt tunes that he strums on Roux's guitar with his own fair hand. That he is also the most thinly sketched in a rich roster of predominantly female characters in the script gives the game away: he is on board merely to be Prince Charming, whose kiss awakens the sleeping Cinderella at the close of the fable.

One reason for Depp's involvement was his professed admiration for Juliette Binoche, a genuine kindred spirit in artistic terms: In 1997, Binoche had won the Best Supporting Actress Oscar for *The English Patient*, having previously turned down roles in *Jurassic Park* and *Mission Impossible* – the first French actress to do so since Simone Signoret in *Room at the Top* (1958) – but she refused to capitalise on her success, returning to domestic features and a £250-a-week role in Pirandello's *Naked* at Islington's Almeida Theatre. 'My aim is not to be an American star,' she said at the time. 'Otherwise, I would have moved there.'

Harris had set her story in the Guyenne region of southern France between Toulouse and Bordeaux, but Hallström had shot in Flavigny to the east, although his town of Lansquenet is made to look as though it is sited much further north, so that evocative snowfalls could be incorporated at appropriate intervals. The overt fairy-tale icing sits uneasily atop a romantic melodrama whose ingredients include wife-beating, sexual frustration, racism and diabetes, and *Chocolat* always seems to be a film of two halves, neither quite matching the other. The novelty concept of chocolate as a metaphor for freedom and self-expression is played to the hilt, sometimes embarrassingly so, but Hallström's lightness of touch kneads the tale's less digestible threads into something softer on the palate. There are a few humorous moments, mostly supplied by Molina's authoritarian mayor, but the suspicion remains that *Chocolat* is a film which was made with Oscar very much in mind.

Depp was cast in *Chocolat* for the very pretty-boy looks that he had always been at pains to disavow, and while he can unarguably play to this, his best asset, one is nevertheless left with the sense of an actor who is trying desperately to rise above the two-dimensionalism of the role as written, but is constantly held back from achieving it. In terms of Johnny Depp's career, *Chocolat* was mere passing frivolity: a delicious dark brown confection, but lacking in 'bite' and of no great gastronomic significance.

> When I awoke, Roux was gone, and the wind had changed again.
>
> Joanne Harris, Chocolat (1999)

Alfred Molina may have been the source of the humour in *Chocolat*, but Depp's propensity for practical jokes was well known among his fellow actors. On *What's Eating Gilbert Grape*, he had paid the young Leonardo DiCaprio $500 dollars to eat a rancid pickled egg, and he was an avid collector of surreal phrases in strange languages, which he culled from every director of foreign nationality for whom he had ever worked: 'I have a small rat in my throat' in Swedish was but one example. He was fond of booking himself into hotels under assumed names, such as William Wilder or Sanchez Del Vecchio (though not Mr Stench or Mr Drip Noodle, as often reported), in order to receive a rib-tickling wake-up call. And he had for years left incongruous messages on his answerphone machine in LA, including one sampled from an advert for breast enlargement which one day greeted a call from his mother: 'I think I must have dropped him on his head as a small child,' she was moved to remark on hearing it.

Depp had played the joker on both *Donnie Brasco* and *Blow* with the liberal deployment of a whoopee cushion and a 'fart machine', which prompted Penelope Cruz, one of his co-stars on the latter, to declare of him, 'Johnny is the funniest man. I don't think people know this, but he is always the joker.' So impressed was she with her scenes being interrupted by flatulent noises off that she was persuaded to purchase a fart machine of her own. 'I think we may have created a monster,' she said, looking around for an unsuspecting victim.

For some time, Depp had carried with him tapes of BBC TV's cult comedy series, *The Fast Show*, a fast-moving (as its name implies!) compilation of satirical sketches, which featured the diverse talents of ex-Harry Enfield straight-man Paul Whitehouse, former Punk-rocker Charlie Higson, comedian Simon Day and actors John Thomson and Mark Williams. Before setting off for his next location, he asked Whitehouse and Higson if he could guest on what was currently shooting as *The Last Fast Show Ever*, for transmission on Boxing Day. He appeared in a sketch with the 'suit you' tailors of Whitehouse and Williams, during which he was able to say 'fuck' on (British) television; when they all assembled for drinks, Whitehouse had to treat his number one fan to endless in-character impressions of the alcoholic Rowley Birkin QC.

Depp had to make the most of the light relief. There were to be very few laughs on his next assignment-other than those which emanated from Jolly Jack.

> Netley: I-It's just, you say we've got to kill another woman. I thought it were finished, sir. I-I can't take it. I've 'ad enough. I mean, i-it's in all the papers. It's everywhere you look... I'm only an ordinary chap, sir. That's all I am. I-I don't know where I am any more, sir, and that's the truth... That's the truth.
> Gull: There, there, Netley. There, there. I shall tell you where we are. We're in the most extreme and utter region of the human mind, a dim sub-conscious underworld. A radiant abyss where men meet themselves... Hell, Netley. We're in Hell.
> Alan Moore, From Hell (1992)

The pressing venue for Johnny Depp was old London Town – but in the Czech Republic, rather than England – as the Victorian police officer who is assigned to the case of 'Jack the Ripper', in 20th Century Fox's big-budget adaptation of Alan Moore's *From Hell*. Daniel Day-Lewis and Brad Pitt originally had been rumoured as the studio's actors of choice to play Detective Chief Inspector Frederick George Abberline, but the role had been offered to Londoner Jude Law, instead. When Law eventually declined in favour of working with Oscar-winning director Anthony Minghella on *The Talented Mr Ripley*, the role came Depp's way. Marlon Brando had availed himself of excellent British accents for *Mutiny on the Bounty* (1962) and *Queimada* (1969). Now, it was going to be Johnny's turn.

From Hell was based on a ground-breaking graphic novel by Moore (of *Watchmen* fame) and illustrator Eddie Campbell. It started out as one component of a now-defunct comic called *Taboo*. When that title folded, it took on a life of its own as a self-contained part-work whose first volume (the novel eventually ran to sixteen) was issued by Mad Love Publishing in February of 1992. In May 2000, all sixteen parts were issued in compendium form by Knockabout. Moore's *From Hell* purports to examine in minute detail the series of murders which were committed on the streets of London's Whitechapel district in 1888 by the pseudonymous Jack the Ripper – the world's first recorded serial killer.

Between 1887 and 1891, the East End of London was struck by a series of street slayings, all centring on the Whitechapel area. The victims were women of the 'unfortunate class', and it was not long before a number of these murders became denominated to a single assailant. The final tally of murders remains open to debate, but students of 'Ripperology' have settled for either five or six, namely those of Mary Ann 'Polly' Nichols, Annie Chapman, Elizabeth Stride, Catherine Eddowes, Mary Jane Kelly and, possibly, Martha Tabram – all of which took place in autumn 1888. *From Hell* played it safe and opted for all six.

These, and others, were designated by Scotland Yard as the 'Whitechapel Murders', though history has chosen to absorb them into the legend of Jack the Ripper. In the event, the murders went unsolved, and the myth of a mysterious assassin in top hat and cape, carrying a surgeon's bag and trawling the backstreets of Whitechapel for his next unwary victim was born. Moore's novel drew heavily for its solution to the crimes on a theory put forward in 1976 by journalist Stephen Knight, in his book *Jack the Ripper: The Final Solution*; that book proposed that the killer was 72-year-old Sir William Withey Gull, physician-in-ordinary to Queen Victoria and stroke victim, who together with a coach-driver named Netley, set out to silence the witnesses to the birth of an illegitimate heir to the throne of England as part of an elaborate Masonic plot. Knight's theory was rapidly discredited but, like all good conspiracies, not before it had taken hold of the willing, for all its implausibilities and errors of fact. *From Hell* the movie was thus bound to an outmoded convention before the first frame of film had even passed through the gate of the camera.

Even Alan Moore had given up on Knight's theory before he and Campbell reached the end of their epic endeavour but, by then, their elaborate fantasy had taken on a life of its own. *From Hell*, the graphic novel, is Jack the Ripper in a parallel universe chock-full of the cosmological claptrap of *The Matrix*. The film's scriptwriters dispensed with Moore's philosophical esoterica but retained his central thesis, though to arrive at the conclusion that Gull is the killer without the leap of astrological faith that Moore had employed required the services of a swami. Enter the swami: Abberline had effectively to be invested with the characteristics of a Neo, minus the ability to alter time and space.

> So – Jack the Ripper isn't just merely killing whores. He's executing traitors. He's a mason fulfilling a duty.
>
> Inspector Abberline (Johnny Depp), From Hell (2001)

The cream of the London detective force were all, at one time or another, allocated the task of tracking down Jack the Ripper, but one man more than any other has come to be associated with the case in the popular mind, even though he had been transferred out of Whitechapel the year before the murders began and was brought back only to investigate the final slaying of the series, that of Mary Kelly. At the time of the Ripper killings, Dorset-born Detective Inspector Frederick George Abberline was 45 years old; he retired from the police force four years later and became a private enquiry agent, in charge of the European branch of the Pinkerton Agency. He died peacefully at his home in Bournemouth in 1929, his wife of 53 years by his bedside; during his long and celebrated career, he had been the recipient of a total of 84 commendations and awards. So much for history; hooray for Hollywood...

From Hell began its transition to the screen at the unlikely venue of Disney (in the form of its Touchstone subsidiary), with producer Don Murphy and scriptwriter Terry Hayes. Assigned to the project as director(s) were the Hughes brothers, Albert and Allen, whose previous films of note included ghetto-dramas *Menace II Society* (1993) and *Dead Presidents* (1995). 'Disney gave us the *From Hell* script with *Con Air* and a couple of other movies,' Albert Hughes said. 'We didn't even read it; we just said, "Not interested". Maybe six months later, we read it, and while we never imagined doing a Jack the Ripper movie, it was really right up our alley.' By this time, it had reversed out of Disney's alley and into New Line's, where it resided for a year before ending up at Fox. The Brothers Grime had stayed the course throughout. 'We were just enthralled,' Allen Hughes recalled. 'Then we got our hands on the comic book. That, mixed with the fact that it's a thriller about a killer, drew us into it.' In the interval, Sean Connery had become the front-runner to play Abberline, but that idea was abandoned along with the original script, in favour of a rewrite by Rafael Yglesias. 'We started looking at the younger version of the movie,' Murphy explained, so in had come

Day-Lewis, Pitt, Law and, ultimately, Depp. In keeping with the Hughes brothers' cinematic preoccupation with urban violence and drugs, the new script turned Abberline into an opium junkie who 'dreams' the murders.

Yglesias drew his concept of a psychic detective from Sax Rohmer's *The Dream Detective*, a pulp-fiction novel of 1920 in which hero Morris Klaw gained intuitive insight into the crimes which he was hired to investigate by sleeping on a 'special' pillow; the pillow of Abberline's acquaintance in the film became that of his bed in an opium den, a further allusion to Rohmer and a nod in the general direction of the ghetto culture so beloved of *From Hell*'s directors. The real Abberline was nothing of the sort, nor did he indulge in anything more mind-expanding than the occasional tot of whiskey.

Depp's methodical propensity for accuracy of characterisation deserted him in the face of such a flagrant abuse of the facts. He had been happy enough to schmooze with the likes of Joe Pistone and Hunter Thompson but was evidently less keen to steep himself in a few volumes of Ripper history, despite adopting a typical promotional pose on the film's release and professing the contrary: 'As a kid, I saw a documentary on television about Jack the Ripper and since then, I've been fascinated by the character and acquired several books about him. Among other things, his crimes fostered the rise of the tabloid press in London, and that's certainly interesting. The *From Hell* comic book was amazingly thorough in its research and was beautifully done. Really painstakingly done. I was impressed by that. It's a great theory that they come up with, and mathematically it works.'

> He's not doing this for fun. This is ritual.
> Inspector Abberline (Johnny Depp), From Hell (2001)

For all of his previously stated aversions to American culture, Depp bought wholesale into the bowdlerised and thoroughly Americanised version of the Ripper saga, as reinvented by the

Hughes brothers and their screenwriters. 'In terms of hero, anti-hero, reluctant hero, whatever, for me, Abberline was an interesting opportunity to play a dedicated police inspector who was not only dealing with the demon of Jack the Ripper and that mystery, but he was dealing with his own demons at the same time. He's a guy who medicates himself, almost to the brink of death, just to be able to cope with life,' he said. Not only was *From Hell* not the history, it was shaping up not to be the comic book either. But none of that stopped Depp from advancing the case that Albert and Allen Hughes, the script and the film were the greatest things since sliced tarts: 'The Hughes brothers were passionate about this. I couldn't say no to them.'

The role of Inspector Abberline in *From Hell* was uncomfortably close to that of Constable Crane in *Sleepy Hollow*, especially when it came to how Yglesias' script chose to interpret the detective – both are policemen whose unorthodox methods solve a series of grisly murders: in the Burton film, it was the alchemy of forensic science, whereas in the Hughes brothers' epic, it is the outright sorcery of 'second sight'. Having effectively essayed this role once, Depp was left with no room to manoeuvre on the second occasion. 'I thought a lot about it, because there are of course some analogies; but when I read the script and understood what kind of character Abberline was, the doubts vanished,' he said. 'This is an inspector who chooses the side of the sub-proletariat and the prostitutes against the Establishment; he is a human character who takes big risks to carry on his investigation. To refuse this part only because I'd already played the role of a detective during the Victorian period seemed absurd to me.' (Burton's film of *Sleepy Hollow* is actually set in the *Georgian* period of British history.)

Depp had initially thought to play Abberline as he had appeared in Campbell's panels in the graphic novel-and in life: with bowler hat and large handlebar moustache. The producers of *From Hell* rejected this notion, and as the Abberline of the film was also to be presented as an opium addict, on whom the 'dragon' bestows precognitive powers, he took the only other route open to an aesthetic actor and turned him into one of the Graveyard Poets, or honorary member of the Pre-Raphaelite Brotherhood: a lank-haired, left-bank radical, hooked on absinthe and the poppy, but with the sensitive soul of the artist. This allowed him to suggest to interviewers who noted the parallel with Ichabod Crane that Abberline would have hated the 'prim and proper' New York constable. On the contrary, the real Abberline would have loved him. 'There wasn't much material on Abberline – I had to make it up or just guess – but when you're playing a real person, there's a lot of responsibility,' he offered, when it came time to promote the film in the States. In point of fact, there is as much material on Frederick George Abberline as there is on Ed Wood, not least the many biographical insights that Moore chose to include in the graphic novel, but all of it plays *against* the character as described in the script for *From Hell*.

In Depp's hands, Abberline became a Byronic hero, a man out of sync with the world in which he is called upon to perform, who takes flight from reality in the pipe of dreams, but who goes to his death on an altar of love and self-sacrifice. This is the very stuff of romance, and it was appropriate that Depp should enter into negotiations to play George Gordon, the real Lord Byron, as soon as *From Hell* was in the can. (The project went unrealised.) But the imposition of a pulp-fictional, quasi-Holmesian mystic on what purported to be a faithful version of events was a pretentious contrivance which allowed the writer to dispense with the necessity of having the hero arrive at his con-clusions by process of deduction. Instead, the film settles for a psychic detective who nabs his man merely by *divining* his pres-ence at the scene of his crimes. No need for unwieldy explana-tions; no need for the sifting of evidence (of which there was none). Gull is the killer because Abberline says that he is the killer, and Yglesias then conveniently has him confess. Case solved. As an interpretation of an historical figure, Depp's rendi-tion of Abberline helped to sink without trace whatever chance

From Hell ever had of being taken seriously as a film about the Whitechapel Murders.

With a mere $30 million at their disposal, the Hughes brothers managed only to turn out the most barefaced example of cultural imperialism that anyone was likely to see (at least until the release of Fox's similarly Moore-inspired *The League of Extraordinary Gentlemen* three years later). And for all of Depp's fine words about the 'responsibility' that he feels when it comes to portraying real people like Pistone or Thompson, he apparently thought nothing of selling poor Fred Abberline right down the river.

> One day men will look back and say I gave birth to the twentieth century. Jack the Ripper – 1888.
>
> screen caption, From Hell (2001)

The bald screen caption which opens *From Hell* is suitably portentous but fundamentally nonsensical, as it would have required foreknowledge to be uttered (as it is by the Ripper at the close). Therein lies the flaw with the film as a whole: foreknowledge is the predominant sensation throughout, and not just on Abberline's part after another night spent 'chasing the dragon'. Unlike Moore's novel, the screen adaptation is played as a mystery-thriller, and yet anyone in the audience who has seen *Murder By Decree* (1979) or even Thames Television's mini-series *Jack the Ripper* (1988), let alone read any book on the case published in the last 25 years, knows right away that the very mention of William Gull's name puts him in the frame for the murders. When Gull is then played by the only other actor of note in the cast besides the leads, game over. To retain some element of mystery about who, of the only possible suspect, Jack might actually be, Ian Holm has to play him as a benign confidante of Abberline's throughout much of the inquiry, but even this had been done before. 'We'd like to make the audience believe that Abberline himself might be Jack the Ripper, committing the murders in an opium stupor, and that aspect made the role a lot of fun to play,' Depp said, and this is attempted by having both characters drink absinthe, though a Cormanesque dream sequence which showed Abberline in the person of the Ripper being confronted with one of his victims was deleted prior to release.

Bereft of mystery, and with few thrills promised between the expected murders, *From Hell* has to fall back on the presumed fascination of squalor and Abberline's unravelling of a larger conspiracy which goes all the way to Queen Victoria herself. To achieve the latter, the screenplay adds a new character to the cast whose name fails to feature in the historical record: Ben Kidney (Terence Harvey), a sinister Special Branch inspector and agent of the Crown, whose officers facilitate Gull's state-sponsored campaign of terror. Under Kidney's auspices, the British police establishment behave like members of the Mafia, while his men on the beat wield all the power of apparatchiks in a banana republic. If this sounds like Los Angeles in a bad B-movie, then it looks like it too.

The misguided attempt to contrive the murders so they approximate what happened for real proves too much of a burden for the brothers and cramps what style they can muster to produce some lifeless assaults, draining the film of tension. In a similar vein, factual titbits which were thought essential for inclusion – the mention of 'Leather Apron'; Netley shouting 'Lipski' at a passer-by as Gull kills Elizabeth Stride – are thrown piecemeal into the narrative like so much dead weight, to give the illusion of veracity. But no amount of casebook facsimiles can combat the treatment meted out to the leading characters; *From Hell* is a painted whore, attractive at a glance but pox-ridden on examination. Particularly risible are scenes dealing with the reactions of the various participants to the Ripper's handiwork, where the film moves from the territory of the unreal into the land of the absurd: a police surgeon vomits at the sight of Polly Nichols' corpse, while Abberline hardly turns a hair. Some actors are good at expressing disgust; Johnny Depp is clearly not one of them. Even the atrocity in Miller's Court – a double-whammy for the inspector in principle as he also assumes the body in the room to be that of his beloved – leaves him largely unmoved, while rank-and-file constabulary take another look at their breakfasts.

In *From Hell*'s scheme of things, Britain is ruled by a medieval clique of master Masons whose disdain for the plebs would put Stalin to shame. But the London that the film depicts is that of Dickens, not Wilde or Shaw. 'No one in Whitechapel, no matter what their trade, could afford grapes,' Abberline says, as though talking about Beluga caviar. The East End set was constructed (at a cost of $1 million) on a 20-acre site near the Barrandov studios in Prague. 'There were about fourteen other productions shooting while we were there,' Depp said. 'There was one time when we were driving to the set and we saw trucks up ahead and started to get out, and someone said, "That's not us – we're two blocks down".' The streets, at least, were accurate enough, but the mood of the film is half a century removed from the smoke-and-steel imperial period which the production design of Martin Childs went to some pains to depict. Albert and Allen Hughes were intent on transplanting a geo-specific, urban nihilism onto a wholly unwilling late-Victorian locale, yet less than three years after the last official Ripper murder, Thomas Edison unveiled his Kinetoscope in New York and cinema came into being. Three years after that saw Carl Benz launch the first production motor car. Twelve months later, and H G Wells published *The Time Machine*. France was on the verge of La Belle Epoque; Britain was on the cusp of modernity.

> Godley: Was it another one? What did you see? What is it?
> Abberline: They don't make any sense. I think it might be time for me to take a little walk.
> Godley: I'm not having you disappearing into some Chinese hole ... Some of that damned dream-stick again.
> Abberline: Then we'll have to search.
> Godley: Search for what – your bloody dreams?
> scene deleted from From Hell (2001)

The deleted scenes included on the DVD release of *From Hell* are unusually instructive. A second dream sequence involved a tracking shot towards the Ripper as he is eviscerating Polly Nichols in the street; he turns and reveals himself to be Ben Kidney. Had this scene remained in the film, it would have served only to further undermine Abberline's supposed precognitive abilities, inasmuch as it shows him perceiving the wrong man to be the killer. Another excision was the murder of Annie Chapman, which formed one of several clumsy nods to Ripper movies that had gone before, in this case, 1959's *Jack the Ripper*, with its whispering, unseen assassin and cowering, spotlighted victim. Two gratuitous scenes of Netley masturbating in his quarters (during the second of which, he is garrotted by a Special Branch lackey) were also edited out, as was an alternative ending which had Abberline meet the same drug-induced death, but many years later (his hair is white) and inexplicably in an opium den on the Hong Kong waterfront.

The part of Gull was to have been played by Nigel Hawthorne, who had to relinquish the role because of illness; he died on Boxing Day 2001. Substitute Ian Holm, though, gives *From Hell* its most chilling moments, from the expression on his face – aided by black contact lenses – when he finally realises that his subterfuge has been uncovered by Abberline, to his pep-talk to Netley (Jason Flemyng) as he ushers him verbally into his own private Inferno. But the pay-off to this scene, in which he dictates the titular 'From Hell' letter to Netley, was also deleted.

As though the experience of *Fear and Loathing in Las Vegas* were not enough, Depp has yet again to spend much of his time on-screen under the influence. 'I can certainly thank past experiences for walking me through some of the more opiated moments in *From Hell*,' he told the *Daily Mirror*. The notional reason this time is the loss of a wife and child, but the scenes in question reek of nothing more than self-pity and bathos. Abberline in the film is supposed to indulge in not only opium but also laudanum (the favoured drug of romantics) and absinthe – *la fée verte* –

a notorious French aperitif of some 80 per cent proof (approximately three times stronger than brandy), whose distinctive flavour was derived from wormwood; famous absinthe-drinkers included Henri Toulouse-Lautrec and the disgraced Oscar Wilde, and it was much in vogue on the artistic fringes around the turn of the nineteenth century. Absinthe was banned in France in 1915, ostensibly for contributing to the spread of alcoholism in Paris but, since the 1980s, it has again become something of a cult among American tourists in Prague, where it had always remained freely available. When he came to shoot *From Hell* in the city, Depp also took to imbibing 'the green fairy' in preparation for his role, though he later commented: 'It's like marijuana. Drink too much and you suddenly realise why Van Gogh cut off his ear.' (When he was a boy, he had a print of the famous self-portrait of the artist, *sans* ear, sited conspicuously in his bedroom.)

The film's Abberline is depicted as a man of destiny ('You're not going to see the twentieth century,' he doomily informs the Ripper, with a sublime sense of timing) who, having nailed the Ripper and saved the tart-with-a-heart, allows himself to succumb fatally to the pipe of dreams in the tale's closing moments. 'The studio wanted Abberline to live,' Depp went on to explain. 'They wanted Abberline and Mary Kelly to end up together on that rocky cliff in Ireland. I was adamant about what happened to my character. I wasn't going to let that happen.' True to the character and Depp's own poetic notions about premature demise, *à la Byron*, Shelley or even Coleridge, it may have been, but it was also an abject betrayal of historical truth. 'I don't regret making any films,' he informed one interviewer. 'Not even the worst of them. I'm sure there's a number of bad ones, but I don't see them all. I worked on a television series for three and half years; I think I was in probably 75 episodes and I saw about five of them. So I'm sure there's some questionable work in there. Over the years, I'm sure I've done some goofy things.' None goofier than *From Hell*. Given that the story opens on a close-up of Abberline's eyes while he lies romantically prostrate in a drug-induced stupor, the entire film could be construed as a bad dream – a Fuselian *Nightmare*. It might be better for all concerned if *From Hell* were indeed to be considered as such.

Not content with having apprehended a serial killer on-screen, Depp pondered briefly over whether to become a cinematic one himself (albeit one who did no actual killing). He had been approached to play Charles Manson, self-styled leader of a violent gang of Californian hippies known as the Family, four of whose number murdered a party of five guests at a rented house on Los Angeles' Cielo Drive on 9 August 1969. Foremost among the victims was eight-months' pregnant Sharon Tate, then wife of *The Ninth Gate* director Roman Polanski. Tate was killed by multiple knife thrusts to the belly, actions which simultaneously ended the life of her unborn child; a rope was trussed around her neck and thrown over a beam; the word 'pig' was scrawled on a door in her own blood. Manson had ordered the murders as part of a 'satanic' campaign of urban guerrilla warfare but, conveniently, had stayed away from the scene of the crimes.

Apparently blind to the impact that such a portrayal might have on a director with whom he had worked only two years before, Depp reportedly sent a letter to Manson, currently resident in California's maximum-security Corcoran State Prison, requesting an interview. 'It's totally up to Manson whether or not Johnny Depp gets the visit he wants,' a prison spokesman stated. 'Mr Depp will have written directly to Manson and if he wants the meeting to take place, he'll send a visitor's pass and Mr Depp can come in here. It's possible he will say yes, although he doesn't have a lot of visitors.' 'I just want to get to know him better,' Depp sought to clarify.

It is said that actors have few scruples and Hollywood none at all. In the case of the Manson film, that notion seemed to apply in spades. Whatever integrity was in play on this occasion, it was left to Manson himself to furnish it by refusing Depp's plea. The actor later denied that he had even considered playing the killer. 'I've been approached,' he admitted, before dismissing the claim as so much hearsay. 'I remember a film called *Helter Skelter* with Steven Railsback. He did such a good job that there's no need for a remake.' ('Helter Skelter', a track from The Beatles' 'white album', was the call sign for Manson's urban revolution; in his warped version of the universe, he was the 'fifth angel' to The Beatles' other four.) Depp once owned a 'clown' painting by homosexual serial killer John Wayne Gacy, so his fascination with the species was nothing new, but playing Charles Manson might have been one Depp eccentric too far.

In the wake of the poor returns from *The Ninth Gate*, Artisan Entertainment, makers of the film, filed suit in the Los Angeles District Court against director Roman Polanski, claiming that he and his R P Productions had siphoned off refunds of value-added tax instead of turning them over to the guarantors who had acted on Artisan's behalf during the shoot. Polanski was alleged to have received $619,000 in refunds, with another $577,000 on the way, and to have 'brazenly deposited the money in a private account', refusing all requests for its return.

If Polanski found himself facing charges of fraud and breach of contract in the first summer of the new millennium, then he was not the only one. While Depp had been investigating crime in Whitechapel, the Los Angeles District Attorney had also set about investigating *him*.

A few months earlier, Peter Nichols, one of the partners in a firm of solicitors called Lichter Grossman Nichols Adler & Goodman Inc., had made a new offer to Anthony Fox, on behalf of Johnny Depp, to buy out his share of the Viper Room. In the course of the negotiations, he had revealed for the first time that licensing rights for the club had now been transferred to Trouser Trumpet, the company owned by Depp and Jenco. For Anthony Fox, it was the last straw.

In July 2000, Fox sued Depp, Jenco and their legal representatives, claiming that the parties had conspired to divert licensing fees from their joint holding company, Safe in Heaven, into Trouser Trumpet, without his knowledge or approval as a

co-owner and co-director of the club. The suit sought an unspecified amount of damages.

This was not the news which Depp had been waiting for. When
his agent telephoned him to break it, he had expected to hear
about the commencement of a different one-man campaign to
right perceived wrongs.

> The financing just fell through for the third time on Don
> Quixote.
>
> Orson Welles (Vincent D'Onofrio), Ed Wood (1993)

The decision to 'turn his back' on America opened the door for
Depp to participate in more European-orientated productions.
His last Hollywood-based film was *Blow* but, before that, *The
Ninth Gate* had been filmed in France, *Sleepy Hollow* in England,
The Man Who Cried also in France and *Chocolat* in both. It was
easier and more convenient for himself and his family if he were
to 'localise' his career for the time being, always assuming that the
work continued to be forthcoming. As it happened, director Terry
Gilliam had at last secured proper financing for his Cervantes
project, and he was now in a position to offer Depp the role of
The Man Who Killed Don Quixote.

The film was originally meant to have been shot on location in
Spain in August 1999, on a budget of $35 million, jointly funded
by Pathé, Canal Plus and a German independent producer named
Rainer Mockert. Mockert dropped out just as the cameras were
making ready to roll and with him went his portion of the budget, a not insubstantial $15 million. By the turn of the year, Gilliam
had a new deal in place with another French company, and the
projected cost of the film had once again risen to a more promising $32 million. But Gilliam had started to tear out his hair over a
different aspect of *Don Quixote*. When it comes to the hiring of
actors, the Hollywood ethic is known as 'pay-or-play', which entitles the star of a film to the contracted fee, even if the film in question is never made. The French industry does not subscribe to

such a practice, and the new producers were unwilling to offer Depp a contract until all the necessary funding was in place. 'It's not for us to commit to Johnny Depp,' said one. 'It's for him to commit to us.' Depp had committed to Terry Gilliam before *Blow*, but even that was on the basis of schedule permitting. 'They just could not, or would not, understand that without the star, the film doesn't get made,' the exasperated Gilliam explained.

In the meantime, Depp had completed both *Chocolat* and *From Hell* and, since August 2000, he had been waiting on tenterhooks for news of *Don Quixote*. All the delays and obfuscations had gone some way to convince him that he was being 'majorly jerked around' by the film's French producers and he was inclined to cry off, in spite of the fact that the project offered an opportunity to act opposite Paradis, who had also been cast.

The extra German finance was eventually forthcoming, and Gilliam's *The Man Who Killed Don Quixote* headed for a definite start date of September. But not before an irate phone call to Gilliam from one Johnny Depp, who only now had been informed of the comparatively meagre size of the pay cheque which he was due to receive. 'Johnny was already becoming obsessional about the film, but when the actual amount was mentioned, he went apeshit,' Gilliam said. 'He told me he wanted twice as much.' After some toing and froing, Depp settled for half as much again, with Gilliam himself taking one quarter of *his* normal fee, and *The Man Who Killed Don Quixote* finally headed off to Navarra, in Northern Spain.

But that was only the start.

In Gilliam and regular collaborator Tony Grisoni's version of Cervantes, Depp was to play a 'really mean' advertising executive named Toby Grosini who is magically transported back to the seventeenth century, where the fabled Quixote mistakes him for his lazy sidekick, Sancho Panza. The character had been written with Depp in mind. 'Terry wanted to expose to the whole world that I'm much shittier than they think I am,' he said in the *Daily Telegraph*. It was a reading of the role with which Gilliam concurred:

'I wanted to take the entire range of Johnny and who he is, and what he's capable of, and play with it. He tends to get these parts where he's lovely or innocent or whatever, and I thought, let's stretch him and let him really play on a broad canvas. He's much more interesting than the world knows. There's a sting to Johnny's tail that most people haven't seen, and I thought we should incorporate some of that.'

Filming was scheduled to begin on the last week of September and, on day one, 70-year-old French actor Jean Rochefort, who was to play Quixote and who had spent the intervening year learning English, was struck down with a prostate infection; trooper that he was, he insisted on carrying on regardless. Day two brought Depp into the picture but, at close of shooting, the set was hit by a sudden flash flood which washed much of it away and caked everything else that remained in a layer of mud when it eventually subsided. Four days later, and Rochefort had to be airlifted to Paris, where he underwent an emergency operation for a double hernia.

Depp was happy to stick around the set until Rochefort recovered, but Vanessa Paradis had work commitments pending, and others in the cast and crew found themselves in the same boat. 'There's no way I could have found a replacement for Jean in that time, plus the other actors had prior commitments and locations had been lined up months in advance for specific dates,' the dispirited Gilliam explained. 'There was about six hours of joy when me and Johnny were shooting together in the desert, getting ideas, inventing stuff. But that was it.' Music up; roll end credits.

In point of fact, the film drifted aimlessly on for two weeks after Rochefort's incapacitation, while its French producers dithered and insurers circled like vultures overhead. When it finally became clear to all concerned that Rochefort was unlikely to return to Spain in any reasonable timescale, and first assistant director Phil Patterson was not about to allow him to mount his nag Rosinante if he did, proceedings ground to an inglorious halt. Gilliam was known to his regular crew (including *Fear and*

Loathing's cinematographer Nicola Pecorini) as 'Captain Chaos', but the chaos which had erupted on the set of *The Man Who Killed Don Quixote* proved too much for even the brave captain to steer his way through. A commiserating Depp was one of the last to leave the sinking ship.

Defeated again in his quest to bring *Quixote* to the screen, as had been Orson Welles many years before him, the eternally optimistic Gilliam felt unusually subdued by the fiasco for some time after. 'I'm going to make this damn film,' he told the *Observer*'s Sean O'Hagen. It has so far remained a cry in the dark.

As Johnny Depp's erratic film career was shunted into another unexpected siding by the premature closure of *The Man Who Killed Don Quixote*, so old flame Winona Ryder's came resoundingly off the rails.

On 12 December, she was arrested outside Saks Fifth Avenue department store at 9600 Wilshire Boulevard in Beverly Hills and charged with shoplifting $5,560 worth of designer clothing, including a $1,595 Gucci dress. Bail was posted at $20,000. She was additionally charged with possession of prescription medicines without a prescription. Celebrity lawyer Mark Geragos (most recently involved with defending Michael Jackson) denied all charges on Ryder's behalf. 'The charges, I'm convinced, once the Beverly Hills PD has a chance to investigate them, will be rejected,' he trumpeted. 'It's a misunderstanding on the part of the store.' Deputy District Attorney Ann Rundle stated that Ryder had been 'shopping doctors', and had used as many as six different aliases, including that of 'Emily Thompson', to obtain the prescriptions for the eight forms of painkiller which were found on her person, ranging from Valium and Demerol to a form of Oxycodone, otherwise known as 'Hillbilly Heroin'. The drug charge was subsequently dropped.

After several delays and deferments, Ryder's trial took place on 6 November 2002. It was revealed during the course of the two-week hearing that the Saks incident was not the first time that the 30-year-old star had indulged in such behaviour: visits to Barney's of New York during May and October, as well as Nieman Marcus in November [both on Wilshire Boulevard], had all produced videotaped evidence of her acting suspiciously and concealing garments about her person; these earlier instances of kleptomania were ruled as inadmissible. 'She came, she stole, she left. End of story,' Rundle concluded. After five hours of deliberations, the jury convicted Ryder of felony grand theft and vandalism.

Winona Ryder was sentenced on 6 December 2002, to three years probation and 480 hours of community service; in addition, she was to undergo drug and psychological counselling. She was ordered to pay $6,355 in costs to Saks Fifth Avenue and a further $1,000 to the court.

'The sentence fashioned today will ensure that if you steal again you will go to jail. Do you understand?' Superior Court Judge Elden Fox asked the actress.

'Yes, I do,' Ryder replied in a hushed voice.

8 THE TWO JACKS

To have a performance acknowledged on this scale is something I'm not used to. Sometimes five people see my movies, sometimes twenty. It feels a little strange because I really didn't do anything different than I've ever done.

JOHNNY DEPP, TALKING TO *USA TODAY* ABOUT *PIRATES OF THE CARIBBEAN* (2002)

You know, the only thing that matters is the ending.
That's the most important part of the story: the ending.
This one ... is very good. This one's perfect.
Mort Rainey (Johnny Depp), Secret Window (2003)

THE FIRST YEAR of the new millennium had ended on a bum note for Johnny Depp; 2001 was not to start out a great deal better. *Chocolat* was released in the States on 5 January, in time for the Oscars, and on 3 February in the UK. Presented with a simple romantic fable of the old school, the critics were generally unimpressed, with most finding the rush to sweetmeat-orientated pun and cliché irresistible: 'It melts in your brain, not in your mouth,' headlined Jonathan Romney in the *Independent*.

Harvey Weinstein's Miramax managed to contrive a total of five Oscar nominations for the film but despite this, and its frolicsome air of feel-good frippery, *Chocolat* was, strangely, not to many tastes, any more than was Depp's performance within it. The *Guardian*'s Peter Bradshaw was particularly scathing: 'Roux is not on the screen for long, but it's quite long enough. Despite his character's name, Mr Depp has evidently decided that he is not comfortable with the *'Allo 'Allo* Franglais voices imposed on everyone else, so he plays him as an Irishman with what is supposed to be an Irish accent. For this he ought to be shot at dawn, or preferably earlier. It's similar to the Gypsy he played in Sally Potter's *The Man Who Cried*, only much, much more embarrassing. He's always to be found a-hummin' and a-strummin' on his guitar, a fascinating lone-wolf figure. Needless to say, Roux is the kindred spirit with whom Juliette elects to get it on for a rare bit of non-chocolate-oriented, off-camera loving. Then he is off, footloose force of nature that he is, taking with him our sincere good wishes and a heartfelt request that Mr Depp give the free-spirit Romany roles a miss from now on.'

The 26 January release of *Before Night Falls* produced another lead balloon, at least as far as Depp was concerned. American reviewers were unconvinced by all except Javier Bardem's extraordinary performance, and their British counterparts reacted much the same way when the film opened in the UK some five months later. 'The film has curious flaws, notably a couple of bizarre vanity cameos from Sean Penn, as a Cuban mule driver, and Johnny Depp who – in the spirit of Ed Wood Jr – plays two roles: a prison drag-queen and an army lieutenant,' was how the *Guardian* saw it. The *Daily Telegraph* nodded in agreement: 'Sean Penn is embarrassing as a Cuban peasant driving an ox-cart, while Johnny Depp does double duty, first as Bon-Bon, a transvestite who smuggles Arenas's manuscripts out of jail and then (in a fantasy sequence) as Lieutenant Victor, a sadistic prison officer who cross-examines Arenas while fondling himself. These scenes are among the weakest in the film.'

With a court battle in the offing, Depp had already taken steps to clean up the image of the Viper Room. He had closed the club down temporarily over Millennium Eve to allow a team of designers to give it a makeover. It had reopened with a concert by Courtney Love and a new art deco interior: gone was the ambience of dingy black, and in its place were creamy white walls and a cherry-wood floor. Now, he let it be known that he was keen to clean up its reputation as well: 'The club took a lot of heat for something it had nothing to do with,' he gravely informed the *Hollywood Reporter* in April, before recalling an incident where he personally had ejected a pair of clubbers after finding them about to snort cocaine in the toilets. 'After what happened to

River, that they thought it was okay to do that really put me in a hideous rage.'

It was a timely rearguard action: *Blow* opened in the US on 6 April, and makers New Line were now coming under attack from anti-drugs agencies for having handed out small mirrors to preview audiences to publicise the film (mirrors being part of the paraphernalia used to 'chop' lines of cocaine). Not that New Line's tongue-in-cheek marketing strategy stopped there. At the 29 March premiere at Mann's Chinese Theatre, the stars had walked along a *white* carpet rather than the traditional red, while at least one launch party had been embellished with glasses filled with powdered sugar and peppermint sticks. The celebrities present must have wondered where the real thing had got to. The company apparently stopped short of punning its own name in the cause of promoting *Blow*. Outrage or no, New Line's line-crossing salesmanship won the day: *Blow* notched up third place at the box office in its opening weekend, raking in more than $12 million dollars. Johnny Depp had another 'hit' on his hands.

The critics were less consistent than the cash registers, but most took note of the inherent contradiction in having a menace to society played by a sensitive and attractive actor. The *Wall Street Journal* set the tone: 'With George being played by an actor of such effortless charm, no slime ever seems to adhere to this man of little demonstrable insight or ability.' 'Rarely since the tale of the Corleones has a movie presented such a compelling, sympa-thetic portrait of a criminal lowlife,' agreed the *New York Post.* The film's overpowering aura of toxic excess was a little too much for some British reviewers, however. 'A *GoodFellas* knockoff down to every culpable detail,' Peter Bradshaw opined in the *Guardian*. 'One coke-head mutters: "I can't feel my face!" By the end of this, I couldn't feel my entire head.' The *Observer*'s Philip French was more sanguine, but he delivered a curiously back-handed compliment to the film's star: 'This is probably Depp's best performance ... He will never be a great actor – you can't see into the head beneath the unchanging mop of long hair – but he is skilled and resilient, and anything deeper would have been biopsy, not biopic.' *The Man Who Cried* followed *Blow* into theatres, where it was met with a murmuring of discontent over the fact that Depp appeared to have imported his gypsy from *Chocolat*; in fact, the two were made in reverse order and *Chocolat* released first in the States to catch the Oscars. Reviewers complained about his gypsy in *Chocolat* as well, so it made no real difference.

As real roles dwindled to the level of guest spots in the films of friends while Depp dallied with his daughter, so the rumours of roles increased. He was mentioned in the same breath as a remake of *It Started With Eve* and was thought to be replacing Mike Myers in *Confessions of a Dangerous Mind*; the film went ahead without either. It was further suggested that he was about to play Lord Byron in a biopic, but he ended in the same out-tray as Marlowe and Burns. Much of this was publicity puff to keep Depp's name in the news until the appeal of bottle-feeding an infant started to fade, and the *Hollywood Reporter* often proved itself to be as discriminating as *National Enquirer* when it came to sifting through insider gossip.

There had been a noticeable shift in Depp's whole attitude to the business since the arrival of Lily-Rose, however, and the suspicion that he was becoming disenchanted with movies was to be given weight by a report that he was looking into the possibility of opening a nightclub in Las Vegas 'for celebrities only'. If true, was it merely a reaction to the birth of his daughter and his new-found need for privacy, or was more than a decade of being a highly paid international movie star, able to satisfy his every whim, finally starting to catch up with him? Up until *Fear and Loathing in Las Vegas*, he had managed to retain his professional integrity, but *The Man Who Cried* was a vanity role if ever there was one, which flew in the face of everything he had ever said about playing against his looks; the same held true for *Chocolat*, which had offered a reprise of the same *Vogue*-style photo-shoot, while his twin cameos in *Before Night Falls* were little more than a peripheral amusement which had appealed on the spur of a particularly boring moment. He had done the Potter film as a favour to Christina Ricci, the Hallström one because he could play his guitar, and the Arenas biopic due to his liking for Schnabel; in all three cases, he had unarguably indulged his preference for artistic merit over commercial judgement but, in each instance, it had been without regard to his own component in the films in question and his continuing credibility as an actor; each of them may have been a product of altruism on Depp's part but, collectively, they were starting to look like a severe case of career carelessness.

At the same time, Depp's promotional pronouncements were becoming as lightweight as his film roles, even though they were designed to seem more profound: for *Sleepy Hollow*, he was suddenly an expert on Hammer Horror; for *Before Night Falls*, he developed a taste for the art of Jean-Michel Basquiat; for *Blow*, it rather incongruously became Cuban revolutionary Che Guevara (although he had been approached to play Simon Bolivar in a biopic); for *The Man Who Cried*, it was gypsy music; for *Chocolat*, it was still gypsy music; for *From Hell*, it was to be various theories about the identity of Jack the Ripper (whereas it should perhaps have been the background of Frederick George Abberline). It was all becoming just a little too pat, and a far cry from the days when love was the drug and he would talk music, or literature, or open his heart up on pleasure and pain. In twelve months' time, he would come off message for a change, but on that occasion, he was to regret it almost as soon as he had said it.

The end of our journey impended. Great fields stretched on both sides of us; a noble wind blew across the occasional immense tree groves and over old missions turning salmon pink in the late sun. The clouds were close and huge and rose. 'Mexico City by dusk!' We'd made it, a total of nineteen hundred miles from the afternoon yards of Denver to these vast and Biblical areas of the world, and now we were about to reach the end of the road.

'Shall we change our insect T-shirts?'

> *'Naw, let's wear them into town, hell's bells.' And we drove into*
> *Mexico City.*
>
> JACK KEROUAC, *ON THE ROAD* (1957)

In June, Mexico loomed into the view of Johnny Depp also, as another camp cameo role beckoned in *Once Upon a Time in Mexico*. The film was the third and final instalment of an unplanned trilogy based around the adventures of a gun-toting guitar player, which had been set in motion in 1991 by a 23-year-old writer-director from Austin in Texas, named Robert Rodriguez. *El Mariachi,* which its director famously shot for a mere $7,000 – $2,000 less than budget, was a homage to the Spaghetti Westerns of Sergio Leone. The production chores on *El Mariachi* were shared between Rodriguez and Carlos Gallardo, who played the Mariachi (guitar player) of the title, and their film went on to make more than $2 million when it was picked up by Columbia Pictures. The success of *El Mariachi* led Rodriguez into a sequel in 1994, called *Desperado*, in which the lesser-known Gallardo was replaced by Spanish actor Antonio Banderas. Fellow low-budget action aficionado Quentin Tarantino played a cameo role in *Desperado*, after filming his own *Reservoir Dogs*, and he persuaded Rodriguez to go for a three-in-a-row: 'Quentin showed up on the set of *Desperado* in 1994 to do his part and said, "This is cool. No one's done this since Sergio Leone. This is your 'Dollars' trilogy and now you've got do *The Good, The Bad And The Ugly* of the series. And you've got to call it *Once Upon a Time in Mexico*",' Rodriguez recalled. After directing the successful *Spy Kids* trilogy in the interim, Rodriguez's thoughts had turned back to his Mariachi, and *Once Upon a Time in Mexico* was finally put into production on 27 May.

Depp's participation in the film had been scheduled to last for a mere eight days, but so much fun did he find the experience of playing a renegade CIA agent to Antonio Banderas' Mariachi that he persuaded Rodriguez to plan him into a ninth day of shooting. 'He'd never shot a full movie in eight days and at the end of it, he was like, "Is there anything else I can do, man?",' the director explained. 'He said, "Who's playing the priest?" and I said I hadn't cast it yet. He said, 'How about I do a Marlon Brando voice and dress up as someone else? Can I do the priest before I leave?' So there's a confessional scene which wasn't supposed to feature Johnny Depp.' Another added scene had Depp drive along a road at sunset, after having disposed of the bullet-riddled body of Cheech Marin, with the fake arm that he uses to mask his gun-hand hanging incongruously out the window of his car.

Depp based agent Sands on a Hollywood suit with whom he once had dealings: 'He refused to call me Johnny – always called me John,' he explained to Gavin Edwards of *Rolling Stone*. 'You knew this guy was aiming to fuck you over, but somehow you stuck around because he was just so fascinating to watch.' He may have walked Sands' 'beat' in Mexico for a mere nine days out of a 35-day schedule, but none of his footage was wasted and that of Banderas was subsequently cut back to accommodate it more fully into the action. The result of the rejig was a film which belongs every bit as much to Johnny Depp as it does to its nominal star.

> My name is Sheldon Jeffrey Sands. I work for the Central
> Intelligence Agency. I throw shapes. I set them up; I watch
> them fall. I'm living la vida loca.
> Sands (Johnny Depp), Once Upon a Time in Mexico (2001)

A title announces 'A Robert Rodriguez flick', which sets the tone for much of what follows. Rodriguez 'shot, chopped and scored' *Once Upon a Time in Mexico*, as he self-effacingly puts it, as well as writing, directing and supervising the visual effects and the production design, so any fault with the film can hardly be put down to too many cooks. On the contrary, its director spoils the broth entirely on his own. The shooting and chopping are both highly proficient, but the finished dish is nothing more than a mess of chilli beans, all the same.

For those interested in plot, agent Sands is kind enough to delineate it: 'Okay. The new president is on a quest to clear out the Barillo cartel, and Barillo has set up a counter-attack by hiring a military general named Marquez, and he wants him to throw a coup d'état while the president's visiting Culiacán. Now, I have a man inside as insurance, just to make sure that Marquez never takes power. The last piece of the puzzle is Barillo. Your tip-off assures that Barillo is out of the picture while the battle ensues. In the aftermath of this very healthy revolution, I will calmly waltz away with the 20 million pesos that Barillo is prepared to pay Marquez for the coup.'

That gives a good indication of the intended narrative but, soon, everyone involved starts to betray everyone else (this is stereotypical Mexico), while sub-plots appear and disappear with the same regularity as the actors who have been brought in to provide the cameos: one of these incidental storylines has cartel-kingpin Willem Dafoe arrange for his appearance to be altered by plastic surgery for no discernible reason, whereas sidekick and once handsome leading man Mickey Rourke now looks as though he has already undergone the procedure.

Once Upon a Time in Mexico is a plotless mishmash of martial arts mediocrity and boring bouts of balletic brutality – one of those movies in which a thousand rounds of ammunition are expended in a fruitless attempt to bring down the hero, yet only a single bullet is ever needed to kill the villain. The wall-to-wall action sequences are effectively staged, but one quickly tires of watching stuntmen being blown into the air or sent careering across floors under the impact of gunshots. The film was photographed using digital high-definition cameras and then blown up to 35mm widescreen for theatrical release. The advantage of this was a relatively short shooting schedule, with Rodriguez adding all of the more complex action and effects after the fact, at his Troublemaker production facility in his home town of Austin. The viewer is thus treated to fire without smoke, explosions without debris, and bullet-hits which defy the laws of physics. And that is just the visual side. The story obviously has been put together in much the same way, by overshooting and making it up on the editing bench, where even style-over-substance is given a bad name by scenes such as the one in which El wakes up in bed to find himself chained to his beloved, just as militiamen start to spray the room with bullets from across the way; seemingly, they went in and chained them together first, so that they could go out again and shoot at them from afar. Missing them, needless to say.

Depp is everything to the piece. He turns a brain-dead B-movie into an acceptable A-feature by his presence alone. 'Agent Sands is a great manipulator. It's like playing chess: he's using all these people as pawns, and putting them all in the position he wants them in. But I think ultimately what Sands wants more than anything is to move all these pieces into a position where it puts *him* in more danger; that there is the possibility that he could be taken out. I think, that's what his goal is,' he said of the role. He, at least, had worked out a motivation. Banderas is nothing more than a sun-bronzed block of sandstone with an infinite supply of guns, and his digitally removed high-wire turns as he wipes out endless numbers of extras are the very height of eye-candy tedium. Seen one, seen 'em all. In a story where action is every-thing, things wind down rapidly in the attention stakes whenever the screen is occupied with the obligatory lyrical flashbacks to El's romantic interludes with his now-dead wife.

Presumably to give the film something of a Sophoclean air, Sands is gratuitously blinded by the bad guys as the coup gets underway, which results in him feeling his way towards the final showdown with the help of a young Mexican boy, as Samson did with Delilah's aid in the Temple of Dagon in DeMille's *Samson and Delilah* (1949). 'This is it,' he says, as he is accorded a splendid death scene (twice!), which also calls to mind the end of the simi-larly black leather-clad Anacleto in *The Singer Not the Song* (1961). But Rodriguez evidently was loathe to part with Depp even then, and Sands is miraculously resurrected at the fade-out, where he looks remarkably unfazed after having been shot in both legs and having his eyes drilled out without anaesthetic. 'Are you all right?' asks his young helper. 'I don't know,' he replies, understandably in the circumstances. No matter how nasty Johnny Depp tries to be – and he tries to be pretty nasty here – he has the ability to evoke sympathy in the viewer; Rodriguez clearly felt much the same way and simply refused to put him down at the climax. In this, he was helped by the fact that he had shot on digital videotape, as opposed to film. There was plenty of additional material available to work with.

'Johnny Depp really doesn't change a script,' Rodriguez marvelled. 'He just comes in and takes it to another level. The thing about Johnny is, we'd be on the set and he'd do a scene and I would be constantly checking the script saying, "Is that the line?" And it was the line in the script, but the way he said it, I didn't recognise my own words.' By the time that *Once Upon a Time in Mexico* was released in theatres, it is doubtful if Rodriguez recognised his own film.

> You want to know the secret to winning? Creative sportsmanship. In other words, you have to rig the game.
> Sands (Johnny Depp), Once Upon a Time in Mexico (2001)

After his two-week stint in San Miguel de Allende with Robert Rodriguez (the town where Neal Cassady, model for Kerouac's Dean Moriarty, died in 1968), Depp returned to France. In a matter of months, Paradis found herself pregnant again. As the happy couple began to savour the prospect of a second child, idly working out possible dates of birth from probable dates of conception, another date burned itself into history with cataclysmic effect: 11 September 2001.

In far-distant New York, the majestic twin towers of the world-famous World Trade Center were sent crashing to earth in a co-ordinated strike by the Islamic fundamentalist terror network which calls itself al-Qaeda, killing thousands. The

shock wave reverberated around the globe, and it reverber-
ates still.

According to Hunter Thompson, Depp telephoned him on the
Sunday after the disaster; he gave this version of the exchange
that followed: 'I freaked out and rushed to the airport,' Depp said.
'But when I got there my flight was cancelled. All flights to the US
were cancelled. All of France is terrified. People went crazy with
fear.'

'Join the club,' Thompson replied. 'Everybody went crazy over
here too.'

Fear and loathing.

Even before the dust had settled over Ground Zero, reports
began to emerge of Hollywood stars who were cancelling trips
abroad through fear of flying. 'Apparently, many people in the
entertainment industry have changed their value scales and their
lifestyles after the tragedy of September 11th,' Depp observed.
'Fortunately, I'd changed my own priorities already and that
horror confirmed that I made the right choice. It's a terrible thing,
but people shouldn't have to wait for such a tragedy to happen to
change their vision of the world.'

Unlike many of his contemporaries, Depp was back on board an
aircraft within weeks of the tragedy for a 14-hour flight to Los
Angeles to promote *From Hell*. The film was premiered on 17
October at the Mann Village Theater in the Westwood area of the
city, but the all-too recent events remained uppermost in the
minds of those in attendance. 'For all of us here, it's already difficult to have to sit around and talk about movies in the midst of
what's happening,' Depp said. 'My immediate plans are to get
back to my family and to be with my girls, and then from there, I
don't know. I can't say that I'm very comfortable putting my 2-
year-old daughter and my girl on a plane.' In the circumstances, it
was impossible for him to work up any enthusiasm in relation to
the opening, even though *From Hell* represented only his second
starring vehicle in two years. 'Is this a movie that people should go
and see? I don't know. We've got to keep moving forward, and

movies are escapism, and if people want to go and get out of reality for a couple of hours, why not?' he offered.

From Hell was released in America five weeks after the trauma of September 11, when the last thing that audiences wanted to see was the brutal dismemberment of the innocent in one of the world's greatest capital cities. Asked in the Spanish magazine *Grazia* what 'Hell' meant for him, Depp replied in sombre mode and with the unparalleled death toll in mind: 'Hell is for me what it probably is for many others, especially after the tragedy of September 11: to see people kill each other because of religion, and to think about the world that our children will live in if terrorism, hate, violence and war get the upper hand.'

The Hughes brothers' Burtonesque ride through sleepy Whitechapel took the top spot at the box office over its opening weekend, but it faced little in the way of competition. $11.3 million in receipts was respectable enough, though *Blow* had done better while only managing to reach number three. The film struggled to gain acceptance from that point on, not helped by a clutch of indifferent reviews on both sides of the Atlantic. *Variety* was first to use the knife: 'Sporting an accent seemingly perfected at the Michael Caine School of Cockney Lads – and which ill fits the thesp's chiselled features behind his long, unkempt hair – Depp evinces a canine dogged-ness as Abberline, relentlessly sniffing out his prey. But with a script that is little more than a smorgasbord of handed-down rumours from the time, he makes little sense of his character and is consistently outmatched by Coltrane's dry one-liners as his cynical assistant.'

But Steven Rea epitomised the American view in the *Philadelphia Inquirer*, when he stated that *From Hell* was 'about as convincing as a visit to a theme-park haunted house.'

British critics were more damning still, despite the fact that the movie's UK release was held back until after the season of goodwill. The *Telegraph*'s Andrew O'Hagen was the first to wield the knife: 'Not so long ago, Johnny Depp was one of the most appealing actors in America ... Depp has hitherto had some of that Brando appeal – dark moods, dark looks – but more recently his judgement has begun to look decidedly dodgy. The person he plays in *From Hell* would no doubt have appealed to his gothic instincts, but he fades into cuteness in the part, and after half an hour of this movie, you begin to wonder if the fight hasn't quite gone out of Johnny Depp.'

The next blow came from Anthony Quinn in the *Independent*:

Depp handles a Cockney accent more adroitly, though there's something too modern in his bearing to pass for a creature of the 19th century ... He looks implausibly well-fed and neatly groomed; poverty doesn't cling to this nether world ... The dreadful failing here is that the filmmakers seem less interested in the piteous death of an individual than in the maniacal brutality of the killing. For all the vaunting of historical accuracy, the sensibility reveals no greater sophistication than your average Hammer horror. As for unlocking the mystery of the Ripper's identity, the theory posited here will convince very few. The Hughes brothers turn out to be in the same boat as everyone else – they don't know Jack.

The *coup de grâce* was delivered by Iain Sinclair in the *Observer*, under the headline 'Jack the Rip-off': '*From Hell* returns to source, as a penny-dreadful, a shocker; a distortion of place and time. An industrial product crafted to stand alongside the wave of predatory development that maligns history and treats the past as the final colony in the American world empire ... Johnny Depp is in the wrong film. He has nothing to do with the historic Inspector Abberline, and demonstrates few traces of Moore's dour West Countryman. He essays a kind of low-key Mockney, tranquillised by Jamie Oliver. Depp is a fin-de-siècle dandy, out of Oscar Wilde or Stevenson. An opium-smoking, absinthe-tippling Shoreditch dude who dreams the crimes. *From Hell* is Depp's posthumous reverie. Which explains the unreal geography, the bloodshot panoramic skies.'

Et tu, Iain?

With the western world still reeling in disbelief at the events of 11 September, dark deeds in Victorian Whitechapel found parallel in modern-day Los Angeles. In December 2001, Anthony Fox, the plaintiff in the Viper Room fraud petition and Depp's nemesis in business for the last five years, suddenly disappeared from his home in Ventura. No rhyme, no reason, no trace. Fox left behind a 16-year-old daughter named Amanda, who was working her way through college. 'There has been no financial or other activity that we can say whether he is alive,' Fox lawyer Jay Stein reported. 'One day he was here; the next day he was missing.'

David Esquibias, a partner in the Camarillo law-firm of Staker & Esquibias which had been brought into the case two weeks after the disappearance, revealed to the press that Fox had left only 'a few thousand bucks in his bank account'. Esquibias took a more dramatic stance on the issue than had Stein: 'It's very odd,' he said. 'Maybe it's the curse of the Viper Room.'

The mysterious disappearance of Ventura businessman Anthony Fox did not bring an end to his long-standing dispute with Johnny Depp, however. Far from it. The next episode in the saga was not to be aired for another two years; even then, resolution would remain a long way off.

Since the arrival of his daughter and all the attendant duties and pleasures of fatherhood (as well as the volatile situation in the USA with regard to the terrorist threat that was now posed by Osama bin Laden's al-Qaeda organisation), Johnny Depp had given serious thought to the prospect of settling permanently in France. It was the country of 30-month-old Lily-Rose Melody's birth, as well as that of her mother, and its government had adopted a significantly softer stance on the potential of an additional threat from Saddam Hussein's Republic of Iraq than had the present bellicose US administration. Consequently, he and Paradis had already begun to look around for a suitable residence, preferably in the quieter south of the country, in addition to their Paris flat. They found it in the shape of a $2 million chateau at Plan de la Tour, near St Tropez on the Côte d'Azur.

The first five months of 2002 were to be like the last five of 2001: Depp made no movies; instead, he had decided to take the better part of the year out to relocate to his new house in St Tropez as well as await the birth of his and Paradis's second child. When he heard the news of the sudden death of director Ted Demme in the third week of January, he was visibly shocked, but it made him more convinced than ever of the rectitude of his decision to turn away from the Hollywood high life and everything that it entailed. (Depp subsequently agreed to contribute to a tongue-in-cheek documentary entitled *In Search of Ted Demme*, in which the director's ashes go on an involuntary trip around LA.)

Jack John Christopher Depp was born without complications on 9 April, and once again at the American Hospital of Paris in Neuilly, where he weighed in at a regulation 7lbs. One death, one birth. With two children now in tow, Depp's transformation from introspective itinerant to cuddly, conservative family man was almost complete. He and Paradis had named the boy Jack to avoid the obligatory generational John Christopher Depp *III*. It was to be a good omen, and Depp celebrated the occasion by having a 12th tattoo with his son's name on it emblazoned over his right forearm.

As his 39th birthday approached and the magnitude of parenthood opened his eyes to a new and different world, it was becoming increasingly clear to him that the tra-la days were over. Just as his screen character had died at the end of *From Hell*, so the 'old' Depp appeared ready to undergo a rebirth into something that was nearer to his heart's desire – the long line of romantic anti-heroes to whom he had gravitated in the past was in need of a makeover more in tune with the escapist philosophy which suddenly had come to dominate the thinking of studio heads in the wake of 9/11. In tabloid terms, it was time for him to 'sell out' – but for the best of reasons. Memories of Brando, Thompson and other of Depp's idols in that rebellious old guard were fading with the receding century. It was time to move forward into a new millennium, and with the birth of Paradis's second child and the unforeseen death of friend Ted Demme, intimations of mortality were giving rise to a radical rethink. 'My movies never seem to make any money,' he confided to one journalist. 'I'm going to have to be a little more circumspect about my film choices because I have a family to support. In the past, money just represented freedom. Now it means security.'

Since appearing in *Ed Wood*, Depp had carved out something of a niche for himself playing misfits and eccentrics, as well as exhibiting a predilection for working with maverick directors like Jarmusch and Schnabel; in consequence, he was still viewed as something of an oddball by casting agents and mainstream filmmakers, both of which remained wilfully determined to pass him by. His youthful looks were on his side, even in his late thirties, but a younger generation of 'edgy' actor like Christian Bale (*American Psycho*), Matt Damon (*The Talented Mr Ripley*) and Jude Law (ditto) were now being offered the films which in other circumstances might well have been his. While he maintained an image of cool detachment in life, his choice of roles had cast him as a weirdo in screen terms, and his oft-stated views on what was hip – the writings of the Beat poets; the music of the Rolling Stones – were no longer moving with the times. Depp had found solace in his new family, but he had at last come to realise that, soon, he would have no choice but to try to move into the mainstream as and when the opportunity arose.

He lost no time in informing the world of his conversion: 'I want to do kiddie movies now,' he declared in the *Daily Telegraph*: 'I'm fed up with adult movies – most of them stink. At a certain point with movies it becomes all about mathematics: this has to lead up to this, this has to lead up to that – you're always bound by some kind of formula. But since having kids and watching lots of animated cartoons and all those great old Disney films, I think they're better, they're much better. They're more fun and they take more risks. Even things like *Shrek* – it's really funny and well made and intelligent.'

Five days after his 40th birthday, Johnny Depp proved to the world that he was as good as his word: he donned the Edwardian 'bags' of Scottish author and playwright James Matthew Barrie, creator of *The Admirable Crichton* and the immortal Peter Pan, for a fictionalised love story based around the events which inspired the latter: *Neverland*. To follow, he had signed up to play a pirate captain (though not Captain Hook) in a Walt Disney adventure yarn which was due to start shooting on the Caribbean island of St Vincent on 9 October. Life, as such, may not begin at 40, but Depp's life in the movies was certainly about to start again.

> He was looking for the inspiration he had lost. They were mourning for the family they once had. What began as a chance encounter will forever change their lives...
> from the American trailer to Finding Neverland (2002)

Neverland is a heavily 'Miramaxed' treatment of the famous episode in English literary history when J M Barrie befriended socialite Sylvia Llewelyn Davies and her five sons, and found in them the inspiration for Peter Pan – 'The Boy Who Wouldn't Grow Up'. Director Marc Forster's film treads much the same ground as a 1978 BBC TV mini-series called *The Lost Boys*, which was written by Andrew Birkin (who also penned a biography of Barrie and his association with the Llewelyn Davies family the following year, entitled *J M Barrie and The Lost Boys*, from the material that he had compiled to produce his teleplay).

Sylvia was the daughter of novelist George du Maurier, the author of *Trilby*, and herself one of five children. In 1897, she met Barrie while walking in Kensington Gardens with two of her three sons, George and Jack, who were aged five and four at the time. (Her third son, Peter, was a babe-in-arms, and Michael and Nicholas were not yet born.) A close friendship developed between Barrie and the Llewelyn Davies family, which was not always regarded as appropriate by Sylvia's solicitor husband Arthur or his sons' nursemaid, Mary Hodgson, but the impotent and unhappily married Barrie became besotted with Sylvia and her charges and was soon declared an 'honorary uncle'. Over the years, their influence on him (and his on them) created the fabric of an imaginary universe through game-play, which led Barrie to write a novel called *The Little White Bird* (1902) in which he introduced a character named Peter Pan, and then to expand the idea into a full-length play called 'Peter Pan, or The Boy Who Wouldn't Grow up', which opened at London's Duke of York's Theatre on 27 December 1904, and rarely closed thereafter.

Peter Pan was actually an amalgam of George Llewelyn Davies and Barrie himself, with the name of the character coming from that of George's younger brother Peter. The concept of the boy who would not grow up had lain dormant in Barrie's mind since childhood, when his elder brother David was drowned in a skating accident at the age of 13 and their mother consoled herself with the idea that he would now remain a boy forever. This was a popular philosophy of the time, when young men were as likely to die on an Imperial field of battle as from any other cause, and Barrie soon became an avid devotee of A E Housman's 1896 collection of romantic poetry, *A Shropshire Lad*, with its melancholic elegies to the passing of youth and innocence, and its yearnings for 'the land of lost content'. It was a book that he read 'year in, year out – over and over again' and in its pages is to be found the darker seed of Pan and the sad dream of Never-Neverland:

Comrade, if to turn and fly
Made a soldier never die,
Fly I would, for who would not?
'Tis sure no pleasure to be shot.

When Arthur Llewelyn Davies died of cancer in 1907, and his wife Sylvia fell victim to the same disease three years later, Barrie became the boys' unofficial guardian by mistranscribing a clause in her will. All five of Arthur and Sylvia's 'lost boys' were both touched and tainted by their association with James Barrie and Peter Pan. George was killed in France in 1915, and the famous line 'To die will be an awfully big adventure', uttered when Peter is trapped on a rock in the middle of the lagoon with the waters rising around him, was removed from Act Three for that year's Christmas revival of the play. In 1921, Michael was drowned in the Thames, either by accident or as part of a suicide pact with another boy. And Peter himself, after a successful career as a publisher, threw himself under a tube train at Sloane Square underground station in 1960, having spent a lifetime referring to 'Peter Pan' as 'that terrible masterpiece'.

Most film versions of Pan are based on the novelised version of the play, *Peter and Wendy*, which Barrie published in 1911. *Neverland* was also based on a play, but one by a New York writer named Allan Knee, which was first performed at his 42nd Street Workshop in 1997: 'The Man Who Was Peter Pan' was optioned by another two members of the small theatre company, Tracey Becker and Nellie Bellflower (wonderful name!), and scripting duties were assigned to a third by name of David Magee. The completed screenplay package was then sold to producer Richard Gladstein and Miramax, who contacted Depp. 'The fascinating thing about Johnny as an actor is that his choices are not typical,' German-born *Monster's Ball* director Marc Forster enthused. 'Ultimately, he represents the person who never grows up, who always has the child alive in him, who's always creative.'

Depp's own take on the film was more pragmatic, although little of it is allowed to surface in the completed product. 'I thought it was a beautiful story and it was interesting the way that he came up with the idea for Peter Pan,' he informed the *Scottish Daily Record*. 'We see titbits of information that inspired it, and there was always some speculation about Barrie that maybe there was some kind of paedophilia going on, which I actually don't think there was. What I do believe is that he was an incredibly dark figure, really depressed … morose.'

> Sylvia: What's it like – Neverland?'
> Barrie: One day, I'll take you there.
> Finding Neverland (2002)

The story is much simplified – even grossly romanticised – for the screen, but Depp makes a creditable job of his first stab at a Scottish accent. After the negative criticism of his cockney inflections in *From Hell*, he had hired a voice-coach in May, in the run-up to production; from the sound of things, they must have worked from a tape of John Hannah. Able as his rendition of a Dundee native may be, he must have breathed a sigh of relief at the end of the film that the proposed biopic of Rabbie Burns from two years before never actually came to pass. As for the rest, only the bare essentials of the Barrie/Llewelyn Davies story remain: Sylvia's tally of five sons is reduced to four, Nicholas being extraneous to the needs of the plot. Husband Arthur is already dead before things get underway, thus clearing a path for a romantic attachment between Barrie and Sylvia. And the focus of Barrie's tacitly homoerotic attention (though not in *this* film) is on young Peter, played by ten-year-old Freddie Highmore, rather than George. In terms of popular biography, however, this is only to be expected. (Highmore, coincidentally, shares a birthday with Depp; both were born on 9 June.)

Sylvia is played by English rose Kate Winslet and her mother by former English Rose Julie Christie, but the star turn in the film comes from Dustin Hoffman, in a cameo as Barrie's friend and theatrical 'angel' Charles Frohman, who betrays a distinctly modern sensibility when faced with the prospect of mounting a production about a gang of boys gathered on a tropical island. 'You have a man who is a fairy … And this girl calls herself Tinker?' he queries. Johnny Depp's buddy from the BBC's *The Fast Show*, Paul Whitehouse, also pops up in a cameo as the stage manager of the Duke of York's, which was filmed at the Richmond Theatre in Surrey.

Neverland's anachronistically modernist take on J M Barrie is not confined to Frohman's wry remarks, however. The film reveals a self-conscious awareness of contemporary thinking in relation to his unorthodox friendship with the Davies boys: fellow Scot and Sherlock Holmes creator Arthur Conan Doyle is foist upon the story for the sole purpose of querying this aspect of things with Barrie himself, only to be regaled by a curt response of 'That's outrageous!' With Magee's script having paved the way for a relationship between Barrie and Sylvia, little is made of it in the event; Winslet evinces nothing but widowly propriety towards Depp throughout, only deigning to let him hold her hand as she lies dying of the Romantics' favoured disease of consumption, rather than cancer. Given the sentimentalist tone of the piece, Forster directs it with a dead hand, seemingly unable to differentiate between dramatic highs and lows. Consequently, *Neverland* is neither magical (in its occasional flourishes of fantasy) nor emotionally compelling, but as unrequited in its promise of uplift as is Barrie's onscreen affair with the mother of his adoptive muse. 'We dream on a budget here, don't we?' he observes of his Drury Lane props, but the film is equally spartan in its own creative design – although one trailer-tailored side-step onto a pirate galleon of the imagination allows Depp a dry-run at the next role on his schedule (in which he was to be joined by several other members of the cast). *Neverland*'s origins as a slight, if engaging, repertory piece stitched together from the bare facts of a primer on James Matthew Barrie are always too readily on display: 'I would be extremely honoured if you would allow me the use of your name for one of the characters,' Barrie asks Peter in respect of his new play. 'I don't know what to say,' comes the reply. 'Say yes,' Barrie predictably retorts; 'This is Peter Pan – how wonderful!' exclaims a first-night guest in the presence of the same Peter, and with wisdom in hindsight. 'I'm not Peter Pan,' the boy demurs, motioning to his mentor. 'He is.' Like the recreation of the theatrical production of Pan which provides the climax to *Neverland*, Forster's mechanical handling of his theme never quite manages to hide the harnesses which have been contrived to enable its characters to 'fly'.

During the shooting, Depp presented Highmore one of his famous fart machines. The young boy's parents turned up subsequently to extend their gratitude in person. 'Thanks very much,' they offered. 'He played with it all weekend.' One can almost picture the scene.

If transformations were the order of the day, then Depp had certainly found himself in good company. 'For me, *Neverland* is about ... being able to transform yourself into something greater than you are,' its director was at pains to explain. 'Even if nobody believes in that or believes in you.' A high ideal, though it is doubtful that Depp would have liked the real James Barrie: the dour Scot had no time for actors *or* acting and thought that the former was a mark of someone with weak intellect, while the latter required no intellect at all.

> Peter: But why did she have to die?
> Barrie: I don't know, boy. When I think of your mother, I'll always remember how happy she looked, sitting there in the parlour, watching you play by the fire. That's her boys, who never grew up ... She went to Neverland. But you can visit her, any time you like, if you just go there yourself.
> Peter: How?
> Barrie: By believing, Peter... Just believe.
> Finding Neverland (2002)

Neverland was originally pegged for release in the late summer of 2003, but the opening in June of an independent production also called *Neverland*, and directed by Damion Dietz, put paid to that and brought about a change of title to *J M Barrie's Neverland*. The film was delayed till later in the year but cancelled again because of the opening of Universal's *Peter Pan* in December. A further change of title resulted in *Finding Neverland*, and Depp's first fully fledged 'kiddie movie' was finally scheduled to see the light on October 29, 2004, in the UK and November 12 in the US.

This is what we call New Orleans Square ... In here, we
have a special attraction; we call it the Blue Bayou lagoon.
People are gonna get on a boat here, ride through the
lagoon, and then as they get around here, we're gonna
take them down a waterfall and take them back into the
past-into the days of the pirates, you know? – when the
whole Caribbean area was full of pirates and they were
always sacking towns and things. You believe in pirates, of
course? – Then you want to see some?
Walt Disney, talking about 'The Pirates of the Caribbean' ride, Disneyland:
From The Pirates of the Caribbean to The World of Tomorrow (1966)

Walter Elias Disney, or Uncle Walt as he was known to children
throughout world, was the James Barrie of cinema, devising
slogans like 'imagineering' to embody the work of the myriad
artists and technicians who brought his fairy-tale fantasies to life.
After 30 years at the sharp end of film animation, nearly 20 of
which had been spent producing some of the best-loved full-
length animated features of all time, Disney had opened his first
theme park, Disneyland, in 1955, at Anaheim in California. In
1966, the park had been expanded for the first time since its inauguration to encompass a whole new village-within-a-village, in the
cotton-candy form of a miniature representation of New Orleans.

Depp had already taken his daughter to Disneyland, as he had
been taken to the newer and larger Walt Disney World in Florida
as a child, and it so happened that the financially troubled Disney
empire had been thinking the previously unthinkable: it planned
to mount a big-budget adventure movie based on one of its own
theme-park rides, and it had approached Depp to play the lead. In
a Hollywood which is constantly criticised for its lack of ideas and
over-eagerness simply to regurgitate winning formulae from the
past, this concept appeared to represent a new low in corporate
brainstorming.

The ride in question was 'Pirates of the Caribbean', an audio-
animatronic experience which basically involved a 15-minute

boat-ride through a cartoon representation of a pirate colony in the West Indies. The 'Pirates' ride had been installed in New Orleans Square at the Disneyland park in Anaheim on 18 March 1967, and it was later adapted in scaled-down form to Florida's Disney World, after the Magic Kingdom opened in 1971. Disney himself did not live to see the ride completed at either venue; he died on 15 December 1966.

With the notion of making movies for children – not least his own – uppermost in his mind, Depp had signed on to play pirate captain Jack Sparrow in what was now called *Pirates of the Caribbean: The Curse of the Black Pearl* regardless of the outcome, be it good or bad. He had earlier decried the idea of 'selling out' to commercial movie-making on Channel 5's *Movie Chart Show* on British television: 'A whole load of money – like some *insane* amount – would probably get me to do that. I mean, maybe not; maybe I'm too ignorant to make the decision to just sell out. Maybe I should. And maybe it would be a kind of interesting experiment to just go in and try that for once. Maybe I will … but it would take an inordinate amount of money.' An inordinate amount of money, namely $14 million, had since been forthcoming from Disney, and he had made the decision to embark on his 'interesting experiment'. Little did he realise at the time that Captain Jack would be a role to die for.

> You'd best start believing in ghost stories, Miss Turner. You're in one.
> Barbossa (Geoffrey Rush), Pirates of the Caribbean (2002)

Every once in a while, a film comes along which hits all the right buttons; where everything *works*; in which the combination of luck and expertise from which all films spring alchemically transforms into something more precious than gold; where every element of the production is in sync with every other; and where all blend perfectly together to make a universally acclaimed work of pop-art – a cinematic classic – a piece of pure movie magic.

Such a film was *Pirates of the Caribbean: The Curse of the Black Pearl*. For Johnny Depp, its like had been a long time in the coming. It was worth the wait.

Producer Jerry Bruckheimer's $125 million production was a rip-roaring seafaring saga of a kind not seen since the high adventure of post-war escapism reigned supreme in Hollywood in the late 1940s and early 1950s. It is to Warners that the screen owes its greatest pirate movies, like *Captain Blood* and *The Sea Hawk* (1935 and 1940, both with Errol Flynn), but aside from an odd jaunt down Jamaica way in films like *The Spanish Main* and *Captain Kidd* (both 1945), it was Walt Disney who breathed new life into the genre in 1950 with a full-blooded adaptation of Robert Louis Stevenson's *Treasure Island*, whose commercial success launched a veritable armada of spectacular swashbucklers, from *Blackbeard the Pirate* and *Abbott & Costello Meet Captain Kidd* and *The Crimson Pirate* (all 1952) to *Pirates of Tripoli* (1955). Robert Siodmak's *The Crimson Pirate* represented the high water mark of pirate movies in the 1950s, and its manifest of sea battles, sword fights and skulduggery was not to be forgotten by the screenwriters of *Pirates of the Caribbean*.

The pirate genre had experienced a brief resurgence of popularity in the early 1960s during the cycle of sword-and-sandal epics that emanated out of Rome's Cinecittà Studios. Films like *The Pirates of Tortuga, Morgan il pirata* (*Morgan the Pirate*, with Steve Reeves) and *Gordon, il pirata nero* (*The Black Pirate*, with Ricardo Montalban and Vincent Price; all 1961) fired the flame of free-booting once again, before audiences tired of starless spectacle and the failure of Lewis Milestone's *Mutiny on the Bounty*, as well as rising costs within the industry, prohibited exotic excursions to faraway places in eighteenth-century galleons. In more recent times, attempts to revive the genre have sunk without trace: Roman Polanski's *Pirates* (1986) and Renny Harlin's *Cutthroat Island* (1995). It was not without trepidation that Disney chose to embark on a major feature on the theme of pirates in the Caribbean. The more so when executives discovered what Johnny Depp was intending to do with his pivotal role of Jack Sparrow, erstwhile captain of the good ship *Black Pearl*.

It is evident from his films that Depp had developed three distinctly different approaches to characterisation. Either he plays the role straight, relying on interior psychology and emotion to carry the day, or he mimics the individual concerned (in the case of living persons like Hunter Thompson and George Jung), or else he pulls a Lon Chaney and turns himself into an archetype by adopting mannerisms from an eclectic mix of cultural influences. In *Ed Wood*, it was Casey Kasem; in *Sleepy Hollow*, it was Roddy McDowell. Given the nature of the material in *Pirates of the Caribbean*, Depp had already decided that Jack Sparrow should fall into the last of these three categories. The models in this instance were going to be more diverse than ever before: a cartoon French skunk courtesy of Warner Bros' 'Looney Tunes' named Pepe Le Pew, and Rolling Stones' guitarist Keith Richards. That was for starters; to these basics, he added Rastafarian dreadlocks, a braided beard, kohl eyeliner, a mouthful of gold and platinum-capped teeth and an angry scar on his chin – and he already had an apposite skull-and-crossbones tattooed on his right ankle. There was method in the madness. 'Pirates were the rock stars of their day,' he said, in explanation of the Richards influence. 'He's not far off being a pirate, is Keith.' The result was the pirate equivalent of Bob Marley or Augustus Pablo, which was well suited to the film's Jamaican setting. (The real 'Jack Sparrow' was a Jamaican session-singer who went on to found 1960s Ska band The Ethiopians under his real name of Leonard Dillon.)

Depp was more effusive when it came to explaining the contribution of the skunk: 'There's something about Pepe Le Pew that I always thought was really beautiful,' he told Emily Blunt: 'The idea of this guy who absolutely had blinders on to reality, and just believed what he thought. He was always really in a good mood, no matter what was going on around him, no matter what the reality of the situation was; he always saw it his way, absolutely his way. Every episode, he was falling in love with this one cat and the cat just despised him, absolutely hated him, and he always interpreted it as 'Oh, she's playing hard to get; she's shy,' or something like that. And so I thought that it worked for the character. I also thought of Jack Sparrow as a sort of a constantly moving organism, who would shape himself to whatever situation, however he needed to be shaped. He would mould himself into that; this organism with a perpetual martini glass in his hand.'

Modelling himself on a cartoon animal was not that wide of the mark either: writers Ted Elliott and Terry Rosso, who previously had scripted Disney's *Shrek* (which Depp so much admired) had in mind Bugs Bunny when they wrote scenes for Jack Sparrow.

The Disney executives remained unconvinced about the efficacy of Depp's characterisation for a full month and a half into filming, but he and director Gore Verbinski stuck with it, going so far as to alter the script so that other actors could 'comment' on the ragbag of idiosyncrasies, such as when Orlando Bloom and Kevin McNally stare in bewilderment at a part of the sky that Sparrow has fixed his gaze upon only a moment before, or when Bloom remarks, 'So that's the reason for all the…' while mimicking Sparrow's mannerisms, after McNally has told him some of his captain's colourful history. 'Originally I had two more gold teeth, and there were a few that wanted them gone,' Depp said of his battles with the corporate suits in *SFX* magazine. 'In fact, they wanted them all gone, and they wanted the braids and the trinkets and the beard gone. I said, "Look, I respect you guys. I'll compromise to some degree, which means I'll take two teeth out. But anything beyond that I feel is compromising the integrity of the character. I'm not willing to do that. You've got to trust me. You've got to let me do what you hired me to do. And if you're not happy with doing that, then you'll have to replace me."'

It goes without saying that Johnny Depp was not replaced. He did what he was hired to do, and Disney was to find itself in the enviable position of never having to look back.

> You don't know what this is, do you? This is Aztec gold –
> one of 882 identical pieces they delivered in a stone chest
> to Cortez himself; blood money paid to stem the slaughter
> he wreaked upon 'em with his armies. But the greed of
> Cortez was insatiable, so the heathen gods placed upon the
> gold a terrible curse. Any mortal that removes but a single
> piece from that stone chest shall be punished for eternity...
> Barbossa (Geoffrey Rush), Pirates of the Caribbean (2002)

Once upon a time in the West Indies...

The film begins with a destitute Captain Jack Sparrow arriving in Port Royal, pirate capital of Jamaica. Ten years before, his ship, the *Black Pearl*, was stolen from him by a mutinous first mate named Barbossa (Geoffrey Rush); since then, he has been trying to steal it back. In the meantime, Barbossa and his crew have fallen victims to a curse placed on a chest full of Aztec gold – a curse which turns them into living skeletons at the time of the full moon. In order for the curse to be lifted, every last piece of the stolen gold must be returned to the chest. Only one piece now remains, and it is in the hands of Elizabeth (Keira Knightley), daughter of the governor of Port Royal.

Barbossa sacks the town and kidnaps Elizabeth, but he is pursued by Sparrow and a young blacksmith named Will Turner (Orlando Bloom). It transpires that blood from the owner of the gold has also to accompany the piece on its return, but when Elizabeth's blood is drawn at the pirates' secret harbour of Isla de Muerta, the curse is not lifted. It is Turner, not she, who is the rightful owner, the piece having been given to him as a boy by his father, who was a member of Barbossa's crew. The pirates turn their attention to Turner, but they have reckoned without the wily Captain Sparrow, while following close to stern is the British navy in the form of doughty Commodore Norrington (Jack Davenport) and his company of jack-tars...

The concept of 'cursed' pirates who turn into rotting skeletons of themselves in the light of the moon had originated with screenwriters Elliott and Rossio, who were hired by Bruckheimer to redraft a first script by TV producer Jay Wolpert. The introduction of a supernatural element into a story which in its original form was pretty standard fare about a damsel in distress who is kidnapped by a black-hearted villain (unoriginally named 'Blackheart') was nothing short of a masterstroke, and it is tempting to suggest that Elliott and Rossio had been mindful of the fact that the only successful pirate film of the previous 25 years had been John Carpenter's *The Fog* (1980), in which a band of ghostly buccaneers laid siege to the small New England town of Antonio Bay. Not only did it supply the traditional tale with a novel twist, but it was instrumental in making a must-see trailer which went a long way to help the film's eventual success. The change allowed for such clichéd plot developments in the earlier draft as Norrington being in league with the pirates after having been spurned by Elizabeth to fall by the quayside.

The director's chair had been assigned to Tennessee-born Gore Verbinski, another ex-Punk band member like Depp, who had begun his career by playing guitar with Little Kings and The Daredevils – the latter of these along with Brett Gurewitz of Bad Religion. Verbinski had come to the film fresh from having directed the American remake of a Japanese supernatural thriller called *Ringu* (*The Ring*, 1998), so he was on familiar ground with ghosts; consequently, what is known in film circles as the 'money shot' in *Pirates of the Caribbean* features Geoffrey Rush's Barbossa turning into a grinning ghoul before the startled gaze of Keira Knightley, while a swig of rum trickles in rivulets through his exposed rib-cage. The horror is of the jaunty sort, though, and no worse than that to which Disney's films have exposed their audiences since *Snow White and the Seven Dwarfs* in 1937.

Given that the film's storyline is meant to have been extrapolated from a theme-park ride, it is only to be expected that elements of the ride should crop up along the way, to tip the wink to the millions of Disneyland customers who have experienced it for themselves. Most of these are confined to Sparrow's arrival at the port of Tortuga, where the bawdy backdrop is composed of real-life recreations of the various animatronic tableaux in the parks, but other incidents are incorporated as well, such as a mutt with the keys to Sparrow's jail cell in his mouth. Verbinski is astute in referencing his film's origins without having them impinge needlessly on a separate and self-contained narrative. The spirit is captured, but the tackiness is not. (Disney was not so lucky when it tried to repeat the experiment five months later in *The Haunted Mansion*, where the opposite proved to be the case.)

> We are cursed men, Miss Turner ... Compelled by greed, we
> were. And now, we are consumed by it!
> Barbossa (Geoffrey Rush), Pirates of the Caribbean (2002)

With a total of four credited screenwriters, and a high quota of revisions even then, it is no surprise that individual sequences in *Pirates of the Caribbean* are often better engineered than the plot overall, in which there are holes the size of cannon fire from a nine-inch gun. Verbinski pastes successfully over the fact that eight years have elapsed since Elizabeth first plucked the one remaining piece of gold from the neck of a young Will Turner whom she helped to rescue from a shipwreck as a child and that, during that time, a pirate as crafty as Jack Sparrow is likely to have succeeded in his quest to retrieve his stolen ship, particularly when he owns a compass which points only to Isla de Muerta! However, he is less diligent in disguising the fact that the gold appears not to exert the same malevolent influence on either Turner or Elizabeth as it does on Barbossa and his crew, yet when Sparrow – who also had no hand in the original theft of the treasure-chest – palms a piece of the gold into his pocket, he is conveniently transformed into a skeleton in the moonlight. Then there is the fact that the *Black Pearl* has herself become cursed along with her crew. The Aztec curse acts in different ways on different people was Elliott and Rossio's equally convenient explanation of the anomalies.

There is evidence in the extant version of how the film was meant to have played, sans the skeletal pirates: in the last reel, Sparrow is sent to the gallows but is saved from hanging at the eleventh hour by a timely piece of derring-do on Turner's part. The sequence is a leftover from another draft of the script, and its retention as an epilogue is pure contrivance; as things stand, even the upright Commodore Norrington is likely to have appreciated that Sparrow's climactic actions in killing Barbossa and thereby defeating his skeleton crew, as they were on the point of victory over his own men, were for the common good and would therefore have weighed in the balance against his past sins. Despite a feeble plea from Jonathan Pryce's Governor Swann that Norrington 'is bound by the law', there is such a thing as pardon as well as parley, and Swann had already extended clemency to Turner. When *Pirates of the Caribbean* was being thought of in more conventional terms, this sequence was to have appeared much earlier in the story, after Sparrow's capture in the blacksmith's shop and before his escape in pursuit of Barbossa.

In addition to this is the matter of how Sparrow's crew managed to escape the clutches of a British naval contingent in disarray at the climax, but the wily Sparrow somehow did not. And not only the navy is in disarray – the timeline of the tale is in a right sailor's knot from the very beginning. When exactly did Sparrow and First Mate Joshamee Gibbs (Kevin McNally) *actually* sail together under the black flag, given that, eight years before, Gibbs was with the Royal Navy and his erstwhile captain was marooned on a desert island by Barbossa? (In dispensing with too much exposition in order to try to keep things simple, the film encourages the false impression that Sparrow has only recently escaped from his island prison.) Belay! Such things matter not a pint of grog, to be sure. Verbinski keeps the action moving along at such a clip that these and other hiccups pass relatively unnoticed – but only just.

The final cut of *Pirates of the Caribbean* came in close to 160 minutes but, even when reduced to 143 for theatrical release, the film was still to prove too lengthy for many reviewers, who found their patience wearing extremely thin at several prolonged sword-fighting sequences which had been retained in full for the benefit of the under-fives in the audience.

> Barbossa: Why, thank you, Jack.
> Sparrow: You're welcome.
> Barbossa: Not you – we named the monkey 'Jack'.
> Pirates of the Caribbean (2002)

Johnny Depp's Captain Jack Sparrow is afforded the most iconic entrance of any actor in a film since Humphrey Bogart's Rick left his desk at the Café Americain in *Casablanca* to sneer at a customer to whom he has just refused entry to his gaming tables, 'Your cash is good at the bar.' Verbinski's camera swoops up behind him, before a cut to a reverse angle reveals him to be standing majestically atop the mast of his sinking longboat, proud and defiant against the setting sun; even though it is only the precursor to a comedy pay-off in which he steps from the mast onto the pier at Port Royal just as the boat goes under, it is a real star entrance. 'You are, without doubt, the worst pirate I've ever heard of,' Norrington notions. 'But you *have* heard of me,' Sparrow replies. By the time *Pirates of the Caribbean: The Curse of the Black Pearl* went into release, everybody was to have heard of Jack Sparrow. 'My pirate is a guy who is able to run between the raindrops,' Depp said of him, waxing strangely poetic. 'It's every boy's dream to be a pirate, and to invent a pirate from the ground up was a great role for me. I can't speak for all pirates but my pirate, I think, stole everything.'

Depp strikes exactly the right note of moral ambivalence in a world too keen by half to fall back on predictable archetypes representative of 'good' and 'evil', and the script affords him at least one line which is every bit as geekishly quotable as any of the many uttered by Humphrey Bogart in *Casablanca*: when Elizabeth berates him for not having escaped from the island and for settling instead for a beach-bum existence of rum-drinking while awaiting inevitable rescue, he looks at her with incomprehension. 'Welcome to the Caribbean, love,' he shrugs, by way of explanation. The scene was originally extended to include a more qualified apology in the first cut of the film, as Sparrow showed Elizabeth wounds that he had received in battle to counterpoint her implicit accusation of cowardice; Verbinski jettisoned this coda when he could see how the character was playing overall:

> Elizabeth: So – is there any truth to the other stories?
> Sparrow: Truth?
> (rolls up his sleeves and opens his shirt to reveal scars and bullet wounds)
> ... No truth at all.
> (scene deleted) from Pirates of the Caribbean (2002)

With the onset of familiarity, it is easy to forget how original Depp's turn as Sparrow really is. He swaggers and sways and grimaces, one minute sly and ingratiating; the next, cheery and charming. He is a laughing cavalier, a gay hussar, a merry musketeer, a tightrope-walker in a tricorn hat, forever teetering on the edge of sanity. He is the crimson-headed pirate. But, always, he is the loveable rogue. Not since the days of Douglas Fairbanks or Burt Lancaster has such a balletic buccaneer so memorably graced the screen, his wit as deft as his prowess with a blade. In a film already full to the gunnels with knowing banter – 'You seem somewhat familiar; have I threatened you before?' – Depp was ever willing to add more of his own, and another deleted scene saw him ad-libbing a punchline straight from *The Fast Show*: 'I'll get me coat,' he says, when one of the pirates contradicts his point of view.

Not even a performer as able and endearing as Depp could carry a film the size and scale of *Pirates of the Caribbean* without an equal measure of support from those around him, though. The ensemble cast are magnificent, particularly Kevin McNally as Gibbs, who rambles through a salty yarn about how Sparrow escaped from his island by lashing together a pair of sea turtles to form a raft, till he is stopped dead in his elaborate tracks when Turner inquires, 'What did he use for rope?' A larger-than-life protagonist requires an antagonist of similar stature to oppose him, and Oscar-winner Geoffrey Rush is one of the best villains in films, a man more than fit to wear Vincent Price's mantle; it can only be a matter of time before he faces up to James Bond (and not by proxy, as he did in *The Tailor of Panama* in 2001). If Depp is the instinctive actor, then Rush is the master craftsman; his Barbossa is a tar-black confection of rolling eyeballs and hissed threats, in the classic tradition of Robert Newton, and he has the additional advantage of being served up with a seafood platter of lip-smacking lines to chew over and spit out: 'You're off the edge of the map we made. Here, there be *monsters*,' he says to Sparrow. Even the *Pearl* itself becomes a living being in the film-its sails in shreds, its hull shrouded in perpetual mist, as it slinks silently towards Port Royal on its nefarious quest, like Darth Vader's battlecruiser in the opening shot of *Star Wars* (now *Star Wars: Episode IV – A New Hope*).

Pirates of the Caribbean: The Curse of the Black Pearl is one of those glorious Hollywood occasions when the pieces of the puzzle fitted together in such a way as to create not only high adventure on the high seas but movie myth. All the familiar ingredients are present and correct, from naval battles and cutlass duels to walking the plank and treasure trove, and all of it to the accompaniment of a rousing score by *Pearl Harbor*'s Klaus Badelt (and seven other incidental composers!), which echoes of the 'epic' orchestrations of Miklós Rózsa or the stirring imperial anthems of Erich Wolfgang Korngold for Errol Flynn's Warners swashbucklers of the 1930s. But there is more; that elusive spark which so many films strive for and so few achieve: magic. 'So this is the path you've chosen, is it? After all, he is a blacksmith,' Governor

Swann queries of his daughter at the close. 'No. He's a *pirate*,' she replies – the designation, by then, having come to embrace every rebel hero who ever was or ever will be. It is an ending to stir the blood of free men everywhere – an inspiring climax, like that in Mel Gibson's *Braveheart*. It raises a silent (maybe not so silent) cheer in the viewer: a feel-good finale hewn from the finest steel, at a time when audiences the world over were desperate to feel good about anything.

Given the film industry's present concerns over video and DVD piracy, it is also something of a paradox. Those in the business would say that there were pirates and *pirates*: Sparrow and Turner represent *good* pirates, an oxymoron in itself. But Hollywood executives are rarely that clear-thinking. Clarity of that sort is the preserve of Superior Court judges, and it was to one of those that Johnny Depp was now about to defer.

> That's what a ship is, you know. It's not just a keel
> and a hold and a deck and sails: that's what a ship needs.
> But what a ship is – what the Black Pearl really is –
> is freedom.
>
> Jack Sparrow (Johnny Depp), Pirates of the Caribbean (2002)

Principal photography on *Pirates of the Caribbean* wrapped on 14 February 2003, just as another alleged act of 'piracy' appeared to be coming to a head. The pirate in this instance was also supposed to be Depp, but the act in question was one of corporate piracy, namely the theft of the Viper Room's trademarks and merchandising rights from its holding company of Safe in Heaven Dead into Depp and Jenco's Trouser Trumpet Inc.

The lawsuit brought by the absent Anthony Fox in July 2000 against Depp, Jenco and their legal team had now rumbled on for the best part of three years. After his client's disappearance, Fox lawyer David Esquibias had created a 'conservatorship estate' to hold Fox's 49 per cent stake in Safe in Heaven Dead, the effect of which was to put Fox's half of the Viper Room out of reach until

2006; were the case to go against Fox, the shares would be worthless, but if damages were eventually to be awarded, then Fox's daughter Amanda would become one of the beneficiaries and part-owner of the Viper Room by proxy.

In February 2003, Los Angeles Superior Court Judge Allan Goodman overturned an earlier lower court judgement which had leaned in Depp's favour and made a temporary ruling which found conversely for Fox, ordering the dissolution of Safe in Heaven Dead in the process. This new ruling put the future of the club – and, by association, Johnny Depp's ownership of it – in grave doubt. 'The facts establish persistent and pervasive fraud and mismanagement and abuse of authority,' Goodman declared, adding that 'Defendant Depp breached his fiduciary duties to the corporation and to Fox as the plaintiff-shareholder and failed to exercise any business judgement with respect to the affairs of Safe in Heaven.'

A final ruling was to follow in April, but the decision left Depp with three choices: he could sell his shares, buy out Anthony Fox's interest, or sell the Viper Room. Alternatively, he could appeal the decision, which would drag the litigation on for many more years. 'I don't think he really has made up his mind yet,' Depp's lawyer, Michael Eidel, told Amanda Bronstad of the *Los Angeles Business Journal*. 'He does have a fondness for the club because it's a business that he built out of scratch.' He appended a disclaimer to the effect that his client had known nothing about the decisions being made on his behalf by his representatives, namely Lichter Grossman. 'I'm not saying we admit that Fox is entitled to anything,' he said. 'But if there are any problems here, Johnny is not the person to whom a finger is pointing.' The actor injected his own plea for understanding into the barrage of claims and counter-claims: 'I don't really know how to do the business side of it,' he said. 'For me, it's just a great place to hang out – initially, because I didn't like any of the other places.'

Depp eventually chose to appeal, which saw to it that things dragged out for a further eighteen months. But Sal

Jenco's days as manager of the Viper Room were effectively over. Within a year, he was to depart the scene under a cloud of confusion, leaving chaos in his wake.

Resolution to the affair would follow less than six months later. In October 2004, United Press International revealed that Depp had relinquished his share of the club to Fox's daughter. A low-key press release from 'unidentified sources' avoided any mention of the legal issues which had dogged Depp for the previous four years and instead laid the blame for his decision on the 'bad memories' which continued to persist over the death of River Phoenix, as well as the upset that was caused to him by the 'death tourists' who still made pilgrimages to the place 'to gawp at the spot' where Phoenix had died. It was the end of an era. "The whole Johnny Depp mystique is over," one visitor to the club was to report, as it was announced that Amanda Fox intended to sell off her newly-inherited stake in Depp's former Sunset Strip watering-hole.

> Son, I'm Captain Jack Sparrow – savvy?
> Jack Sparrow (Johnny Depp), Pirates of the Caribbean (2002)

Three months to the day after the birth of his son Jack, Johnny Depp's Disney swashbuckler *Pirates of the Caribbean: The Curse of the Black Pearl* opened in theatres across the USA after receiving its world premiere at Disneyland, California, on 28 June. The jaded press critics were largely unmoved by the film's epic sweep, rousing score, superb digital effects or plentiful acts of derring-do and thought that, at 143 minutes, it was 'bloated' (*New York Post*) or even 'a nice little 90-minute B-movie' that 'outstays its welcome' (*Chicago Sun-Times*). They were moved to a man (or woman), however – and significantly so – by Depp's perform-ance as Sparrow.

Jamie Bernard in the *New York Daily News* concluded that 'Depp's peculiar buccaneer is an instant classic of actorly charisma. His performance – with kohl-smudged eyes, beaded beard and a constantly shifting centre of gravity – elevates *Pirates* to one of the summer's must-sees.' Ann Hornaday in the *Washington Post* wrote that 'Depp is the single best reason to see *Pirates of the Caribbean.*' *The New York Post*'s Lou Lumenick waxed equally positive about 'Johnny Depp's endearingly eccentric performance'. *Variety* was reminded of another screen eccentric: 'Depp's turn here ... puts one in mind of some of Marlon Brando's more oddball screen outings, which often ended up being the most interesting elements in those pictures even if they weren't particularly coherent or even plausible.' Last but by no means least, Roger Ebert threw his hat into the same ring of endorsement: 'Depp and Rush fearlessly provide performances that seem nourished by deep wells of nuttiness.' A similar reaction greeted the film when it opened in the UK less than a week later, typified by Sukhdev Sandhu in the *Daily Telegraph*: 'At the heart of the film ... is a quite extraordinary performance by Johnny Depp,' he marvelled. 'Whether in a good or a bad way is hard to say.' The *Observer*'s Philip French was less equivocal: 'Depp's Sparrow is the sly, charming trickster with a curious cockney accent, a fatalist and a bit of a dandy with bells on the black braids of his beard ... It is arguably the best of its kind since *The Crimson Pirate* fifty years ago.'

Not everyone was impressed by Depp's turn as Jack Sparrow. Charlotte O'Sullivan in the *Independent* found it tiresome and predictable: 'From *Benny & Joon* on down, the actor has long shown a penchant for these kind of counter-culture parts (pale freaks, tanned Gypsies – so long as they don't work in a bank, they're alright with Johnny). Also horribly familiar is Depp's Brechtian, punkish desire to alienate us from the action, his deter-mination to signal – via camp pouts, wacky accents, whimsical walks and childlike hand wiggling – that all is illusion. Poor Depp. He's apparently unaware that what he mostly offers is a lifestyle model for wealthy slummers. *Chocolat*, anyone?'

In the course of her piece, O'Sullivan confessed herself to be a 'Johnny-hater', though, so her view can be discounted as being less than objective.

In the critical fraternity, there had been an almost audible intake of breath. They seemed to have been bewildered by Depp's atypical interpretation of the eponymous hero of such a film, perhaps because their collective psyches had been press-ganged into submission by a surfeit of stereotypes in the two available parts of the *Lord of the Rings* trilogy, but Depp's inter-pretation was by no means without precedent in the annals of Hollywood hokum: Kirk Douglas played nominal hero Ned Land as a drunken, self-obsessed lout in Disney's *20,000 Leagues Under the Sea* in 1954, and Robert Newton, the real hero of the company's *Treasure Island* (1950), could hardly have been mistaken for a member of the Jamaican social scene in his oft-mimicked guise as the tic-infested Long John Silver. Jack Sparrow was merely the latest – and most universally acceptable – in a long line of camp characterisations which had begun on the set of *Jump Street* (where Depp had turned up as Hanson in a turban or a powdered George Washington wig), and ended, for the present, with the look that he adopted for Sands in *Once Upon a Time in Mexico*, where he had opted for a selection of cheesy T-shirts sporting slogans such as 'CIA – Cleavage Inspection Agency' and 'I'm With Stupid'.

Critical opinion notwithstanding one way or the other, *Pirates of the Caribbean* proved to be a sell-out sensation for the Disney organisation, helping it to become the first film studio in history to take over $3 billion at the box office in the course of a single year. The same term found itself applied to Johnny Depp in the wake of the movie's surprise success.

'I'm so pleased you're selling out,' Terry Gilliam had said on visiting the set, 'This can be a giant hit, and we can get Quixote back and running.' Be that as it may, whatever 'selling out' Depp may have engaged in was no worse than that perpetrated by Bob Dylan in 2003, when the former folk-poet of the protest movement in the 1960s appeared in a TV commercial for Victoria's Secret lingerie to the accompaniment of 'Lovesick' from his own 1999 Grammy Award-winning album, *Time Out of Mind*.

The film passed quickly into popular iconography (its title was to be purloined by television commentators to refer to the England cricket squad when it won its first Test series for 36 years against the West Indies in Barbados, in April 2004). Having originally been voted the 'world's sexiest star' by the readers of *Empire* magazine in August 1995, Depp found that as a result of *Pirates of the Caribbean*, he was still considered the 'sexiest man alive' eight years later. 'For a guy like me, who's been dangling in this business for the last twenty years, to finally have something hit, it's unexpected and very touching,' he told *Entertainment Weekly*.

Depp was back. And he was bigger than he had ever been before.

Johnny Depp greeted the surprise success of *Pirates of the Caribbean* with an atypical bout of self-pity, which seemed to hint that the lack of self-esteem that he had suffered as a teenager still lurked beneath the sophisticated surface, ready to cut through the veneer of superstardom like a knife. 'Mine has been a career of failures. I'm getting all this attention right now because people feel sorry for me,' he needlessly confessed. 'I'm an underdog. Other actors look at me and think, 'That poor bastard is still hacking away at it'.' In truth, other actors were looking at him and wishing that they had what Depp had – a unique and unpredictable talent, which could be relied upon to bring something fresh and unusual to the most formulaic of projects. 'I think he's probably the premier actor of his day,' confirmed Miramax boss Harvey Weinstein, whose Dimension Films subsidiary had co-financed *Once Upon a Time in Mexico* along with Sony's Columbia Pictures. 'He's been frozen out for years. He was looked at as too risky for a lot of the top stuff. A lot of people are going to be kissing his butt now.'

One of those who had done so already was David Koepp, writer of the newly released Jody Foster thriller *Panic Room* and currently intent on directing his first feature since *Stir of Echoes* in 1999. (*A*) *Stir of Echoes* had been adapted from the 1958 novel of almost the same name by Richard Matheson, the horror maestro of the rock 'n' roll generation. What Koepp had in mind for Depp was a film based on a novella by the horror king of the MTV generation.

> *'You stole my story,'* the man on the doorstep said. *'You stole my story and something's got to be done about it. Right is right and fair is fair and something has to be done.'*
> STEPHEN KING, 'SECRET WINDOW, SECRET GARDEN', *FOUR PAST MIDNIGHT* (1990)

Secret Window is based on 'Secret Window, Secret Garden', the second of four novellas in a 1990 compendium called *Four Past Midnight*, by Maine-based gonzo horrormeister Stephen King. King's chatty, conversational style and prolific output have confirmed him as the world's bestselling author of horror stories, though his ingratiating 'dear reader' approach harks back to the earliest days of mass-market Gothic fiction, while his overriding tendency to pad out thin material has marked him down as the modern equivalent of James Malcolm Rymer.

'Secret Window, Secret Garden' thuds resoundingly into this category; essentially a retread of ideas already advanced in *The Dark Half* and his more successful *The Shining*, the novella is King in typically voluminous mode, spinning a short-story premise into an unwieldy 150 pages, by which time the twist in its tedious tail has long since been guessed by any 'dear reader' with a passing knowledge of Jekyll and Hyde. The basic concept appeared compelling enough for its author to have reached out for another ream of foolscap, however: Mort Rainey is in the throes of writer's block, reeling from the prospect of an impending divorce and holed up in a cabin in the Maine woods with a few unsatisfactory pages of a new novel. His self-imposed solitude is interrupted by the unsolicited entrance of one John Shooter, who accuses Rainey of plagiarising a story of his own, entitled 'Secret Window, Secret

Garden', and who desires redress. Rainey at first refuses to discuss the matter but Shooter is insistent, strangling Rainey's pet cat in order to gain his attention before moving on to murder those around him who subsequently are enlisted to help in the ensuing battle of wills. Unlike Rainey in the story, the alert reader can see the end coming a mile off: the two are one and the same, Shooter being merely the literal embodiment of Rainey's various neuroses. All is revealed to Rainey's wife, when she turns up unexpectedly at the cabin in shades of *Psycho*, and Rainey is shot dead by an insurance investigator.

King felt duty-bound to comment on the subject of plagiarism in his jocular introduction to the piece, revising the history of his own fictions like *Salem's Lot* as he did so, but the debt that 'Secret Window, Secret Garden' owed to William F Harvey's short story 'W.S.', let alone RLS and his *Strange Case of Dr Jekyll and Mr Hyde*, somehow managed to pass without mention. The resultant film was not so adept at disguising the source of its less than original storyline.

In its tale of a writer secreted away in isolated retreat, saddled with neuroses and subject to perceived persecution, *Secret Window* is a one-hander for much of its running time. Depp rises to the challenge, coming up with another virtuoso perform- ance as the dishevelled Rainey which perfectly conveys the semi-somnambulant nature of the self-absorbed obsessive. He brings much flair and conviction to the role, from the old, torn, dressing gown in which he passes his days to the unruly mop of blonde hair which typifies the turmoil beneath it – so prominently do Depp's famous locks feature in the piece, in fact, that many reviewers thought they deserved a credit all of their own. Rainey's nemesis arrives in the versatile form of John Turturro, herein donning an Amish hat and an accent that is kissing cousin to that which he adopted for *Oh Brother Where Art Thou?* and the two play off one another in assured and absorbing style during the early part of the film. But as the coincidences and killings start to stack up in the face of logic and reason, any pretence at suspense begins to desert the story as surely as does the sanity of its protagonist when he comes eventually to uncover the truth about Shooter's charge.

For all its self-conscious allusions to Alfred Hitchcock and his films, including a reverential score by Philip Glass, *Secret Window* aspires rather to the intricate psychological thrillers of Patricia Highsmith, author of *The Talented Mr Ripley* and especially *Strangers On a Train*, to whose plot in particular it owes more than a passing debt. But the difference between aspiration and achievement is often a significant one.

Incidental details start to nag in the mind about *Secret Window*, and not in the way that was intended, such as the punning play on the villain's name: Shooter (a variation on 'Red Rum' in *The Shining*). Shoot 'er – geddit? When Amy enters Rainey's house at the climax, she finds the name (or words) carved on every surface, yet he ends up pummelling her with a shovel instead so the name should perhaps have been 'Spader'. This is typical of King: it seems clever enough on the surface, but scratch a little at the veneer and it makes less sense. When Rainey holds the conversation with his alter ego which reveals the Jekyll and Hyde twist (in a modern rendering of the old mirror scene in film versions of the Stevenson story), the wonders of digital effects offer up two Johnny Depps for the price of one as he *literally* talks to himself. This only points out what has been wrong with *Secret Window* from the start. It is conducted throughout on the realistic level of a mystery-thriller, but King's novella is horror-fantasy, in which the characters are merely ciphers along the road to yet another of pulp fiction's unending series of predictable twists in the tail. Watching the film is like setting out for *Fargo* and ending up in *Twin Peaks*, a directorial misjudgement which jarred with most of those who saw it. Because the twist is so trite, so uninventively unoriginal, Koepp was moved to disguise it as much as possible, which effectively meant removing the clues which a more conventional narrative would have seen him include. Even those that do remain – Amy's boyfriend having been born in 'Shooter's Bay'; the private detective's use of Shooter's term 'Pilgrim'; Rainey sleeping and waking, then sleeping and waking again – are treated so dismissively that they are all but ignored. And the revelatory flashback reveals things which King had seen fit to embed into the fabric of his story but which Koepp keeps hidden, like the fact that Rainey had once bought a hat like the one which Shooter is shown to wear. Had such tell-tale elements been more to the fore, all would have guessed the ending within the first reel, thus the subterfuge. But the effect is like different films having been grafted together in a desperate attempt to keep an audience on its toes, rather than a satisfactory resolution to an entertaining mystery.

(In Koepp's original version of the film, the final tracking shot down into the cornfield was extended to show the two corpses buried in the soil; this graphic denouement was excised from the release print, ostensibly to obtain a PG-13 rating in the USA, but more probably because its inclusion would have made a mockery of the police chief's supposed search of the property.)

King offers up several alternative endings to the story in his novella, variously derived from *Psycho* or the 'Method For Murder' episode of Amicus's *The House That Dripped Blood* – no single one of which apparently was considered satisfactory enough in itself to do justice to the contrived nature of what had gone before. Koepp jettisons all of these and opts instead for a bit of plagiarism of his own. In the story, Shooter is Rainey/Shooter is an entity brought into being by the power of imagination/ Shooter is a real person from Rainey's past whose story he had stolen (the last and least explicable of the three); in the film, Shooter is Rainey as per the first of King's endings, but in a climactic departure from 'Secret Window, Secret Garden', in which he is shot dead before he can do further harm, Koepp has him kill both his wife and her lover and bury their bodies in Amy's 'secret garden'. King's story was about a writer on the verge of a nervous breakdown. Koepp's script turns this idea into another variant of the eternal triangle, whose resolution would better have slotted into an episode of *Tales of the Unexpected* (where it had indeed already featured).

While he never quite cuts the mustard as the monster that he is revealed to be in the finale, Depp does supply the film with its creepiest moments – of which there are otherwise relatively few – by involuntarily stretching his jaw into a caricature of a yawn at times of stress, as though he were trying to suppress a latent desire to eat something unspeakable. This is a very effective touch and cleverly in tune with the implicit cannibalism of Koepp's revisionist text.

Depp gave Koepp several alternatives from which to choose in his final confrontation with Amy, even going so far as to play the scene in mimicry of both Marlon Brando and Christopher Walken. He would appear to have overlooked the obvious: Jack Nicholson. All that is missing from *Secret Window*'s hokey climax, in which Amy finds her husband outfitted as the very man whom he has been accusing of persecuting him and realises that he is in fact stark, staring mad, is Depp's utterance of the line: 'He-e-e-re's *Johnny!*'

> Turn around. Turn around… Turn the car round, and get the hell out of here. Right now. Don't go back. Do not go back there…
> Mort Rainey (Johnny Depp), Secret Window (2003)

A showcase for Johnny Depp, then, if a highly unsatisfactory one. His star power as a result of *Pirates of the Caribbean* had assured *Secret Window* a slot on the Sony production slate, but that in itself could prove to be a mixed blessing for the actor in future. 'It's classic Stephen King, and then suddenly you go: "Oh crap! Are you kidding?"' Depp said of the twist at the end of the film, presumably meaning that it would leave audiences gasping; *Secret Window* is more accurately reflected in how his remark can be taken at first reading.

After *Secret Window*, Depp was asked by Disney to participate in another story with a twist in the tail. He was to play himself as a 'real' interviewee in a mock-documentary being made in conjunction with television's Sci-Fi Channel to promote *The Village*, the latest Disney-backed fright-film by M Night Shyamalan, director of *The Sixth Sense* and *Signs*. *The Buried Secret of M Night Shyamalan* was an elaborate, two-hour hoax which purported to expose the dark secret of the director's past (a revelation which aped the plot of *The Sixth Sense*), and Depp added to the fraudulent air by appearing to bear witness to Shyamalan's obsessive desire for secrecy and 'confidentiality agreements'. A month before the film was due to be screened in the USA on 18 July 2004, two weeks ahead of the nationwide release of *The Village*, a press release was issued which stated that Shyamalan had tried to have it suppressed.

In response to probing questions from the press, Sci-Fi Channel president Bonnie Hammer was forced to admit that the whole thing was a 'guerrilla marketing campaign' (corporate-speak for a hoax) on behalf of *The Village*, that Shyamalan had been involved with the project since the beginning, and that the channel had purposefully misled the news media. A spokesman for NBC, which by then had taken over the channel with its acquisition of Vivendi Universal's TV holdings, said that such a marketing strategy was 'not consistent' with NBC policy.

The Sci-Fi Channel was forced to apologise on air, three days before the film was due to be shown in the USA (though not in the UK, where it was transmitted without demur on 22 August). As was the case with the Internet campaign for *The Blair Witch Project* in 1999, many viewers were nevertheless fooled, thus ensuring *The Village* of an opening weekend which flew in the face of the mostly damning reviews which it received prior to release. Had *The Buried Secret of M Night Shyamalan* been broadcast on 1 April instead of 18 July, things might not have got quite so out of hand.

When *Once Upon a Time in Mexico* arrived in cinemas only two months after *Pirates of the Caribbean*, not only the film had been transformed. The original theatrical trailer had naturally majored on star Banderas, with Depp's involvement signalled by a single mention of his name and a few brief shots of him in action. The revisited version in the wake of the good returns for *Pirates* made it appear as though he was the star of the film, with poor Banderas much reduced in importance. Rodriguez had taken the opportunity in the interim to elaborate Depp's scenes at the expense of the other actors (one of the few to benefit was Ruben Blades, with whom Depp interacts and who treats his role with commendable seriousness). The critics reviewed the result as a starring vehicle for the current box-office champ, rather than one which merely contained a disposable cameo of the kind to which they had been giving short shrift a year before.

Rodriguez's supposed homage to Leone was generally condemned out of hand: 'The only thing missing is a coherent story, or even, for that matter, an interesting idea for one,' was the view of the *New York Times*; 'The plot practically demands that you board a tour bus to navigate it,' echoed the *Boston Globe*. Depp's performance within it, however, was singled out for rare praise. The *Washington Post* called him 'the most larcenous man in show business by stealing every movie he's in.' It was a sentiment with which the *Chicago Tribune* concurred – 'Depp pulls off more movie piracy' – as did *Variety*: 'Depp … follows his enormously enjoyable work in *Pirates of the Caribbean* with another inventive turn, finding the sly comedy and even an unexpected paternal side behind his character's cool cruelty.' But it was left to the *Toronto Star* to quantify the new perception: 'For the second time this year, the actor transforms a moribund movie into a watchable one merely by *being* there.' Across the pond, even traditional British reserve was wavering in the face of that old-time religion.

In a review of the film entitled 'Depp rises above the mad Mex factor', the London *Evening Standard* typified the born-again attitude of commentators in general to what its show business correspondent had christened 'the Depp effect', the box-office phenomenon of 2003: 'Johnny steals the movie in a performance that keeps faith with itself, while including a series of wicked impersonations of, among others, Marlon Brando and Chow Yun Fat. He risks visual gags that only the most gifted silent comedians could have pulled off – especially in the latter stages when, blinded by the really bad guys, he stumbles like Oedipus through the carnage, bumping into window-ledges and shooting in all directions.'

Clearly, Johnny Depp had come a long way in the eyes of his critics since the days of *Benny and Joon*.

The $29 million *Once Upon a Time in Mexico* took $24 million in its first weekend; within another month, *Pirates of the Caribbean* would become only the second film of the year to pass the $300 million-dollar mark during its initial run, the other being *Finding Nemo*. No one was more surprised about the reception accorded to agent Sands than 'Sands' himself: 'I thought it was like a cameo, you know? A little in-and-out thing,' Depp said, bewildered. 'Suddenly, it was my agent or my sister – someone saw the movie and said, "Man, you're through the whole thing." I had no idea – especially after nine days of shooting.'

With *Once Upon a Time in Mexico* following hot on the heels of *Pirates of the Caribbean: The Curse of the Black Pearl* in the USA, and the two films playing virtually concurrently in the UK (where a little under seven weeks was all that had separated them in release), Johnny Depp, on-screen and in person, was unquestionably the biggest hit of summer 2003. But storm clouds of controversy were once again gathering around Hollywood's most unpredictable star.

Ever since railing against the 'fascist' undertow of *21 Jump Street*, Depp's adopted posture of rebel artist had confined itself to occasional sideswipes at the Hollywood establishment and public declarations of admiration for the rebels of the 1950s Beat movement, such as Kerouac and Ginsberg. He had never consciously promoted himself as a 'political' actor, in the activist style of Tim Robbins or his wife Susan Sarandon, for example, and yet the writers and artists of yesteryear whom he claimed so much to admire were *all* political animals – up to and including Brando – who often utilised their art to communicate larger truths in the pursuit of a just cause or social advance. In his 20 years as a rebel icon, the closest that Johnny Depp had come to supporting a cause was to get himself involved with the Make-a-Wish Foundation while still on *Jump Street* or plead in interview for the release of a convicted drugs dealer.

Amid the now-familiar protestations about a 'failed' career and his overindulged disdain for the mechanics of the Hollywood machine, Depp's jet-setting lifestyle and extravagant displays of wealth and celebrity power were signally at odds with his much-vaunted image of rebel chic and deference to the likes of the habitually impoverished Jack Kerouac. He may have believed himself immune to the blandishments of fortune and fame, but he had for some time past been a fully paid-up member of the super-rich élite, and his well-publicised deeds in that respect were starting to tell a different story. When one is given the chance to preach from the mountaintop on any subject which might spring to mind, before a press corps which hangs reverentially onto every syllable, it is easy to become carried away with a sense of one's own importance; having spent half a lifetime verbalising from the hip, Depp's sometimes intemperate affection for the taboo topic or loose phrase finally got the better of him.

In March 2003, while *Pirates of the Caribbean* was still in post-production, the Bush White House had launched an invasion of Saddam Hussein's Iraq in alliance with a so-called coalition of the willing, which included Britain, Spain and Australia in rapidly descending order. The issue split the United Nations down the middle, and it was left to the leaders of France and Germany to take up the batons of those calling for moderation in the face of a new and more belligerent American foreign policy. Since 1999, Depp had virtually been resident in France full-time, and with feelings running high in the run-up to war, he suddenly found himself called upon to opine on the actions of his government, rather than his own acting.

To a rising tide of questions about US behaviour on the international stage, Depp's replies were typically immoderate and largely in sympathy with the French position: 'Three years ago, I had the foresight to leave the USA before Bush had even become a small sparkle in the eye of "Uncle Sam",' he was quoted as saying, with respect to the man in charge on Capitol Hill. 'You really believe that this guy controls the country? I'm not at all sure about it. The way he was elected seems, in a way, suspicious.' He was more forthright still when it came to commenting on reports in the American press that anti-French sentiment in the country was demanding that French fries should be renamed 'Freedom fries': 'My favourite thing of all was the brilliant government officials who decided to change the name of French fries and French toast to Freedom fries and Freedom toast. That was the ultimate revelation. They basically woke up one morning and addressed the globe and said, "How do you do. We're idiots. We're childish. Just in case you wanted some proof, here it is. We're dumb-asses".'

The European media understandably lapped up such remarks from someone whom they had begun to think of as one of their own, with his home in St Tropez, his brasserie in Montmartre, his children by a woman who was herself born on the Isle de France and his self-confessed love of all things Euro-cultural. Sensing the mood of those around him as troop numbers mounted in preparation for the impending land assault on Iraq, Depp was encouraged to travel even further along the same rocky road. As though to prove that he had lost none of his erstwhile talent for iconoclasm, he went so far as to call the US President a 'liar' (though conversely, when he later met British Prime Minister Tony Blair, he was impressed with his sincerity).

In September 2003, seven months after the initial invasion of Iraq but six months before the impending Academy Award celebrations, Depp gave an interview to respected German magazine *Stern*, in which he claimed that 'America is dumb; it's like a dumb puppy that has big teeth that can bite and hurt you, aggressive,' adding, for good measure, 'My daughter is four and my boy is one. I'd like them to see America as a toy, a broken toy. Investigate it a little, check it out, get this feeling and then get out.' When news of this interview reached the shores of a United States of America whose peoples were now caught up in a frenzy of patriotic fervour over the fate of their fighting forces abroad, his remarks provoked an outcry in the domestic media.

As an indication of how high passions had run, one enterprising Internet columnist by the name of Joseph Farah even went so far as to suggest that Hollywood should reinstate the 'blacklist' that resulted from Senator Joe McCarthy's House Un-American Activities Committee hearings in the early 1950s. To give his readers some encouragement in compiling names for inclusion, he suggested the following list for starters: Michael Moore, Martin Sheen, Mike Farrell, Sheryl Crow, Janeane Garofalo, the Dixie Chicks, Richard Gere, Sean Penn, Harry Belafonte, Danny Glover, George Clooney, Jane Fonda, Tim Robbins, Susan Sarandon, Ed Asner, Alec Baldwin, Barbra Streisand... and Johnny Depp – none of which, if Farah and his followers had their way, would ever be allowed to work in America again.

Depp was branded disgraceful and *unpatriotic* – the most heinous charge that can be levied against an American citizen. In the meanwhile, word had filtered through to Depp's agent that her client might be in line for an Oscar nomination for his portrayal of Captain Jack Sparrow in *Pirates of the Caribbean*. With the slippery proficiency of Sparrow himself, verbally wriggling his way out of another sticky situation, Depp quickly issued a humiliating retraction which laid the blame for the mess on those two staples beloved of the political class: 'misquoted' and 'out of context': 'Taken in context, what I was saying was that, compared to Europe, America is a very young country and we are still growing as a nation. It is a shame that the metaphor I used was taken so radically out of context and slung about irresponsibly by the news media.' Given that he was now resident in France – the country to which Roman Polanski had fled in 1976 to escape an American-imposed jail-term – his change of heart seemed a trifle unnecessary, but he still owned property and had business interests in America, not to mention the prospect of that newly burgeoning career on the back of potential success at the Academy.

With France widely perceived in the States as having been the main stumbling block to the Bush administration's more bellicose stand on the whole Iraq problem, this was not the time to alienate sections of American public opinion. The 'dumb puppy' was turned from allusion into metaphor, and the rest was blamed on mistranslation. 'There was no anti-American sentiment. In fact, it was just the opposite,' Depp moved to correct. 'I am an American. I love my country and have great hopes for it. It is for this reason that I speak candidly and sometimes critically about it. I have benefited greatly from the freedom that exists in my country and for this I am eternally grateful.' For its part, Stern stuck by its original interview, but the Germans had sided with the French over Iraq, so he was given the benefit of the doubt.

It was the second time in weeks that Depp purportedly had been taken 'out of context'. The first had been over the misreporting by syndicated showbiz news series *Entertainment Tonight* of an interview that he had given about how he would educate his daughter on the dangers of drugs. ('If she comes to me in 15 or 20 years and says, "I'm curious about marijuana", then I'd be able to say, "Let's experiment; let's investigate together." I mean, I wouldn't want her to score a bag of weed on the street that's laced with PCP or something horrible,' he had said originally.) On that occasion, he had boycotted the programme during the promotional tour for *Once Upon a Time in Mexico*; on this latest, it was programme-makers who threatened to boycott him. 'That was a nasty moment,' Depp sighed with relief when things calmed down. 'But it's all cleared up now. I got to say what I needed to say.'

In any such piece in a 'foreign' press, one might expect the odd nuance of conversation to prove elusive, or for some stumbling to occur over more extreme examples of idiom (to which Depp is particularly prone), but not the mistranslation or misinterpretation of an entire train of thought – even though it did allude curiously to puppy-dogs. In his unabashed volte-face, Depp revealed himself to be as selective as any other star of his stature when it came to dealing with the media: it was useful when it stayed on message, less so when it chose to act arbitrarily. His mentor Marlon Brando had been prepared to tolerate the wrath of the Hollywood establishment when, in 1973, he had despatched a Native American to the Academy in his stead (actually an actress whom he had hired to play the part) to collect his Best Actor Oscar for *The Godfather*. Johnny Depp, it seems, is rather more circumspect. Not that it mattered, in the event. Elegantly tuxedoed and more conservatively coiffured than usual for the glittering occasion on 29 February, Depp was indeed nominated for the Academy Award for Best Actor for his role in *Pirates of the Caribbean: The Curse of the Black Pearl*, along with Jude Law for *Cold Mountain*, Bill Murray for *Lost in Translation* and Ben Kingsley for *The House of Sand and Fog*. All of them lost out to Sean Penn, for his performance as Jimmy Markum in *Mystic River*.

What can you do? There's a game to be played here. You can play it to the hilt and make shit-piles of money. I don't want to be ninety years old and look back and see how full of shit I was. The people I admire didn't do that.
JOHNNY DEPP, INTERVIEWED BY DAVID BLUM, *ESQUIRE* (1995)

In April 2004, the same Disney organisation of Chairman Michael Eisner with which Depp had been involved when he backtracked on his anti-Bush sentiments in the run-up to the Oscars pulled

out of a prearranged deal to distribute the Michael Moore documentary *Fahrenheit 9/11*, citing as its reason the upcoming
Presidential election. Moore's *Fahrenheit 9/11* went on to win
the Palme d'Or at the 57th Festival de Cannes, under the jury-
presidency of Quentin Tarantino, and found itself another distributor in the shape of Lion's Gate and Bob and Harvey Weinstein
of the ubiquitous Miramax Corporation. The anti-Iraq war, anti-
Bush White House *Fahrenheit 9/11* (a title punned on Ray
Bradbury's 1953 novel *Fahrenheit 451*) has since become the most
successful documentary in cinema history, taking more than $143
million in revenue.

Moore is a genuine 1960s-style radical, of the kind that Johnny
Depp has long held in high esteem; for his street cred to remain
intact, Depp should perhaps begin to refer less to the likes of
Kerouac and Thompson and more to the likes of Moore. Vietnam
is over; the Middle East is the problem now. But that might not sit
too well with his newly bankable status in the present climate.
Despite his professed distaste for the Hollywood ethic, Depp
bowed to the notion that nothing could be allowed to stand in the
way of the dollar. In the process, he made himself out to be a lot
less principled than the natives of his adopted France, whom he
claims to respect so much, when it came to the matter of
protesting a war.

Love him or loathe him, Sean Penn risked a jail term and the
vitriol of the right-wing media by going on a three-day 'fact-
finding' mission to Iraq in December 2002, as American bombers
were preparing to fly. But it was Penn who won the Oscar.

DISSOLVE TO...

EPILOGUE TWENTY YEARS AFTER

One evening, when Charlie went in to see his grandparents, he said to them, 'Is it really true that Wonka's Chocolate Factory is the biggest in the world?'

'True?' Cried all four of them at once. 'Of course it's true! Good heavens, didn't you know that? It's about fifty times as big as any other!'

'And is Mr Willy Wonka really the cleverest chocolate maker in the world?'

'My dear boy,' said Grandpa Joe, raising himself up a little higher on his pillow, 'Mr Willy Wonka is the most amazing, the most fantastic, the most extraordinary chocolate maker the world has ever seen! I thought everybody knew that!'

ROALD DAHL, *CHARLIE AND THE CHOCOLATE FACTORY* (1964)

PIRATES OF the Caribbean: The Curse of the Black Pearl was classic studio filmmaking, harking back to the great days of the Hollywood machine, and the fact that it went unrecognised by an Oscar community which seemed to be swept along on a tidal wave of synthetic appreciation for the pseudo-mythology of Tolkien's Middle-earth was a tragic sin of omission by the Academy in 2004. Depp nevertheless professed himself to be honoured by his nomination and happy just to be in the running for once, and he lapsed into Kerouac mode to reflect upon the experience: 'Sometimes you make a right turn and go down a bumpy road, and then you go on a highway and it smoothes out for a while, and then you get on another bumpy road. I'm just enjoying the ride, whether the road is bumpy or smooth,' he told *Screen International.* He had been equally gracious in defeat. 'I'm very thankful. I'm very grateful for this past year and for the things that have happened. I had no expectations at all – certainly not nominations of any sort, so I'm very touched, very moved.' But he *should* have won the Oscar, just for once, and not only because of his audaciousness in going out on a limb and creating an unforgettable character in a magical movie that will play down the ages and for generations to come. Instead it went to *Mystic River* and Sean Penn for a powerful if predictably pained peformance, but in a film that was destined to be forgotten before the DVD was even released.

Oscar night turned out to be anti-climactic, but the character of Jack Sparrow did not prove a total write-off in the prize-giving stakes: the week before, Depp had picked up the Best Actor gong at the 10th annual Screen Actors Guild Awards (where he beat Sean Penn) and on 5 June he was to do the same again at the MTV Movie Awards. All the while, the engagement diary of the hottest property on the Hollywood scene had been filling up more projects than Depp could shake a sea-leg at, to the extent that, by March 2004, he was booked for the next two years!

No sooner had the sun set on his chances of winning an Oscar for *Pirates of the Caribbean* than Johnny Depp was heading back to England to pick up where he had left off in the kind of small, independent endeavour on which he had built his reputation in the 1990s. According to the Brando principle, he had just made two commercial movies in a row, so he could afford to take some time out on another artistic one:

The Libertine was adapted from a play by Stephen Jeffreys, which was originally performed at London's Royal Court Theatre in December 1994, after a brief tour of the provinces. It deals with the last years in the short and debauched life of John Wilmot, 2nd Earl of Rochester, who was poet and profligate at the court of 'Merry Monarch' Charles II, and who died of syphilis in 1680 at the age of 33.

When Jeffreys' play opened in the USA in February 1996, at Chicago's Steppenwolf Theatre, Rochester was played by John Malkovich, who had been trying to mount a film version ever since. By 2003, Malkovich had been able to secure a production deal through British funding house First Choice and his own Mr Mudd, the company that he co-owns with producers Russell

Smith and Lianne Halfon. With a deal in place and a date finally set, Malkovich was too old at 50 to play the 30-year-old Earl and a younger actor was sought, with Malkovich stepping into the role of Charles II instead. First-time director Laurence Dunmore had Depp in his sights from the start and reportedly pursued him 'like a stalker' to try to persuade him to sign, although given that Depp and Malkovich are partners in Paris's Man Ray bistro, Dunmore presumably did not have to stalk for long. Even Johnny Depp was too old at 40 to give the Earl his historical due, but he could at least pass for thirty-something.

Location shooting for *The Libertine* stretched over the length and breadth of England and Wales: Wadham College at Oxford – the real Earl's college of learning and one of the earliest examples of 'Jacobean Gothic' – stood in for Adderbury, Rochester's country seat and the scene of his death in the film. Other authentic backdrops of note were the great Tudor houses of Charlecote Park in Warwickshire and Montacute in Somerset (which last appeared in Ang Lee's *Sense and Sensibility*; 1995), National Trust properties both. After several weeks spent in the West Country, *The Libertine* had been scheduled to move into the recently refurbished Ealing Studios in London on 23 February, but on 10 February, the British government had dropped a bombshell on the domestic industry. An edict from the Inland Revenue removed at a stroke a tax subsidy which had allowed producers to claim a tax-loss refund against a production budget before the film in question had even been made. Over the years, this loophole had encouraged inflated budgets and 'cowboy' exploitation of the system and it was closed off without warning, to the detriment of several films already in production. As a consequence of the Revenue's action, *The Libertine* suddenly was deprived of one third of its proposed $23 million budget – $1.4 million of which was earmarked for Johnny Depp – and DreamWorks' *Tulip Fever* (from the book by Deborah Moggach and starring Jude Law and Keira Knightley), had to be abandoned altogether. 'It was a big blow because we've been working on this film for seven years,'

Malkovich explained. 'To get someone like Johnny to do it takes a long time, and it's not an easy film to get financed because, to be blunt about it, it's not retarded. As the French say, this fell like a hair in our soup.'

Malkovich had an ace up his sleeve, however. He had just completed *Colour Me Kubrick* at the Lezayre studios at Ramsey on the Isle of Man, and he came to a substitute arrangement with the Manx Film Council to switch production to the island. It was not a moment too soon; along with other investors in *The Libertine*, Malkovich already had put $560,000 of his own money into the kitty to maintain cash-flow. 'We were in trouble for those ten or twelve days. We were trying everything,' he told Nigel Bunyan of the *Daily Telegraph*. 'In this business, you're used to the sky falling on your head. It was awfully sudden, but maybe they needed a billion pounds for the NHS. And anyway, who has sympathy for a bunch of prancing Hollywood luvvies who can't do their movies?' Steve Christian, director of Isle of Man Film, was the answer to that, and the film had found itself with a new start date of 3 March, on a self-governing tax haven in the middle of the Irish sea.

Charles II: Anyone can oppose, it's fun to be against things, but there comes a time when you have to start being for things as well. The time is now.

FROM STEPHEN JEFFREYS' PLAY, *THE LIBERTINE* (1994)

The role of John Wilmot is a continuation of the long line of artistic outsiders whom Depp has taken it upon himself to characterise since the days of *Edward Scissorhands*, although their innate impotence and desire to drown the pain of living with drink or drugs appears to increase disproportionately with each film. *The Libertine* presents him at his lowest ebb yet: Wilmot is a dissolute and disillusioned Restoration rebel, who cannot summon up the strength of character required to do anything about the wrongs which he rails against, and settles instead for bleating forlornly and wallowing in his cups. In many ways, he is a man of our times, as he was a 'Man of Mode' in his own – a living representation of a culture so shallow and hedonistic and lacking in moral clarity that he could never quite decide whether to be Christian or atheist, monarchist or republican, sinner or saint; an inspiration and source of amusement to others, but a source of shame and squandered opportunities to himself. His rebelliousness is a foppish pose, inspired by insecurity and the need to prove that he is his own man. As such, he writes pornographic poetry (which would neither be published nor appreciated till after his death) and leaves a friend to die in the street as a result of a fight which he has set in train. Wilmot is rebel hero as celebrity, full of sound and fury, signifying nothing. To the actor who portrayed him, those were still qualities to be admired: 'He had no tolerance for bullshit,' Depp explained to *Empire*'s Will Lawrence during an interview-break at the 2004 Venice Film Festival. 'He was able to tell King Charles II, "Fuck you, you're an asshole." He medicated himself to death; dead of drink and syphilis by the time he was 32. I loved him.'

There are many striking actorly scenes in the play, such as when Wilmot and the King square off against one another in the way that Depp described, and Jeffreys' sharp exchanges make some timely allusions to the betrayals and broken promises of Britain's Blair government: 'The thing is this, Charlie, we expected so much of you. We thought you would *transform* everything just with your solemn and glittering presence. We wanted a Sun King,' Wilmot recriminates. *The Libertine* is an exquisitely crafted piece and Stephen Jeffreys is a playwright of quite outstanding brilliance, but like so much art in this post-millennial age, it somehow lacks resolution and point. Aside from George Etherege (Tom Hollander), who rises above the pubescent preoccupations of Wilmot's 'Merry Gang' to model a successful stage show around his former mentor, the one character who triumphs over antipathy is the actress Elizabeth Barry (Samantha Morton) with whom Wilmot belatedly falls in love. She alone finds purpose to life in the pursuit of her craft, and at the expense of her love for the degenerate Earl. In exploring the literal and spiritual fall from grace of this seventeenth-century Sid Vicious, *The Libertine* is a soliloquy to self-destruction; it is Depp's *Hamlet*, a direction in which he was advised to go by Marlon Brando all those years before. Whether Jack Sparrow or the likes of Earl of Rochester will be the mark of Johnny Depp's screen career in years to come remains to be seen. Dunmore's film was provisionally set for UK release on October 22, 2004, but the subsequent clash with *Finding Neverland* pushed it back to November; at time of writing, a final date is as yet unknown.

Nine days after Depp settled into the studio shoot for *The Libertine*, *Secret Window* opened in America. *Variety* captured the prevailing mood among US critics: the film was lacklustre but the Deppster could now do no wrong. 'What might have been a pedestrian thriller adapted from a self-referentially recycled Stephen King novella is elevated several notches by Johnny Depp, who continues to ride the wave of a remarkable mid-career high.' John Anderson in Newsday went further: 'Johnny Depp has emerged as the world's coolest actor,' he decreed, to which the *Washington Post* added that 'Depp's cool presence and quirky mannerisms are the only thing to keep your eyelids from shutting down like Venetian blinds.'

When the film arrived in the UK on 30 April, it was a different story. The dangers inherent in the success of *Pirates of the Caribbean* being attributed to the performance of its lead player had been hinted at in the favourable reviews which had greeted *Once Upon a Time in Mexico*, but they were made more apparent in the less favourable ones for *Secret Window*. Whereas the odd-ball character of Sands was felt to have added sparkle to an undistinguished actioner in the euphoria that led up to Depp's entry into the Oscar race, the equally oddball character of Mort Rainey was felt to swamp the style the Stephen King thriller that came in the wake of his defeat at the hands of the Academy. The *Daily Telegraph*'s Tim Robey set the tone by suggesting that Depp had delivered the film of 'an oddball tour-de-force' that it hardly knew how to house, and that director Koepp was left with little to do but 'fiddle around with incidental comedy while Depp eats the cabin furnishings for breakfast'. The implication was that Depp was being given his head in the hope of another box-office bonanza along the lines of *Pirates*, and that the wiser councils which had prevailed in the past were suddenly prepared to step aside and let the actor do exactly as he pleased – none of which was helped by the fact that all three films had opened inside nine months, with *Pirates* and *Mexico* separated by a mere two. Johnny Depp was simply doing what he had always done, which was to take each project on its merits and try to invest it with something new, but too many idiosyncratic turns in a row seemed now about to turn some reviewers off him as fast as they had been turned on. Notwithstanding, *Secret Window* took $18 million on its first weekend in the States and $80 million worldwide within its first six months, rivalling the recent returns for *Once Upon a Time in Mexico*. The days of Johnny Depp making nothing but 'flops' seemed well and truly to be over.

Depp went straight from *The Libertine* into a fourth collaboration with Tim Burton, by way of a quick detour to Paris and a cameo in a romantic comedy entitled *Ils se marièrent et eurent beaucoup d'enfants* (*They Married and Had Lots of Children*) for director Yvan Attal. If *Secret Window* had something in common with the macabre stories of Roald Dahl, Depp's next major project was to consolidate the connection: Burton had it in mind to remake Dahl's most famous children's novel, 1964's *Charlie and the Chocolate Factory*.

Dahl, who died in 1990, had been a native of Wales but was originally of Norwegian origin; his childhood traumas – his father and elder sister both died when he was four, and one of his own daughters died when she was eight – and unhappy years at public school coloured his fiction in terms of the way that it treated adults as 'the enemy', which resulted in Dahl producing some of the strangest children's stories ever written. *Charlie and the Chocolate Factory* is one such: a cynical and sharp-edged satire which forever seems to teeter on the edge of outright horror, but which ostensibly concerns the adventures of a young boy named Charlie who turns up a Golden Ticket that entitles him to a tour of the titular Chocolate Factory, a Victorian-Gothic edifice run by the strange and reclusive Willy Wonka. Dahl's narrative is a typical nursery allegory, with the good, kind but impoverished Charlie eventually winning out in a secret contest over the fat, selfish, spoilt and slobbish quartet who accompany him to the Chocolate Factory. In its tale of what exactly *happens* to the other winners of said Golden Tickets, however, *Charlie and the Chocolate Factory* is right up Burton's street.

The screen's first and, until 2004, only 'Willy Wonka' was comedian Gene Wilder, the manic protégé of producer Mel Brooks, who had played the role in a 1971 film directed by Mel Stuart and retitled *Willy Wonka and the Chocolate Factory*: Wilder's Wonka was much as described by Dahl in the book, minus the beard: 'He had a black top hat on his head. He wore a tail-coat made of a beautiful plum-coloured velvet. His trousers were bottle green. His gloves were pearly grey. And in one hand he carried a fine gold-topped walking cane. Covering his chin, there was a small, neat, pointed black beard-a goatee. And his eyes – his eyes were most marvellously bright.'

Some would say that Wilder was an impossible act to follow, with his Danny Kaye-like penchant for wild-eyed mugging and exaggerated physical tics in films like *The Producers* (1968), *Young Frankenstein* (1974) and *The Lady in Red* (1979); others might think, on the contrary, that his frenzied antics in the field of slapstick were almost as irritating as those of Jim Carrey. Either way, Wilder has been the personification of Dahl's conniving candy man for more than 30 years, so it would be a curious choice of role for an erstwhile Hollywood bad boy to assume – were it not for the fact that most of Depp's screen roles have been curious choices, and he had little hesitation in accepting the part when it was offered to him by Tim Burton after Christopher Walken and Michael Keaton had been crossed off the provisional list of candidates. 'You'll never escape that memory that's seared into your consciousness of Gene Wilder as Willy Wonka,' he said. 'It was really amazing to watch as a kid growing up and I've watched it with my kids. So it's, okay, where do I go from there? Gene Wilder did something very beautiful, but it's time to take it somewhere else.' The film commenced in production across five of Pinewood Studios' sound stages in Buckinghamshire on 5 June 2004, with *Finding Neverland*'s Freddie Highmore as Charlie.

And after that?

First out of the starting gate is the return of a certain pirate captain. In an echo of his sentiments about the character of Edward Scissorhands 13 years before, Depp waxed reflective about the prospect of reprising the role of Sparrow: 'I went through a decompression period after the first film. If you're really connected with a character, you always do to some degree. You miss the guy. You miss being that person. The only thing that was in the back of my mind was the hope that there would be a sequel some day, so that I could meet him again.' With *Pirates of the Caribbean* having attained a global box-office take of a staggering $650 million and counting, his wish was certain to have been granted, and *Pirates 2* ('Treasures of the Lost Abyss') and 3 are now scheduled to be shot back-to-back in St Vincent and the Grenadines towards the end of the year. Acknowledging the fact that the inspiration for the character of Jack Sparrow was Stones' guitarist Keith Richards, Depp asked for the ageing rocker to be included in the cast of the sequels as Sparrow's *father*.

It took me a long time and most of the world to learn what I know about love and fate and the choices we make, but the heart of it came to me in an instant, while I was chained to a wall and being tortured.

GREGORY DAVID ROBERTS, *SHANTARAM* (2003)

Depp has also signed to play Jean-Dominique Bauby, editor of French *Elle*, who suffered a stroke which paralysed his entire body, in Julian Schnabel's *The Diving Bell and the Butterfly*, and he will be the voice of Victor in Tim Burton's animated feature *The Corpse Bride*. There is also talk of him playing Ozzy Osbourne, the wild-man of rock, in a biopic, as well as starring opposite Vanessa Paradis in *The Gypsy's Curse*. And then there is *The Rum Diary*, a supposed 'lost' novel of Hunter Thompson's from 1959, which charts the semi-autobiographical fortunes of a writer who takes a job on a Puerto Rican newspaper while battling the bottle and the local yokels; Depp was pencilled in for the role of Thompsonesque hero Paul Kemp. Last but not least, there is *Shantaram*, another quasi-autobiography by Australian first-time author Gregory David Roberts. Roberts' 940-page adventure epic was a runaway best-seller on its home turf, which initially sparked the adaptive interest of Russell Crowe, but Depp and Warners managed to acquire the screen rights to the book in what *Daily Variety* called 'one of the biggest film rights deals of the year.' *Shantaram* is set in the 1980s and follows the trail of one-time heroin addict Roberts as he journeys from maximum security prison (and a 19-year sentence for armed robbery) to the back-streets of Bombay and then on to Afghanistan, where he fights alongside the Mujaheddin against the invading Russian army.

Undoubtedly there will be more. Many more. In the meantime, Depp's cultural status grows in line with the number of projected films to which his name now attaches.

Episodes of *21 Jump Street* have just been released on DVD, whereas previously they had been virtually unobtainable; at the same time, Paramount is touting the idea of turning the show into a feature film to be written by its original creators, Stephen Cannell and Patrick Hasburgh. And following the success of his Broadway musical adaptation of *Hairspray* in 2002, director John Waters is planning to follow up with a similar adaptation of *Cry-Baby*. Between that and *Jump Street* the movie, the public image of Johnny Depp looks set to become more iconic than iconoclastic with each passing year: he recently provided the voice for a character called Yogi Victor in the 'Hank's Back' episode of the Fox cartoon television series *King of the Hill*, and a pop video for the single 'Girls Lie Too' by Canadian country singer Terri Clark featured a Jack Sparrow lookalike in a dream sequence. Depp is a commodity again, as he was once before, but on his own terms this time.

Finding Neverland received its UK premiere at the Odeon Leicester Square on Sunday, October 17. Depp and Winslett were both in attendance, and the proceeds from the event went to the Great Ormond Street Hospital for Children, to which august institution Barrie had also bequeathed the rights to *Peter Pan* on his death in 1929. Ever the chameleon, Depp lopped off his locks for the occasion and turned up in J M Barrie guise, while Winslett settled for a regal Ben de Lisi dress. Also in attendance were Freddie Highmore, Ian Hart (who plays Sir Arthur Conan Doyle in the film) and director Marc Forster, who found himself having to defend the numerous departures from historical fact which reportedly had left descendants of the Llewelyn Davies family less than pleased with the finished result. 'For me, it was about how [Barrie] was inspired to write *Peter Pan*, so basically the most important thing is dealing with the characters who inspired him. Otherwise you're making a biography and it wasn't about that.' When asked about the Oscar buzz that already had begun to surround his latest release, Depp was typically self-effacing: 'Freddie or Kate? Me? Oh, no—not again!'

The belated release of *Finding Neverland* ahead of the 2005 Oscars showed no signs that the born-again fervour for Hollywood's pirate king among the critical establishment was in any danger of abating. No film of Depp's had experienced a delay of such inordinate length between production and distribution since *Arizona Dream*, but trade reviews in advance of its November release were satisfyingly upbeat – not only in terms of the piece as a whole but of its star's performance in particular. *Variety*'s Todd McCarthy, handkerchief in hand, was the first to fall under the spell of director Marc Forster's expertly crafted 'tear-jerking' flourishes: 'Many moments of the film's final stretch will have audiences welling up and blubbering away,' he sobbed, dry-ing his eyes just long enough to heap unreserved praise on Depp's 'delicate and inviting portrait' of Barrie: 'Depp takes a cue from the soft lilt of his beautifully rendered Scottish accent to create a gently nuanced portrayal of an artist who at least this once found a way to transform troubled reality into an imaginative work for the ages.' Mike Goodridge, for *Screen International*, was equally moved. While appreciating the fact that *Finding Neverland* was likely to play havoc with 'historical purists', and damning the maudlin Elton John/Bernie Taupin ditty ('Peter's Song') that plays over the end credits of US prints, he was nevertheless Kleenexed into submission by the *Chocolat*-style sentimentality and Depp's 'knockout performance': 'Adopting a note-perfect upper-crust Scottish accent, the American actor is in almost every scene and he is the model of restraint,' he wrote, adding, 'He is assured another Oscar nomination for his work.' With *The Libertine* already heading on a parallel track, one might not be enough.

> *Rochester: When I poured away the last bottle of wine I saw the blood of Christ streaming onto the floor and it took all my effort not to throw myself on my face and guzzle. But I desisted and my mind cleared and I made an inventory of my life and found much wanting: injuries to divers people: want of attention to my affairs: a lifetime spitting in the face of God, and I knew I was to be cast down. I had long ago discarded the layer of formal politeness with which we negotiate the world, but now I had to wade through the slough of my licentiousness until I found level ground underfoot, a ground of true sensibility and love of Christ. Now I gaze upon a pinhead and see angels dancing. Well. Do you like me now? Do you like me now?*
>
> **FROM STEPHEN JEFFREYS' PLAY, *THE LIBERTINE* (1994)**

Nowadays, Depp is almost less of an actor than he is an *artiste*. He has become what he had always fated himself to be: the perfect Rochester-like expression of the free spirit in the flesh. Existentially slouched in the elegant palaces of man, he muses and philosophises on the nature of things, while contemplating his next artistic challenge. He names as friends some of the most famous artists and musicians of the twentieth century, while himself laying claim to some of the most respected cult films of the last 25 years. In his leisure hours, he reads, paints and tends to the vegetable garden in his chateau in the Provence countryside, sipping red wine and listening to the gypsy strains of Taraf de Haïdouks or the Blues music of Howling Wolf. When he was filming *Pirates of the Caribbean* in St Vincent, he lived in a yacht moored on the quay: 'You should have seen this boat!' co-star Orlando Bloom exclaimed in *GQ*. 'Shag pile carpet; mirrors on the ceiling; velvet everywhere – like an Austin Powers boat. It was mad. I love the fact that he lived on a boat. How cool is that?' As an international entrepreneur, Depp is also a man of eclectic (and casually expensive, rattle-ring-wearing) tastes, acquired from a lifetime of Romany roving around the film capitals of America and Europe. He alters his image to suit his mood, and his screen persona to suit almost every film he makes. He has been there, seen it, done it – and bought the 'I'm With Stupid' T-shirt to go along with it all. Oscar Wilde would have been proud. The decadent Victorian once told André Gide, 'I put my talent into my work, but my genius into my life.' Johnny Depp appears to do both. He watches Disney cartoons with his children and plays along with Paradis on her albums and on stage, his 'first love', music, as strong as ever. Of late, he has even cut down his lifelong habit of hand-rolling cigarettes out of Bali Shag tobacco and chocolate-flavoured papers in favour of jogging (yes, jogging). Age and responsibility appear to be transforming him out of all recognition. Or are they?

Depp's salary demands have now risen to a reported $20 million per film (a figure which he previously labelled 'obscene') and he recently abandoned the mobile trailer in which he had been domiciled during the shooting of *Charlie and the Chocolate Factory* in favour of a 'Bedouin' tent, constructed by Pinewood's technicians at a cost of $450,000. 'Johnny already had the biggest trailer on-set but he wasn't happy with it,' a studio 'insider' told the *Sun*. 'He's a real hippie at heart and he wanted his trailer to look like a Bedouin tent' – this, on top of the $950,000 that the film incurred when an expensive camera-rig tumbled into a vat of chocolate.

'Maybe I should do what Brando did thirty years ago – buy an island,' he had mused to Sophie Cooper in 1999. 'Maybe take my girl and some friends and just go there and sleep. And read, and swim and think clear thoughts.' Five years later, in May 2004, he did exactly that, paying $1.9 million for a 35-acre retreat in the Bahamas, 60 miles south of Nassau. He also has set up another production company, called Infinitum Nihil, through which he intends to produce and star in *Shantaram*. But as though to show that the old, rakish Depp has not entirely vanished, he recently totalled his brand new Mercedes sports car by reversing it into the gates of his Plan de la Tour chateau.

'We live a very boring life,' Paradis has said in interview. 'We go to the market, cook, eat, and watch our children grow' – the simple life of the French peasant, interrupted only by the occasional film premiere, or the acquisition of another club, bar or expensive piece of real estate in one of the great capitals of the world. To Lisa Grainger in the *Sunday Times*, she intimated the following about her domestic situation: 'We've never said we don't want to get married, but we're neither opposed to it nor excited about it. You know, we might do it for the kids one day. But we are more than married: we have two children. It's not like we need to.' Herself a victim of vitriolic headlines in the past, Paradis shares Depp's antipathy towards the press. 'My life is away from silly magazines, which are good for one thing – making fires.' But making fires was the last thing that anyone in the south of France thought of doing in July 2000, when a spate of wildfires destroyed 30,000 hectares (22,000 acres) of forest, left 19 firefighters injured, five tourists dead and nearly cost the couple their exclusive home.

'Vanessa and my children have taught me that the only thing that matters in life is being a good parent,' Depp summarised. 'I

can't say that the darkness has completely gone; it's still there –
but I've never been closer to the light than I am these days.'

> They even had these quotes that I was to memorise if I was
> asked anything – responses, basically, that I was supposed
> to give if I was asked questions, which was pretty weird.
> Johnny Depp, The Buried Secret of M Night Shyamalan (2003)

It is difficult to think of a star of his calibre who has been more
honest and approachable to the media about every aspect of his
life and career than Depp and yet, since 1995, he has gained
a completely unwarranted reputation for privacy and publicity-
shyness – presumably disseminated by those whom he has barred
from aspects of his private life, such as the more intrusive
paparazzi; in reality, 'private' actors are men like Michael
Gambon (with whom he worked on *Sleepy Hollow*) or the late
Alec Guinness, who studiously avoid the glare of the media spotlight and give little of themselves beyond their talents. With literally hundreds of press and television interviews to his name, Depp
could hardly be described as private, and yet he continues to be
so, even though he has reverted more to his former self since
settling down in St Tropez with Paradis and his children and
reaching the pinnacle of his profession through his acclaimed
performance in *Pirates of the Caribbean*. He balances his
apparent frankness in interviews by quoting an adage which he
attributes to Jean Cocteau (ironically, the words were actually
spoken by Kate Moss!): "The more visible you make me, the more
invisible I become', implying, in the process, that no matter what
he says or whatever might be written about him, he retains the
'privacy' of his innermost thoughts; that only *he* knows the real
Johnny Depp. To a large extent, this is true, but he has been such
an open book for so long now that the rest of the world has managed to garner a pretty good idea, and what it sees, it is finally
beginning to find attractive and endearing instead of quirky,
eccentric and conversationally scatological.

There remains the matter of how Depp's public utterances about his life and philosophy can be weighed in the balance against the obvious examples of spin. Of late, his comments have sounded increasingly anodyne and indistinguishable from those of any other cog in the wheel of the dollar-hungry Hollywood machine: every screenplay is the best, every story the most interesting, every producer/director the most brilliant to work with, every co-star the most fascinating to work alongside. Like a tape playing on a continuous loop, with only the names interchanging. Same old, same old. 'Lies – it's all lies,' he once conceded, referring to interviews that he had given to promote his filmwork. 'You can never say what you want to say; it's impossible.'

In an article in the November issue of *Vanity Fair*, he again attempted to defend his pre-war stance on US-British involvement in Iraq—almost a year's distance from the affair allowing him a little more leeway in terms of shoulder-shrugging on this occasion: 'I used the metaphor of a puppy-dog, but I never said ignorant puppy-dog. I said it's a very young country compared to Old Europe, or Asia. I was misinterpreted. I was talking about the government, and especially the current administration. Never about the troops, even if I was not particularly enthusiastic about going to Iraq or whatever. I love my country. But fuck, if I want to say that I don't agree with the President's choices or words or intentions, so what? Even if I had said what they printed—which I didn't—what's the big deal? Some actor blurts out this thing— who gives a shit? He's an actor!'

As though to reconnect himself further with the rednecks who bombarded his agent's office with electronic hate-mail in the wake of his initial outburst (several of whom he telephoned personally in order to explain himself), Depp took the opportunity presented by the *Finding Neverland* premiere to reveal to the *Daily Telegraph* what he considered to be the press's latest Big Lie about him: 'The big lie is that I live in France now,' he confided to Charlie Methven, the *Telegraph*'s 'Spy.' 'The French papers are always making out that I do, but I don't. In fact, I divide my time equally between LA and France. Sure, I like France, and it has some pretty good wines, but, you know, I really miss America.' Even Paradis appeared to join him in his new-found antipathy towards the country that he had adopted so vocally only four years before: 'There are so many rumours about me there, and most of them are wrong,' she echoed.

So given these latest confessions, what are we left with? — What is the truth about Johnny Depp?

Is he really a radical of unassailable integrity in the face of the commercial pressures which are part and parcel of his profession? Or is it all an illusion, like the plain-glass spectacles that he is prone to wearing when he is out and about in public? Have he and his Hollywood agent, Tracey Jacobs, merely made a virtue out of necessity and between them orchestrated one of the most astute personality campaigns in the history of the movies, in a world that values celebrity above all else and where the cool and the crazy are hailed as the new demigods of this earthly Olympus? A little of both is the likely answer. 'To play a role, you have to be in love with the character,' he has said. 'I can only love characters who aren't like me; I don't like myself. Not to be yourself for two months gives a nice, sheltered feeling.'

The *essence* of acting is character, not the ability to speak dialogue with conviction (which is what most so-called actors strive for), and characters are what Johnny Depp will continue to play: 'When I age, I'll be able to do more character parts, which is what I want to do. It's why the movies I've been in were so welcome to me – all character parts. From the moment I started acting, I wanted to be a character player. I tell you, I look forward to getting old.'

It was a trait in Depp that was observed long ago by Peter Hedges, author of *What's Eating Gilbert Grape*. 'He's a character actor in a leading man's body,' he said. But after two decades in the business, how much of Johnny Depp is the character, and how much the actor?

My friend, you have just seen the story of Edward D Wood,

> Junior. Stranger than fact, and yet every incident based on
> sworn testimony... A man. A life. Can you prove it didn't
> happen?
> Criswell (Jeffrey Jones), Ed Wood (1993)

An actor's life is the *creation* of illusion, but exactly how far that illusion might stretch can vary from individual to individual. What we *can* know for certain about an actor named Johnny Depp is up there on the screen, for all to see. It speaks for itself, and it reveals him to be one of the finest performers of his generation. The other certainty is that like many in his position, he would be more than happy for that to speak for him – and that *alone*. Any human life is the sum of what it achieves, rather than how it might be conducted, and Depp's life to date undoubtedly has achieved a great deal.

Johnny Depp has put together a cinematic *oeuvre* like no other in Hollywood. He may have amassed more than his share of commercial failures among the films in which he has chosen to appear, but this is as nought compared to those which he can count as artistic successes. With one or two notable exceptions, there is hardly a bad movie in the bunch, due, primarily, to the unique qualities which he has brought to them, but to use the analogy which he coined for *Rolling Stone* in relation to the Beat poets, those that walked 'a little higher off the ground' must include *Ed Wood, What's Eating Gilbert Grape, Dead Man, The Brave, Fear and Loathing in Las Vegas, Blow* and, of course, *Pirates of the Caribbean*. Of these, he should be particularly proud. If he were never to make another film, they would stand as testament to the consummate skills and persuasive screen presence of a truly magical 'actor's actor'.

> It seems to me now that the closer that one can come to
> death in life makes the passage into death all the more
> easy. And it also leaves behind the greatest gift that any-
> one can give another, which is the courage to face death.
> McCarthy (Marlon Brando), The Brave (1996)

Marlon Brando died on 2 July 2004, of heart failure; he was 80 years old. With him, went the soul of a whole generation of actors who owed him their style, their technique and their inspiration, in the way that musicians might talk of Presley or Chuck Berry or John Lennon. An entire era of the American screen has passed into history. Brando's singular talent and peerless contribution to cinema was a 'pearl of great price', possession of which must now pass to the next in line.

As an actor, Johnny Depp is at the peak of his powers: he has been honing his craft for over twenty years. Having reached the ripe old age of 41, he is now one of the elder statesmen of the new brood of dedicated artist which is taking over from the likes of Al Pacino, Robert De Niro and Mickey Rourke as they, in their turn, took over from Paul Newman, Steve McQueen and, yes, Marlon Brando.

This is the story of what has been.

From Johnny Depp, however, the best is surely yet to come.

EXT. BLACK PEARL-DAY

Ana Maria: Captain Sparrow... the Black Pearl is yours.

Jack runs a hand lovingly along the rail, then takes the wheel. It feels good – right – in his hands. He opens the compass, takes a reading, and adjusts the course. Opens up a bottle of rum, takes a swig. Begins to hum to himself...

Jack Sparrow: Drink up, me hearties... Yo, ho!

The orchestra takes over, and the Black Pearl sails away, into the sun...

CUT TO BLACK as CREDITS and orchestra continue on...

THE END

from the screenplay of Pirates of the Caribbean (2003)

APPENDIX CAST AND CREDITS

1984

A Nightmare on Elm Street
CAST
Lt Thompson ....John Saxon
Marge Thompson......Ronee Blakley
Nancy Thompson......Heather
Langenkamp
Tina Grey ....Amanda Wyss
Rod Lane ....Nick Corri
Glen Lantz ....Johnny Depp
Dr King ....Charles
Fleischer
Sgt Parker ....Joseph Whipp
Freddy Krueger ....Robert Englund
Teacher ....Lin Shaye
Sgt Garcia ....Joe Unger
Nurse ....Mimi
Meyer-Craven
Minister ....Jack Shea
Mr Lantz ....Ed Call
Mrs Lantz ....Sandy Lipton
Foreman..................David Andrews
Coroner ....Jeffrey Levine
Tina's Mom ....Donna
Woodrum
Cops ....Shashawnee
Hall,
Carol Pritikin
Brian Reise
Surfers....................Jason Adams
Don Hannah
Hallguard.................Leslie Hoffman
Tina's Mom's Boyfriend
Paul Grenier
With ....John Richard
Petersen

SELECTED CREDITS
Director: Wes Craven
Producer: Robert Shaye
Screenplay: Wes Craven
Associate Producer: John
Burrows
Music: Charles Bernstein
Song, 'Nightmare': Steve Karshner,
Martin Kent, Michael Schurig
Cinematography: Jacques Haitkin
Production Designer:
Greg Fonseca
Editors: Pat McMahon,
Rick Shaine
Sound Mixer: James LaRue
Production Manager: John
Burrows
1st Assistant Director: Nick
Batchelor
Makeup: Kathy Logan
Special Makeup Effects: David
Miller, Louis Lazzara
Hair Stylist: RaMona
Costumes: Dana Lyman
Executive Producers: Stanley
Dudelson, Joseph Wolf
NEW LINE 91 MINUTES

1985

Private Resort
CAST
Ben..........................Rob Morrow
Jack Marshall ....Johnny Depp
Patti ....Emily
Longstreth
Dana........................Karyn O'Bryan
The Maestro.............Hector
Elizondo
Mrs Rawlings ....Dody Goodman
Reeves ....Tony Azito
Shirley ....Hilary Shapiro
Bobbie Sue ....Leslie
Easterbrook
Scott ....Michael Bowen
Alice ....Lisa London
Curt ....Andrew Clay
The Barber...............Ron House
Mike ....Greg Wynne
Kelly ....Nora Gaye
Aerobics Instructor..Susan
Mechsner
Georgie ....Matthew
Levine
Wanda ....Lucy Lee
Flippin Dog Lady ......Phyllis
Franklin
Fred ....Jonathan
Prince
Phillip.......................Jeremy
Lawrence
Bikini Girl ....Vickie Benson
Georgie's Mom ....Nancy Raffa
Bartender ....Raymond
Forchion
Lead Singer ....Mark
Scandariato
Sumo Wrestlers ....Ed Nakamoto
Lonnie Wun
Officer Sturgeon ......Steve Fifield
Strong Guy...............Christopher
Wolf

Resort Guests:
Jill Selkowitz, Karen Chase, Barbara
Szubota, Jacqueline Pare, Victoria
Wilburn, Wendi Morrison, Pamela
Barry, Jamie Massalas, Michelle
Harbour, Nancy Herbrecht, Pamela
Joy, Rae Naritomi, Walter Naritomi,
William Yamadera

SELECTED CREDITS
Director: George Bowers
Producers: R Ben Efraim,
Don Enright
Screenplay: Gordon Mitchell,
Ken Segall, Alan Wenkus
Cinematography: Adam Greenberg
Production Designer: Michael
Corenblith
Editor: Samuel D Pollard
Sound Mixers: Jonathon 'Earl'
Stein, James Thornton
Production Manager: Russell
Vreeland

1st Assistant Director: Ernest
Johnson
Makeup: Deborah Figuly
Hair Stylists: Donna Felix,
Peter Tothpal
Costumes: Jill M Ohanneson
Stunt Coordinator: Gary Jensen
TRISTAR 82 MINUTES

Slow Burn
CAST
Jacob Asch ....Eric Roberts
Laine Fleischer ....Beverly
D'Angelo
Ron McDonald ....Dennis
Lipscomb
Raymond J Barry ....Gerald
McMurtry
Mona ....Anne Schedeen
Pam Draper ....Emily
Longstreth
Donnie Fleischer ......Johnny Depp
Robert ....Henry Gibson
Simon Fleischer........Dan Hedaya
Norton ....Frank Schuller
Erica ....Victoria Catlin
George ....Edward Bunker
Mrs Poulson..............Ruth Richards
With ....
Pat Ast, Linda Rae Barrs, Tomasa
Bazan, Gary Boswell, Cliff Courtney,
Patrick Delinger, Jean Poitras,
Teresa Prater, Gigi Valente,
Kay Younker

SELECTED CREDITS
Director: Matthew Chapman
Producer: Mark Levinson
Screenplay: Matthew Chapman
From the novel *Castles Burning* by
Arthur Lyons
Music: Loek Dikker
Cinematography: Tim Suhrstedt
Production Designer: Bo Welch
Editor: T Battle Davis
Production Manager: Henry Kline
1st Assistant Director: Scott Easton
Makeup: Teresa Austin
Hair Stylist: Kathy Webright
Costumes: Gale Parker Smith
Executive Producers:
Joel Schumacher, Stefanie Staffin
Kowal MCA
UNIVERSAL 92 MINUTES

1986

Platoon
CAST
Staff Sgt Bob Barnes..Tom Berenger
Sgt Elias Grodin........Willem Dafoe
Pvt Chris Taylor ......Charlie Sheen
Big Harold ....Forest
Whitaker
Rhah ....Francesco
Quinn

Sgt Red O'Neill..........John C
                         McGinley
Sal ....Richard Edson
Bunny ....Kevin Dillon
Junior ....Reggie Johnson
King ....Keith David
Lerner ....Johnny Depp
Tex ....David Neidorf
Lt Wolfe ....Mark Moses
Crawford ....Chris Pedersen
Sgt Warren...............Tony Todd
Manny ....Corkey Ford
Tony ....Ivan Kane
Doc ....Paul Sanchez
Sanderson ....J Adam Glover
Francis....................Corey Glover
Pvt Gardner.............Bob Orwig
Morehouse ....Kevin
                        Eshelman
Ace ....James Terry
                        McIlvain
Capt Harris ....Dale Dye
Parker ....Peter Hicks
Flash ....Basile Achara
Fu Sheng ....Steve Barredo
Rodriguez................Chris
                        Castillejo
Tubbs ....Andrew B
                        Clark
Village Chief............Bernardo
                        Manalili
Village Chief's Wife
......................................Than Rogers
Village Chief's Daughter
......................................Li Thi Van
Old Woman...............Clarisa Ortacio
One-Legged Man.......Romy Sevilla
Terrified Soldier.......Mathew
                        Westfall
Mechanized Soldiers Nick
                        Nickelson,
                        Warren
                        McLean
Rape Victim.............Li Mai Thao
Medic ....Ron Barracks
Soldier with Mohawk Haircut
......................................H Gordon Boos
Pfc Ebenhoch..........Mark Ebenhoch
Alpha Company Major in Bunker
......................................Oliver Stone

SELECTED CREDITS
Director: Oliver Stone
Producer: Arnold Kopelson
Screenplay: Oliver Stone
Music: Georges Delerue
Cinematography: Robert
Richardson
Production Designer: Bruno
Rubeo
Art Director: Rodell Cruz, Doris
Sherman Williams
Editor: Claire Simpson
Sound Mixer: Simon Kaye
Production Manager: Joe
Constantino
Assistant Director: Tim Minear
**Special Makeup Effects and
Visual Continuity**: Gordon J Smith
Special Effects Supervisor: Yves
De Bono
Stunt Coordinator: Gil Arceo
Executive Producers: John Daly,
Derek Gibson
HEMDALE/ORION 120 MINUTES

1987

21 Jump Street
(2-part pilot episode)
CAST
Officer Tom Hanson
......................................Johnny Depp
Captain Richard Jenco
......................................Frederic
                        Forrest
Officer Judy Hoffs ....Holly Robinson
Officer Doug Penhall
......................................Peter DeLuise
Officer Harry Truman
......................................Ioki Dustin Nguyen
Officer Charlie Dunnigan
......................................Barney Martin
Tyrell 'Waxer' Thompson
......................................Reginald T
                        Dorsey
Cappie ....Charles Payne
Kenny Weckerley .....Brandon
                        Douglas
Noreen ....Margaret
                        Langrick
Mrs Futterman ....Karen Austin
Mike Summers ....David Brener
Breeze ....Blu Mankuma
Bartender ....Richard
                        Sargent
Trig.........................Ken Douglas
Jackson ....Bernie Coulson
Mr Ritz ....Doug Tuck
With Claude Earl Jones,
Sheryl Anderson, Scott Kraft,
Niles Brewster, Noelle Harling
Regular series cast members:
Steven Williams (Seasons 1 - 5),
Sal Jenco (Seasons 1-4)
Gina Nemo (Season 2)
Yvette Nipar (Season 3)
Richard Grieco (Seasons 3-4)
Michael Bendetti, Michael DeLuise,
David Barry Grey, Alexandra Powers
(Season 5)

SELECTED CREDITS
Director: Kim Manners
Producer: Steve Beers
Created by: Patrick Hasburgh
Stephen J Cannell
Screenplay: Patrick Hasburgh
Associate Producers: Joan Carson,
James S Geritlian
Music: Peter Bernstein
Title Theme: Liam Sternberg
Sung by: Holly Robinson
Cinematography: Jose Luis
Mignone
Art Director: Michael Nemirsky
Editors: James S Geritlian, Michael
Robison
Sound Mixer: Frank Griffiths
Production Manager: Mary Eilts
Makeup: Pearl Louie
Hair Stylist: Janet Sala
Costumes: Glenne Campbell
Special Effects: Michael Clifford
Stunts: Gary Combs
Executive Producer: Patrick
Hasburgh
**FOX TELEVISION 50 MINUTES
(SERIES RUNNING TIME)**

1989

Cry-Baby
CAST
Wade 'Cry-Baby' Walker
......................................Johnny Depp
Allison Vernon-Williams
......................................Amy Locane
Ramona Rickettes....Susan Tyrrell
Mrs Vernon-Williams
......................................Polly Bergen
Uncle Belvedere Rickettes
......................................Iggy Pop
Pepper Walker ....Ricki Lake
Wanda Woodward......Traci Lords
Hatchet-Face aka
Mona Malrovawski
......................................Kim McGuire
Milton Hackett ....Darren E
                        Burrows
Baldwin ....Stephen Mailer
Lenora ....Kim Webb
Toe-Joe Jackson.......Alan J Wendl
Hatchet's Father .....Troy Donahue
Hatchet's Mother .....Mink Stole
Milton's Father ....Joe
                        Dallesandro
Milton's Mother.......Joey
                        Heatherton
Wanda's Father ....David Nelson
Wanda's Mother.......Patricia Hearst
Hateful Guard ....Willem Dafoe
Snare-Drum.............Jonathan
                        Benya
Susie Q....................Jessica Raskin
Dupree ....Robert Tyree
Dupree's Girlfriend ..Angie Levroney
Whiffles ....Drew Ebersole,
                        Kenny Curtis,
                        Scott Neilson
Judge ....Robert Walsh
Inga ....Jenni Blong
Conks ....Craig Wallace,
                        Phillip
                        Broussard,
                        Reggie Davis,
                        Nick Fleming,
                        Robbie Jones
Mrs Tadlock.............Vivienne Shub
Angelic Boyfriend ....Robert
                        Marbury
Strip Pokers.............Skip Spencer
......................................Holter Graham
Night Court Parent ..Susan Lowe
Snake-Eyes Hood ......Dan Griffiths
Convicts..................Kirk McEwen,
                        Eric Lucas,
                        Frank
                        Maldonado,
                        Patrick
                        Mitchell
Picnic Mother ....Mary Vivian
                        Pearce
Mean Guard.............Steve Aronson
Pepper's Baby ....Kelly Goldberg
Mean Policeman ......Brad Baker
Dancers ....Patrick Egan,
                        Elizabeth Gue
Square ....Cindy Geppi
Baltimore Reporter ..Michael
                        Stanton
                        Kennedy
Corrections Officer
......................................Peter Koper

Howling Square-Boy Stephen William Moore
Obnoxious Photograper ....Joey Perillo
Goody Two-Shoes ......Carmen Renee Reynolds
2nd Reporter ....Gary Wheeler

SELECTED CREDITS
Director: John Waters
Producer: Rachel Talalay
Screenplay: John Waters
Associate Producer: Pat Moran
Music: Patrick Williams
Cinematography: David Insley
Production Designer:Vincent Peranio
Art Director: Dolores Deluxe
Editor: Janice Hampton
Sound Recordists: Richard Angelella, Dwayne Dell
Production Manager: Karen Koch
1st Assistant Director: Mary Ellen Woods
Makeup:Van Smith
Hair Stylist: Denise Cellucci
Costumes:Van Smith
Special Effects: Steve Kirshoff
Stunts: Jery Hewitt
Executive Producers: Jim Abrahams, Brian Grazer
UNIVERSAL 85 MINUTES

1990

Edward Scissorhands
CAST
Edward Scissorhands Johnny Depp
Kim Boggs ....Winona Ryder
Peg Boggs ....Dianne Wiest
Jim............................Anthony Michael Hall
Joyce Monroe.........Kathy Baker
Kevin Boggs ....Robert Oliveri
Helen ....Conchata Ferrell
Marge.......................Caroline Aaron
Officer Allen.............Dick Anthony Williams
Esmeralda ....O-Lan Jones
The Inventor ....Vincent Price
Bill Boggs ....Alan Arkin
Tinka ....Susan J Blommaert
Cissy ....Linda Perri
Talk Show Host ....John Davidson
George Monroe.........Biff Yeager
Suzanne...................Marti Greenberg
Max ....Bryan Larkin
Denny......................John McMahon
TV Newswoman ....Victoria Price
Retired Man.............Stuart Lancaster
Granddaughter ....Gina Gallagher
Psychologist.............Aaron Lustig
Loan Officer ....Alan Fudge
Dishwasher Man ......Steven Brill
Editor......................Peter Palmer
Reporters.................Marc Macaulay, Carmen J Alexander, Brett Rice
Beefy Man ....Andrew B Clark

Pink Girl...................Kelli Crofton
Older Woman/TV ......Linda Jean Hess
Young Woman/TV ......Rosalyn Thomson
Red-Haired Woman/TV ....Lee Ralls
Teenage Girl/TV ....Eileen Meurer
Rich Widow/TV..........Bea Albano
Blonde/TV.................Donna Pieroni
Policemen..................Ken DeVaul, Michael Gaughan
Teenage Girl ....Tricia Lloyd
Other Teen ....Kathy Dombo
Police Sergeant ....Rex Fox
Max's Mother ....Sherry Ferguson
Little Girl on Bike ....Tabetha Thomas
Girl in Diner..............L A Rothman
Neighbourhood Extras:
Tammy Boalo, Jackie Carson, Carol Crumrine, Suzanne Chrosniak/Ellen Dennis, Kathy Fleming, Jalaine Gallion, Miriam Goodspeed, Dianne L Green, Mary Jane Heath, Carol D Klasek, Laura Nader, Doyle Anderson, Harvey Bellman, Michael Brown, Gary Clark, Roland Douville, Russell E Green, Cecil Hawkins, Jack W Kapfhamer, Bill Klein, Phil Olson, Joe Sheldon, James Spicer, Nick Carter

SELECTED CREDITS
Director:Tim Burton
Producer:Tim Burton, Denise Di Novi
Original Story:Tim Burton, Caroline Thompson
Screenplay: Caroline Thompson
Associate Producer: Caroline Thompson
Music: Danny Elfman
Cinematography: Stefan Czapsky
Production Designer: Bo Welch
Art Director:Tom Duffield
Editors: Colleen Halsey, Richard Halsey
Sound Recordists: Kathy McCart, Gary Ritchie
Sound Mixer: Petur Hliddal
Production Manager: Bill P Scott
1st Assistant Director: Jerry Fleck
Makeup: Selena Miller, Matthew W Mungle, Rick Stratton, Brad Wilder
Special Makeup Effects: Stan Winston
Hair Stylists: Irene Aparicio, Rick Provenzano, Liz Spang, Lynda Kyle Walker
Costumes: Colleen Atwood
Special Effects: Michael Arbogast, James Reedy, Gary Schaedler, Brian Wood, David Wood
Stunt Coordinator: Glenn R Wilder
Executive Producer: Richard Hashimoto
20TH CENTURY FOX 105 MINUTES

1991

Freddy's Dead: The Final Nightmare
CAST
Freddy Krueger ....Robert Englund
Dr Maggie Burroughs, Katherine Krueger....Lisa Zane
John Doe ....Shon Greenblatt
Tracy ....Lezlie Deane
Carlos......................Ricky Dean Logan
Spencer ....Breckin Meyer
Doc ....Yaphet Kotto
Childless Woman ......Roseanne
Childless Man ....Tom Arnold
Orphanage Woman ..Elinor Donahue
Teen on TV ....Johnny Depp
Little Maggie ....Cassandra Rachel Frel
Kelly ....David Dunard
Mrs Burroughs ....Marilyn Rockafellow
Woman in Plane.......Virginia Peters
Stewardess ....Stella Hall
Carlos' Mother.........Angelina Estrada
Tracy's Father ....Peter Spellos
Teen Freddy ....Tobe Sexton
Spencer's Father .....Michael McRab
Springwood Teacher Matthew Faison
Officers ....Vic Watterson Carlease Burke
Cop in Shelter ....Warren Barrington
Security Guard ....Mel Scott-Thomas
Angry Boy ....Jonathan Mazer
Loretta Krueger........Lyndsey Fields
Soul From Freddy's Chest ....Linnea Quigley
Young Freddy...............Chason Schirmer
Ticket Seller.............L E Moko
Freddy's Father ....Alice Cooper

SELECTED CREDITS
Director: Rachel Talalay
Producers: Robert Shaye, Aron Warner
Original Story: Rachel Talalay, Wes Craven
Screenplay: Michael De Luca, Aron Warner
Associate Producer: Michael N Knue
Music: Brian May
Cinematography: Declan Quinn
Production Designer: C J Strawn
Editor: Janice Hampton
Sound Mixer: James Thornton
Assistant Director: James Cohen
Special Effects Makeup: Rodd Matsui
Stunt Coordinator: Dan Bradley
Executive Producer: Michael De Luca
NEW LINE 96 MINUTES

1992

Arizona Dream
(The Arrowtooth Waltz)
CAST

Axel Blackmar ....Johnny Depp
Leo Sweetie ....Jerry Lewis
Elaine Stalker ....Faye Dunaway
Grace Stalker............Lili Taylor
Paul Leger ....Vincent Gallo
Millie ....Paulina
Porizkova
Paul ....Michael J
Pollard
Blanche ....Candyce Mason
Angie ....Alexia Rane
Betty ....Polly Noonan
Carla ....Ann Schulman
MC, Announcer ....Patricia
O'Grady
Lawyer.....................James R
Wilson
Man with Door.........Eric
Polczwartek
Mechanical Doll ....Kim Keo
Boatman ....James P
Marshall
Eskimo Man..............Vincent
Tocktuo
Mariachi Band Members:
Santos Romero, David Rodriquez,
Juan Urrea, José Luis Ávila,
Sergio Hlarmendaris, Frank Turley,
Manuel Rodríguez, Cayetano Acosta,
Manuel Ruiz, Narcisco Domínguez,
Benjamin S Gonzales,
Serafino Flores, Miguel Moreno,
Raphael Salcido, Chanaia Rodriguez
The Priest ....Jackson
Douglas
Lindy ....Tricia Leigh
Fisher
The Doctor ....Michael S John
Man at the Phone ....Sal Jenco
Man in the Bar ....Emir Kusturica

SELECTED CREDITS
Director: Emir Kusturica
Producers: Yves Marmion,
Claudie Ossard
Co-Producer: Richard Brick
Screenplay: David Atkins,
Emir Kusturica
Music: Goran Bregovic
Cinematography: Vilko Filac
Production Designer: Miljen
Kreka Kljakovic
Art Director: Jan Pascale
Editor: Andrija Zafranovic
Sound Mixer: Jim Stuebe
Production Manager: Jay Sedrish
1st Assistant Director: Sergio
Mimica-Gezzan
Makeup: Karoly Balazs, Patty York
Hair Stylist: Deborah Ann Piper
Costumes: Jill M Ohanneson
Special Effects Coordinator:
Ken Estes
Stunts: Ron Petruccione
Executive Producer: Paul
R Gurian
WARNER BROS 142 MINUTES

Benny & Joon
CAST

Sam ....Johnny Depp
Juniper 'Joon' Pearl..Mary Stuart
Masterson
Benny Pearl ....Aidan Quinn
Ruthie ....Julianne Moore
Eric ....Oliver Platt
Dr Garvey ....C C H Pounder
Thomas ....Dan Hedaya
Mike ....Joe Grifasi
Randy Burch ....William H
Macy
Claudia.....................Liane
Alexandra
Curtis
Mrs Smail ....Eileen Ryan
UPS Man ....Don Hamilton
Waldo ....Waldo Larson
Orderlies ....Irvin Johnson,
Shane Nilsson
Nurse, Emma Sherman Memorial
Hospital ....Leslie Laursen
Video Customer ....Faye Killebrew
Video Clerk at American Classic
Video Store...............Ramsin
Amirkhas
Female Customer ....Lynette Walden
Young Joon...............Amy Alizabeth
Sanford
Young Benny ....Brian Keevy
Policeman ....John Grant
Phillips
Local ....Tony Lincoln
Patrons ....Dan Kamin,
Noon Orsatti

SELECTED CREDITS
Director: Jeremiah Chechik
Producers: Susan Arnold,
Donna Roth
Original Story: Barry Berman,
Leslie McNeil
Screenplay: Barry Berman
Associate Producer: Leslie McNeil
Music: Rachel Portman
Cinematography: John
Schwartzman
Production Designer: Neil Spisak
Art Director: Pat Tagliaferro
Editor: Carol Littleton
Sound Recordist: Scott Austin
Sound Mixer: James Thornton
Production Manager: Bill Badalato
1st Assistant Director: K C
Colwell
Makeup: Patty York
Hair Stylist: Frida Aradottir
Costumes: Aggie Guerard Rodgers
Special Effects: J D Streett IV,
Stunt Coordinator: Noon Orsatti,
Executive Producer: Bill Badalato
M-G-M, UA 98 MINUTES

1993

What's Eating Gilbert Grape
CAST

Gilbert Grape ....Johnny Depp
Arnie Grape ....Leonardo
DiCaprio
Becky ....Juliette Lewis
Betty Carver ....Mary
Steenburgen

Bonnie Grape ....Darlene Cates
Amy Grape................Laura
Harrington
Ellen Grape ....Mary Kate
Schellhardt
Ken Carver ....Kevin Tighe
Tucker Van Dyke ....John C Reilly
Bobby McBurney ......Crispin Glover
Becky's Grandma ....Penelope
Branning
Mr Lamson ....Tim Green
Mrs Lamson ....Susan
Loughran
Minister...................Robert B
Hedges
Todd Carver ....Mark Jordan
Doug Carver.............Cameron Finley
Sheriff Jerry Farrel..Brady Coleman
Deputy ....Tim Simek
Boys ....Nicholas
Stojanovich,
Daniel
Gullahorn
Waitress...................Libby Villari
Police Secretary........Kay Bower
Burger Barn Manager
................................Joe Stevens
FoodLand Bakery Worker
................................Mona Lee Fultz
Dave........................George Haynes
Burger Barn Employee
................................Brent Bratton
With Kirk Hunter

SELECTED CREDITS
Director: Lasse Hallström
Producers: David Matalon, Bertil
Ohlsson, Meir Teper
Screenplay: Peter Hedges
From the novel *What's Eating
Gilbert Grape?* by Peter Hedges
Music: Björn Isfält, Alan Parker,
Joseph S DeBeasi
Cinematography: Sven Nykvist
Production Designer: Bernt Capra
Art Director: John Myhre
Editor: Andrew Mondshein
Sound Mixer: David Brownlow
Production Manager: Richard
J Gelfand
1st Assistant Director: David
B Householter
Makeup: Patty York
Hair Stylist: Deborah Ann Piper
Costumes: Reneé Ehrlich Kalfus
Special Effects Coordinator:
Howard Jensen
Stunt Coordinator: Rusty
McClennon
Executive Producers: Alan C
Blomquist, Lasse Hallström
PARAMOUNT 118 MINUTES

Ed Wood
CAST

Edward D Wood Jr....Johnny Depp
Bela Lugosi...............Martin Landau
Dolores Fuller ....Sarah Jessica
Parker
Kathy O'Hara............Patricia Arquette
Criswell ....Jeffrey Jones
Reverend Lemon ......G D Spradlin
Orson Welles ....Vincent
D'Onofrio

397

John 'Bunny' Breckinridge
..................................Bill Murray
Georgie Weiss ....Mike Starr
Paul Marco................Max Casella
Conrad Brooks ....Brent Hinkley
Vampira ....Lisa Marie
Tor Johnson..............George 'The
Animal' Steele
Loretta King ....Juliet Landau
Ed Reynolds..............Clive
Rosengren
Cameraman Bill ......Norman Alden
Makeup Man Harry...Leonard Termo
Dr Tom Mason ....Ned Bellamy
Soundman ....Danny Dayton
Camera Assistant ....John Ross
Tony McCoy ....Bill Cusack
Teenage Kid ....Aaron Nelms
Rude Boss ....Biff Yeager
Security Guard ....Joseph R
Gannascoli
Old Crusty Man ....Carmen Filpi
Secretaries...............Lisa Malkiewicz,
Melora Walters
Bartender ....Conrad Brooks
Salesman ....Don Amendolia
Tough Boy ....Tommy Bertelsen
Stage Guard.............Reid
Cruickshanks
Mr Feldman ....Stanley
DeSantis
Executives ....Lionel Decker,
Edmund L Shaff
Ring Announcer........Gene Le Bell
Wrestling Opponent ..Jesse
Hernandez
TV Show Host ....Bobby Slayton
TV Host's Assistant Gretchen
Becker
Conservative Man .....John Rice
Conservative Wife ....Catherine
Butterfield
Backer's Wife...........Mary Portser
Hick Backer ....King Cotton
Southern Backer ......Don Hood
Doorman ....Frank Echols
Valet.........................thew Barry
Waiter ....Ralph Monaco
Busboy ....Anthony
Russell
Stage Manager ....Tommy Bush
Potential Backer ......Gregory
Walcott
Another Backer ....Charles C
Stevenson Jr
Old Man McCoy ....Rance Howard
Professor Strowski ..Vasek Simek
Vampira's Assistant Alan Martin
Vampira's Girlfriend Salwa Ali
Vampira's Friend......Rodney Kizziah
Indian Musician ......Korla Pandit
Greta Johnson ....Hannah
Eckstein
Karl Johnson ....Luc De Schepper
TV Horror Show Director
..................................Vinny Argiro
Nurse ....Patti Tippo
Doctor ....Ray Baker
Rental House Manager
..................................Louis Lombardi
Theatre Manager.....James Reid
Boyce
Angry Kid.................Ben Ryan
Ganger

Frantic Usher ....Ryan Holihan
High School Punk ....Marc Revivo
Tourist ....Charlie
Holliday
Photographers.........Adam Drescher
Ric Mancini
Pilot, Strapping Young Man
..................................Daniel Riordan
Hammy Alien............Mickey Cottrell
Organist...................Christopher
George
Simpson
Choir Members:
Robert Binford, Herbert Boche,
Linda Rae Brienza, Marlene Cook,
Sylvia Coussa, Audrey Cuyler,
Joseph Golightly, Carrie Starner
Hummel, Ramona Kemp-Blair,
Carolyn Kessinger, Nancy Longyear,
Matthew Nelson, Robert Nuffer,
William Michael Short, Susan Eileen
Simpson, George F Sterne, Charles
Alan Stephenson, Cheri A Williams,
Cynthia Ann Wilson
Wrestling Referee ....Bill Anderson
Editor on Studio Lot Patrick
Cranshaw
Orson Welles ....Vincent
D'Onofrio
(Maurice LaMarche: voice)
Car Vandal...............Rayder Woods
With ....Paul Marco

SELECTED CREDITS
Director: Tim Burton
Producers: Tim Burton, Denise
Di Novi
Co-Producer: Michael Flynn
Screenplay: Scott Alexander,
Larry Karaszewski
From the book *Nightmare of Ecstasy*
by Rudolph Grey
Music: Howard Shore, Jay
Livingston
Cinematography: Stefan Czapsky
Production Designer: Tom
Duffield
Art Director: Okowita
Editor: Chris Lebenzon
Sound: Edward Tise
Sound Recordist: Dave Luke
Production Manager: Michael
Polaire
1st Assistant Director: Mike
Topoozian
Makeup: Carrie Angland, Ve Neill
Hair Stylist: Yolanda Toussieng
Costumes: Colleen Atwood
Special Effects Coordinator:
Howard Jensen
Stunt Coordinator: John Branagan
Executive Producer: Michael
Lehmann
TOUCHSTONE 127 MINUTES

1994

Don Juan DeMarco
CAST
Dr Jack Mickler........Marlon Brando
Don Juan ....Johnny Depp
Marilyn Mickler........Faye Dunaway
Doña Ana ....Géraldine
Pailhas

Dr Paul Showalter ....Bob Dishy
Doña Inez.................Rachel Ticotin
Doña Julia ....Talisa Soto
Woman in Restaurant
..................................Marita Geraghty
Detective Sy Tobias ..Richard C
Sarafian
Grandmother DeMarco
..................................Tresa Hughes
Dr Bill Dunsmore.....Stephen Singer
Don Antonio.............Franc Luz
Don Alfonzo ....Carmen
Argenziano
Sultana Gulbeyaz ....Jo Champa
Nurse Alvira ....Esther Scott
Nurse Gloria ....Nada
Despotovich
Judge Ryland...........Gilbert Lewis
Rocco Compton ....'Tiny' Lister Jr
Baba, the Eunuch ....Tom
Mardirosian
Woman's Date ....Al Corley
Nicholas ....Nick LaTour
Sultan ....Bill Capizzi
Doña Querida............Patricia
Mauceri
Delivery Man ....Cliff Weissman
Young Don Juan.......Michael Malota
Flower Girl...............Renee
Sicignano
Waiter ....Trevor Long
Auctioneer ....Sanjay
Night Duty Nurse ....Diane Lee
Nurses ....Joni Kramer,
Shirlee Reed
Doctor ....Ken Gutstein
Social Worker...........Adriana
Jardini
Priest ....Robert Polance
Rodriguez
Nuns ....Roberta Danza,
Bridget Mariano,
Christine Wolfe
Bandleader...............José
Hernández
Singer......................Selena Pérez
Mariachi Band:
Rosendo Casillas, Esperanza
Donlucas, Filiberto Ramírez,
Santiago García, Ernesto V Molina,
Fernando C Moreno
Harem Girl...............Sara Newman

SELECTED CREDITS
Director: Jeremy Leven
Producers: Francis Ford Coppola,
Fred Fuchs, Patrick Palmer
Screenplay: Jeremy Leven
Based on characters created by
Lord Byron
Music: Michael Kamen, Robert
John Lange
Cinematography: Ralf Bode
Production Designer: Sharon
Seymour
Art Director: Jeff Knipp
Editor: Tony Gibbs
Sound Mixer: Richard Lightstone
Production Manager: Patrick
Palmer
1st Assistant Directors: Jerry L
Ballew, Eric Jewett
Makeup: Ron Berkeley
Hair Stylist: Lucia Mace
Costumes: Kirsten Everberg

Special Effects: James Fredburg
Stunt Coordinator: Victor Paul
Executive Producers: Michael De Luca, Ruth Vitale
NEW LINE 97 MINUTES

Dead Man
CAST
William 'Bill' Blake ..Johnny Depp
Nobody ....Gary Farmer
Cole Wilson...............Lance Henriksen
Conway Twill ....Michael Wincott
Thel Russell ....Mili Avital
Salvatore 'Sally' Jenko
.................................Iggy Pop
Train Fireman ....Crispin Glover
Johnny 'The Kid' Pickett
.................................Eugene Byrd
Nobody's girlfriend ..Michelle Thrush
Marvin.....................Jimmie Ray Weeks
Lee ....Mark Bringelson
Charles Ludlow 'Charlie' Dickinson
.................................Gabriel Byrne
John Scholfield ....John Hurt
Trading Post missionary
.................................Alfred Molina
John Dickinson ....Robert Mitchum
Man with Gun in Alley
.................................Gibby Haines
Man at End of Street
.................................George Duckworth
Man with Wrench ....Richard Boes
Mr Olafsen ....John North
Drunk......................Peter Schrum
Young Nobodies ....Thomas Bettles, Daniel Chas Stacy
Big George Drakoulious
.................................Billy Bob Thornton
Benmont Tench ....Jared Harris
Old man with 'wanted' posters
.................................Mike Dawson
Men at trading post John Pattison, Todd Pfeiffer
Makah villagers.......Leonard Bowechop, Cecil Cheeka, Michael McCarty
Bartenders...............Steve Buscemi, Mickey McGee
SELECTED CREDITS
Director: Jim Jarmusch
Producer: Demetra J MacBride
Co-Producer: Karen Koch
Screenplay: Jim Jarmusch
Music: Neil Young,
Cinematography: Robby Müller
Production Designer: Robert Ziembicki
Art Director: Ted Berner
Editor: Jay Rabinowitz
Sound Recordists: Coll Anderson, Stacey Tanner
Sound Mixer: Drew Kunin
Production Manager: Beth DePatie
1st Assistant Director: Todd

Pfeiffer
Makeup: Neal Martz
Special Effects: Makeup: Tom Irvin
Hair Stylist: Scott W Farley
Costumes: Marit Allen
Special Effects: Lou Carlucci
Stunt Coordinator: Al Jones
MIRAMAX 121 MINUTES

1995

Nick of Time
CAST
Gene Watson ....Johnny Depp
Lynn Watson ....Courtney Chase
Huey........................Charles S Dutton
Mr Smith ....Christopher Walken
Ms Jones ....Roma Maffia
Gov Eleanor Grant....Marsha Mason
Brendan Grant ....Peter Strauss
Krista Brooks ....Gloria Reuben
Officer Trust ....Bill Smitrovich
Mystery Man............G D Spradlin
Gustino ....Yul Vazquez
Irene........................Edith Díaz
Hector ....Armando Ortega
Mixologist ....C J Bau
Beverage Server ......Cynthena Sanders
Transport Reception Manager
.................................Dana Mackey
Comestible Server ....Christopher Jacobs
Sanitation Engineer Charles Carroll
Franco ....Miguel Nájera
Chief Aide.................Jerry Tondo
Weapons Security .....Lance Hunter Voorhees
Security Associate....John Azevedo Jr
Personal Security ....Lance August
JBN Reporter...........Peter Mackenzie
JBN Videographer ....Rick Zieff
Asian Man ....Michael Chong
Asian Woman............Cynthia Noritake
Physically Attractive Woman
.................................Holly Kuespert
Centerpiece Poacher Pamela Dunlap
Rally Orienter ....Jan Speck
Personal Waste Facility User
.................................Tom Lawrence
Illegal Security Access Carrier
.................................Robert Buckingham
Hackney Transportist
.................................J Clark Johnson
French Man ....Antonio Sandoval
French Woman.........Isabel García Lorca
Young Hispanic Girl..Nicole Mancera
Young Hispanic Girl's Mother
.................................Yolanda Gonzáles
Mrs Wentzel.............Antonette Saftler
Union Station Security

.................................Teddy Beeler
Verbally Abusive Spouse
.................................Alison Stuart
With ....Tom Bradley
SELECTED CREDITS
Director: John Badham
Producer: John Badham
Screenplay: Patrick Sheane Duncan, Ebbe Roe Smith
Associate Producer: Cammie Crier
Music: Arthur B Rubinstein
Cinematography: Roy H Wagner
Production Designer: Philip Harrison
Art Director: Eric Orbom
Editors: Frank Morriss, Kevin Stitt
Sound Mixer: Willie Burton
Production Manager: Richard H Prince
1st Assistant Director: John Hockridge
Makeup: John M Elliott Jr
Hair Stylists: Janice Alexander, Hazel Catmull, Dale Miller
Costumes: Mary E Vogt
Special Effects: Jeff Jarvis
Stunt Coordinator: Shane Dixon
Executive Producer: D J Caruso
PARAMOUNT 90 MINUTES

Cannes Man
CAST
Sy Lerner ....Seymour Cassel
Frank 'Rhino' Rhinoslavsky
.................................Francesco Quinn
Rebecca Lerner ....Rebecca Broussard
Kitty Monaco ....Ann Cusack
French Actor ....Marc Duret
Producer ....Robert Evans
Tawny ....Therese Kablan
Troma Chief.............Lloyd Kaufman
Investor ....May Hall Ross
Exasperated Director
.................................Jim Sheridan
Frenchman ....François Petit
American ....Robert Hockley
Agent on Phone ....Luana Anders
Minister ....Jack Ong
Studio Exec ....Lawrence Kasanoff
Duquesne Cameron ..Duncan Clark
Producer ....Gary W Goldstein
Betting Producer ......Jim Stark
Director ....Randal Kleiser
Hollywood Reporter ..Alex Ben Block
Screenwriter ....Nat Bernstein
Screenwriter ....Michael Katlin
Ronnie Mills.............Veronica Heif
Leslie ....Leslie Carleton
Kari ....Kari G Peyton
Michele....................Michele Sublette
Ehu ....Ehu Ursulu
Richard Hedd...........Cameron Dye
Actor & Guy on Phone
.................................Tim Ryan
Attorney ....Nancy Rainford
'Chain of Title' Producer
.................................Johan Schotte

Norwegien Distributor Ed Harridsteff
French Distributor ..Jean Paul
    Jacobi
Pakistani Distributor
  ....Sam Anwar
Mourner....................Lori M Cincotta
Director ....Richard
    Martini
With Jim Sheridan, Johnny Depp,
Treat Williams, Lara Flynn Boyle,
James Brolin, Nino Cerruti, Benicio
Del Toro, Dennis Hopper, Julian
Lennon, John Malkovich, Kevin
Pollak, Frank Whaley, Bryan Singer,
Peter Gallagher, Harvey Weinstein
Cameos ....Jim Jarmusch,
Jon Cryer, Chris Penn, Charley
Boorman, Menahem Golan
SELECTED CREDITS
Director: Richard Martini
Producers: Tom Coleman, Holly
MacConkey, Johan Schotte
Screenplay: Deric Haddad, Richard
Martini, Irwin Rappaport, Susan
Shapiro
Music: Richard Martini
Cinematography: Denise Brassard,
Dean Lent
Editor: Richard Currie
Sound Mixer: Jon Ailetcher
Makeup: Lori Matyska
Executive Producer: Jon Turtle
ROCKET 88 MINUTES

1996

Donnie Brasco
CAST
Benjamin 'Lefty Two Guns' Ruggerio
  ....Al Pacino
FBI Special Agent Joseph D Pistone,
Donnie Brasco ....Johnny Depp
Dominick 'Sonny Black' Napolitano
  ....Michael
    Madsen
Nicky Santora ....Bruno Kirby
Paulie ....James Russo
Maggie Pistone ....Anne Heche
Tim Curley ....Zeljko Ivanek
Dean Blandford ....Gerry Becker
Alphonse 'Sonny Red'Indelicato
  ....Robert Miano
Bruno 'Whack-Whack' Indelicato
  ....Brian
    Tarantina
Richie Gazzo ....Rocco Sisto
Dr Berger ....Zach Grenier
Sheriff ....Walt
    MacPherson
Annette ....Ronnie Farer
Strip Club Owner.......Terry Serpico
Sonny's Girlfriend ....Gretchen Mol
Philly Lucky.............Tony Lip
Big Trin ....George Angelica
Santo Trafficante ....Val Avery
Jilly ....Madison
    Arnold
Daughters ....Delanie
    Fitzpatrick,
    Katie Sagona,
    Sara Gold
Tommy Ruggerio .....Larry Romano
FBI Technicians ....Tim Blake
    Nelson,

    Paul Giamatti
FBI Agent ....James Michael
    McCauley
US Attorney ....Jim Bulleit
Hollman ....Andrew Parks
Japanese Maitre D'
  ....Keenan
    Shimizu
Trafficante's Men ....
Rocco Musacchia, Joe Francis
Mare Chiaro Bartender
  ....Sal Jenco
Communion Party Man
  ....Billy Capucilli
Communion Party Woman
  ....Laura Cahill
Mob Girlfriends ....Doreen Murphy,
    Elle Alexander,
    Denise Faye,
    Elaine del Valle
FBI Directors ....John Horton,
    Dan Brennan
Singers.....................LaJuan Carter,
    Sandy Barber,
    Joyce Stovall
Wiseguys ....Frank Pesce,
Randy Jurgensen, John Di
Benedetto, Richard Zavaglia,
Tony Ray Rossi, Edward Black,
Gaetano LoGiudice, Carmelo
Musacchia, Pat Vecchio
Carmine Galante's Bodyguard
  ....Garry Pastore

SELECTED CREDITS
Director: Mike Newell
Producers: Louis DiGiaimo, Mark
Johnson, Barry Levinson, Gail
Mutrux
Screenplay: Paul Attanasio
From the book *Donnie Brasco: My
Undercover Life in the Mafia* by
Joseph D Pistone, Richard Woodley
Music: Patrick Doyle, Jay Livingston
Cinematography: Peter Sova,
Production Designer: Donald
Graham Burt
Art Director: Jefferson Sage
Editor: Jon Gregory
Sound Recordist: Joel Holland
Sound Mixer: Tod A Maitland
Production Manager: Richard
Baratta
1st Assistant Director: Joseph Reidy
Makeup: John Caglione Jr, Margot
Boccia
Hair Stylists: Milton Buras, Nathan
Busch II
Costumes: Aude Bronson-Howard,
David C Robinson
Special Effects: Ronald Ottesen Jr
Stunt Coordinator: G A Aguilar
Executive Producers: Alan
Greenspan, Patrick McCormick
SONY, TRISTAR 127 MINUTES

The Brave
CAST
Raphael ....Johnny Depp
McCarthy..................Marlon Brando
Larry ....Marshall Bell
Rita ....Elpidia Carrillo
Lou Sr ....Frederic
    Forrest

Father Stratton........Clarence
    Williams III
Lou Jr ....Max Perlich
Luis ....Luis Guzmán
Frankie ....Cody Lightning
Marta......................Nicole Mancera
Papa ....Floyd 'Red
    Crow'
    Westerman
Strange Man in Office
  ....Chuck E Weiss
Louis's Girl ....Elena St John
With Bruce Corkham, Gibby Haynes,
Iggy Pop, Tricia Vessey

SELECTED CREDITS
Director: Johnny Depp
Producers: Charles Evans Jr, Carroll
Kemp
Co-Producer: Diane Batson-Smith
Screenplay: Paul McCudden,
Johnny Depp, D P Depp
From the novel *The Brave* by
Gregory McDonald
Associate Producer: Buck Holland
Music: Mark Governor, J J Holiday,
Iggy Pop, Chuck E Weiss
Cinematography:Vilko Filac
Production Designer: Miljen
Kreka Kljakovic
Art Director: Branimir 'Bane'
Babic
Editor: Pasquale Buba
Sound: Paul Ledford
Production Manager: Dara
Weintraub
1st Assistant Director: Lisa
Campbell
Makeup: Judy Yonemoto
Costumes: Lindy Hemming
Executive Producer: Jeremy
Thomas
MAJESTIC 123 MINUTES

1997

Fear and Loathing in Las Vegas
CAST
Raoul Duke ....Johnny Depp
Dr Gonzo ....Benicio Del
    Toro
Hitchhiker ....Tobey Maguire
Waitress....................Ellen Barkin
Highway Patrolman Gary Busey
Lucy ....Christina Ricci
Magazine Reporter ..Mark Harmon
Blonde TV Reporter ..Cameron Diaz
Desk Clerk ....Katherine
    Helmond
L Ron Bumquist ......Michael Jeter
Carnie Talker...........Penn Jillette
Lacerda ....Craig Bierko
Road Person.............Lyle Lovett
Musician ....Flea
Frog-Eyed Woman ...Laraine
    Newman
Judge ....Harry Dean
    Stanton
Hoodlum ....Tim Thomerson
Uniformed Dwarf......Michael Lee
    Gogin
Car Rental Agent.....Larry Cedar
Parking Attendant....Brian Le Baron
Bell Boy ....Michael

Warwick
Reporter....................Tyde Kierney
Dune Buggy Driver
..................................Richard Riehle
Dune Buggy Passengers
..................................Ransom Gates,
Frank Romano
Desert Inn Doormen Gil Boccaccio,
Gary Bruno
Wine Colored Tuxedo Richard
Portnow
Goon ....Steve Schirripa
Wee Waiter ....Verne J Troya
The Black Guy ....Will Blount
Clown Barker............Ben Yeagar
Bazooka's Circus Waitress
..................................Christopher
Callen
TV Crew Man ....Ben Van Der
Veen
Stockbroker ....Alex Craig
Mann
Clerk at Mint Hotel ..Gregory Itzin
Police Chief ....Troy Evans
Police Chief's Wife ....Gale Baker
Sven, Clerk at Flamingo Hotel
..................................Christopher
Meloni
Executive Director ..Chris Hendrie
Cop in Back ....Larry
Brandenburg
Alice the Maid ....Jenette
Goldstein
Human Cannonball ..Stephen
Bridgewater
Shoppers ....Buck Holland,
Mary Gillis,
Jennifer Elise Cox
Car Rental Agent – Los Angeles
..................................Robert Allen
Man in Car ....David Brisbin
Newscasters ....James
O'Sullivan,
Milt Tarver
Lounge Lizards:
Kathryn Alexander, Mia Babalis,
Kristin Draudt, Kim Flowers,
Nan Friedman, Judith Lieff,
Tane McClure, Diana Mehoudar,
Geoffrey B Nimmer
Trapeze Artists:
Marlene Bologna, Chobi Gyorgy,
Karen E Castoldi, Lisa S Hoyle,
Joseph S Griffo
Hooker ....Kacee DeMasi
American Flag Girl ..Eva Ford
Lizard Performer......Trudi Forristal
Man With White Elephant
..................................Bryce Ingman
Medical Angel ....Brian D Kline
Mark Allen Race Official
..................................Walt G Ludwig
Other Duke in Matrix Flashback
..................................Hunter S
Thompson

SELECTED CREDITS
Director: Terry Gilliam
Producers: Patrick Cassavetti, Laila
Nabulsi, Stephen Nemeth
Co-Producer: Elliot Lewis
Rosenblatt
Screenplay: Terry Gilliam, Tony
Grisoni, Tod Davies, Alex Cox
From the novel *Fear and Loathing in*

Las Vegas by Hunter S Thompson,
Associate Producer: John Jergens
Music: Ray Cooper, Michael
Kamen
Cinematography: Nicola Pecorini
Production Designer: Alex
McDowell
Art Director: Chris Gorak
Editor: Lesley Walker
Sound Mixer: Jay Meagher
Production Managers: Mark Indig,
Elliot Lewis Rosenblatt, Lorie
Zerweck
1st Assistant Director: Philip
Patterson
Makeup: Cheryl Nick, Patty York
Special Effects Makeup: Matthew
Mungle, Mike Smithson
Hair Stylists: Bridget Cook, Lynn
Del Kail, Ellen Powell, Cindy Rose
Costumes: Julie Weiss
Special Effects: Ray Svedin, Steve
Galich
Stunt Coordinator: Noon Orsatti
Executive Producers: Harold
Bronson, Richard Foos
UNIVERSAL 118 MINUTES

1998

The Astronaut's Wife
CAST
Commander Spencer Armacost
..................................Johnny Depp
Jillian Armacost .....Charlize
Theron
Sherman Reese ....Joe Morton
Nan ....Clea DuVall
Natalie Streck ....Donna Murphy
Capt Alex Streck .....Nick
Cassavetes
Dr Patraba...............Samantha
Eggar
NASA Director ....Gary Grubbs
Shelly McLaren ....Blair Brown
Jackson McLaren ....Tom Noonan
Allen Dodge ....Tom O'Brien
Shelly Carter ....Lucy Lin
Pat Elliott ....Michael Crider
Calvin.......................Jacob Stein
Wide Eyed Kid ....Timothy Wicker
Paula ....Sarah Dampf
Spencer's Doctor .....Charles Lanyer
Doctor ....Carlos
Cervantes
Reporter...................Conrad
Bachmann
Dr Conlin ....Rondi Reed
Yuppie Shark ....Seth Barrish
Dried Up Socialite ....Ellen Lancaster
Waiter ....Julian Barnes
Women ....
Priscilla Shanks, Jennifer Burry,
Susan Cella, Linda Powell
Screaming Girl
.............Lyndsey Danielle Bonomolo
Security Guard ....Elston Ridgle
Maitre D' ....Robert Sella
Reporter...................Samantha
Carpel
Taxi Driver...............Lahai
Fahnbulleh
Doorman ....Stephen Berger
Waiter at Party ....Michael Luceri

Storage Facility Client
..................................Ben Van Bergen
Pilot ....Edward Kerr
Twins ....Cole Sprouse,
Dylan Sprouse
Excited Fourth Grader
..................................Brian Johnson
Nurse ....Dawn Landon

SELECTED CREDITS
Director: Rand Ravich
Producer: Andrew Lazar
Co-Producer: Diana Pokorny
Screenplay: Rand Ravich
Associate Producer: Jody Hedien
Music: George S Clinton
Cinematography: Allen Daviau
Production Designer: Jan Roelfs
Art Director: Sarah Knowles
Editors: Tim Alverson, Steve
Mirkovich
Sound Mixer: Paul Ledford
Production Manager: Mari-Jo
Winkler-Ioffreda
1st Assistant Director: K C
Colwell
Makeup: Deborah K Larsen
Hair Stylist: Candy L Walken
Costumes: Isis Mussenden
Special Effects: Thomas R
Homsher, Gregory C Tippie, Brian
Tipton
Stunt Coordinator: Tim A Davison
Executive Producers: Mark
Johnson, Donna Langley, Brian
Witten
NEW LINE 109 MINUTES

The Ninth Gate
CAST
Dean Corso................Johnny Depp
Boris Balkan ....Frank Langella
Liana Telfer ....Lena Olin
The Girl ....Emmanuelle
Seigner
Baroness Kessler ......Barbara
Jefford
Victor Fargas ....Jack Taylor
Pablo & Pedro Ceniza,
Workmen in shop......José López
Rodero
Liana's Bodyguard....Tony Amoni
Bernie ....James Russo
Andrew Telfer ....Willy Holt
Witkin ....Allen Garfield
Old Man ....Jacques
Dacqmine
Old Man's Son ....Joe Sheridan
Daughter-in-Law ......Rebecca Pauly
Concierge ....Catherine
Benguigui
Secretary ....Maria
Ducceschi
Gruber ....Jacques Collard
Desk Clerk ....Dominique
Pozzetto
Baker ....Emmanuel Booz
Hotel Porter ....Lino Ribeiro
de Sousa
Cabby ....Asil Raïs
Cafe Owners.............Bernard
Richier, Marinette Richier
Extra in Paris ....Pierre-Benoist
Varoclier

SELECTED CREDITS
Director: Roman Polanski
Producer: Roman Polanski
Co-Producers: Mark Allan,
Antonio Cardenal, Iñaki Núñez,
Alain Vannier
Screenplay: Roman Polanski, John
Brownjohn, Enrique Urbizu
From the novel *El club Dumas* by
Arturo Pérez-Reverte
Associate Producer: Adam
Kempton
Music: Wojciech Kilar
Cinematography: Darius Khondji
Production Designer: Dean
Tavoularis
Art Director: Gérard Viard
Editor: Hervé de Luze
Sound Mixer: Jean-Marie Blondel
1st Assistant Director: Michel
Cheyko
Makeup: Paul Le Marinel, Liliane
Rametta
Hair Stylist: Jean-Pierre Berroyer
Costumes: Anthony Powell
Special Effects: Gilbert Piéri
Stunt Coordinators: Dominique
Fouassier, Patrick Cauderlier
Executive Producers: Michel
Cheyko, Wolfgang Glattes
ARTISAN 133 MINUTES

Sleepy Hollow
CAST
Constable Ichabod Crane
...............................Johnny Depp
Katrina Van Tassel ..Christina Ricci
Lady Van Tassel, Western Woods
Crone ....Miranda
Richardson
Baltus Van Tassel ....Michael
Gambon
Brom Van Brunt ......Casper Van
Dien
Reverend Steenwyck Jeffrey Jones
Burgomaster ....Christopher
Lee
Magistrate Samuel Philipse
...............................Richard
Griffiths
Dr Thomas Lancaster
...............................Ian McDiarmid
Notary James Hardenbrook
...............................Michael Gough
Young Masbath ....Marc Pickering
Ichabod's Mother ....Lisa Marie
Mr Killian ....Steven
Waddington
Hessian Horseman ..Christopher
Walken
Midwife Elizabeth Killian
...............................Claire Skinner
High Constable ....Alun
Armstrong
Jonathan Masbath ..Mark Spalding
Sarah ....Jessica
Oyelowo
Van Ripper ....Tony Maudsley
Ichabod's Father ......Peter Guinness
Glenn ....Nicholas
Hewetson
Theodore ....Orlando Seale
Thomas Killian ....Sean Stephens
Dr Lancaster's Wife Gabrielle Lloyd

Dirk Van Garrett ......Robert Sella
Spotty Man ....Michael Feast
Thuggish Constable ..Jamie Foreman
Constable ....Philip Martin
Brown
Young Ichabod Crane
...............................Sam Fior
Young Lady Van Tassel
...............................Tessa Allen-Ridge
Young Crone.............Cassandra
Farndale
Girl ....Lily Phillips
Little Girl ....Bianca
Nicholas
Rifleman ....Paul Brightwell
Widow.......................Layla
Alexander
Peter Van Garrett ....Martin Landau
Widow Emily Winship
...............................Keeley O'Hara

SELECTED CREDITS
Director: Tim Burton
Producers: Scott Rudin
Adam Schroeder
Co-Producers: Kevin Yagher,
Andrew Kevin Walker
Screenplay: Andrew Kevin Walker,
Tom Stoppard
From the story *The Legend of Sleepy
Hollow* by Washington Irving
Associate Producer: Mark Roybal
Music: Danny Elfman
Cinematography: Emmanuel
Lubezki
Production Designer: Rick
Heinrichs
Art Directors: Ken Court, John
Dexter, Andrew Nicholson
Editors: Chris Lebenzon, Joel
Negron,
Sound Recordists: Harry Higgins,
Bob Olari
Sound Mixer: Tony Dawe
Production Manager: Dusty
Symonds
1st Assistant Director: Chris
Newman
Makeup: Elizabeth Tag
Hair Stylist: Paul Gooch
Costumes: Colleen Atwood
Special Effects: Carmila Gittens,
Joss Williams
Stunt Coordinator: Nick Gillard
Executive Producers: Francis Ford
Coppola, Larry Franco
PARAMOUNT 105 MINUTES

1999

The Source
CAST
Jack Kerouac ....Johnny Depp
William S Burroughs Dennis Hopper
Allen Ginsberg ....John Turturro

SELECTED CREDITS
Director: Chuck Workman
Producer: Chuck Workman
Screenplay: Chuck Workman
Associate Producer: Mark Apostolon
Music: David Amram, Philip Glass
Cinematography: Andrew
Dintenfass, Tom Hurwitz, Don

Lenzer, José Louis Mignone, Nancy
Schreiber
Production Designer: Marc
Greville-Masson
Editor: Chuck Workman
Executive Producer: Hiro Yamagata
WINSTAR 88 MINUTES

Before Night Falls
CAST
Reinaldo Arenas ......Javier Bardem
Lázaro Gómez Carriles
...............................Olivier Martinez
Pepe Malas...............Andrea Di
Stefano
Bon Bon, Lieutenant Victor
...............................Johnny Depp
Herberto Zorrilla Ochoa
...............................Michael Wincott
Reinaldo's Mother ....Olatz Lopez
Garmendia
Young Reinaldo ....Giovani Florido
Reinaldo's Grandmother
...............................Loló Navarro
Reinaldo's Father ....Sebastián Silva
Teacher ....Carmen Beato
Smallest School Children
...............................Cy Schnabel,
Olmo Schnabel
Teenage Reinaldo......Vito Maria
Schnabel
Reinaldo's Grandfather
...............................Pedro
Armendáriz Jr
Carlos.......................Diego Luna
Lolin ....Lia Chapman
Cuco Sánchez............Sean Penn
Professor ....Jerzy
Skolimowski
Translator ....Aquiles Benites
Pretty Blonde Student
...............................Eva Piaskowska
María Teresa Freye de Andrade
...............................Patricia Reyes
Spíndola
Virgilio Piñera ....Hector Babenco
Women in Car ....Marlene Díaz,
Olga Borayo
Tomás Diego..............Santiago Magill
Faustino....................Manolo García
Girl With Keys ....Lola Schnabel
Landlady ....Ofelia Medina
Woman (UNEAC) ......Lois Barragán
Nightclub Singer .....Eduardo
Antonio
Valeria ....Stella Schnabel
José Lezama Lima ....Manuel
González
Nicolás Abreu ....Maurice
Compte
María Luisa Lima ....Claudette
Maillé
Juan Abreu ....John Ortiz
José Abreu...............Vincent
Laresca
Recruit Driver..........Rene Rivera
Blonde on the Beach Chanel Puertas
Royal Gay.................Manolo Rivero
Pedro the Bus Driver Nemo
French Tourist..........Andrea Fassler
Santería Dancer ......Magda
Violent Soldier ....Julian Bucio
Prosecutor ....Jorge Zárate
Fina Zorrilla Ochoa ..Najwa Nimri

Jorge Camacho ....Francisco
Gattorno
Margarita Camacho Marisol Padilla
Sánchez
Kid with Kite ....Jorge Zamora
Policeman on Beach..Noel Medina
State Security on Beach
................................Jorge Zepeda
Teenagers.................Yulian Díaz,
Eduardo
Arroyuelo
Stranger in Lenin Park
................................Antonio Zavala
State Security in Lenin Park
................................Eloy Ganuza
Young Man with Bird Khotan
Antonio ....René Pereyra
Hungry Inmate ....Abel Woolrich
Gay Inmate ....Mario Oliver
Singing Prisoner ......Robertico
Valdez
Guard at El Morro....Claudio Osoria
Armando García ......Alfredo Villa
Blanca Romero ....Diahnne Déa
Dancer in the Convent
................................Caridad
Martinez
Zulema.....................Zulema Cruz
Blanca's Teenage Daughter
................................Annie Gil
Dwarf.......................Filiberto
Estrella
Immigration Officer Juan Cristóbal
Murillo
Man at Mariel harbourMelanio
................................Filiberto Hebra
Officer at Mariel harbour
................................Matthias
Ehrenberg
Mr Greenberg...........Jack Schnabel
Mrs Greenberg.........Esther Schnabel
Death ....Xavier Domingo
Orderly....................Eric Springer
Taxi Driver..............Jimmy Nugent

SELECTED CREDITS
Director: Julian Schnabel
Producer: Jon Kilik
Screenplay: Cunningham O'Keefe,
Lázaro Gómez Carriles, Julian
Schnabel
From the book *Before Night Falls* by
Reinaldo Arenas
Associate Producer: Matthias
Ehrenberg
Music: Carter Burwell
Cinematography: Xavier Pérez
Grobet, Guillermo Rosas
Production Designer: Salvador
Parra
Art Director: Antonio Muño-
Hierro
Editor: Michael Berenbaum
Sound: Christian Wangler
Production Manager: Pamela
Jaeckle
Assistant Director: Sebastián Silva
Makeup: Ana Lozano
Hair Stylist: Manolo García
Costumes: María Estela Fernández
Special Effects Coordinator:
Alejandro Vazquez Effeccine
Executive Producers: Olatz Lopez
Garmendia, Julian Schnabel
FINE LINE 133 MINUTES

The Man Who Cried
CAST
Suzie ....Christina Ricci
Lola ....Cate Blanchett
Dante Dominio.........John Turturro
Cesar ....Johnny Depp
Felix Perlman...........Harry Dean
Stanton
Father ....Oleg Yankovsky
Men in Village:
Thom Osborn, Frank Chersky, Daniel
Hart, Peter Majer
Grandmother............Hana Maria
Pravda
Children:
Ayala Meir, Abraham Hassan, Lloyd
Martin, Uri Meir, Sophie Richman,
Theo Wishart
Boys in Cart.............Michael Mount,
Harry Flinder
Man in Cart ....Danny
Richman
Man at Port ....Victor Sobchak
Red Cross Woman ....Sue Cleaver
English Port Official Clifford Barry
Second Official.........Paul Clayton
Foster Mother ....Diana Hoddinott
Foster Father...........Richard
Albrecht
Playground Bullys... Ornella Bryant,
Sam Friend, Isabella Melling
Welsh Teacher ....Alan David
Audition Mistress ....Imogen Claire
Man in Suit ....Danny
Scheinman
Madame Goldstein....Miriam Karlin
Mother of Man in Suit
................................Anna Tzelniker
Party Hostess ....Consuelo De
Haviland
Man in Village.........Barry Davis
Young Suzie ....Claudia
Lander-Duke
Pianists ....Katia Labeque,
Marielle Labeque
Reporter...................George
Yiasoumi
Dancing Romany .....Pablo Verón
Opera Chorus...........Odile Roire,
Brigitte Boucher, Norah Krief,
Hélène Hardouin
Romany Brothers ....Hugues
Dalmagro,
Cedric Gary
Romany Boy ....Saïfi Ghoul
German Officer ....Manfred
Andrae
German Officer Pianist
................................Richard Sammel
Father of Boy............Ahmet Ziyrek
Joe ....Don Fellows
Refugee Worker ....Joyce Springer
Older Man in Sweatshop
................................Cyril Shaps
Woman in Sweatshop
................................Anna Korwin
Men in Sweatshop... Mark Ivanir,
Alfred Hoffman, Bernard Spear
Studio Assistant .....David Puckler
Studio Lawyer ....David Baxt
Father's New Wife ...Katherine
Hogarth
Son ....Patrick Clarke
Daughter ....Bridget Clarke
Nurse ....Chris Gillespie

SELECTED CREDITS
Director: Sally Potter
Producer: Christopher Sheppard
Writer: Sally Potter
Music: Osvaldo Golijov
Cinematography: Sacha Vierny
Art Directors: Carlos Conti,
Laurent Ott, Ben Scott
Editor: Hervé Schneid
Production Managers: Michael
Manzi, Patrick Millet
Assistant Directors:
Chris Newman
Janet Nielsen
Makeup: Nathalie Tissier
Hair Stylist: Beya Gasmi
Costumes: Lindy Hemming
Special Effects Supervisor:
Dominic Tuohy
Stunt Coordinators: Joëlle Baland,
Andy Bradford, Pascal Madura
Executive Producers: Simona
Benzakein, Tim Bevan, Eric Fellner
UNIVERSAL 100 MINUTES

2000

Blow
CAST
George Jung ....Johnny Depp
Mirtha Jung ....Penélope Cruz
Barbara Buckley ......Franka Potente
Ermine Jung ....Rachel
Griffiths
Derek Foreal ....Paul Reubens
Diego Delgado...........Jordi Mollà
Pablo Escobar ....Cliff Curtis
Augusto Oliveras......Miguel
Sandoval
Tuna.......................Ethan Suplee
Fred Jung ....Ray Liotta
Leon Minghella ....Kevin Gage
Kevin Dulli ....Max Perlich
Young George ....Jesse James
Alessandro..............Miguel Pérez
Cesar Toban ....Dan Ferro
Sanchez ....Tony Amendola
Mr T ....Bobcat
Goldthwait
Dr Bay ....Michael Tucci
Maria ....Monet Mazur
Rada........................Lola Glaudini
Inez ....Jennifer
Gimenez
Young Kristina Jung Emma Roberts
Kristina Jung ....James King
Jack Stevens ....Charles Noland
Beach Women...........Pamela Abdy,
Tracy Falco, Genevieve Maylam,
Kathleen Mullan, Sophie Tsirnel
FBI Waiters ....John
Harrington Bland, Jimmy Burke,
Brantley Bush, Dale Snowberger,
Pamela Walker
DEA Eastham ....Kevin H
Chapman
Archie Zigmond ....Edward Demme
Emilio Ochoa ....Daniel Escobar
Guards ....Jean-Carlos
Felix, Ralph Kampshoff, Roberto
Lopez
Band Singer ....Lazaro
Galarraga
Guard Gus ....Brian Goodman

Stewardesses:
Vanessa Greyson, Elif Guertin, Faith Hoover, Meriah Nelson, Crystal Erickson, Leslie Schirrmacher
Detectives ....
Josh Herman, Richard LaGravenese
GG..............................Brad Hunt
Bank Manager ....Patrick Husted
James Trout ....Ajgie Kirkland
Customs Agent ....Skip O'Brien
Inmates ....
Lydell M Cheshier, Mike Ralph, Matthew Robinson
Judge ....Dorothy Lyman
Nurse ....Jodie Mann
Bank Employee ....Charles Martiniz
Ramon Ochoa ....Gonzalo Menendez
Benny.....................Mauricio Mendoza
Tony ....Carlos Mendoza
Young Tuna ....Alan James Morgan
Employee ....Randy Mulkey
Bank President ....Tony Perez
Ben...........................Jack Polick
Rafael Ojeda.............Raoul N Rizik
Martha Oliveras .....Elizabeth Rodriguez
Bank President (Panama)
..............................Bert Rosario
Clara Blanca ....Julia Vera
Juan Carlos ....Santiago Verdu
Restaurant, Bar Patron
..............................Ricardo Azulay
Derek Foreal's Party Girls
Anastasia Blue, Melissa Renée Martin
Man in Derek's Salon
..............................Nick Cassavetes
Beach Cyclist ....Dana Emberson
Bodyguard for Pablo Escobar
..............................Miguel Ángel Fuentes
Biker ....Jacque Lawson
FBI Undercover Agent
..............................Rayder Woods

SELECTED CREDITS
Director: Ted Demme
Producers: Ted Demme
Denis Leary, Joel Stillerman
Screenplay: David McKenna, Nick Cassavetes
From the book *Blow* by Bruce Porter
Associate Producers: Tracy Falco, Susan McNamara, Hillary Sherman
Music: Money Mark, Graeme Revell, Ronnie Van Zant, Nikka Costa, Justin Stanley
Cinematography: Ellen Kuras
Production Designer: Michael Z Hanan
Art Directors: David Ensley, Bernardo Trujillo
Editor: Kevin Tent
Sound Recordist: Eric Flickinger
Sound Mixer: Allan Byer
Production Manager: Georgia Kacandes
Assistant Directors: Anne Berger, Rosemary C Cremona, Maria

Mantia
1st Assistant Director: Nicholas Mastandrea
Makeup: Desne J Holland, Jamie Kelman
Hair Stylists: Rita Troy, Karl Wesson
Costumes: Mark Bridges
Special Effects Coordinator: Ron Bolanowski
Stunt Coordinator: Rick Avery,
Executive Producers: Michael De Luca, Georgia Kacandes
NEW LINE 124 MINUTES

Chocolat
CAST
Vianne Rocher ....Juliette Binoche
Comte de Reynaud ..Alfred Molina
Caroline Clairmont ..Carrie-Anne Moss
Luc Clairmont ....Aurelien Parent-Koenig
Jean-Marc Drou.......Antonio Gil-Martinez
Francoise 'Fuffi' Drou
..............................Hélène Cardona
Dedou Drou ....Harrison Pratt
Didi Drou ....Gaelan Connell
Yvette Marceau.......Elisabeth Commelin
Alphonse Marceau...Ron Cook
Baptiste Marceau ....Guillaume Tardieu
Pere Henri ....Hugh O'Conor
Guillaume Blerot ......John Wood
Josephine Muscat ...Lena Olin
Serge Muscat...........Peter Stormare
Madame Audel.........Leslie Caron
Anouk.......................Victoire Thivisol
Armande Voizin........Judi Dench
Madame Rivet ....Michèle Gleizer
Madame Pouget ....Dominique MacAvoy
George Rocher ....Arnaud Adam
Chitza ....Christianne Gadd
Roux........................Johnny Depp
Gati ....Marion Haudcoeur
Thin Grizzled Man....Esteban Antonio
Musicians ....J J Holiday, Malcolm Ross, Ged Barry, Iain Stoddart
Charlie the Dog ....Sally
Man in Photo...........David Brown
Countess ....Dominique Delany

SELECTED CREDITS
Director: Lasse Hallström
Producers: David Brown, Leslie Holleran, Kit Golden
Co-Producer: Mark Cooper
Screenplay: Robert Nelson Jacobs
From the novel *Chocolat* by Joanne Harris
Music: Rachel Portman
Cinematography: Roger Pratt
Production Designer: David Gropman

Art Directors: John Frankish, Louise Marzaroli, Lucy Richardson
Editor: Andrew Mondshein
Sound Recordists: Terry Laudermilch, Bob Olari
Production Manager: Mark Cooper
1st Assistant Director: Stephen P Dunn
Makeup, Hair Stylist: Norma Webb
Costumes: Renee Ehrlich Kalfus
Special Effects: Stuart Brisdon
Stunt Coordinator: Richard Hammatt
Executive Producers: Alan C Blomquist, Meryl Poster, Bob Weinstein, Harvey Weinstein
MIRAMAX 121 MINUTES

From Hell
CAST
Inspector Fred Abberline
..............................Johnny Depp
Mary Kelly ....Heather Graham
Sir William Gull ....Ian Holm
Sergeant Peter Godley
..............................Robbie Coltrane
Sir Charles Warren ..Ian Richardson
Netley.....................Jason Flemyng
Dark Annie Chapman
..............................Katrin Cartlidge
Benjamin 'Ben' Kidney
..............................Terence Harvey
Liz Stride ....Susan Lynch
Dr Ferral ....Paul Rhys
Kate Eddowes ....Lesley Sharp
Ada.........................Estelle Skornik
Officer Bolt...............Nicholas McGaughey
Polly ....Annabelle Apsion
Ann Crook ....Joanna Page
Albert Sickert, Prince Edward
Albert Victor ....Mark Dexter
Constable Withers ....Danny Midwinter
Martha Tabram.......Samantha Spiro
McQueen ....David Schofield
Robert Best ....Bryon Fear
Lord Hallsham.........Peter Eyre
Mac Bartender ....Cliff Parisi
Victoria Abberline ...Sophia Myles
Gordie......................Ralph Ineson
Gull's Maid...............Amy Huck
Doss Landlord ....Rupert Farley
Hospital Director.....Donald Douglas
Marylebone Governor
..............................John Owens
Queen Victoria ....Liz Moscrop
Robert Drudge ....Ian McNeice
Special Branch Constable
..............................Steve John Shepherd
Stonecutter ....Al Hunter Ashton
Alice Crook...............Poppy Rogers
Ann Crook's Father ..Bruce Byron
Ann Crook's Mother Melanie Hill
Carpenter ....Andy Linden
Carpenter, Letter Writer
..............................David Fisher

Constables ....Gary Powell, Steve Chaplin, Dominic Cooper
George Lusk ....Vincent Franklin
Bold Hooker ....Louise Atkins
John Merrick............Anthony Parker
Masonic Governor ....James Greene
Police Photographer Carey Thring
Rag & Bone Man ......Vladimir Kulhavy
Records Clerk ....Graham Kent
Sailor ....Rupert Holiday Evans
Thomas Bond............Simon Harrison
Young Doctor ....Paul Moody
Young Labourer ....Glen Berry
Labourer ....Charlie Parish
Funeral Minister, Letter Writer
...............................Gerry Grennell
Preacher ....Roger Frost
Medical Student ......Stephen Milton
Opium Den Owner ....Tony Tang

SELECTED CREDITS
Directors: Albert Hughes, Allen Hughes
Producers: Jane Hamsher, Don Murphy
Screenplay: Terry Hayes, Rafael Yglesias
From the graphic novel by Alan Moore, Eddie Campbell
Music: Trevor Jones,
Cinematography: Peter Deming
Production Desiger: Martin Childs
Art Director: Jindra Koci
Editors: George Bowers, Dan Lebental
Sound Recordists: Tim Gomillion, Matt Patterson, Dennis Rogers
Sound Mixer: Franklin D Stettner
Production Managers: Michal Skop, Elena Zokas
1st Assistant Directors: Jan Mensik, John Woodward
Makeup: Jiri Farkas
Hair Stylist: Jiri Farkas
Costumes: Kym Barrett
Special Effects Supervisor: George Gibbs
Stunt Coordinator: Pavel Voukan
Executive Producers: Thomas M Hammel, Albert Hughes, Allen Hughes, Amy Robinson
20TH CENTURY FOX 122 MINUTES

2001

Once Upon a Time in Mexico
CAST
El Mariachi ....Antonio Banderas
Carolina ....Salma Hayek
Sheldon Jeffrey Sands
...............................Johnny Depp
Billy ....Mickey Rourke
Ajedrez....................Eva Mendes
Cucuy.....................Danny Trejo
Lorenzo ....Enrique Iglesias
Fideo.......................Marco Leonardi

Belini ....Cheech Marin
Jorge FBI ....Rubén Blades
Barillo ....Willem Dafoe
Marquez...................Gerardo Vigil
El Presidente ....Pedro Armendariz
Advisor ....Julio Oscar Mechoso
Cab Driver ....Tito Larriva
Dr Guevara ....Miguel Couturier
Chicle Boy ....Tony Valdes
Alvaro ....José Luis Avendaño
Omar ....Rodolfo d'Alejandre
Mariachi's Girl ....Natalia Torres
Right Hand ....Steven Constancio
Romero ....Troy Robinson
Qui-Que ....Ermahn Ospina
Pistolera ....Luz María Rojas
Cook ....Mario Simon
Blascoe....................Bernard Hacker
Waitress...................Cecilia Tijerina
Hospital Administrator
...............................Carola Vázquez
Chief Federale ....René Gatica
Bachelorette ....Silvia Santoyo
Bull Fighter ....Juan Pablo Lladuno
Teacher ....Ignacio Torres
Manny ....Rogelio Gonzalez Grau
Taco ....Jorge Becerril
Left Nut ....Víctor Carpinteiro
Que Pasa ....Dagoberto Gama

SELECTED CREDITS
Director: Robert Rodriguez
Producers: Elizabeth Avellan, Carlos Gallardo, Robert Rodriguez
Co-Producers: Sue Jett, Tony Mark, Luz María Rojas
Screenplay: Robert Rodriguez
Music: Robert Rodriguez
Cinematography: Robert Rodriguez
Production Designer: Robert Rodriguez
Art Director: Melo Hinojosa
Editor: Robert Rodriguez
Sound Recordist: Kevin Globerman
Sound Mixer: Ed Novick
Production Manager: Arturo Del Rio
1st Assistant Director: Brian Bettwy
Makeup: Ermahn Ospina
Special Effects Makeup: Robert Kurtzman, Gregory Nicotero
Hair Stylist: Ermahn Ospina
Costumes: Graciela Mazón
Special Effects Coordinator: Mike Reedy
Stunt Coordinators: Jeff Dashnaw, Troy Robinson
COLUMBIA 102 MINUTES

2002

Finding Neverland
CAST
James Matthew Barrie
...............................Johnny Depp
Sylvia Llewelyn Davies
...............................Kate Winslet
Mrs du Maurier.......Julie Christie
George Llewelyn Davies
...............................Nick Roud
Mary Barrie.............Radha Mitchell
Jack Llewelyn Davies
...............................Joe Prospero
Peter Llewelyn Davies
...............................Freddie Highmore
Charles Frohman......Dustin Hoffman
Wendy Darling ....Kate Maberly
Michael Llewelyn Davis
...............................Luke Spill
Peter Pan ....Kelly Macdonald
Set Mover ....Tony Way
Stage Hand ....Murray McArthur
Sir Arthur Conan Doyle
...............................Ian Hart
Stage Manager ....Paul Whitehouse
Theatre Ushers ....Mackenzie Crook, David Decio
John Darling ....Matt Green
Smee ....Toby Jones
Mary McCormack ....Suzy Kewer
Emma ....Kali Peacock
Lost Boy...................William Tomlin
Hook/'Lord Carlton' ..Tim Potter
Nanna the Dog..........Angus Barnett
With Raymond Waring, Eileen Essel

SELECTED CREDITS
Director: Marc Forster
Producers: Nellie Bellflower, Richard N Gladstein
Co-Producer: Michael Dreyer
Screenplay: David Magee
From the play The Man Who Was Peter Pan by Allan Knee
Associate Producer: Tracey Becker
Music: Jan A P Kaczmarek
Cinematography: Roberto Schaefer
Production Designer: Gemma Jackson
Art Director: Peter Russell
Editor: Matt Chesse
Sound Mixer: David Crozier
1st Assistant Director: Martin Harrison
Makeup: Christine Blundell
Hair Stylist: Christine Blundell
Costumes: Alexandra Byrne, Mary Kelly
Special Effects: Stuart Brisdon
Stunt Coordinator: Lee Sheward
Executive Producer: Gary Binkow
MIRAMAX 101 MINUTES

Pirates of the Caribbean: The Curse of the Black Pearl

CAST

Jack Sparrow ....Johnny Depp
Barbossa ....Geoffrey Rush
Will Turner...............Orlando Bloom
Elizabeth Swann ......Keira Knightley
Norrington ....Jack
.................................Davenport
Governor Weatherby Swann
..............................Jonathan
.................................Pryce
Pintel ....Lee Arenberg
Ragetti ....Mackenzie
.................................Crook
Lt Gillette.................Damian O'Hare
Murtogg ....Giles New
Mullroy ....Angus Barnett
Cotton ....David Bailie
Twigg ....Michael Berry Jr
Bo'sun ....Isaac C
.................................Singleton Jr
Joshamee Gibbs.......Kevin R
.................................McNally
Koehler....................Treva Etienne
Anamaria.................Zoe Saldana
Harbourmaster ....Guy Siner
Mr Brown.................Ralph P Martin
Estrella ....Paula Jane
.................................Newman
Butler......................Paul Keith
Young Will ....Dylan Smith
Young Elizabeth.......Lucinda Dryzek
Officer ....Greg Ellis
Sentry ....Dustin Seavey
Steersman ....Christian
.................................Martin
Grapple ....Trevor Goddard
Jacoby ....Vince Lozano
Seedy Prisoners ....
Michael Sean Tighe, Ben Wilson,
Antonio Valentino, Mike Babcock
Scarlett ....Lauren Maher
Mallot......................Brye Cooper
Town Clerk..............Owen Finnegan
Sailors ....Ian McIntyre,
.................................Paul Cagney
Giselle.....................Vanessa
.................................Branch
Crying Boys ....Sam Roberts,
.................................Ben Roberts
Marty.......................Martin Klebba
Pirate......................Gregory R
.................................Alosio
Marine ....Brazil Joseph
.................................Grisaffi III
Sparrow's Crew:
Moises ....Félix Castro
Kursar ....Mike
.................................Haberecht
Matelot ....Rudolph
.................................McColam
Tearlach..................Gerard Reyes
Duncan ....M Scott Shields
Ladbroc ....Chris 'Sully'
.................................Sullivan
Crimp......................Craig Thomson
Quartetto.................Fred Toft
Barbossa's Crew:
Weatherby ....D P FitzGerald
Ketchum ....Jerry Gauny
Maximo ....Maxie J
.................................Santillan Jr
Monk ....Michael
.................................Lane

Dog Ear ....Tobias
.................................McKinney
Clubba ....David
.................................Patykewich
Scarus ....Tommy
.................................Schooler
Simbakka.................Michael A
.................................Thompson
Hawksmoor ....Michael W
.................................Williams
Katracho ....Jose Zelaya
Scratch ....Finneus Egan
Nipperkin................Don LaDaga

SELECTED CREDITS

Director: Gore Verbinski
Producer: Jerry Bruckheimer
Screenplay: Ted Elliott, Terry
Rossio, Jay Wolpert
Associate Producer: Pat Sandston
Music: Hans Zimmer
Cinematography: Dariusz Wolski
Production Designer: Brian
Morris
Art Directors: Derek R Hill, James
E Tocci, Donald B Woodruff
Editors: Stephen Rivkin, Arthur
Schmidt, Craig Wood
Sound Mixer: Lee Orloff
Production Managers: Paul
Deason, Bruce Hendricks, Douglas
C Merrifield
1st Assistant Director: Peter Kohn
Makeup: David DeLeon, Zoe Hay,
Anne-Maree Hurley, Marese
Langan, Deborah Patino, Don
Rutherford
Special Effects Makeup: Greg
Cannom, Art Anthony
Hair Stylist: Nina Paskowitz
Costumes: Penny Rose
Special Effects Coordinator: Terry
D Frazee
Stunt Coordinator: George
Marshall Ruge
Executive Producers: Paul Deason,
Bruce Hendricks, Chad Oman,
Mike Stenson
DISNEY, BUENA VISTA
143 MINUTES

2003

Secret Window

CAST

Mort Rainey..............Johnny Depp
John Shooter ....John Turturro
Amy Rainey..............Maria Bello
Ted ....Timothy
.................................Hutton
Ken Karsch ....Charles
.................................S Dutton
Sheriff Dave Newsome
.................................Len Cariou
Mrs Garvey ....Joan Heney
Tom Greenleaf ....John Dunn-Hill
Fire Chief Wickersham
.................................Vlasta Vrana
Detective Bradley ....Matt
.................................Holland
Fran Evans ....Gillian
.................................Ferrabee
Greta Bowie ....Bronwen
.................................Mantel

Juliet Stoker ....Elizabeth
.................................Marleau
Busboy ....Kyle Allatt
Motel Manager ....Richard Jutras
Public Works Guys....Kevin
.................................Woodhouse,
.................................Vito DeFilippo
Sheriff's Niece ....Sarah Allen

SELECTED CREDITS

Director: David Koepp
Producer: Gavin Polone
Screenplay: David Koepp
From the novella *Secret Window,
Secret Garden* in *Four Past Midnight*
by Stephen King
Music: Philip Glass, Geoff Zanelli,
Alan Elliott
Cinematography: Fred Murphy
Production Designer: Howard
Cummings
Art Director: Gilles Aird
Editor: Jill Savitt
Sound: Patrick Rousseau,
Production Manager: Manon
Bougie
1st Assistant Director: Pedro
Gandol
Special Effects Makeup: Adrien
Morot
Costumes: Odette Gadoury,
Executive Producer: Ezra
Swerdlow
COLUMBIA 96 MINUTES

2004

The Libertine

CAST

John Wilmot, Earl of Rochester
.................................Johnny Depp
King Charles II.........John
.................................Malkovich
Elizabeth Barry ....Samantha
.................................Morton
Elizabeth Malet ....Rosamund Pike
Billy Downs ....Rupert Friend
George Etherege.......Tom Hollander
Agnes Jessop ....Maimie McCoy
17th Century Bard ..Shane
.................................MacGowan
Charles Sackville......Johnny Vegas

SELECTED CREDITS

Director: Laurence Dunmore
Producers: Lianne Halfon, John
Malkovich, Russell Smith
Screenplay: Stephen Jeffreys
Music: Michael Nyman
Production Designer:
Ben van Os
Art Directors: Patrick Rolfe, Fleur
Whitlock
Editor: Jill Bilcock
Sound Recordist: John Hayes
Production Manager: Marshall
Leviten
1st Assistant Director: Max Keene
Special Effects: Rob Tucker
Stunts: Peter Pedrero
Executive Producers:
Chase Bailey, Louise Goodsill,
Ralph Kamp
ODYSSEY 130 MINUTES

Ils se marièrent et eurent beaucoup d'enfants

CAST

Gabrielle	Charlotte Gainsbourg
Vincent	Yvan Attal
Georges	Alain Chabat
Fred	Alain Cohen
Nathalie	Emmanuelle Seigner
Florence	Marie-Sophie Wilson-Carr
La maîtresse de vincent	Angie David
L'inconnu	Johnny Depp
Le père de Vincent	Claude Berri
La mère de Vincent	Anouk Aimée
La mère de la maîtresse de Vincent	Aurore Clément
Le client du garage	Jérôme Bertin

With Carolina Gynning

SELECTED CREDITS
Director: Yvan Attal
Producer: Claude Berri
Screenplay: Yvan Attal
Music: Brad Mehldau
Cinematography: Rémy Chevrin
Production Designer: Katia Wyszkop
Editor: Jennifer Augé
Sound: Didier Sain,
Production Manager: Nicole Flan
Assistant Director: Laurent Goldztejn
Costumes: Jacqueline Bouchard
PATHE 100 MINUTES

Charlie and the Chocolate Factory

CAST

Charlie Bucket	Freddie Highmore
Willy Wonka	Johnny Depp
Mrs Bucket	Helena Bonham Carter
Oompa Loompas	Ty Dickson, Lance Smith
Mike Teavee	Jordan Fry
Grandpa Joe	David Kelly
Ms Beauregard	Missi Pyle
Violet Beauregarde	Annasophia Robb
Augustus Gloop	Philip Wiegratz
Veruca Salt	Julia Winter

With James Fox, Christopher Lee, Noah Taylor

SELECTED CREDITS
Director: Tim Burton
Producers: Liccy Dahl, Brad Grey, Richard D Zanuck
Screenplay: John August
From the novel *Charlie and the Chocolate Factory* by Roald Dahl
Associate Producers: Brenda Berrisford, Derek Frey
Music: Danny Elfman
Cinematography: Philippe Rousselot
Production Designer: Alex McDowell
Art Directors: Kevin Phipps, Andy Nicholson, Leslie Tomkins
Editor: Chris Lebenzon
Sound Mixer: Tony Dawe,
Production Manager: Nikolas Korda
Assistant Director: Joseph Bond,
Costumes: Gabriella Pescucci
Special Effects Supervisor: Joss Williams
Stunt Coordinator: Jim Dowdall
Executive Producers: Bruce Berman, Felicity Dahl, Patrick McCormick, Michael Siegel
WARNER BROS

BIBLIOGRAPHY

JOHNNY DEPP has been the subject of literally hundreds of magazine and newspaper articles and interviews since 1987, and there are, in addition, numerous fan sites on the web which are devoted to the actor – but few substantive materials on Depp exist in conventional book form, bar the two biographies which have been included in this list. Websites which proved time and again to be particularly informative are also included, but the remainder of the list is occupied by titles that relate to the films in which Depp has appeared and which therefore were instrumental in aiding me in the writing of this book. My thanks go to their authors.

Reinaldo Arenas, *Before Night Falls* (New York: Penguin Books, 1993)

Paul Begg, Martin Fido and Keith Skinner, *The Jack the Ripper A to Z* (London: Headline, 1991)

Andrew Birkin, *J M Barrie and the Lost Boys* (New York: Random House, 1988)

Richard Bojarski, *The Films of Bela Lugosi* (Secaucus: Citadel Press, 1980)

Lord Byron, *The Works of Lord Byron* (Ware: Wordsworth, 1994)

Roald Dahl, *Charlie and the Chocolate Factory* (London: Allen & Unwin, 1967)

Nigel Goodall, *What's Eating Johnny Depp? An Intimate Biography* (London: Blake Publishing, 2004)

Rudolph Grey, *Nightmare of Ecstasy: The Life and Art of Edward D Wood Jr* (Portland: Feral House, 1992)

Joanne Harris, *Chocolat* (New York: Doubleday, 1999)

Christopher Heard, *Depp* (Toronto: ECW Press, 2001)

Peter Hedges, *What's Eating Gilbert Grape* (New York: Simon & Schuster, 1999)

Washington Irving, *The Legend of Sleepy Hollow and other stories* (London: Penguin, 2000)

Stephen Jeffreys, *The Libertine* (London: Nick Hern Books, 1994)

Jack Kerouac, *On the Road* (New York: Penguin Books, 1991)

Stephen King, *Four Past Midnight* (New York: Signet Books, 1991)

Gregory McDonald, *The Brave* (New York: Barricade Books, 1991)

Denis Meikle, *Jack the Ripper: The Murders and the Movies* (London: Reynolds & Hearn, 2002)

Alan Moore and Eddie Campbell, *From Hell* (London: Knockabout, 2000)

Joseph D Pistone, *Donnie Brasco: My Undercover Life in the Mafia* (New York: Signet Books, 1997)

Bruce Porter, *Blow: How a Small-Town Boy Made $100 Million with the Medellin Cocaine Cartel and Lost It All* (New York: St Martin's Press, 1993)

Arturo Pérez Reverte, *The Dumas Club* (London: Harvill Press, 1996)

Jim Smith and J Clive Matthews, *Tim Burton* (London: Virgin Books, 2002)

Hunter S Thompson, Fear and Loathing in Las Vegas (New York: Vintage Books, 1998)

Websites
www.imdbpro.com
www.johnnydeppfan.com
www.variety.com

INDEX

PICTURE CREDITS

Jacket
Front: Goffredo/Rex Features
Back: Alessia Pierdomenico/Reuters/Corbis

Picture section 1
Page 1: Fox Television/Snap/Rex Features; *2a* Universal; *2b* Dave Lewis/Rex Features; *2c* M-G-M/UA; 3 20th Century Fox; *4a* Paramount/The Joel Finler Collection; *4b* Joyce Silverstein/Rex Features; *5* Touchstone; *6* New Line/The Joel Finler Collection; *7a* Miramax/The Joel Finler Collection; *7b* Araldo Di Crollalanza/Rex Features; *8a* Universal/Rex Features; *8b* New Line/Rex Features; *8c* Artisan.

Picture section 2
Page 1a Araldo Di Crollalanza/Rex Features; *1b* Paramount; *2a* Universal/The Joel Finler Collection; *2b* Miramax; *3a* New Line; *3b* 20th Century Fox; *4* Buena Vista; *5a* Buena Vista/Rex Features; *5b* Alex Berliner/BEI/Rex Features; *6* Columbia; *7a* Columbia; *7b* Miramax; *8* Action Press/Rex Features.